Jacques Tourne

Jacques Tourneur

the cinema of nightfall

by

Chris Fujiwara

with a foreword by

MARTIN SCORSESE

NEW ENGLAND INSTITUTE
OF TECHNOLOGY
LEARNING RESOURCES CENTER
The Johns Hopkins University Press

Baltimore and London

Cover photograph and frontispiece: Jacques Tourneur during the shooting of *Days of Glory* (1944). Courtesy of the Academy of Motion Picture Arts and Sciences

Published by special arrangement with McFarland & Company, Inc., Publishers, Jefferson, North Carolina
Johns Hopkins Paperbacks edition, 2000
9 8 7 6 5 4 3 2 1

The Johns Hopkins University Press
2715 North Charles Street
Baltimore, Maryland 21218-4363
www.press.jhu.edu

Library of Congress Cataloging-in-Publication Data

Fujiwara, Chris.
   Jacques Tourneur : the cinema of nightfall / by Chris Fujiwara ; with a foreword by Martin Scorsese.
      p.   cm.
   Includes bibliographical references and index.
   ISBN 0-8018-6561-1 (alk. paper)
   1. Tourneur, Jacques, 1904–1977—Criticism and interpretation.
I. Title.

PN1998.3.T6 F85 2000
791.43′0233′092—dc21

                                    00-033045

A catalog record for this book is available from the British Library.

To Julia

Acknowledgments

For responding to my inquires about Jacques Tourneur, and in some cases for providing me with unpublished materials, I am indebted to Jean-Claude Biette, Jack Elam, Richard Goldstone, Bert and Charlotte Granet, Peter Graves, Jane Greer, Jacques Manlay, Rhonda Fleming Mann, Richard Matheson, Virginia Mayo, Gregory Peck, Philippe Roger, Robert Schiffer, George Sidney, Robert Stack, Maurice Vaccarino, Paul Valentine, and Michael Henry Wilson.

For encouragement, support, consultation, and various services — including providing prints, videotapes, and textual materials — I wish to thank Ed Bansak, Diego Curubeto, John Gianvito, Scott Hamrah, Kent Jones, Bill Krohn, Tim Lucas, Juan Mandelbaum, Dennis Millay, Federico Muchnik, Charlotte Fay Pagni, Max Schaefer, Martin Scorsese, Tom Weaver, and my mother and father.

For putting me up and driving me around L.A., I am grateful to Marilynn Eden; Mark, Lisa, and Tyler Engel; Kenny Fujiwara; and Patty Masumi.

I gratefully acknowledge the assistance of the staffs of the following archives and research collections: the Margaret Herrick Library, Academy of Motion Picture Arts and Sciences (Faye Thompson); the Library of Congress Motion Picture, Broadcasting and Recorded Sound Division (Rosemary Hanes, Madeline Matz); the New York Public Library for the Performing Arts; Special Collections, University Research Library, University of California at Los Angeles (Brigitte Kueppers, Ray Reece); the UCLA Film and Television Archive; the Cinema-Television Library and Archives of the Performing Arts, University of Southern California (Ned Comstock); and the Wisconsin Center for Film and Theatre Research, State Historical Society of Wisconsin.

Contents

Foreword

by Martin Scorsese

It's appropriate that so many of Jacques Tourneur's movies deal with the supernatural and the paranormal, because his own touch as a filmmaker is elusive yet tangible, like the presence of a ghost — in a way, you could say that Tourneur's touch is so refined and subtle that he haunts his films. It's as though he cast a spell over each project, from a movie that actually deals with the supernatural like *Cat People* to one that only seems to deal with it, like *The Leopard Man*, to a western like *Canyon Passage,* a period piece like *Experiment Perilous*, a noir like *Out of the Past* or a routine B assignment like *Nick Carter, Master Detective*. Which may be the reason why he remains so under appreciated. Tourneur was a great director, fully deserving of the thoroughly researched and perceptive treatment he receives from Chris Fujiwara in the pages that follow. But in comparison to the directorial stars of American cinema — Hitchcock, Ford, Capra, Hawks — he remains a shadowy figure, apt to portray himself in public as a craftsman and content to work in B-movies. Throughout his long career, Tourneur stayed in what critic Manny Farber called "termite" territory. He never made grand statements and he never worked with large budgets or big stars. He cultivated the most fleeting and elusive aspects of experience, things that other filmmakers would never bother with but that, for Tourneur, were the essence of movies.

Tourneur was an artist of atmospheres. For many directors, an atmosphere is something that is "established," setting the stage for the action to follow. For Tourneur it is the movie, and each of his films boasts a distinctive atmosphere, with a profound sensitivity to light and shadow, and a very unusual relationship between characters and environment — the way people move through space in Tourneur movies, the way they simply handle objects, is always special, different from other films. Bertrand Tavernier and Jean-Pierre Coursodon have noted that Tourneur tended to record dialogue at low levels, and he always encouraged his actors to underplay (which must be why he preferred to work with minimalists like Robert Mitchum, Dana Andrews, or Victor Mature) and to move at a slightly slower pace than usual. Places, objects and atmospheres are living presences in his work, while emotion and drama speak very softly, the better to show how deeply they are affected by the physical world around them — which is why I think the films have such a hypnotic quality. Farber, again, might have been the first person to describe the way that Tourneur equalized people and objects, in his obituary for the great producer of *Cat People* and *I Walked with a Zombie* (Tourneur's favorite), Val Lewton.

Take *Canyon Passage*, an example of the short-lived but very interesting sub-genre of the "noir western" and a picture that's very special to me. It's one of the most mysterious and exquisite examples of the western genre ever made. When you think of "westerns" you immediately picture the plains or the desert, vast spaces that stretch on and on for miles. But this film, Tourneur's first in color, is set in a small town in the mountains of Oregon, and it is lush, green, muted, and rainy (one of the first scenes in the movie shows the cramped main street of Portland turned into a muddy bog by a downpour). Even the open spaces in this movie are just small mountain clearings. If you study *Canyon Passage* carefully you'll see that Tourneur constantly composes diagonally into small spaces, showing people walking up or down inclines, and it gives you the feeling that this is a real settler's town. One of the first shots in the movie is of Hoagy Carmichael singing a song as he slowly rides his donkey up the steep little main drag of the town — it's repeated in the end (it's in this movie that Carmichael also sings "Ole Buttermilk Sky," a song that instantly transports me back to my childhood whenever I hear it). And it embodies the muted, understated beauty of the entire film.

There are some beautiful set pieces in *Canyon Passage* like the Indian attack and the barnraising, but the overall tone is so carefully controlled that every small variation or nuance has an impact. That's what makes Tourneur's films so unsettling, this strange undercurrent that runs through every scene but that somehow enhances the dramatic impact of the whole film. For instance in the famous sequence in *Cat People* where Jane Randolph walks alone to the bus stop in Central Park, the evenness of the tone keys the viewer to the subtlest changes in sound and light to such an extent that the climax of the scene (hair-raising each time you see it) is the sound of a bus hitting its air brakes. In *Easy Living*, the decadent party thrown by pretentious and greedy Manhattanites is surveyed by Tourneur with such control that one shot of a lonely model sitting off by herself in a corner is enough to suggest her eventual suicide. And there is also a suggestion of magic at the oddest moments in Tourneur's work. Look at the scene in *Out of the Past* where Dickie Moore saves Robert Mitchum by hooking the arm of the man who's trying to kill him with his fishing line and yanking him to his death. Tourneur films this scene in a unique way — where any other director would have pumped music into the background and cut to close-ups of a struggle, Tourneur lets us listen to the rushing water of the river below and shoots the action mostly in long shot, giving it a strange, dreamlike inevitability.

Tourneur's films are very special to me, and they've been a great inspiration throughout my career. He's one of those directors whose work renews your enthusiasm for movies — whenever I look at one of his films on tape or on screen, I remember why I wanted to make movies in the first place. The craft, taste, and extraordinary fluid artistry of his cinema make most other movies look bloated and synthetic. I'm glad that there is finally a book about his work, and especially glad that it is as thoughtful and scholarly as this one.

Jacques Tourneur

Introduction

Appearances are a glimpse of the unseen.

ANAXAGORAS

Jacques Tourneur appears in the third rank of directors, "Expressive Esoterica," in Andrew Sarris's definitive account of the "auteur theory," *The American Cinema*. The terms in which Sarris describes Tourneur's work ("a certain French gentility ... subdued, pastel-colored sensibility ... unyielding pictorialism ... a triumph of taste over force") show that he regards the director as a pleasant stylist without a strong personal vision. This remains the standard take on Tourneur. Robin Wood, for example, acknowledges the visual consistency of Tourneur's films but denies that Tourneur is a major creative force because in several of his films, visual style "is simply *applied* to the subject-matter externally, without in any way transforming it."[1]

Addressing auteurism's inability to come to terms with Tourneur, Claire Johnston and Paul Willemen state flatly, "It is impossible to consider Tourneur as an artist expressing a coherent world-view, a coherent and individual thematic." They find "the principle(s) of coherence of a Tourneur text, not in some thematic unity, but in a procedural unity.... [T]he Tourneur text demands to be approached as a textual practice, a practice of signification."[2] These claims suggest that Tourneur has a unique position in film studies: before becoming canonized as an auteur, he was identified as a kind of post- or anti-auteur.

In France, especially since the early 1970s, Tourneur has become a cult figure, thanks to such perceptive admirers of his work as Jacques Lourcelles, Louis Skorecki, Michael Henry, Bertrand Tavernier, Gérard Legrand, and Jean-Claude Biette. The belatedness of this attention (Tourneur was not among the American directors whom the critics of *Cahiers du cinéma* championed during the heroic period of their discovery of the American cinema in the fifties) is undoubtedly due to accidents of distribution that kept some of Tourneur's major films off French screens until the late sixties.

Tourneur's achievement remains underappreciated and misunderstood. His films are mostly relatively obscure thrillers, Westerns, and adventure films that, at first glance, have little in common. Of the five best-known films he directed, three of them — *Cat People, I Walked with a Zombie*, and *The Leopard Man* — are more often credited to their producer, Val Lewton, than to their director, whereas the other two, *Out of the Past* and *Night of the Demon* (as it is known in Britain, where it was produced; in the United States it was released as *Curse of the Demon*), tend

I

to be praised as quintessential genre pieces rather than as personal works. *Experiment Perilous, Canyon Passage, Stars in My Crown, Anne of the Indies, Way of a Gaucho*, and *Wichita* are rarely shown or discussed.

The question of Lewton's coauthorship of the Tourneur films he produced deserves attention. The films Lewton produced at RKO unmistakably constitute a coherent cycle, and Lewton played a key role in conceiving them, developing their scripts, and bringing them to fruition, as has been well documented and as many of his collaborators, including Tourneur, have confirmed. Joel E. Siegel concludes that Lewton was "unarguably the artistic creator and prime mover of his films."[3] Siegel and others see Lewton's directors — principally Tourneur, Mark Robson, and Robert Wise — as having merely executed his creative will, albeit with varying degrees of skill (they usually grant that Tourneur's films for Lewton have a visual fluidity lacking in Robson's and Wise's).

Yet the features cited as distinguishing the Lewton films also characterize Tourneur's films without Lewton. "In spite of their sensationalistic titles," J. P. Telotte notes, "films like *Cat People, I Walked with a Zombie*, and *The Leopard Man* are most marked by a lack — of monsters, of gruesome presences, and even of concrete evidence of a malevolent force at work in the human environment." This undemonstrativeness is typical of Tourneur's direction, not only of *Night of the Demon*, his return to the horror genre, but also of films as disparate in their overt concerns as *Experiment Perilous, Canyon Passage*, and *Out of the Past*. Telotte identifies the "substantial sense of the everyday" of Lewton's films as an equally important aspect of his art, which emphasizes "characters who can be identified by their station in life or occupation, and who thus seem like a natural part of this texture of the commonplace." The emergence of the fantastic in this context results in "a subtle dialectic between substance and lack, presence and absence."[4] This dialectic also functions in virtually all Tourneur's non–Lewton films, which similarly lavish immense care on their social and visual textures.

Tourneur's pre–Lewton work enables us to evaluate Tourneur's crucial contribution to *Cat People, I Walked with a Zombie*, and *The Leopard Man*. Paul Willemen's summing-up of the Lewton-Tourneur question is clearly inadequate:

> The films in dispute happen to be the first three important
> works in the filmographies of both Lewton and Tourneur.
> No conceivable auteur analysis of Lewton's work would be
> able to dispel at least a suspicion that the producer was
> merely trying to recapture and recreate the successful ele-
> ments of the films Tourneur had directed for him. Obviously
> this argument could equally be applied to Tourneur, who
> could be seen to have spent the rest of his career elaborating
> on the work of Lewton.[5]

Anyone who has seen the shorts Tourneur directed for MGM from 1936 to 1942, in particular such masterpieces as "The Rainbow Pass," "Killer-Dog," "Romance of Radium," "The Ship That Died," "The Face behind the Mask," "What Do *You* Think? Tupapaoo," and "The Incredible Stranger," can affirm that *Cat People* was not, in fact, Tourneur's first important work and that the main features of Tourneur's directorial style, along with a number of his thematic preoccupations, were already firmly in place by 1937, five years before *Cat People*.

Beneath the surface inconsistencies of Tourneur's post–Lewton career lies a paradoxical unity. Tourneur said in 1977, the year of his death: "I always did what I wanted. I never turned down a script."[6] His refusal to acknowledge a contradiction between these two propositions suggests why the division between stylists and directors with a worldview, fundamental to Andrew Sarris's auteur system, is irrelevant to Tourneur. The attributes of Tourneur's style — the lighting, cinematography, and performance characteristics that we shall examine shortly — cannot be separated from a set of narrative concerns and procedures that, though perhaps failing to add up crushingly to "a coherent and individual thematic," mark a personal approach to a variety of genres.

Tourneur's "themes" are conceptual oppositions between whose terms his characters seek to define themselves, boundaries that are simultaneously or fluctuatingly real, imaginary, and symbolic: the boundaries between human and animal (*Cat People*, *The Leopard Man*), between living and dead (*I Walked with a Zombie*), between health/sanity and sickness/insanity ("The Magic Alphabet," *Cat People*, *Experiment Perilous*, *Easy Living*, *Stars in My Crown*), between town and wilderness or open country (the Westerns, *Way of a Gaucho*), between law and crime (*Out of the Past*, *Nightfall*), between male and female (*Anne of the Indies*), and "between the powers of darkness and the powers of the mind" (*Night of the Demon*). Tourneur's special territory is the space between these poles. As Paul Willemen writes, "Although the films dramatise the conflict between terms A/B, it is the '/' which constitutes the enigmatic pivot upon which Tourneur's films turn."[7]

The typical Tourneur narrative is full of confusion and ambiguity, signs that point in no clear direction, and messages that circle back on the sender. The director's narrative and stylistic choices constantly underline absence and distance. Significant events take place offscreen or before the start of the film; exposition is omitted or, when needed, made empty and incomprehensible, so that the motives of characters, even the protagonists, remain mysterious to the audience. Tourneur's films revolve around communications that are misunderstood or blocked: "The Incredible Stranger" and *Out of the Past* both feature mute characters; in *Cat People*, the husband wrongly discredits the heroine's fear of "something evil" in herself; in "Night Call," Tourneur's masterly *Twilight Zone* episode, the heroine receives repeated phone calls that are at first incomprehensible (coming, as she eventually finds, from her dead fiancé). Other Tourneur films hinge on written texts that are uninterpretable or that play a crucial, occult part in the life or death of their bearers, like the check that passes from endorser to endorser in the ironic short "The Grand Bounce," the maps in *Anne of the Indies* and *Appointment in Honduras*, and the parchment that dooms its recipient in *Night of the Demon*.

Tourneur's films on the supernatural pose questions whose answers are unknowable. "What Do *You* Think?" "What Do *You* Think? (Number Three)," "The Ship That Died," and "What Do You Think? Tupapaoo" all center on such enigmas. In *Cat People*, whether Irena turns into a cat, as she believes, can be discovered only at the cost of the narrative's life: as long as we, along with the film's "normal" characters, can doubt the truth and hesitate between two readings, the narrative may continue, but as soon as Oliver, her husband, can say "She never lied to us," the narrative must end. In *I Walked with a Zombie*, the most radical and total of Tourneur's enigmas, the narrative's central question is structurally

Jacques Tourneur during the shooting of *Berlin Express* in 1947 (courtesy of the Academy of Motion Picture Arts and Sciences).

undecidable. The film cannot say whether voodoo has turned Jessica Holland into a zombie; it can only raise possibilities, show parallels. In *Night of the Demon*, the unknowable is, paradoxically, known: from the beginning, we're not in doubt that the demon can be summoned to appear and destroy its victim. The film becomes a mystery because of the disavowal of Holden, its protagonist, a disavowal so strong that it ultimately overwhelms evidence and appeals for support, no longer to sensory experience and logic but to the good: "it's *better* not to know."

In Tourneur's nonhorror films, even when their mysteries aren't finally insoluble (as are those of "The King without a Crown," "The Man in the Barn," "The Face Behind the Mask," and "Strange Glory"), the improbable often takes the place of the unknowable, implying an unpredictable context for the characters' actions. Near-miracles save a number of Tourneur characters, including Faith, apparently dying of typhoid, in *Stars in My Crown*, and Pierre and Molly, abandoned on a desert island in *Anne of the Indies*. The plot of *Nightfall* foregrounds to an unusual extent the key role played by chance and coincidence in most Tourneur films: in *Nightfall*, all the decisive events in the hero's life happen by chance. The unknowable also returns in the endings of certain Tourneur films that leave characters uninformed about significant events in their lives: Ann thinks that Jeff was going away with Kathie in *Out of the Past*; Pentecost is unaware that Boston, the woman he loves, is dead in *Great Day in the Morning*.

Tourneur loves situations that allow him to present character and story ambiguously. In the long flashback section of *Experiment Perilous*, we don't know at what point Cissie, whose notebooks about the life of her brother, Nick, provide the material for the narrative, becomes aware of Nick's insanity. In *Canyon Passage*, George Camrose attributes his compulsive gambling to envy of Logan Stuart, his successful, enterprising friend; for Logan, however, "that's no answer," and the audience is left free to accept or reject this interpretation. *Circle of Danger*, *Appointment in Honduras*, and *Timbuktu* all keep us in uncertainty for some time about the protagonists' motives and alliances. For the first half of *Anne of the Indies*, we are ignorant of Pierre's secret mission to deliver the pirate Captain Providence to the English, just as in *Out of the Past*, we remain in the dark about the real nature of Kathie, the film's femme fatale, until the end of the long flashback. In several scenes of *Nightfall*, Vanning's suspicion of Marie leads us at least to question her motives if not to share fully his assumption (which proves false) that she is in league with the criminals persecuting him.

The mystery of Tourneur's films comes not only from the complex, clouded plots that his protagonists seek to unravel but also from the unexpressed motives and unresolved interior conflicts of the protagonists themselves. Betsy, the nurse-heroine of *I Walked with a Zombie*, may unconsciously want her patient to die; the hero and the heroine of *The Leopard Man* face their own indirect responsibility for the murders they investigate. For much of *Out of the Past*, Tourneur keeps the audience uncertain about the motives and intentions of Jeff, the detective-hero, through a process that Roger McNiven describes as "keeping the audience's intellectual identification with the protagonist one step behind its emotional identification."[8] Owen Pentecost, the hero of *Great Day in the Morning*, is an enigmatic figure whose motives are called into question incessantly throughout the film.

Jacques Lourcelles sees Tourneur's characters as "active shadows; men of action who have nothing to say or to communicate." Stripping away the mythic and erotic elements of genre, Tourneur, according to Lourcelles, leaves only the beauty of "action at the moment at which it is accomplished."[9] His heroes seem outside themselves, far away, indifferent to what happens to them (in this they perhaps reflect the personality of their director). *I Walked with a Zombie*, *Experiment Perilous*, and *Out of the Past* highlight this strange self-remoteness in a unique way by having characters narrate sections of the action in voice-over and by emphasizing the disjunction between the act of narration and the unity of the represented events. (Tourneur's shorts, *Berlin Express*, and *Stars in My Crown* use voice-over narration somewhat more conventionally; Tourneur also intended to use a narrator in his unfilmed *Whispering in Distant Chambers*.)

With rare exceptions, such as Anne of the Indies and Martín the gaucho, Tourneur's characters are not heroic or tragic. The typical Tourneur heroes are the pragmatic, determined Logan in *Canyon Passage* and the stoic Jeff in *Out of the Past*: defined by their circumstances, they act in ways that they seek neither to explain nor to justify. Tourneur has an affinity for characters who are helpless and passive (Lindley, trapped in the huge brewery vat in *Berlin Express*, is unable to come to the aid of his colleagues as they are apparently about to be killed) or who sacrifice themselves (Anne at the end of *Anne of the Indies*). For Tourneur, resignation isn't a moral ideal in itself but comes as the inevitable result of the displacement of the hero in history (the prolonged aporia of *Way of a Gaucho*) or as a convulsion or exhaustion, like the confessions of characters in *I Walked with a Zombie*, *The Leopard Man*, and *Great Day in the Morning* and like the surrender of Vanning in front of the church in *Nightfall*. Tourneur's sense of passivity and inevitability colors even his most straightforward and positive protagonist, Wyatt Earp in *Wichita*, who has to be goaded into action by events and who apologizes to his enemy in advance for the bullet with which he kills the latter in a duel.

Tourneur's characters invariably lack the psychological density of the heroes of, for example, Anthony Mann and Nicholas Ray: psychological depth is irrelevant to Tourneur, as it is to Raoul Walsh and Budd Boetticher, for example, but not because he is concerned with the characters only as existential subjects (as Walsh is) or only as they affect each other (as Boetticher is) but because he sees them in terms of their freedom or unfreedom. Logan speaks for Tourneur near the beginning of *Canyon Passage* when he says, "A man can choose his own gods." Camrose and Bragg in the same film are typical of the many Tourneur characters who become trapped in cycles of compulsive destruction.

Tourneur is drawn to marginal characters, figures who are situated at once both inside and outside their communities, who typically play minor roles in the plots but who embody the ambiguity of their worlds. Bertrand Tavernier notes, "Often in Tourneur the film is prolonged after the last word, and a secondary character becomes the center of the story, illuminates it differently, and opens it ... toward 'something else.'" Robin Wood points out the "special status" of such characters as the gentle Hi Linnet in *Canyon Passage* and the mute Kid in *Out of the Past*, "more spectator than participant, detached, belonging to no one." As Wood notes, these characters are related to the zombie Carrefour in *I Walked with a Zombie*, a "speechless intermediary between the shadowy other-world and the world of consciousness."[10] Other characters in Tourneur films also stand at the crossroads of different worlds, functioning variously as intermediaries for the audience, interpreters for the director, and ambassadors from the world of art (in particular, music): the property master in "The Rainbow Pass," Tourneur's extraordinary short about the Chinese theater; the calypso singer in *I Walked with a Zombie*; the troubadour in *The Flame and the Arrow*; and the medium in *Night of the Demon*.

Himself a figure at the crossroads of two worlds, his native Europe and his adoptive home America, Tourneur persistently explores in his films the antagonisms and misunderstandings that arise from cultural difference. The heroes of Tourneur's three films for Val Lewton are normal, uncomplicated North Americans who become embroiled in doubt, guilt, and moral ambiguity through contact with a foreign culture: "Serbia" in *Cat People* (rather than designating a precise cultural-geographical entity, the name functions as a sign of foreignness in the film); "St. Sebastian" or Haiti in *I Walked with a Zombie*; and the predominantly Hispanic New Mexico town in *The Leopard Man*. In each of these deeply antiracist films, conflict and anguish arise not from the permanent characteristics of a foreign culture but from the reaction between two cultures. In *Cat People*, Oliver's and Dr. Judd's refusal to take Irena's fears at face value lead to disaster; in *I Walked with a Zombie*, several whites, including a nurse and a missionary's wife, become susceptible to voodoo, provoking catastrophe; and in *The Leopard Man*, the Anglo visitors from the East bring terror and violence with them, unconsciously imitating the conquistadores whose slaughter of the town's indigenous population is recalled by the procession of penitents in the last section of the film.

The skeptical Holden in *Night of the Demon*—who, on a mission to debunk all forms of belief in the supernatural, ends up a believer—is the most fully developed embodiment of the type of Tourneurian hero who enters a sort of "parallel world" (to cite one of the director's favorite themes) and emerges humbled. *Night of the Demon* is the central work in a group of Tourneur films about Americans in Europe, a group that also includes *Berlin Express* and *Circle of Danger*. Because the heroes of the latter two films are less personally implicated by the unpleasant discoveries they make, the dramatic force of these two films is attenuated, but not their mystery. The same could be said of *Experiment Perilous* (set, like *Cat People*, in New York), which deals with the prototypical triangle of a rationalistic American hero, a woman in distress, and her cultured, misogynistic, impotent European husband, trying to convince the world that she, not he, is mad.

Tourneur was one of several European directors who, working in Hollywood during the 1940s, evolved an alternative (some might argue, oppositional) film practice. In order of their first American feature directing credits, they include Edgar G. Ulmer, Fritz Lang, Otto Preminger, Tourneur, Billy Wilder, Jean Renoir, Robert Siodmak, Douglas Sirk, and Andre De Toth. The group members share several characteristics: they almost all started directing in Hollywood in the late 1930s or early 1940s (Ulmer, the exception, directed his first American film in 1932); they all have an affinity for what has become known as film noir; and many of them express a politically liberal viewpoint in their films. The liberalism of Lang, Renoir, Preminger, and Sirk is explicit. That of Tourneur is less definite but no less perceptible: the liberalism of *Berlin Express* probably owes more to its producer, Bert Granet, than to its director, but the sympathetic treatment of blacks and other minorities throughout Tourneur's films is a clear-enough sign of the director's attitude.

Within the language of Hollywood cinema, Tourneur, like his European colleagues, developed a variant mode of expression. According to Gilles Deleuze and Félix Guattari, in a "minor" literature, "the expression must break forms, mark ruptures and new branch-lines. A form being broken, reconstruct the content which will necessarily be in rupture with the order of things."[11] Tourneur's films enact this rupture in various ways: in the tearing of Irena's unfinished sketch at the beginning of *Cat People*, in the splintering of narrative in *I Walked with a Zombie* and *Experiment Perilous*, and in the sudden eruptions of violence in *Anne of the Indies*, *Appointment in Honduras*, and *Wichita*. *The Leopard Man* openly courts incoherence, both by breaking down into a series of mininarratives (each with its own heroine and each ending in her death) and by stressing motifs that ostensibly function as unifying devices but whose recurrence is marked by a notable failure to unify, such as the fountain at the hotel, the film's metaphor for the lack of insight that it sees as characteristic of the human condition. Even *Stars in My Crown*, a beautifully wrought but seemingly anomalous work that, by its optimism, constitutes an enigma of its own within a career based on enigma, can be related to this subversive impulse in Tourneur's work. *Stars in My Crown* examines "the order of things" itself— a homogeneous, organic pattern that is precisely what the narratives of Tourneur's other films exclude as unrealizable.

The breaking of form is most noticeable in Tourneur's approach to genre. A number of Tourneur films belong to more than one genre: *I Walked with a Zombie* is both a kind of horror film and a loose transposition of *Jane Eyre*; *The Leopard Man* is a combination of horror film, murder mystery, and film noir; *Berlin Express* combines the murder mystery and the didactic semidocumentary. *Out of the Past, Anne of the Indies, Appointment in Honduras*, and *Nightfall* all subvert their genres by playing against audience expectations, whereas *Easy Living* and *Way of a Gaucho* are genre-like films that belong to no existing genre. Jacques Lourcelles sees the originality of Tourneur's approach in the "touch of the fantastic" the director slips into each of his films and in their peculiar rhythm, created by

> an irregular, depressing, non-dynamic succession of
> moments of lassitude and moments of terror, in which,
> moreover, the rigor of the author reappears curiously.... He
> prefers to show that action has its *temps morts*, that it has its
> own contrasts, notably that contrast of lassitude and terror
> that he succeeds admirably in painting; for the cycle of
> action — fear, fatigue, suffering, and death — which is a terri-
> fying cycle, is also a monotonous cycle.[12]

Even in the Western, the least flexible of Hollywood genres, Tourneur creates an unusual atmosphere through the homogeneity of his visual style and the hypnotic slowness of his narrative development. As Robin Wood writes, "The key to Tourneur's Westerns ... is the fact that he approaches the genre as an outsider."[13] Tourneur doesn't so much deconstruct the Western tradition as patiently let it explain itself, a process we watch in the opening sequences of *Wichita*, which introduce, in orderly succession, first the cowboys, possessing an equal potential for generosity and for violence, then the solitary hero, and finally the town of Wichita, its commercial enterprises devoted to the cowboys' needs, and its newspaper, the voice of principled criticism. The thematic and iconographic similarities to Ford are obvious, but Tourneur is more concerned than Ford with exploring the social chain of the western town and the links between commerce, politics, and crime. Similarly, the entrepreneurial heroes of *Canyon Passage* and *Great Day in the Morning*, drawn unwillingly into conflicts in spheres beyond their private interests, have a family resemblance to the heroes of Anthony Mann's *Bend of the River* and *The Far Country* but are conceived in more modern terms. They are fallible, fluid, and motivated unpredictably by various desires and attachments. We never see them definitely as figures who stand either for or against the community.

In an article on *Berlin Express*, Michael Henry points out, "The feeling of insecurity that Tourneur likes to instill in each of his films is not confined to the conventions of a particular genre, but derives from the *uncertainty* in which his creatures find themselves plunged as soon as they have been uprooted, placed out of their element, literally sidetracked."[14] Linked with this uncertainty is the strongly oneiric atmosphere of several of Tourneur's films. Many Tourneur films show characters waking up from sleep to confront situations that they never succeed in perceiving clearly, that they are never fully able to control, and that we interpret as partly created by their unconscious desires: Oliver in *Cat People*, Betsy in *I Walked with a Zombie*, Consuelo in *The Leopard Man*, Nina in *Days of Glory*, Bailey at the beginning of *Experiment Perilous*, Jeff in the Acapulco bar where he first sees Kathie in *Out of the Past*, John recovering from fever in *Stars in My Crown*, Teresa apprehending the absolute strangeness of the pampa in *Way of a Gaucho*.

Tourneur's compositions and lighting schemes insistently involve the characters with their surroundings, creating a sense of human interaction as a tapestry. The transitions from character to character in *The Leopard Man* show this aspect of his cinema well, as do the elaborate camera movements in *Canyon Passage*. In one of the most illuminating comments ever made about Tourneur's style, Manny Farber found in *The Leopard Man* "a way to tell a story about people that isn't dominated by the activity, weight, size and pace of the human figure."[15] This freedom from anthropocentrism, which we sense throughout Tourneur's films, allows him to express a view of man that is simultaneously detached and compassionate. Tourneur favors long and medium-long shots, in which people are shown full-figure, with much head room in the composition; *Out of the Past* is filmed as much as possible in such shots. Frequently, Tourneur poses a character in the frame so that his or her body is in profile while the face is turned toward the camera — a position that emphasizes temporariness, the person held by the camera as if interrupted in the act of departing: in *Experiment Perilous*, the shot of Alec agreeing with Nick's suggestion of whisky; in *I Walked with a Zombie* and *Out of the Past*, the similarly angled and composed shots of Carrefour and of Jeff on beaches.

The expressive use of light and shadow in nearly all Tourneur's films makes them instantly identifiable as his. The legendary shadows on the walls of the swimming pool in *Cat People*, the two-shot of Professor Walther and his shadow in *Berlin Express*, and the shadows of the officers chasing Teresa in the cathedral in *Way of a Gaucho* all bear the stamp of the same extraordinary inventiveness.

Night scenes and scenes in which only certain areas of the composition are lit are prevalent in all Tourneur films. Of the countless shots in Tourneur that make striking use of darkness, a few that come readily to mind are the scene in which Irena hums her lullaby to Oliver in the dark apartment in *Cat People*, the close-up of Irena's face in a pool of darkness in Dr. Judd's office in the same film, the scene in which George stalks and kills McIver in *Canyon Passage*, the duel between Dardo and the marchese in *The Flame and the Arrow*, and the shot of Pierre entering Molly's empty room at the inn in *Anne of the Indies*. Tourneur invariably derives dramatic and emotional power from darkness, for example in his scenes of lovers in silhouette: Jeff and Kathie rekindling their flame in *Out of the Past*; Dardo and Anne in *The Flame and the Arrow*; Pentecost and Ann in *Great Day in the Morning*. At other moments, the lighting throws shadows on faces, bodies, and decor, creating an undefinable mood of disquiet: the horizontal bars of light admitted through jalousies in *I Walked with a Zombie*; the dim light projected, through curtains, on people sleeping uneasily in *The Fearmakers* and "Night Call."

Tourneur always gives prominence to light sources in his sets: lamps, windows, and sometimes torches, car headlights, and flashlights. By placing these sources within compositions and underlining the characters' relationship to them (for example, by having actors move to the light in order to read, as in *Experiment*

Perilous and *Night of the Demon*), Tourneur makes the conditions of visibility an overt concern of his films. With his systematic placement of light sources within shots, Tourneur is the director who best represents an "expressionistic" style of lighting, as Marc Vernet describes it:

> In a seemingly paradoxical way, there is a constant attempt
> to diegeticize this light as a function of the situation (night)
> and of the light sources (streetlights, lamps), although the
> light is also exhibited, since the spectator's attention is
> drawn by its violence, its apparent rarity and the deforma-
> tions it provokes. But this exhibition is diegeticized in its
> turn, since the light can be what pursues and threatens the
> character (it is a persecutory force).[16]

Tourneur even gives the image of a pursuing, threatening light its ideal embodi-ment in the sequence of Holden being chased through the woods by a cloud in *Night of the Demon*.

Tourneur's expressionism rigorously excludes the distorted perspectives, odd angles, and subjective effects typical of what has been called expressionism in Hollywood cinema. (His restraint is all the more remarkable in view of the high number of horror films and films noirs in his output.) *Stars in My Crown* was originally to have included a sequence in a child's sickroom filmed so as to suggest his blurred, intermittent vision and time-perception; as finally shot, this sequence is entirely "objective" and achieves its overwhelming power by concentrating on the emotions of the child's adoptive parents, portrayed in a naturalistic visual context.[17]

The settings of Tourneur's films are atmospheric and richly detailed, in color no less so than in black-and-white. The hermetic wonders of the soundstage jun-gle in *Appointment in Honduras* and the brooding calm of the western towns in *Wichita* and *Great Day in the Morning* are as specific and identifiable as the superbly drawn microcosms of the Lewton films, *Days of Glory*, and *Experiment Perilous*. Tourneur's films also show unusual sensitivity to weather and its effect on lighting and mood: the viewer can almost feel the sweltering heat at the beginning of *Nightfall* and the barely moving summer air of Frankfurt in *Berlin Express*.

Many of Tourneur's films offer a distinctive experience of space. In the open-ing sequence of *Canyon Passage*, Logan enters, successively, a stable, an assayer's office, and a dry-goods store, repeatedly returning to the street that joins them, itself a "canyon passage" between the buildings (as an initial high-angle shot leads us to perceive it). At the beginning of *Out of the Past*, Stefanos drives down a country road into the town of Bridgeport, California, then gets out of his car and walks into a diner. The fluidity of these sequences suggests a progressive opening-up of contiguous spaces — a kind of funneling of action through space most suc-cinctly visualized in the trains and corridors of *Experiment Perilous*, *Berlin Express*, and *Night of the Demon* and in the streets and "transverses" of *Cat People*, *The Leopard Man*, and *Canyon Passage*. Tourneur's spaces frequently conceal unpre-dictable dangers (such as the leopard in the tunnel in *The Leopard Man*), resonate mysteriously with each other (Vanning's apartment in *Nightfall* as seen from Fraser's window in the boardinghouse across the street, and the apartment opposite

Irena's in *Cat People*), or unfold in unexpected ways (the open apartment adjacent to Leonard Eels's in *Out of the Past*, and the area curtained off from the banquet room where Philippides fights the wrestler in *La Battaglia di Maratona*). Tourneur's fluid camera movements cause us to see the narrative as a series of revelations and discoveries: the tracking shot that picks up Betsy and Jessica leaving the house in *I Walked with a Zombie*; the shot that tracks with Jeff and Whit in the foreground while Kathie emerges from the background in *Out of the Past*; and the tracking shots of Holden in the woods in *Night of the Demon*.

The experience of space in Tourneur's films is as different from that in Preminger's films, in which arrivals and departures become occasions for celebrating man's freedom of movement, as from the claustral preoccupations of Lang. Tourneur's films are voyages of exploration: in *Cat People*, *I Walked with a Zombie*, and *The Leopard Man*, the camera follows characters on long walks that become extended journeys into fear; the circular investigations of *Circle of Danger* and *Night of the Demon* are metaphorical journeys as adventurous as the itinerary of *Berlin Express* and the trek through the jungle in *Appointment in Honduras*. The motif of characters retracing their steps in Tourneur's adventure films (e.g., *Appointment in Honduras*) relates to the strange sense of time characteristic of several other Tourneur films: the viewer of *Experiment Perilous*, for example, is at once pulled back into the past (by the flashback) and drawn forward into the future (along with Bailey, with whom the viewer makes discoveries about the other characters); on the other hand, the flashbacks interspersed with the present-time action in *Nightfall* constitute a second narrative, running parallel to the first.

The cutting in Tourneur's films gives a sense of dislocation and disorientation to spaces that characters inhabit precariously. The three murder sequences in *The Leopard Man* evoke a dangerous, fragmented world through varying camera distances, high and low angles, and unexpected cutaways. *Experiment Perilous*, *Berlin Express*, *Anne of the Indies*, and *Way of a Gaucho* have similarly baroque visual fields. Several Tourneur films use a quasi–Wellesian device in which a shot of a foreground character looking at an object in the background is followed by a shot that shows the object from approximately the same angle and distance but in which the foreground character is now absent: the street scenes in *Experiment Perilous* have several instances of this effect, whose vertiginous potential is exploited more fully in *The Leopard Man* and *Night of the Demon*.

Tourneur's sound practice represents a deliberate attempt to make use of an often neglected potential of the film medium.[18] Frequently in Tourneur films, off-screen sounds disrupt the images, accentuating the instability of the narratives: the weeping that awakens Betsy in *I Walked with a Zombie*; the castanets heard over the first shot of *The Leopard Man*; the ringing of the telephone and the various noises and fragments of speech it transmits in "Night Call." Tourneur loves murmurs and reverberations, sounds filled with gaps, and weak, fading sounds. Often, he forces us suddenly to listen to silence or near-silence. Carrefour's intrusion in Fort Holland in *I Walked with a Zombie* takes place in a totally empty sound-scape punctuated by small, discrete sounds. In *Circle of Danger*, we listen along with Elspeth and Clay to a Scottish landscape that seems to be "waiting"; in *Anne of the Indies*, Anne and Dr. Jameson listen from the ship deck for the sounds of Pierre's returning longboat. Dardo's whispered "Now, Marchese, we're in the dark" in *The*

Flame and the Arrow makes a magical contrast to the loud clashing of swords earlier in the scene. Such a contrast illustrates the dramatic value of the eruptions in Tourneur's sound tracks of prolonged screams (the swimming pool in *Cat Peuple*), cacophonous animal sounds (*Cat People*), or interminable, random blasts of gunfire (*Wichita*) and fist blows (*Out of the Past*).

The quietly convincing acting style typical of Tourneur's films is crucial to their muted tone. Tourneur recalled the pains he took to elicit natural delivery from his actors:

> I've always used the same method with actors. I set up a rehearsal in a completely empty studio and I let them act. Then I ask them each in turn to come and tell me, and me alone, what they have to say in the scene. I have them sit close to me, and they say their lines. Since they're so close, they lower their voice, eliminate inflections, and give the sentences a different, less dramatic rhythm. And that's what I want to get on the screen. I don't like actors to dramatize their dialogue, because they always use the same procedures.[19]

No confession in any other film is more memorable than Mrs. Rand's in *I Walked with a Zombie*, in which the soft, placid delivery of the actress Edith Barrett conjures a remembered, faraway emotion. The excellence of the performances throughout *Anne of the Indies* enhances the subtle emotional richness of the film, for example in the movingly underplayed scene in which Anne confronts the treacherous Pierre alone in her cabin.

The director himself seems to speak, through his films, as softly and remotely as his characters. Unlike the classic auteur who imposes his vision on his film, Tourneur effaces his vision, not by the absence of style but by a style that emphasizes absence. The abundance of long shots, the restraint of the performances, the unity of mood sustained through lighting and decor, the muted tone that transmits a deep unease — all these marks of Tourneur's reticence suggest not uninterest or timidity but rather the desire to raise his material to the highest degree of truth. There, paradoxically, it becomes fleeting and indefinite. Tourneur's cinema, obsessed with the unshowable and with the conditions of its own impossibility, is the antithesis of the cinema of spectacle. He respects his audience as much as he does reality, risking being misunderstood and unheard but giving us all the more reason to listen to him attentively.

Maurice Tourneur

...the old time of directors who were dictators.

JACQUES TOURNEUR

Maurice Tourneur, Jacques Tourneur's father, was born Maurice Thomas in Paris on February 2, 1876, the oldest of three children of a jeweler who also manufactured imitation pearls.[1] After graduating at 18 from the Lycée Condorcet (where he became friends with the painter François Jourdain and the poet Léon-Paul Fargue), Maurice started a career in the arts, illustrating books and magazines, designing fabrics, lace curtains, and stage settings, and doing interior decoration. He served as assistant to the sculptor Auguste Rodin and to the painter and muralist Pierre-Cécile Puvis de Chavannes, working on the latter's sketches for the decoration of the grand staircase of the Boston Public Library. The future director later recalled: "I left painting because it gave me more pain than enjoyment. So much beauty was lost between the brain, which conceived the idea of the picture, and the fingers which portrayed it."[2]

After three years in the French Army as an officer of artillery, Maurice became a stage actor in 1900. His first engagement was with a road-show company, which on some evenings called on him to play nine parts in four successive one-act plays. He was good enough to be given the chance to tour the world as part of the company of the famous actress Mme. Gabrielle Réjane.

Early in his theatrical career, he abandoned his real name "because it sounded too English," according to George Geltzer.[3] His reasons for choosing the pseudonym Tourneur are unknown. The only well-known figure in the arts to bear the name was, paradoxically enough, English — the Jacobean dramatist Cyril Tourneur, whom Maurice may have known as the author of the macabre *The Revenger's Tragedy* and *The Atheist's Tragedy*. In French, *tourneur* most commonly means someone who works with a lathe (*tour*) or with another rotating object such as a millstone, spinning-wheel, or roller. As the noun associated with several of the various meanings of the verb *tourner*, it can also mean, for example, someone who causes things to turn or someone who turns. Perhaps the name was meant to honor Maurice's having abruptly "turned" to a new profession. Whatever the reason, the choice proved prophetic in a way that Thomas/Tourneur was unlikely to have foreseen in 1900, around which time *tourner* acquired a new meaning, one that is still generally used — "to shoot film." The first use of *tourneur* to mean someone who operates a movie camera (i.e., someone who rolls film), noted in *Trésor de la langue française,* is dated 1913. By extension, the term could also mean film director

13

and was recommended for adoption as the standard designation for that profession in an article published in 1921.[4] By then Maurice Tourneur was recognized as one of the leading film directors.

Back in Paris after his tour with Réjane, Tourneur became associated with the actor-director André Antoine. A renowned figure in the French avant-garde of the late 19th century, Antoine had become one of the leading forces in the movement toward naturalism in theater. Jacques Tourneur later recalled: "Antoine was a man of iron who forced his actors to underplay. He was fifty years ahead of his time, and his adaptations of Ibsen and Chekhov were played exactly as we'd play them today. I believe my father brought to America everything he'd learned from Antoine."[5] Maurice Tourneur started as an actor with Antoine, then graduated to régisseur, a position whose closest equivalent in the American theater would be stage manager. In February 1904, Tourneur married Fernande Petit, who under the name Van Doren was a star of Antoine's company. Their son, Jacques, was born on November 12.

After working with Antoine on over 400 plays over seven years, first at the Théâtre Antoine and then (from 1906 on) at the Théâtre National de l'Odéon, Maurice Tourneur left Antoine in 1909 after a dispute and became an actor and designer at the Théâtre de la Renaissance. In 1910, Emile Chautard, who had acted on stage for Tourneur and who was now director general of the Compagnie Eclair, persuaded Tourneur to switch from the stage to the cinema. Tourneur acted in several of Chautard's films and then began directing films for Eclair in 1912, including war pictures in Africa and an adaptation of a Grand Guignol based on Poe's "The System of Doctor Tarr and Professor Fether."

Eclair sent Tourneur (who had learned English as a touring actor) to head its production unit at Fort Lee, New Jersey, where the company had built a glass-enclosed studio. Maurice arrived in May 1914. His wife and his son joined him shortly after.

Maurice Tourneur achieved success with his first American films, which were distributed through William Brady's World Pictures. Many of these films were literary adaptations, notably *The Wishing Ring* (1914), *The Pit* (1915), and *Trilby* (1915). The future director Clarence Brown started in the industry after approaching Tourneur on the set of one of these pictures, *The Cub* (1915), and offering his services as assistant. Brown's description of Tourneur's visual style is informative:

> He was a great believer in dark foregrounds. No matter where he set his camera up, he would always have a foreground. On exteriors, we used to carry branches and twigs around with us. If it was an interior, he always had a piece of the set cutting into the corner of picture, in halftone, to give him depth. Whenever we saw a painting with an interesting lighting effect, we'd copy it. We had a library of pictures. "Rembrandt couldn't be wrong," we'd say, and we'd set the shot up and light it like Rembrandt. At least we stole from the best!
>
> Tourneur was great on tinting and toning. We never made a picture unless every scene was colored. Night scenes were blue, day scenes amber, sunsets blue-tone pink or blue-tone

green. The most beautiful shots I ever saw on the screen
were in Tourneur's pictures. He was more on the ball photo-
graphically than any other director.[6]

In late 1915, Tourneur was made head of production of a new company,
Paragon, financed by Jules Brulatour, who had become wealthy as the primary agent
for the sale of Eastman film stock to the film industry. In 1917, Tourneur switched
to the Artcraft company, for whom he made some of his best-known films, including *The Pride of the Clan* (1917) and *Poor Little Rich Girl* (1917), both starring Mary
Pickford; *The Bluebird* (1918); and *Prunella* (1918). In an article he wrote for the
September 1918 issue of *Motion Pictures Magazine*, Tourneur cited the last two
films, along with his *A Doll's House* (1917) and Raoul Walsh's *Carmen* (1915), as
examples of "stylization in motion picture direction." This he defined as "an
endeavor to express to others one's mental reactions upon studying a drama." He
continued: "The time has come when we can no longer merely *photograph* moving
and inanimate objects and call it art. We are not photographers, but artists — at
least, I hope so. We must present the effect such a scene has upon the artist-direc-
tor's mind, so that an audience will catch the mental reaction." This impressionist
credo is in character for the Tourneur depicted in a brief article written at about the
time of *Poor Little Rich Girl*: he was a man who liked to wander around New York
City and find spots that reminded him of Paris, Rome, and Naples. "If one knows
where to look, he can get almost anything in the way of scenic effects right in and
about New York that will represent Broadway to Hong Kong."[7]

Tourneur formed his own production company with Brulatour, Maurice
Tourneur Productions, in 1918. A *Motion Picture World* article announcing this
move declared, "He studied everything that bears upon the making of pictures that
he might qualify as an expert at every angle." His first picture for the new company was *Sporting Life*, an adaptation of a Drury Lane melodrama. The film had
no stars, and in publicizing the film, Tourneur attacked the star system, which had
already become entrenched in the American film industry:

> The star system of today is proving its fallacy. Consider the
> problem of the producer with a chain of stars. He must
> manufacture films regularly, using these stars at systematic
> intervals, in order to succeed.... The independent producer,
> on the other hand, can afford to select the star to fit his pho-
> todrama.... He can put time, undivided attention and care
> into his efforts as against the machine-made productions of
> the star system.[8]

In 1918, Tourneur moved to Hollywood, where Brulatour rented space in the
Goldwyn studios at Culver City. Tourneur's family accompanied him west (Mme.
Tourneur arrived after some delay, for she was acting in French-language plays in
New York under her stage name of Van Doren as late as December 1918).

In a profile of the director in the July 1918 *Photoplay*, Dorothy Nutting confessed to being seduced by "the boom of his voice making baritone solos of perfect
English phrased in the French manner, the twinkle of the poet's humor in his eyes —
a twinkle most English or American men might scorn as a symptom of triviality."

He made a somewhat different impression on the author of a 1920 profile that appeared in *Motion Picture Classic*: "Mr. Tourneur is somewhat larger than the average Frenchman, and indeed, looks more like a husky athlete than an artist and poet, yet the moment he spoke I felt as if I were in the audience chamber of an Oracle, for every word he utters is heavy with meaning and significant of deep thought." Accompanying the article is a photograph showing the director, in high boots, beside two large dogs.[9]

In a 1961 article, George Geltzer offered a revealing portrait of Tourneur: "He was a tall and introverted man who had never adjusted to American ways and lived in a large house on a Hollywood hilltop that had been built in '20. He did not get on too well with people and resented, e.g., people wondering why he had absented himself from France during World War I. He was one of the first of the Hollywood film colony to be 'psychoanalyzed.'"[10]

Jacques Tourneur recalled his father as having been "fascinated by scientific, medical, and philosophical research. His library was incredible. He followed very closely all the discoveries of psychoanalysis. It was through him that I discovered Freud, Jung, Adler, Havelock Ellis."[11] Psychoanalysis and psychiatry would occasionally figure prominently in Jacques Tourneur's films, in particular *Cat People* and *Experiment Perilous*. In 1971, he told an interviewer that one of his cherished projects was a film on the life of the pioneering neurologist Jean-Marie Charcot.

Clarence Brown, who regarded Maurice Tourneur as his "god," acknowledged: "He had only one failing in his pictures—he was cold. He had no heart." Aware of this deficiency himself, Tourneur sometimes asked Brown to retake scenes that he had already accomplished, seemingly to perfection. "So I'd get the actors in a corner of the set and we'd talk and kid around awhile. Then we'd take the scene again, the same way as he had taken it. But now it had a little something that it didn't have before—warmth." Jacques Tourneur recalled that his father "could be very hard with actors, something that I've always tried to avoid."[12]

Abandoning Brulatour's financial shelter against the latter's advice, Maurice founded Associated Producers, Inc., in 1920, joining Thomas Ince, Mack Sennett, Marshall Neilan, Allan Dwan, George Loane Tucker, and J. Parker Read, Jr. The company was formed in the hope of escaping the control of distributors, which Tourneur saw as damaging the quality of pictures:

> I should like to make pictures that dealt simply in humanity, but I always hear the distributor asking, "What's the big punch in your picture?" or "Has it got a ballroom scene in it, or something else that will get 'em?" He wants to catalogue my picture in his mind, and if I try to tell him that none of his labels will describe it but that it reflects human life, I talk in language he doesn't understand ...[T]he distributor must anticipate the judgment of the public in determining whether he will risk his money on the picture, and his judgment, and not the public's, determines the fate of the photoplay. It is the fact that his judgment is based on considerations that do not take the real quality of the picture into account that makes the trouble.[13]

Tourneur's first film for Associated Producers, *The Last of the Mohicans* (1920), was one of his great artistic and commercial successes and remains his most widely known work. (While on location for the film, Tourneur came down with either ptomaine poisoning or pleurisy;[14] Clarence Brown took over the film and directed much, perhaps most, of it.) The new production company failed, however, and was merged with First National in 1921. That year, Maurice Tourneur became a U.S. citizen and had the name Tourneur legalized. He spent the next few years in Hollywood working for various studios.

In the January 1, 1924, issue of *Kine Weekly*, Maurice published "A Protest," which George Geltzer aptly called "one of the most curious and self-contradicting outcries ever uttered by a talented man."

> The making of motion pictures is an Industry. It is an Industry demanding the services of men of talent, of men of artistic learnings. But it is not an Art. Its primary object is not the creation of beauty, the satisfaction of the yearning for expression of men with great souls.
>
> The aim of the men who make motion pictures is to line their pocket books. People go to see movies in the same spirit in which they read the works of frothy novelists or attend a vaudeville show — in order to pleasantly pass a few hours of idle time. There is nothing in a motion picture audience of the spirit which prompts a man to attend a performance of Duse, an exhibition of Claude Monet, a Wagnerian concert.
>
> And to speak of the future development of the art of the cinema is futile. It cannot be. It costs a great deal of money to produce a motion picture. The only way the financial backer of a motion picture can get his money back, to say nothing of a profit, is to appeal to the great masses. And the thing which satisfies millions cannot be good. As Ibsen once wrote, it is the minority which is always right....
>
> Motion pictures an art?
>
> They can never be![15]

The disillusioned tone of this diatribe contrasts strikingly with the idealism of Tourneur's interviews in the late teens and can undoubtedly be attributed to his disappointment over the failure of Associate Producers and the desultory nature of his subsequent assignments.

Tourneur's American career ended in 1926 over a dispute with MGM about the studio's insistence on assigning a supervising producer to *The Mysterious Island*. As Jacques, who was present, recalled, four days into the shooting, a man apparently unconnected with the production appeared; Maurice had him thrown off the set. An irate Louis B. Mayer called to inform Tourneur that the man was the film's producer, who, under MGM's new policy, would supervise Tourneur's direction. When the producer returned the next day, Tourneur stopped production, saying, "I won't work until this man leaves the set." The producer left again; Mayer called again, adamant; this time, Tourneur walked off the set.[16] Three days later, Maurice Tourneur was on his way back to France, leaving his son behind. Soon after, he and his wife separated, although they were never to divorce. (*The Mysterious Island* was taken over by Benjamin Christensen, was later suspended, and was eventually completed by Lucien Hubbard in 1929.)

Tourneur directed *L'Équipage* in France in 1927, then *Das Schiff der verlorenen Menschen* in Germany in 1928; Jacques rejoined him as assistant director on the latter film. Returning to Paris after *Das Schiff*, Maurice Tourneur signed a contract with the film company Pathé-Natan; again, Jacques followed him, working both as assistant director and as editor. Among Maurice Tourneur's films that Jacques edited were some that Jacques considered his father's greatest, including *Accusée, levez-vous* (1930), *Les Gaîtés de l'escadron* (1932), and *Les Deux Orphelines* (1933).[17]

After Jacques returned to Hollywood to pursue his directing career, Maurice Tourneur continued directing in France, making a number of films that are today virtually unknown outside France and are hardly familiar even there but that are highly prized by those who have seen them: *Justin de Marseille* (1935), *Avec le sourire* (1936), *Katia* (1938), *Volpone* (1940), *La Main du diable* (1941). On October 16, 1945, he wrote a strange letter to *Variety*, in which he introduced himself as "the Michelangelo of the movies" and signed off as "the Frank Sinatra of the Riviera." In this letter, he reported on his activities, listed some property damages he suffered during the war, reminisced about his days at World Pictures, and noted: "I am awfully pleased that my son Jack (RKO director) is doing very well, and at last has got big pictures assigned to him. He is a very capable fellow, and I always knew he had it in him."[18] (At that time Jacques was shooting *Canyon Passage* for Walter Wanger.)

Maurice Tourneur's last film was *Impasse des deux anges* (1948). In 1949 he suffered a catastrophic car accident. According to Clarence Brown, while Tourneur was driving, a suitcase fell from the top of his car onto the road; he pulled over and, while running into the road to retrieve it, was hit by another car. One of his legs was amputated; "he was fitted with a pegleg he could hardly walk on. Finally, he became bedridden."[19] Tourneur spent his last years translating detective novels from English into French and died on August 4, 1961, after a six-month bout of edema.

Having seen only six Maurice Tourneur films, one of them (*La main du diable*) made after Jacques was already an accomplished director, I can't speak authoritatively on whether his directorial style directly influenced that of his son. I believe that if such an influence exists, it is slight. One could cite the frequent use of foreground silhouettes in Jacques Tourneur's films as an inheritance from his father, for whom they were a stylistic trademark as early as 1913. By the time Jacques Tourneur was directing, however, foreground silhouettes had entered the standard vocabulary of filmmaking, and his use of them cannot be traced to any particular model. The proscenium-like staging in parts of *The Flame and the Arrow* also strongly suggests Maurice Tourneur's early films, but this is an isolated example of a stylistic option taken for specific purposes.

Maurice influenced Jacques, I think, in general aesthetic principles and in visual culture more significantly than in specific procedures. An extreme attention to detail, particularly of lighting and decor, a naturalistic acting style, and a love of unusual and striking scenic effects are features that characterize the work of both men, and the example set by Maurice in such matters could hardly have failed to have made an impression on his son. Asked what he had learned from his father, Jacques replied simply, "I learned the profession with everything that it includes."[20]

In any case, Jacques remained proud of his father's achievement. He was pleased to hear Clarence Brown say that his father was as important as D. W. Griffith for the American filmmaker. During the shooting of *Anne of the Indies* in 1951, Jacques met actor Holmes Herbert, who told the director that he had made his screen debut in Maurice's *The White Heather* (1919). Jacques replied, "I'll be happy if I'm half as great a director as my father."[21]

Jacques Tourneur: I

Everything came to me all by itself, and I think it's because I made no effort to make
things come to me; if I had made an effort, maybe I would have hurt myself.

JACQUES TOURNEUR

Jacques Tourneur remembered an incident from his early childhood as his
first encounter with fear.

> I was about four years old and we lived near the Luxemburg
> Gardens. My father, who before becoming a filmmaker,
> painted a lot and had worked with Puvis de Chavannes, lived
> in the latter's house. His studio was a big mysterious room
> that filled me with fear. It was there that on Christmas Eve,
> my parents would put my gifts, and they would say to me,
> "Go find them yourself." There was a very long corridor,
> completely black, and I could make out in the distance the
> white spots that were my presents. I walked forward all
> alone, torn between desire for the toys and a fear that almost
> made me faint, especially as the toys in their packages started
> to take on a phantom-like appearance.

This story makes us think of the filmmaker-father in Michael Powell's *Peeping
Tom*, experimenting on his young son by exposing the boy to sources of fear. Consider also the following anecdote: "And then if I hadn't been a good boy, my parents would send the maid into the cupboard. In there she shook a bowler hat,
while my parents said, 'It's the Thunderman.' That's the source of one of my
obsessions: to suddenly introduce inexplicable things into a shot, like the hand on
the banisters in *Night of the Demon*, which disappears in the reverse shot."[1]

Jacques Tourneur's widow, (Marguerite) Christiane Tourneur, told an interviewer in 1992 that she believed that her husband "never had what's called the
affection of his parents.... His mother didn't want to think about anything but her
husband." Present at the same interview, her nephew, Jacques Miermont, added
that Maurice Tourneur had little time to spend with Jacques and that his wife was
"a *grande tragédienne* who was embarrassed by dragging along a son who was growing up and who therefore made her look older."[2] Jacques's upbringing was largely
entrusted to his governess, the family's Alsacian cook.

Jacques attended first the Lycée Montaigne and then the Lycée Lakanal. Joining his father in America in 1914, he was enrolled in the New York Public School.
He later remembered this school, located in a poor neighborhood, as a place of
violence and suffering.

> I was the only child to wear suspenders. My father insisted
> on it. So the other children spent their time pulling on my
> suspenders, very hard, in order to let them snap into my
> back. I didn't dare wear them any more and I walked around
> holding up my trousers. I think that was what led me to put
> in my films comic touches in a dramatic moment, to better
> highlight the dramatic side: the magician disguised as a
> clown in *Night of the Demon*. It's fascinating to mix fear and
> the ridiculous, as in the death of the clown in *Berlin
> Express*.[3]

Joining his father in California in 1918, Jacques was enrolled first at the Private School of Santa Barbara and then at Hollywood High School, where he excelled at tennis; one of his friends there was Joel McCrea, one year his junior. He became an American citizen in 1919.

While in high school, Jacques decided he wanted to enter the film industry. He watched his father at work, sold story ideas to him for ten dollars apiece, and appeared as an extra in Rex Ingram's *Scaramouche* (1923). After finishing school in June 1924, Jacques accompanied his father to Tahiti to assist him as script clerk on *Never the Twain Shall Meet*. He continued as script clerk on several of his father's subsequent pictures.

Jacques was 21 when Maurice Tourneur returned to Europe after the debacle of *The Mysterious Island*. His remembered his father's farewell: "He gave me a hundred-dollar bill, saying, 'Now, get by.'" Jacques found work as a stock player at MGM at $50 a week, appearing in, among other films, Sam Wood's *The Fair Co-ed* (1927), Edmund Goulding's *Love* (1927), and Clarence Brown's *The Trail of '98* (1928). His experience as an actor gave him insight into the problems of actors, serving him well later when he became a director. "I always put myself in their place," he said. "They're all afraid." Jacques also did production work, serving as second assistant to Brown and to John Stahl and making sure that the extras on Fred Niblo's *Ben Hur* (1926) took off their glasses and watches before the cameras rolled. He also acted on stage and worked as an usher at the Hollywood Bowl, which allowed him to listen to music, he said.[4]

On the night of May 5, 1928, according to the *Los Angeles Examiner*, Tourneur was arrested for drunkenness at a gin party in a Hollywood bungalow. The article reporting his arrest described him as "an assistant film director and son of a well-known producer and director" and gave his name as Maurice Tourneur, Jr. On May 12, he was sentenced to ten days in jail; his attorney gave oral notice that the sentence would be appealed.[5] This incident is the earliest evidence of Tourneur's fondness for alcohol, a trait remarked on by several of his acquaintances. (This isn't merely a point of gossip or anecdote: alcohol figures significantly or at any rate prominently in many Tourneur films, in particular *Toto*, "What Do *You* Think?" *I Walked with a Zombie*, *The Leopard Man*, *Canyon Passage*, *Out of the Past*, *Easy Living*, *Circle of Danger*, *Anne of the Indies*, *Wichita*, *Great Day in the Morning*, *Night of the Demon*, and *The Comedy of Terrors*.)

Jacques's career as an actor was getting nowhere when, in 1928, his father cabled him to join him in Berlin, where Maurice was directing *Das Schiff der verlorenen Menschen*. Jacques worked on the film as his father's assistant and also seized the opportunity to learn editing, realizing that he could rise more quickly to directing from editing than from being an assistant.

During the making of *Das Schiff*, Jacques met Marguerite Christiane Virideau, an actress. They married in 1930 and remained married until his death. Her sporadic later career (under the names Christiane Tourneur or Christiane Gebb) included appearing in several French films and at least one Hollywood film (Joe May's *Society Smugglers* [1939, Universal]) and, perhaps most notably, dubbing the voice of Snow White for the French version of the Disney film.

Jacques Tourneur was assistant director, editor, or both on all his father's French films from 1930 to 1934, as well as editor of Marco de Gastyne's *Rothschild* and Jacques Natanson's *La Fusée* (both 1933). In 1977, the French television channel FR3 presented a retrospective of Maurice Tourneur's films. Jacques was asked for his thoughts on revisiting the films:

> I saw one of them: *Maison de danses* [1931]. There's my name
> beneath it: "Editing: Jacques Tourneur." I guarantee you
> that I never edited this film, or else I really have a bad mem-
> ory. I saw it yesterday night, I said: that's not me. Because I
> know my way of editing: it links together, it rolls along;
> there, it was too static. But you're going to see a film that's
> called *Les Gaîtés de l'escadron*, which I cut; instead of staying
> one minute on me, one minute on you, now, that one
> moves.[6]

Jacques, who said that his father was "more difficult" with him than with anyone else, told a revealing story related to his period as his father's editor: "I cut eight films for my father and one day, on his boat, at a time when I had been given a big film to direct, he said in front of me—[actor Charles] Vanel was present—he said, 'You know, I'm in the middle of making a film, I saw the cut, and it's the first time one of my films has been well edited'—not laughing, very seriously; and I had spent years of my life editing eight films for him—well, that's not nice!"[7]

The only Maurice Tourneur film from this period that I have been able to see is *Obsession* (1933). Jacques is not credited in the titles to this film; Edouard Lepage is credited as assistant. Since no editor is credited, presumably Jacques fulfilled this function on the film. Perhaps his father omitted his credit deliberately as part of a program of harsh treatment of which the above anecdote is an example. At any rate, *Obsession* is revealing, since it deals with a father-son relationship in a way that can be read as a commentary on the relationship of Maurice and Jacques Tourneur.

The film opens as a woman (Louise Lagrange) who has had her paranoiac husband committed to an asylum reluctantly submits to pressure from his brother (Charles Vanel) to have him released. A long sequence at the asylum shows the husband (Jean Yonnel) pretending not to believe in his own delusions in order to fool the director of the asylum into authorizing his release. After returning home to his terrified wife, the husband rapidly succumbs to his madness. He is about to strangle her while she's asleep when the voice of their little boy (Jean Bara) interrupts him. The boy's innocent affection restores his father to lucidity long enough for him to telephone the asylum director and demand to be picked up and recommitted.

The psychiatric theme of *Obsession* bears out Maurice's interest in psycho-analysis, as testified to by Jacques, although the portrait of the psychotic husband appears to owe more to melodrama (the film is based on a play) than to clinical case studies. The climactic episode between the father and son shows that the psychosis need not be given much weight and that it functions merely as a device (as it does in Nicholas Ray's *Bigger Than Life*) to allow the film to examine the inner structure of the family. Initially, the father, stunned after his attempt to kill his wife, behaves in a distant, distracted manner while the son is frank and affectionate. Then the father becomes almost violent in his expression of remorse and need, frightening the boy, who is now reluctant to put his hand in his father's.

It would be presumptuous to suggest, without more evidence, that the character of the father is a conscious or even unconscious autocriticism on Maurice Tourneur's part. Yet the father-son scene strangely echoes Jacques's accounts of his father's cruelty and coldness. Moreover, Jacques Tourneur returns to this theme in *Experiment Perilous*, which exactly repeats the configuration of *Obsession*: again, a little boy's paranoiac father tries to kill his wife while she's asleep.

Obsession has another moment that foreshadows Jacques's work as a director. In a flashback to the attack that led the wife to commit her husband, Tourneur shows the struggle between the two as a play of shadows thrown on the wall by a lamp that has been knocked to the floor. The conjunction of these visual ideas — the fallen lamp and the fight rendered in shadow — will recur in *Cat People* and *Out of the Past*.

As a work of editing, *Obsession* is, if anything, too terse and tightly paced. The most striking effects that have to do with editing occur in the flashback sequence. The dissolve that opens the flashback is unconventional in that the image dissolved from — a close shot of the wife recalling the event — is held in superimposition over a series of cut-together shots (part of the flashback) before fading out. Later in the flashback, an expressionist montage superimposes images of hands and the husband's face over a shot of the wife fleeing down a street — a tour de force in a style that Jacques Tourneur would avoid in his own movies.

While working on other directors' films, Jacques Tourneur continued to nurture an ambition to direct. As he told it, he kept pestering studio head Emile Natan with requests to be allowed to direct until finally Natan ordered the studio manager to give him a film. His father's influence probably played some part in Jacques's elevation.

The first film directed by Jacques Tourneur was *Tout ça ne vaut pas l'amour* (1931), originally known as *Un Vieux Garçon*. It was followed by *Pour être aimé* (1933), *Toto* (1933), and *Les Filles de la concierge* (1934). According to Maurice Vaccarino, who worked as assistant director on the second and fourth of these films, Jacques was then already "a very precise director who knew exactly what he wanted."[8]

Jacques Tourneur: II

In 1934, Jacques Tourneur felt he had enough filmmaking experience to risk a return to Hollywood. His portfolio was a copy of *Toto*, which he took from studio to studio: "It was in French, they didn't understand it at all and they couldn't care less. I had to start from zero."[1]

With the aid of friends he had made while working at MGM as a script clerk in the twenties, Tourneur managed to land a contract at MGM at $100 a week, twice what he had been earning as a contract director for Pathé-Natan.[2] Tourneur worked at MGM from 1934 to 1939 as second-unit director on features and as director of numerous short subjects. In 1939, he managed the transition to feature direction with *They All Come Out*, a film that was planned (and initially shot) as a short. After two more low-budget films, MGM apparently dropped Tourneur's contract, which meant that he was available in 1942 when Val Lewton, with whom he had worked on the second unit of *A Tale of Two Cities* (1935), wanted him to direct Lewton's first film as producer for RKO, *Cat People*. This B film was a surprise hit, instantly making the reputations of both Tourneur and Lewton. They made two more films together, *I Walked with a Zombie* and *The Leopard Man*, before RKO decided to promote Tourneur to A productions with *Days of Glory*. Tourneur did four more A features for RKO — *Experiment Perilous*, *Out of the Past*, *Berlin Express*, and *Easy Living*— along with the Universal loanout *Canyon Passage*.

After his RKO contract expired in 1948, Tourneur began freelancing, making *Stars in My Crown* for MGM, *The Flame and the Arrow* for Warner Brothers, *Circle of Danger* in England for David E. Rose's Coronado Productions, and *Anne of the Indies* and *Way of a Gaucho* for 20th Century–Fox. *Way of a Gaucho*, an expensive, troubled production and a commercial failure, marked a turning point in Tourneur's career. He followed it with several smaller-budget films, mostly for independent producers. Starting in 1954, he also directed frequently for television. His last film, *War-Gods of the Deep*, was made in 1964 and released in 1965; his last known directing credit was on an episode of the TV series *T.H.E. Cat* in 1966.

The testimony of Tourneur's friends and acquaintances is consistent in portraying him as a shy man, averse to socializing; he never raised his voice and was a director of great skill and tact. Richard Goldstone, a writer and producer in the shorts department, recalled:

> He was very charming and affable, very intelligent, round-faced, very French, loved good food, loved good wine. He was a very, very nice guy and an excellent director, very sensitive, very acute cinematically, of course, he knew camera

Jacques Tourneur directing *Days of Glory* (1944) (courtesy of the Academy of Motion Picture Arts and Sciences).

angles like the back of his hand. He was a very talented man.
He also had a great personality with the cast, his sets were
always very genial and happy. He was very relaxed and very
knowledgeable about what he was doing. Therefore he was
not under great pressure. He had a very soft voice, a very
cultured voice. Not particularly a French accent.[3]

Bert Granet, who first met Tourneur when Granet served as producer of
Berlin Express and who became a close friend of the director's, stated, "Jacques was
a six footer, basically a very shy man with a wonderful sardonic French sense of
humor." To Charlotte Granet, Bert's wife, Tourneur was "a big teddy bear. The
people who loved him loved him very much, and understood him. Not many people did understand him."[4]

In an interview with Philippe Roger, Christiane Tourneur remembered her
husband as "very human, very simple." On the sets of his films, she recalled, "the
first day, people were always a little frightened of him because he had a rather cold
air. But after two or three days, everyone loved him, finally."[5] She added, "He
wasn't at all what one calls 'Hollywood,' not enough." By this she seems to have
meant that he was incapable of self-promotion and that he was more apt to invite a
prop man aboard his yacht than a producer or a star. "He never talked about himself, really.... He was never impressed by people, and he never wanted to impress
them."

Bert Granet thought that Tourneur "was frequently misunderstood because of
his shyness and the extrovert qualities of his wife." Granet remembered Christiane
as "effervescent, probably an American's idea of what a French woman should be
like if they had never visited France." Charlotte Granet, who became a friend of
Christiane's, found that the latter "was not any help" to her husband: "She was
charming, but she was so dynamic.... She did all the talking." The Granets
remembered that Tourneur occasionally visited their house and sat in silence while
others carried on a conversation around him. "Jacques kept so much inside of
him," Bert Granet said, "it was hard to tell what troubled him. Occasionally he
would drink a bit too much, but even then nothing was revealed about his feelings."

Tourneur was passionate about sailing, an interest he shared with Dana
Andrews, Bert Granet, and the makeup artist Robert Schiffer, who frequently
accompanied him on trips on his beloved yacht, the *Shearwater*. Schiffer (who
when interviewed for this book was surprised to hear the litany of the credits of a
man he had known mainly as a sailing buddy) recalled: "He never really appeared
to me to be zeroed in on anything in particular.... He was always kind of laid
back, and there was never any pressure. It was delightful to be with him. And very
funny at times."[6]

Tourneur was an amateur painter with a predilection for landscapes and
boats. Christiane Tourneur recalled that Henry Miller liked one painting very
much and that Tourneur gave it to him (it would be interesting to know under
what circumstances the authors of *Black Spring* and of *The Leopard Man* met and
what they talked about). Robert Schiffer remembered his painting style as "kind of
fey," but Philippe Roger remarked, "The strokes are always very decided, but at
the same time, not aggressive, but soft."

Tourneur also collected artworks. His nephew, Jacques Miermont, who accompanied Tourneur on trips to museums during the latter's visit to France in 1957, described him as "a man constantly in search of the new. And thus, he was interested in everything, he was interested in all art.... He would go to second-hand bookstores and spend the whole day in them."[7]

In Hollywood during the war, Tourneur was part of the sizable colony of French émigrés in California, which included directors Jean Renoir and Julien Duvivier and actors Charles Boyer, Annabella, and Victor Francen (who chose Tourneur as his son's godfather). Despite having spent much of his youth in America, Tourneur considered himself French. "When you were in the Tourneur house," Charlotte Granet recalled, "they spoke nothing but French. Everything was translated for you. If they were in your house, they addressed each other in French; otherwise they spoke in English." Jacques Miermont, who became acquainted with Tourneur relatively late in the latter's life (from 1957 on), noted that he spoke French with an American accent but recognized him as someone "fundamentally French in culture."

Tourneur's mother had spent the war in Normandy; he and his wife brought her back to live with them in 1947 after the location shooting of *Berlin Express*. Bert Granet recalled her as "a *grande dame* ... who only spoke French." Jacques and Christiane Tourneur had no children. Christiane later recalled that they had wanted to adopt a child: "We went to Chicago. In Chicago there were 2,800 people ahead of us." Then they tried to adopt a French child but found that children weren't allowed to leave France before they were 11 years old.

Except for *Stars in My Crown*, which he wanted to do, Tourneur never fought to do a particular film rather than another, and he accepted with apparent equanimity his position as a director-for-hire. "You know, I have a pretty strange reputation in the United States. They say, 'You have a bad script? Give it to Jacques Tourneur, he'll manage.'" He rarely turned down a script but invariably cited his rejection of *Devil's Doorway*, which Anthony Mann eventually directed in 1950. This was another example of Tourneur's congenital inability to promote his self-interest by pleasing the great: Tourneur turned the script down not realizing that the writer was Dore Schary's best friend. Tourneur is known to have turned down another Schary project, *A Woman's Secret* (1949), which then went to Nicholas Ray, and also *The Set-Up* (1949), which Robert Wise directed.[8]

Tourneur liked working quickly and under constraints: "I work much better when it's necessary to go fast. The films that I made in twelve or eighteen days are better than those that I shot in eighty days. It's bad to think too much. Everything must come from instinct." Tourneur contradicted himself on this point, however; he cited both *Canyon Passage* and *Berlin Express*, two of his longest-schedule films, as films he liked. And he said in another interview: "We don't have a chance to do anything interesting on a 12 or 14 day film like *The Fearmakers*. The script is written for a quickie. When you're making a long, long schedule thing, the script is written with many situations — and you do much more coverage, spend much more time rehearsing, you get a much better film."[9]

Tourneur thought the direction of actors was the most interesting part of directing. Before shooting, he would try to arrange a day or two for sitting down with the actors and reading through the script, changing lines they felt uncomfortable with. Then he would go with them to see whatever sets were ready so that while memorizing their dialogue at home, they would be able to imagine themselves saying their lines in the settings where they would have to say them on film.[10]

Tourneur's first principle was to give his actors the freedom to do what they wanted. Frequently, he limited his corrections to suggesting that an actor speak more quietly and naturally. After listening to the actor in rehearsal, he would say: "That's very good. Do exactly the same thing, but speak half as loudly." At a lower volume, the actor's performance "immediately takes on a stature, a truth, that it didn't have before. People often object to me that, in this fashion, my scenes become a little dull, a little gray. That may be, but I find that that adds to them all the same an element of truth."[11]

Members of the cast of *Out of the Past* remember Tourneur as a quiet, calm, and humane man, so sparing in his direction that the single instruction Jane Greer could recall receiving from him was to be "impassive. No big eyes." Rhonda Fleming remembered him as someone who "ruled quietly" and was "very much in control. He would be sure that you were in a comfortable position. He would run the rehearsal only once.... I didn't feel any pressure from him.... He liked actors, which was wonderful." Paul Valentine, who made his screen debut in the film, said: "Tourneur was a delightful, lovely man, and he treated everybody like they were his own family members. And we enjoyed it. There was never a loud word, never an argument. He gave me absolute freedom to do anything I wanted." Dick Moore added: "It turned out to be the most fun I ever had on a movie. I think it was the first time I'd felt a total absence of pressure on a movie set.... Jacques Tourneur was one of the best directors I've ever had — kind, sensitive, very laid back. If someone were to ask me to name my five favorite directors among those I worked with, he'd be right up there with Ernst Lubitsch, Howard Hawks, and a couple of others."[12]

In her autobiography, Hedy Lamarr remembered *Experiment Perilous* fondly: "Everyone treated me like a queen. Never did a movie go so smoothly." Presumably the director had something to do with making her experience agreeable. Virginia Mayo remembered Tourneur as "contemplative"; Robert Stack thought him "shy and pleasant"; Gregory Peck said he was "smiling, easygoing." To Peter Graves, he was "a kind man and a good director.... So many Hollywood directors were gruff and abrupt. I remember him as kind and patient. If you had a problem with the scene, he'd say, 'Take it easy, and let's do it again.'" Richard Matheson, visiting the set of *The Comedy of Terrors*, Tourneur's second-to-last film, watched the director "do a brief scene with Joe E. Brown who couldn't remember his speech. Tourneur was endlessly patient through about 25 takes."[13]

He could also be hard on actors, especially stars. On the set of *Cat People*, Jane Randolph recalled, Simone Simon "was always upstaging" Randolph. "So Jacques Tourneur really bawled her out — in French — and she didn't like that either. She was very difficult with everyone." During production of *The Flame and the Arrow*, Tourneur "walked off the set because Burt [Lancaster] had been terribly rude with a technician without any reason." Tourneur explained: "I detest people who insult those who can't defend themselves. I told him that if it happened again I would abandon the film, and he was very docile after that." He scolded his friend Joel McCrea in front of the rest of the cast and crew for being late for an early-morning call for *Wichita*.[14]

Tourneur claimed to have sometimes worked closely on his scripts, especially during the late forties, although this is contradicted by Daniel Mainwaring, who, under the pseudonym Geoffrey Homes, received sole screen credit for the screenplay of *Out of the Past*. Bert Granet faulted Tourneur for not having challenged the producer over the weaknesses of the script of *Berlin Express*: "[He should have] evaluated characterizations more.... He's not what I'd call a script director. Some directors come in, and they immediately start fighting you over the script.... It takes a lot of courage, and if you're a smart producer, you listen. You may not always accept what they have to say, but it's a sign of wanting to put their own touch on it. Now this is something I never noticed with Jacques. His work was satisfying visually. I think he got lucky when he got good actors." Louis M. Heyward, who later foisted on Tourneur a far worse script than *Berlin Express*, similarly faulted him for being "overly agreeable" in accepting the stupidities of *War-Gods of the Deep*.[15]

However easygoing he may have been with his casts and scripts, Tourneur was exacting regarding the cinematography of his films. He stated: "I always give my cameramen a hard time. I tell them exactly what I want. When I rehearse a scene, ... to put the actors and the technicians in the mood, I tell everybody to sit down. We turn out the lights and turn on just a gas lamp. The cameraman watches, and the actors perform better when they are lit by a real gas lamp, in the dark. When it's all done, I say to the cameraman, 'That's what I want for lighting, figure out how to get it.'" Tourneur also said: "I never look in the camera — cameramen hate a director who is always looking in that thing — because I know pretty well what's on it. But I'm very adamant and descriptive about the source of lighting, and if he doesn't give it to me I can tell on the set and I say, 'Look, this won't do. There's no logical source.' Most directors from my observation take much too much time looking into the camera for the framing and forget the essential part which is the lighting."[16]

Tourneur applied the same visual principles to his color films as to his black-and-white ones. "What color the sets are has no importance; what's essential is the lighting of the sets." Tourneur preferred real locations, both exterior and interior, and liked his sets to have windows so that they would take on more of the character of a real location. "A set must have a window because this window not only allows you to breathe but is, especially, a source of light, and I believe very strongly in the value of natural light."[17]

"A fighter against the cliché," Tourneur constantly sought to add details that would give his scenes a sense of happening in a real world. "In the average film you'll see someone receive a letter — well, I'll make a deliberate point of having that person if it's a day scene get up, go to the window and read it — if it's a night scene, go to the lamp and read it." He also cited a scene in *Night of the Demon* in which a man, in order to answer a phone in a hotel room, must pull the phone around on the table because it's turned the wrong way.[18]

Tourneur also paid close attention to the sound design of his films:

> I always follow the synchronization and the sound editing of
> my films very closely. Sometimes I take great liberties. If
> someone is talking, and he gets up and starts walking, I cut

the sound and you don't hear the sound of footsteps. If a bad
guy enters a house and has to go up a staircase, I know that,
after I'm gone, the technicians will keep all the sounds, the
staircase, the door, the footsteps. That's why I do my own
sound dubbing on the set. As soon as the actor has finished
talking or opening the door, I cut the sound and there is
complete silence while he goes upstairs and while he crosses
the room. That way I know that when the film is finished
and I'm not there anymore, the technicians won't do anything stupid in the dubbing.[19]

Like Ford, Tourneur edited with the camera: "It's an old editor's habit. I
always shoot so few shots that the producer can't do anything other than what I
filmed." Bert Granet confirms this: "You didn't know exactly what you were going
to get from Jacques.... Looking at Jacques's rushes, you wouldn't think you had
much of a picture, till you assembled it, because the scenes would be short." This
habit may help explain why an RKO executive wanted to fire Tourneur from *Cat
People* after seeing the first three days' worth of rushes.[20]

During the period when Tourneur was under studio contract, he was usually
able to see his films cut to his wishes. Problems with producers who recut his films
against his will arose only in his later years, when he was working for independent
producers: he regularly cited *Night of the Demon* and *Timbuktu* as examples.[21]

As his Hollywood career approached its end in the mid-sixties, Tourneur
became the object of attention from a generation of young cineastes. He told
Patrick Brion and Jean-Louis Comolli, who interviewed Tourneur for *Cahiers du
cinéma* in Paris, "I intend to choose my stories and my actors, for the first time in
my life." He acknowledged, however, that the initiative and the persistence needed
to launch and complete his own projects not only were against his nature but also
were irrelevant to the art of directing. "I am a director, it's my profession. I consider it to be a profession that takes all your time: you can't be at the same time
producer, director, writer, and everything. To be an honest director, you must
dedicate all your time and all your energy."[22]

In interviews from this period, the director of *Cat People*, *I Walked with a
Zombie*, and *Night of the Demon* professed a firm belief in certain aspects of the
supernatural, including the theory that the past, the present, and the future constitute "parallel worlds." He told *Films and Filming* in 1964 that he had been a "student" of this subject for forty years.[23] While making *Night of the Demon*, he had
taken advantage of his stay in London to meet witches and magicians.

"The true horror film has not yet been made," he told Brion and Comolli.
Shortly before the start of production on *War-Gods of the Deep*, Tourneur
announced: "I'd like to make almost a documentary on parapsychology—using
actors. I'm going to use all the scientific things as against ghosts." This project,
which he also outlined at around the same time in an interview with Chris Wicking, evolved into *Whispering in Distant Chambers*, which exists in the form of a
rough treatment, dated 1966. The story, told by a narrator to a group of little girls,
concerns an American multimillionaire who brings advanced technology into a
British haunted house in order to test for signs of life after death. The millionaire's
recording devices succeed in capturing the voices of the legion of the dead. During

a further experiment, he passes briefly into the world of the dead, from which he emerges chastened, only to die shortly afterward in an accidental (?) plane crash. *Whispering in Distant Chambers* would have been Tourneur's personal testament, the fullest exposition of his belief in "parallel worlds." He proposed this project to American-International and to Hammer Films, both of which turned it down.[24]

Tourneur had other ideas for films during this period, none of which came to fruition. He told Brion and Comolli that he wanted to "make films that would be shot around the world and that would be films of high adventure, in the style of Conrad's novels," as well as films concerned with the social and material problems of "man and woman at this moment."[25] In addition to *Whispering in Distant Chambers*, two of Tourneur's other original story ideas with supernatural or horror themes have been preserved. One, called simply "Satanique" or "The Horror Story," is a piece reminiscent of Grand Guignol about twin brothers, one of whom is insane; the other story, with the unlikely title "Fat Witch on a Bent Broom," is an offhand extension of the "parallel worlds" theme in which a married couple discover a camera that can photograph the future. The most detailed and extended of Tourneur's treatments was for a black comedy, called *Lazare*, about the repeated attempts by a Marseilles gas station operator to do away with his friend. Tourneur also told Bertrand Tavernier about two other projects he wanted to make in France: *La Bande à Bonnot* and *Charcot de la Salpêtrière*.[26]

Tourneur's tastes in other people's films are largely unrecorded. He liked *The Uninvited* (a film clearly indebted to Tourneur's own work with Lewton), *Lilies of the Field*, and *Ride the High Country* (of which, in 1964, he said, "It was John Ford when John Ford was good, 10–15 years ago").[27] He apparently disliked virtually all horror films, including those of Roger Corman and even James Whale.[28]

In interviews during the late sixties and seventies, Tourneur expressed a generally favorable opinion of the contemporary cinema. He applauded the progress made in getting rid of dissolves and transitional shots in general: "You see people leave an apartment and there's a cut: they're in their car or walking. Why not? There's nothing more boring in a film than seeing a car arriving, the people getting out, paying the taxi (they never carry change), and leaving."[29]

In the summer of 1971, with his money gone and now dependent on his small pension from the Screen Directors' Guild, Tourneur and Christine went to Bergerac, France, to be near his wife's sister and her family. Jacques Miermont believed Tourneur wanted to rediscover his French roots and to compensate for the lack of human warmth in his childhood by seeking it in an adopted family.

At Bergerac, Tourneur had many acquaintances but no close friends. Of the French friends whom he and his wife had entertained in Hollywood during the war, only one — the actor Charles Vanel — now invited them to visit.[30] Tourneur would sometimes spend a whole day without talking, simply listening to his wife, his relatives, and their guests. Jacques Manlay, a television director, came to know Tourneur in the last months of his life. "He was a very discreet and very modest man; I think he had only a single passion: the cinema."[31]

On December 19, 1977, Tourneur, walking in Bergerac, fell on a sidewalk and had a heart attack. He was taken to a hospital, where he died a few hours later — six days before the death of Charles Chaplin and seven days before Howard Hawks died.

French Films
(1931-1934)

Thus I made four films, all comedies. Why comedies?
No doubt because I'm not funny at all.

JACQUES TOURNEUR

The account Tourneur gave of his four early films seems calculated to discourage research: "All those films are mixed up with each other in my mind. They resembled each other so much! It was always the same formula: musical, happy, young."[1]

Tourneur's first film, *Tout ça ne vaut pas l'amour* (1931), tells the story of an old man (Marcel Levesque) who takes in a poor young woman (Josseline Gaël) and falls in love with her, only to lose her to a young neighbor (Jean Gabin) who sings and dances. If the Oedipal triangle in this film may make it a remote predecessor of *Experiment Perilous*, the identity-exchange theme of his next film, *Pour être aimé* (1933), looks forward to *Berlin Express*: Pierre Richard Willm plays a young businessman who, jilted by his mistress, changes identities with a bartender on the French Riviera, only to fall in love with an aristocratic young widow (Suzy Vernon).

The third of Tourneur's French films, *Toto* (1933), is enjoyable on its own terms as a modest farce and, without being particularly suggestive of Tourneur's later style, demonstrates the young director's inventiveness and early mastery of the medium.

Toto has the thinnest of plots. Escaping from a policeman who has caught him with a stolen dog, Toto (Albert Préjean), a petty crook, hides in the apartment of a typist, Ginette (Renée Saint-Cyr). The two quickly fall in love, and after a brief incarceration, Toto returns to her and schemes to have her win a beauty contest. Bruno (Jim Gérald), a "financier" who met Toto in prison, briefly comes between the couple, but they are reunited at the end.

The film relies heavily on its main actors' charm, which is considerable. Préjean brings music-hall extroversion and skill to his performance, and Saint-Cyr (whom Tourneur had encountered earlier that year playing a supporting part in his father's *Les Deux Orphelines*) is likable. Their rapport makes the film sparkle.

The film is briskly paced, fluid, and attractively shot, making good use of contrasting angles and shot sizes. Tourneur keeps his camera on the move, starting with the first shot, which tracks rapidly alongside Toto and his pal (Robert Goupil) as they stride down a street. This lateral movement becomes a motif in the film. When Toto is arrested, the camera tracks with him and the policeman as they walk left to right in front of a long poster for René Clair's *A nous la liberté*, the words of the title gradually unscrolling as the shot progresses. In the film's most visually striking shot, the camera, at a high angle, tracks from right to left above a row of curtained changing booths for the beauty contestants; the booths are unceilinged, giving the camera a view inside each.

The sequence in which Toto and his partner steal a rich woman's dog has no dialogue except for a brief exchange between Toto and a policeman; it shows Tourneur drawing on silent comedy style for inspiration as Toto's partner tries to use pantomime to warn him of the policeman's presence and as Toto mimes his incomprehension.

Occasionally Tourneur uses long takes as a basis for visual humor, demonstrating the bias toward realism that would be a hallmark of his career. In the hallway of Ginette's building, Ginette and her landlady yell at each other from doorways at opposite sides of the foreground of the set while in the background, two other tenants emerge from their doors to see what is going on; at the end of the shot, all four people disappear into their rooms, shutting doors behind them. Shortly afterward, there is another long take with the camera in the hallway, shooting through the doorway of Ginette's apartment as the landlady, to prevent Ginette from leaving with Toto, takes Ginette's suitcase from her, carries it back inside the apartment, and puts it beneath a window at the back of the set. Toto and Ginette leave the frame in the foreground, then the landlady leaves, and finally Toto appears at the back of the set to reach through the window and retrieve the suitcase. Later in the film, Toto enters a dressing room at the beauty contest to pick out a bathing suit for Ginette. The wardrobe mistress, sewing in a chair, completely ignores his entrance, his presence, and his question ("Where are the bathing suits for the beauty contest?"). After he leaves, shutting the door behind him, she speaks for the first time: "*Entrez!*" Tourneur shoots the entire enigmatic incident in a deadpan medium shot.

Tourneur's later films aren't strongly marked by humor, the unfortunate exception being the broad burlesque of *The Comedy of Terrors* (which he once claimed, oddly, to be "a little bit in the old René Clair tradition").[2] More in keeping with the director's sensibility as it is revealed in his major films, the humor of *Toto* comes from realistic situations that are pushed toward craziness by slight exaggeration and caricature, just as the supernatural events in Tourneur's horror films and the violence in his Westerns develop within carefully realized contexts.

If *Toto* resembles any of Tourneur's later films thematically, it is, strangely enough, *The Leopard Man*. The beauty contest foreshadows the rivalry among women entertainers in the later film; the Toto-Ginette relationship, in which Toto acts as a sort of promoter, anticipates Jerry and Kiki in *The Leopard Man*; and *Toto* has a recurrent motif of animals (including a dog that lives in one of the apartments on the ground floor in Toto's building and is never seen but barks whenever there is noise).

The last and, in his opinion, best of Tourneur's French films was *Les Filles de la concierge* (1934), which he described as "a little comedy, unanimistic, realistic, and which described a social milieu pretty accurately. There were many amusing touches in it, especially for the period." This description suggests that Tourneur directly expressed his political sympathies in this film and in fact *Les Filles de la concierge* is concerned with class issues, but it handles them in the typical manner of a lightweight romantic comedy. Jeanne Cheirel stars as Madame Leclercq, a concierge with three attractive daughters. Loyal, sweet Lucie (Ghislaine Bru) marries Albert (Paul Azais), a chauffeur whose rich English boss, Henry Robertson, falls in love with Lucie's sister, Suzanne (Josettte Day). Robertson and Suzanne marry, but on Madame Leclercq's advice, they keep her lowly background (and Madame Leclercq's profession) a secret from him. Meanwhile, the third daughter, Ginette (Germaine Aussey), becomes the mistress of a rich couturier, Gaston Rival (Marcel André). Robertson misunderstands his wife's apparent friendship with his chauffeur and becomes jealous, but the truth is revealed harmlessly, and all ends well, with Ginette ditching her womanizing lover and taking up with Jacques (Pierre Nay), a pastry cook who's been in love with her all along.

The film is brisk, fluid, and cheerful, but with dark overtones. Emotionally it is structured on a contrast between inside and outside. Inside is the home of Madame Leclercq, a place of family unity, affection, and mutual tolerance, enhanced by the constant, reassuring presence of Albert and Lucie, who live with her mother after they are married. Outside is a world of dangerous attractions and false images linked to the wealthy Robertson and Gaston. Significantly, Madame Leclercq is never shown leaving her boardinghouse, while Lucie's major departure from it, to go to the posh Saturne club with Ginette, leads to disaster when Albert sees her dancing with another man (Robertson, who has coincidentally gone there alone to mourn his wife's supposed infidelity). The inside-outside opposition is central to most of Tourneur's major works, and it's interesting to find him developing it in a subtle and sustained manner in *Les Filles de la concierge*. As in *The Leopard Man*, the family home is a safe haven, while a nightclub is the major nexus for the class and cultural interactions portrayed in the film. The long sequence of Lucie and Albert's wedding party (which takes place, inevitably, in the concierge's apartment) anticipates the cabin-raising in *Canyon Passage*: both are placed centrally in the films as partly symbolic representations of harmony, and yet both involve exclusions that hint at underlying conflicts: in *Les Filles de la concierge*, Suzanne is absent from her sister's wedding, while in *Canyon Passage*, George and Lucy don't participate in the cabin-raising.

Les Filles contains a number of striking scenes. The sequence at the toy store where Suzanne works ends with an extraordinary montage linking close-ups of the characters with shots of mechanical toys, a juxtaposition that anticipates Renoir's famous shot of Marcel Dalio and his mechanical orchestra in *La Règle du jeu*. Later, an unusual crane shot, taken with a wide-angle lens, glides down the length of a tall window toward Robertson and Suzanne, dining at a table at the foot of the window. At the end of the film, when Madame Leclercq at last tells all to Robertson in the foyer of the boardinghouse, the light goes out four times as the result of a defective electric timer, leaving the two characters briefly in near-total darkness and forcing Madame Leclercq to switch the light back on before resuming the conversation. The repeated interruption, culminating at the end of the single-take scene when the light goes out for the fourth time just as the actors leave the frame, is an example of an unexpected and seemingly irrelevant element that ends up controlling the mood and rhythm of a scene.

One of the most interesting aspects of the film is its morality, which is much more liberal than that of Hollywood films of the period. In particular, no ignominy is attached to Ginette's becoming Gaston's mistress for money. Madame Leclercq is always willing to perform or encourage a questionable act if it seems to benefit her daughters: she insists on pretending to Robertson that she is a resident of the boardinghouse rather than its concierge, and she gets Lucie to overcome her scruples against going out at night without her husband.

Thirty years later, Tourneur expressed the desire to remake *Les Filles de la concierge*: "One could make a marvelous film out of it…. People don't make enough films about concierges, they're an amazing group."[3]

Second-Unit Work
(1934-1938)

Tourneur's first assignment at MGM was as second-unit director of Charles
F. Riesner's *The Winning Ticket* (1935), a mild B comedy about a barber (Leo Carrillo) who wins the Irish sweepstakes but misplaces the ticket. Despite Tourneur's
account of having shot "miles and miles of footage," including Shuftan effects, for
his sequence of the sweepstakes drawing,[1] this sequence, which lasts only a little
over a minute, is visually unremarkable.

Nevertheless, Tourneur's work on *The Winning Ticket* came to the attention
of David O. Selznick, who was preparing *A Tale of Two Cities* and wanted a person
of French background to direct the scenes of the storming of the Bastille. Tourneur
got the job. While working on *A Tale of Two Cities*, Tourneur first met Val Lewton, Selznick's story editor and personal assistant whom Selznick had assigned as
producer of the second unit.

Working independently from the rest of the *Tale of Two Cities* production,
Tourneur and Lewton developed a rapport that led, seven years later, to Lewton's
choosing Tourneur to direct the first film in Lewton's contract as full producer at
RKO: *Cat People*. Tourneur recalled: "He had a Russian background, and he was a
dreamer and an idealist. I am a realist: I always brought him back to earth. You
need that in a partnership. He'd go off into flights of fancy and I'd say, 'Well, look,
this can't be done.' I'd pull him down and he'd bring me up."[2]

Selznick was so pleased with the work of the second unit that he gave Lewton
and Tourneur a special credit, which was highly unusual: "Revolutionary
sequences arranged by Val Lewton and Jacques Tourneur." Tourneur thought
Selznick put his name on "because, since it sounded so French, it would give a
look of greater authenticity to the picture!"[3]

The scenes that Tourneur directed for *A Tale of Two Cities* are the only
moments in the film that move. Despite Ronald Colman's excellent performance,
the rest of the film is a literary classic embalmed in the dreariest Hollywood tradition, with painstakingly dull direction by Jack Conway, one of the smoothest and
most anonymous MGM artisans. (Robert Z. Leonard filled in for Conway during
the latter's intermittent bouts of pleurisy;[4] the possibility that even the most dedicated specialist could distinguish between the two men's contributions to the picture is unlikely.)

The revolutionary sequence begins as a starved, enraged crowd watches servants feeding dogs from a wagon load of meat. The crowd bursts through the gate

and seizes the food; cavalrymen arrive and swipe at the crowd with their swords. Watching with horror as a peasant is trampled by a horse, Madame DeFarge (Blanche Yurka) yells, "Why?" The word is repeated in increasingly big letters by superimposed titles as the camera, on a crane, swings from window to window of a Paris tenement to show the occupants gazing out excitedly.

Tourneur organizes the scenes of the mob marching toward the Bastille as a succession of bold, sweeping verticals and horizontals: a peasant at the head of a formation stoops to pick up a sheet and waves it aloft like a banner; as he does so, the camera swoops up over the street on its crane, showing the vast body of people behind him. Tourneur was especially proud of an idea he suggested for the scene of the mob arriving at the Bastille: instead of, as Selznick proposed, setting up the camera in front of the building while 3,000 extras arrive *en masse*, Tourneur exploited the possibilities for surprise inherent in the urban design, starting the shot with, as he put it, "six hundred people who come toward us in the narrow street" and then, "at the last moment," revealing with the crane the other 2,400 converging on the square from a larger street and from the boulevard behind the camera.[5]

Tourneur's background as an editor is suggested in the suspenseful use of extremely brief close-ups of people in the crowd, just as his future as a director is heralded not so much in the monumentality of the scene (Tourneur never again had a chance to direct 3,000 extras, or even one-tenth that number, except for his later chore on the second unit of *Marie Antoinette*) as in the predilection for high angles and unpredictable patterns of movement.

After the surrender of the Bastille, a brief section intimates the beginning of the Terror: a series of night scenes with anonymous figures riding on horseback and carrying torches dissolves to glimpses of fiery destruction and finally to the image of a guillotine. Then the narrative involving the principal actors resumes its course. The Tourneur section constitutes a seven-minute oasis of cinema in a two-hour-plus desert of dullness.

An earlier scene in *A Tale of Two Cities* looks as if it was also shot by the second unit: the scene in which peasants rush to drink the wine spilled in the street from a fallen barrel. The incident is effectively staged as sudden flurries of movement, organized visually in strong verticals and horizontals and lines receding from the camera (the narrow street, the line of heads bowed at the gutter).

Tourneur's only other known second-unit job was on *Marie Antoinette*, a former Irving Thalberg project that had been delayed several times and at last went before the cameras in 1938. W. S. Van Dyke II, the director, was noted more for his breakneck speed than for any other quality and was not associated with European costume subjects; assigning him to the project seemed to be a sign that MGM wanted to get *Marie Antoinette* in the can as quickly and as cheaply as possible. The ramshackle film that resulted reflects this haste; Van Dyke's direction is more visually forceful than Conway's (and Leonard's) on *A Tale of Two Cities*, but he failed to make anything meaningful of the script and was saddled with the insufferable Norma Shearer, who is on-screen almost constantly. (Oddly, *Marie Antoinette* was released in the same year as Jean Renoir's *La Marseillaise*, in which Lise Delamare delineates a completely convincing Marie Antoinette in her ten or so minutes on-screen.) In the large cast, only Robert Morley as Louis XVI, Gladys George as Madame Du Barry, and Joseph Schildkraut as the Duc d'Orléans make an impression.

Tourneur had already done duty for the project by shooting the short "The King without a Crown" (1937) to whet the public's appetite for a French Revolution feature. He was a logical, almost an inevitable, choice to help Van Dyke wrap up *Marie Antoinette*. In the absence of external evidence, we cannot affirm with certainty which scenes Tourneur shot. But one sequence stands out sharply from the rest of the film in style, involves none of the principals (except Schildkraut, who delivers an offscreen exhortation), and strongly recalls Tourneur's work on *A Tale of Two Cities*. After the birth of the dauphin, the film dissolves to a peasant woman carrying a child on her back; successive shots show peasants tilling fields and working in a mine; next follows a series of close-ups of grim, worn-faced peasants. The sequence, which lasts slightly over a minute, gives a disturbingly effective glimpse of an alternate reality to the aristocratic world that has been the film's exclusive preoccupation until this point.

Some of the mob scenes later in the film are overacted and shot in a routine manner, although there are occasional shots that one would ascribe more happily to Tourneur. The only other sustained scene that suggests his style is a nighttime pursuit through a forest. The atmospheric, natural lighting in these exterior long shots and the scale of the natural surroundings to the coach and its riders are reminiscent of Tourneur's use of landscape in *Days of Glory* and *Out of the Past*.

MGM Shorts
(1936–1942)

Tourneur hoped that his impressive work on *A Tale of Two Cities* would lead to promotion to full feature direction. Instead, he was assigned to MGM's short subjects department, where he went on to direct 20 one- and two-reel films. The assignment wasn't prestigious, but it had advantages. MGM's shorts makers enjoyed greater freedom from studio supervision than their counterparts in feature production and were able to tackle a wider range of subjects, often using techniques that were unconventional for features.

> The big producers, busy working with Greta Garbo, John Gilbert, and the others, left us entirely in peace. We formed an enthusiastic, young group, and with no supervision from the bosses, we could make films that were honest, free, and even meticulous. In fact, I think the producers never saw our films. They projected them as program-fillers with MGM features. Thus, for example, with a big Garbo film, they showed "Romance of Radium." But in my opinion, "Romance of Radium" was ten times better than the Garbo, than all those big machines that rang false, with the studio stars.[1]

The shorts series served as a training ground for directors who later moved on to features, including Fred Zinnemann, George Sidney, Felix Feist, David Miller, and Harold S. Bucquet. Richard Goldstone, who began as a writer in the shorts and later moved up to producer, recalled that the average budget of a one-reel short was about $10,000 and the average shooting schedule two to three days.[2] This was a comfortable time frame, allowing the filmmakers to pay attention to the visual qualities of the films. In later years, Tourneur would find himself allotted the same amount of time for a 25-minute television series episode.

"These shorts," Tourneur said, "taught me the need for great concision in story-telling. That's what's lacking, if I can allow myself to give my opinion, in many films nowadays. What matters is not that the rhythm be very fast, but to show what's important with a great economy of means, and avoiding slow stretches."[3]

Because of their rarity and intrinsic interest, I'll discuss Tourneur's shorts in detail. They prove that several years before *Cat People*, Tourneur was already a talented director with an individual visual style.

"The Jonker Diamond" (1936)

"The Jonker Diamond" has a narrative, visual, and thematic density startling in a ten-minute film. The first part of the film deals with Jacobus Jonker, a Dutch adventurer who brings his family to South Africa in the hope of finding a fabled, enormous diamond. Despondent after years of fruitless searching, Jonker decides, during a violent storm, to give up the search. Miraculously, the storm brings the diamond to the surface, where it is discovered by Jonker's son. The second part shifts to New York, where jewel magnate Harry Winston buys the Jonker diamond and has it shipped by common carrier in order to thwart thieves. The third and last part shows how, after preparatory study, expert jewel cutter Lazarre Kaplan plans and executes the splitting of the 726-carat diamond into smaller stones to be sold by Winston.

The film glides swiftly between narrative modes, from the realistic drama of the opening section, with its emphasis on toil, poverty, and abjection, to something approaching the urban crime film in the middle sequences, to mock documentary in the final part. The first part of the film is the most visually arresting, with its forceful tracking shots and credible decor, but the last part is especially interesting because here the process of cutting, smoothing, and polishing diamonds becomes a metaphor for cinema. Kaplan's search for the lines of cleavage of the Jonker diamond is like a film director's search for the dramatic values of a script or an editor's search for the moment to make a cut (also, the preoccupation with what can't be seen has a clear relevance to Tourneur's later films). As the narrator speaks of diamond cutting as an art handed down traditionally from father to son, the film highlights the presence of Kaplan's grown son, watching his father at work: in the round-faced son and the severe-looking, spectacled father, we may recognize the traits of Jacques and Maurice Tourneur (whose own father was a jeweler). "The Jonker Diamond" can thus be read as a personal meditation on the cinema as the intersection of the father-son relationship (note that Jonker, Sr., is on the verge of giving up when his son finds the stone), transcontinental movement, arcane craft, and the creation of beauty.

"Master Will Shakespeare" (1936)

Jacques Tourneur stated: "A tour de force. The entire life of Shakespeare and extracts from eight of his plays in ten minutes!"[4]

Visually, the film is richly Tourneurian—filled with life and movement, yet studied, never flamboyant. Camera movement unifies the film: a traveling shot from right to left of young Will Shakespeare going on foot to London dissolves to a traveling shot in the same direction, following someone carrying a torch to light the way for the crowd at the Blackfriars Theater, where Shakespeare, discovered at the end of the camera movement, now works as an ostler. This shot dissolves to one that starts close on Shakespeare, now at a prompter's table with a script; next it pans left and cranes up to show actors on a stage, one of them brandishing a sword, then continues left and down to show the groundlings, and finally goes up to show the spectators watching the play from a window.

A scene at the Mermaid Tavern contains a shot that could have come from *Anne of the Indies*: the camera tracks left from a keg as drafts are pulled, crosses several groups of drinkers, and continues past the backs of Ben Jonson and Thomas Dekker, at the edge of the crowd, to frame — in medium-long shot — Shakespeare alone brooding in a chair by the fireplace.

Irving Thalberg commissioned "Master Will Shakespeare" as part of the pre-release promotional campaign for *Romeo and Juliet*. Fortunately, the short devotes only about a minute to this propaganda purpose, showing the Thalberg production of *Romeo* as the culmination of a movement toward increasing realism in performance. According to the narrator (Carey Wilson), as stage director, Shakespeare "fought stubbornly against the crude traditions of the Elizabethan theater, demanding realism in place of the usual stilted gestures." The film briefly sets forth the performance tradition of *Romeo* in shots of an Elizabethan production with a boy playing Juliet, then of the David Garrick production, in which a chandelier stands in for the moon above Juliet's balcony. Finally we are shown a movie camera and a spotlight — in a telling example of the MGM shorts' constant emphasis on the apparatus of representation — as the narrator speculates what Shakespeare will think "when he sees from high in the seventh heaven his *Romeo and Juliet* on the motion picture screen." We see a few shots from the film, showing the lavish garden and balcony sets, and we see the actors speaking, but we don't hear their voices.

"Harnessed Rhythm" (1936)

A semi-documentary study of the training of Dixie Dan, a "trotter" (i.e., a harness racing horse), "Harnessed Rhythm" has a lackadaisical air, keyed to Pete Smith's jocular narration. The film uses slow motion and stop motion to analyze the horse's trot and demonstrate the workings of the harness. At the end of the film, Dixie Dan, hampered by accidents, unexpectedly loses the big race of the season, becoming, as Smith concludes, "the screen's first hero horse to lose a movie horse race." It seems almost pointless to add that the film has little to offer anyone not interested in the subject and that only two shots — the opening pastoral long shot of horses grazing under trees and a long shot of Dixie Dan's van on its way to the "final meeting" — are suggestive of Tourneur.

"Killer-Dog" (1936)

Tourneur disliked this short and scoffed at its having won a medal (the "Grand Shorts Award" from Jay Emanuel Publications readers in 1937).[5] Nevertheless, despite its melodrama and dog heroics, "Killer-Dog" is a small masterpiece.

The opening shot introduces us to Major the dog, seen through a wire fence: suspected of killing sheep, Major is on trial for his life. In a tracking shot, we see the muzzled dog led into a courtroom along a balustrade that separates him from Betty Lou, the little girl who owns him. A flashback shows the first meeting of Major and Betty Lou on her father's farm. Major's mother is a peaceful collie, but his father is a wolf dog who has been caught slaughtering sheep and is shot ("The beast in whose veins flows the blood of the wolf is led to his doom," narrator Pete Smith comments). Major gets a chance to prove his worth one day when Betty Lou falls in the driveway, unnoticed by her mother, who is backing the car out. Quickly sizing up the situation, Major uses his teeth to drag Betty Lou out of the way of the car.

One night, Major escapes through Betty Lou's open window and roams outside. "Pounding within him is a strange instinctive force that excites the lust to kill," the narrator says. The next morning, the dog returns home with a wound on his back, and the same rancher who, three years before, executed Major's father finds two of his sheep slaughtered and blood on the barbed-wire fence of the corral. Major falls under suspicion and is impounded.

We return to the present time of the narrative. The judge at Major's trial consents to a test. At night, while the rancher, an armed policeman, and Betty Lou and family all watch tensely from hiding places, Major is released near the sheep corral. He approaches the corral as if preparing to attack. The officer is about to shoot when the real culprit, a coyote, betrays itself by leaping into the corral. Major jumps the fence and attacks the coyote, killing him after a harrowing fight in the dust. The end of the film returns to the farm for an extreme long shot of Betty Lou and Major running away from the camera together.

Absurd as all this may sound, "Killer-Dog" has a remarkable intensity. It's at once both one of Tourneur's most lyrical and one of his darkest films. The several pastoral long shots show Tourneur's love of nature in a way that anticipates *Stars in My Crown*. (Another detail that recalls *Stars in My Crown* is the brief nighttime scene of Betty Lou's illness, consisting of a single shot that tracks in toward her sickbed.) The scenes on the farm are held back from sentimentality by the almost neorealist quality of their starkly sunlit, unfiltered exteriors (cf. the close shot in which the girl and the puppy are startled by the sound of the gunshot that destroys Major's father).

The extraordinary climactic night scene of the testing of Major opens with a long shot of the corral, surrounded by fences; we cut first to a two-shot of the rancher and an armed policeman waiting tensely in the barn, their faces starkly lit through slats (so that the rancher's eyes are in a horizontal band of light, his forehead is covered by a broad hat, and the lower part of his face is in shadow), then to a low-key three-shot of Betty Lou and her parents watching from inside their car. High-angle shots show Major slowly approaching the corral. With its tension, air of doom, and emphasis on visual barriers, the scene strongly recalls the climax of Nicholas Ray's *They Live by Night*, in which Bowie returns to the motel while the police wait in ambush for him. (Tourneur's first American feature, *They All Come Out*, also anticipates the Ray film.)

In the most striking shot of the film, the camera remains inside a van that drives Major away after he is apprehended on suspicion of killing the sheep. Through the wire mesh at the back of the van, we see Betty Lou run from the house toward the camera; crying, she grabs the mesh, reaching toward Major, in the foreground. Betty Lou's mother restrains and comforts her as the van pulls away, the camera inside it; the shot is held for some length, the people getting smaller and smaller in the background.

"Killer-Dog" has remarkable connections to *Cat People*. Both films involve slaughtered sheep and inherited blood thirst. Both Major and Irena are subject to a similar "strange instinctive force," although unlike Irena, Major triumphs over it.

"What Do *You* Think?" (1937)

This "miniature" inaugurated a miniseries of fictional stories, each built around an extraordinary event that could be explained either as a coincidence or as a result of the supernatural, also the theme of *Night of the Demon*. Tourneur directed the first, third, and fourth of the "What Do *You* Think?" films (the second was directed by Felix Feist).

Narrated by Carey Wilson, the first "What Do *You* Think?" opens in a house "high on the hills overlooking Hollywood" on a dark and stormy night. Among the people gathered around the fireplace, all of them shown discreetly in shots that conceal their faces, are a "prominent film director" (smoking, perhaps, John Ford's pipe), a matinee idol with a tennis racket, and someone named Basil who proceeds to relate to the others a strange event in the life of a screenwriter named John Dough. We flash back to the story-within-a-story, where *another* Hollywood party is in progress, also one at which a story is being told: as a parlor game, John's guests must try to solve a murder mystery he has propounded. (One of the guests firing questions at him is a blonde woman; kneeling on the floor, she shows more aggressiveness and more cleavage than would have been tolerated in a feature in the same year.)

The next morning, as John is about to drive to a meeting at the studio, he thinks he hears his mother repeatedly calling his name. He shrugs this off as a minor hallucination and tries to start the car, only to find that he has left the key in the house. Returning inside to retrieve the key from his dresser (next to his mother's photograph), he has a mysterious vision of a woman's body lying face-up on the bed (the shot of the woman is superimposed lightly over a shot of the bed). Again, John rationalizes away the phenomenon. Then, driving to the studio, he witnesses an unavoidable, fatal collision on the road ahead of him: the body of the female victim, stretched out on the road, reminds him of the vision in his room.

Obsessed by the event, John uses a stopwatch to determine that the delay caused by his having forgotten the ignition key—57 seconds—was equal to the time it would have taken to drive from the point where he saw the collision to the point where it took place. Thus, he would have been in the fatal place of the accident victim, had it not been for the "chance" delay, coinciding with his mother's voice. John is still struggling to free himself from his obsession when a phone call from his brother confirms that he has had a brush with the marvelous: that morning, John learns, his mother started awake from a vision in which she saw John about to do "something foolish" and called out to him to stop him.

The narrator, Wilson, rhapsodizes: "If the clumsy fingers of mortal man can concoct a contraption of metal and glass and wire that will pluck out of the thin air words that were tossed into the sky many miles away, by a purely mechanical apparatus, why is it impossible to believe that the unfathomable machinery of a mother's love could send a message to such a delicately sensitive receiver as the brain of an adoring son?" Over this speech, a montage leads from shots of a radio, tubes, a tower, and an announcer to shots in which the mother and John are linked by a dramatic sky. Finally, we return to the situation of the framing story — the fireplace, the house in the storm — as Wilson puts the question to the viewer: "Coincidence or telepathy: what do *you* think?"

The first "What Do *You* Think?" is an elegant treatment of an eminently Tourneurian theme. The film tempers its sentimentality with humor and irony. The plot develops with the same compulsiveness and the same sense of the accumulation of overwhelming evidence that we find in *Night of the Demon*. Like Holden in that film, John Dough constantly seeks to rationalize the mysterious events that transform his life. Returning home after his experiment with the stopwatch, he sees the shadow of a female figure on his bed; he determines that the shadow is created by the conjunction of a cypress tree and a lamppost outside his window and disperses it by switching on his bedside lamp.

The film has one of Tourneur's most obsessive narratives, with its Chinese-box structure, its multiple storytelling situations, and especially its compulsive repetition of the minute before the car crash —first shown "live" in the sequence of John's drive, then reconstructed with the stopwatch, and finally represented in terms of a different narrative situation and set of characters in the flashback that accompanies the brother's phone call.

"The Grand Bounce" (1937)

"The Grand Bounce" is a neat, ironic tale. The hero, Jimmy Clark, signs a $1,000 check to pay off a gambling debt; although he can't cover it, he hopes to be able to recover the amount from his own debtors in time for the check to clear. The rest of the film follows the check as it moves from one endorser to another: the gangster to whom Jimmy wrote the check signs it over to his girlfriend so that she can buy a fur; the furrier uses it to pay for an operation on a poor little girl whom he accidentally hits with his car; the surgeon endorses it to a friend to replenish his funds at a casino; the check is stolen from the casino cashier in a holdup, after which the robber uses it to pay off a debt to a prize-fight promoter; the promoter then awards it to a victorious boxer, Leadhead Hogan, as an advance on a contract. At this point, Jimmy closes the circle by claiming the check from Leadhead, who, as it happens, owes him $1,000.

The film is exceptional for the fluidity with which it moves through a large number of locations. An elegant camera movement starts on a medium shot of the gangster's girlfriend, standing before a full-length mirror, tracks toward her slightly as she walks left and picks up her purse, then pans with her right and down as she sits at a desk, her back to the camera in close shot, to endorse the check to the furrier. Later, an excellent traveling shot adopts the point of view of the furrier's moving car, passing several parked cars; a little girl runs into the shot, chasing a ball; as the camera bears down on her, she suddenly turns to face us with a look of fear.

In its shifting of interest from one character to another, "The Grand Bounce" anticipates *The Leopard Man* and *Canyon Passage*; it is more schematic and contrived, but not unacceptably so for a short. A slip of paper endowed with life-or-death power, Jimmy's check resembles both the map in *Appointment in Honduras* and, more obviously, Karswell's parchment in *Night of the Demon*: like both those pieces of paper, it is finally burned. Over an extreme close-up insert of the back of the check, showing its long list of endorsing signatures, the narrator emphasizes its purely symbolic value: "It paid several debts, it bought a fur coat, it was payment on a contract, yes, and it even saved a human life, yet it's not worth the paper it's written on."

"The Rainbow Pass" (1937)

A tie-in with the MGM feature *The Good Earth*, "The Rainbow Pass" opens with a short montage combining shots probably from that film with stock footage of China as the narrator (Carey Wilson) talks about the endurance of Chinese cultural traditions and the close dependence of the Chinese people on the land. These observations lead to the film's subject: the midautumn festival thanking Shan Nung, the god of agriculture. In a series of tracking shots of a crowded street at night, people carry a statue representing the god to the local theater. Yuan, a young farmer, buys tickets for himself, his wife, and his little boy.

The camera tracks in a circular manner from a close shot of the effigy of the god, seated at the back of the house, to a long shot that takes in the audience and a dancer on stage. The narrator prepares us for the imaginative reversal that will be one of the main themes of the film: "To appreciate the performance, we must know that its realism exists principally in the minds of its audience. For instance, if an actor carries a whip in his hand, one instantly recognizes that he is riding on a horse. Trained from childhood to recognize these conventional symbols, the audience is as interesting as the performance."

The film connects the use of symbolism in Chinese theater and the role of the audience, which is to interpret and complete these symbols. Since the audience has an active role, the film appropriately differentiates and personalizes this audience, in shots that show groups of children and a group of respected old critics, one of them rolling walnuts in his fingers to keep them supple for writing. Instead of a mass of spectators, the audience becomes "interesting," a varied set of loci of activity.

Part of the audience's function is to segregate the real from the unreal; "The Rainbow Pass" is preoccupied with locating the line of this separation, which cuts across the space of the film at several places. The narrator urges us to ignore, for example, the coolies wringing towels in pots of hot water as subordinate elements in the spectacle; yet the film insists on pointing them out to us, performing a double gesture of exclusion and inclusion that gives these subordinates the same status as everything else that takes place.

The property master, dressed in black, is supposed by the audience to be invisible, we're told; yet he is on stage almost constantly and could be considered the protagonist of the play (also called "The Rainbow Pass"). Hidden and yet exposed, he stands at the crossroads between the "story" that is ostensibly the point of representation and the apparatus that permits the story to be. The property master is perhaps the first avatar of a recurring figure in Tourneur's cinema — the one who joins different worlds, like Carrefour in *I Walked with a Zombie*. Usually marginal both to the society portrayed in the film and to the narrative, this character becomes central through his affinity with the power of cinema to join, translate, and transform. Frequently, as in "The Rainbow Pass," this crossroads figure has some involvement with performance (e.g., Hi Linnet in *Canyon Passage* and the troubadour in *The Flame and the Arrow*) or, in a more abstract way, with narration and communication (e.g., the Kid in *Out of the Past*, who conveys information between Jeff and the gangsters and finally provides the message that frees Ann from the circuit of the narrative).

In "The Rainbow Pass," the property master is the agent for a crucial reversal in the relationship between imagination and reality. According to the narrator, we merely "imagine" that we see the property master stacking chairs on tables; to the Chinese, the chairs are mountains rising from a plain. The space between them is the rainbow pass — a site both real and imaginary — which gives its name and its dual status both to the epic historical drama attended by the on-screen audience and to the film in which play and audience form an educational spectacle for a Western audience. This richly symbolic "space between" is nothing less than the space of art, an absence that makes present, a sacred, timeless space cut out from the world.

The film's three pivotal moments are all set in this symbolic space. The first is the close-up of the property master on stage smoking his pipe, an interested but neutral witness to the grief of the widow (in the play) beside her slain husband. At this point, by an imperceptible movement, the property master's function in the physical mise-en-scène merges with the function of the audience: to be the subject of belief in the story, to create its realism — a belief that is visible on his face (or, at any rate, that we read into it).

The second pivotal moment is the time transition during the middle of the performance, covered by two shots linked by a dissolve: in the first shot, Yuan hands his sleeping son over to his wife; in the second shot, the boy is asleep in the hollow of his mother's arm. Over both shots, we hear the voices-off of actors. On the simplest level, the dissolve merely marks the passage of time, but this passage is mirrored both by the "passage" of the child from father to mother and by the "passage" from the world of the play to the world of the "real" family. The magical nature of the latter transition is highlighted by the child's being asleep, which suggests both the oneiric character of the spectacle and the unconscious character of cultural transmission, as if the words of the play's text, heard from offscreen, were passing into or emanating from the mind of the sleeping child.

The third pivotal moment comes during the fight between the conquering general and the widow of his victim. The two clash their sticks together and hold a pose, gazing at each other: their enmity is transformed into love. The film emphasizes the significance of the moment by intercutting it with close-ups of Yuan and his wife, rapt: we see the transformation occurring on stage *through* the sudden recognition of its meaning by the married couple in the audience.

After the end of the play, the film again underlines the magical transaction between play and audience. In a shot that will be exactly repeated in the medicine show sequence of *Stars in My Crown*, the camera tracks along a row of astonished

children in close-up; this cuts to a shot that tracks along the tables of the spectators, then to a shot tracking in on Yuan's face. In a new twist on the theme of
modes of representation, the film proceeds to verify the power of imagination by
calling forth a bizarre image of the drama as it took form in Yuan's mind: the rainbow pass of his imagination is obviously a fake set, resembling an elaborate theatrical mise-en-scène. The end of the film returns us to the fields; the last shot of this
beautiful film is a low-angle track-in on the statue of Shan Nung.

"The Boss Didn't Say Good Morning" (1937)

"The Boss Didn't Say Good Morning" catches the ambiguity and openness
that the short form, as practiced at MGM, made possible. "Let's you and I write a
letter," begins narrator Carey Wilson — a letter addressed to bosses everywhere, to
a corporate "Mr. Boss," a letter particularly needed "today in these days of ever-
growing misunderstanding between boss and employee" (this is possibly code for
the organized labor movement). Like other Tourneur shorts, the film refers to
means of communication — an airplane carrying mail, a radio tower — to place
itself within the circuit of the mass media. The cinema is both one of these media
and a meta-medium that encompasses the others, carrying a message that is simultaneously highly generalized and somewhat specific.

This message concerns one John Jones, typical American office worker: in his
thirties, married, with a small child and with a mortgage nearly paid off. "Let's
find out," Wilson exhorts the unseen "boss" whom he continues to address
throughout the film, "whether John Jones is happy, and what relation to life John
Jones has that gives him inspiration and the ability and willingness to live."
Despite the interestingly sociological sound of this pronouncement, the film
immediately contents itself with the external indices of what it calls "happiness,"
which the mere physical presence of an obedient wife and a cute little boy is
apparently sufficient to guarantee.

A trivial incident at Jones's office provokes a violent upheaval in Jones's "relation to life" and a reversal of the meaning of all the signs surrounding him. Jones,
seeing his boss enter the office, looks up at him with an ingratiating slave's smile;
the boss ignores him with a frown and proceeds into his private office. Immediately Jones is plunged into alienation and doubt. His fellow employees grin at him
maliciously and whisper to each other, in shots that expose the envy and rivalry
that apparently lie just underneath a thin surface of solidarity at Jones's office.

Jones's sour mood transforms his home into a dismal trap: in a characteristically Tourneurian high angle on the front lawn, Jones berates his son after bump-
ing into the latter's perennially misplaced tricycle. Observing that the family has
been "robbed of the richness that makes life possible and tenable," Wilson doesn't
hesitate to add: "Your fault, Mr. Boss. Aren't you ashamed of yourself?"

A dissolve leads to a Tourneurian shot of Jones lying restlessly in his bed, the
wind rustling the curtain in the background. The narrator discerns an existential
epiphany: "Here indeed is the only time that mankind is really alone. Alone with
himself. Alone sometimes with a god he can never quite understand." The film's
visuals continue to be ironic: on the first utterance of the word "alone," the film

cuts to a shot showing Mrs. Jones (in her separate twin bed) also lying awake, her husband out of focus in the background.

Realizing the next morning that in his anguished preoccupations, he forgot to ship a big order he was entrusted with, Jones reaches the bottom of despair and writes a letter of resignation, which he gives to his son to mail. A chance meeting with the boss at the golf lodge clears up the problem as quickly as it started: the boss's ill humor was caused by indigestion; Jones's inadvertent failure to ship the order has turned out for the best, since the customer is a deadbeat. All that remains is for Jones to rush home and ascertain that his son fortunately neglected to mail the fateful letter of resignation (repeating his father's lucky failure to fulfill a command).

The film's final movement is its most startling. The film dissolves from Jones hugging his son on the front step to a shot of the sky at twilight as Wilson talks about man's need for hope. A further dissolve returns us to the office, where we see that hope continues to do its work: Jones is back at his desk; the boss, walking by, this time returns Jones's smile. Wilson's conclusion is pessimistic, however: "I wonder if you know what this letter is about. Do you, Mr. Boss? Do you, John Jones? I wonder."

"The Boss Didn't Say Good Morning" is less a triumph of mise-en-scène than a multilayered construction of ideological discourse, cinematic irony, and psychological study. Anguish and insecurity dominate the film, derailing its tentative movement toward a picture of social cohesion. In this respect, the film looks forward to *Easy Living*, the closest Tourneur came in his features to what is now called the "family melodrama" and another film that portrays society as a net of tensions and compromises. But "The Boss Didn't Say Good Morning" is more explicit and unremitting. The reversal of meaning at the end is remarkable: from its opening, in which the film inserts itself within technologies of mass communication to deliver to one group of everymen a simple message about another group, the film goes on, after a series of transformations, to admit finally that its message may be incomprehensible to both.

"Romance of Radium" (1937)

"Romance of Radium" is one of the densest and most satisfying of Tourneur's short films. In slightly less than ten minutes, it takes the viewer through a complex experience that spans 40 years, switches between heroic drama, impersonal historical chronicle, and staged documentary, covers three continents, and ends with a glimpse into the future.

The film traces the development of man's knowledge about radium, from its accidental discovery by Antoine Henri Becquerel in 1896, through experiments by Pierre and Marie Curie in refining it and using it for medical purposes, to contemporary storage procedures. The adventures of Becquerel and the Curies give the film its heroic section and are filled with emotion: Becquerel's disappointment at the apparent failure of his experiments with pitchblende; his astonishment on accidentally discovering the ore's effects on photographic plates; the terror of a superstitious "Oriental nobleman" for whom the Curies demonstrate the photosensitivity of uranium; Marie

Curie kneeling beside the broken fragments of the glass that contained the precious uranium, which the nobleman has just dashed to the floor. On the other hand, Tourneur handles the episode of Becquerel's apparent imminent death and miraculous recovery with remarkable dryness: the look that passes between the bedridden Becquerel and Pierre Curie is sympathetic but restrained; then, when the startled Curies (standing behind a tree, like Barney taking aim at Frank in *Doctors Don't Tell*) witness Becquerel in animated conversation with the nuns on the hospital grounds, Pierre simply narrows his eyes, registering not joy at his friend's recovery but a scientist's understanding of its significance.

This look into the psychology of medicine links "Romance of Radium" to Tourneur's later studies of doctors, nurses, and scientists in *Cat People*, *I Walked with a Zombie*, his National Nursing Council promotional short "Reward Unlimited," and *Experiment Perilous*. The film with which "Romance of Radium" is linked most closely is undoubtedly *I Walked with a Zombie*: "highly beneficial yet extremely dangerous," radium has the same double character possessed by insulin in *I Walked with a Zombie* (a shock that "can kill, but it can also cure").

"Romance of Radium" devotes an entire section to the convergence between "primitive" and "scientific" belief systems, a major concern of *I Walked with a Zombie*. In the Belgian Congo, a native boy is found by two white hunters on the verge of death after being lacerated by a leopard (another link with Tourneur's later work). They take him to his village and later return there to find the boy in a hut, where he is immersed up to his neck in mud (cf. the shot of the slain rebel buried up to his neck in the emir's garden in *Timbuktu*). In two extraordinary close-ups, the boy slowly turns his head and then opens his eyes. Prevented by the tribesmen from intervening, the horrified whites return again covertly to try to save the boy from what they perceive as unsanitary treatment. This time they do not find the boy where he was before (in an evocative shot, the beam of the flashlight of one of the hunters prowls the empty ground); then, turning, they see him, healthy, participating in a tribal dance.

As the hunters realize, the mud has curative properties (it proves to be uranium-rich). For the natives, the power to cure can't be dissociated from ritual. Over the shots of the boy's head planted in the mud, we hear the slow beat of a single drum. In the next scene, when the hunters return, the rhythm of the drum has become a dance rhythm. The fire around which the tribesmen dance echoes the shot of the bonfire in which the Curies immolate their carpets and furniture in an effort to recover their spilled uranium.

"Romance of Radium" is a film of dualities: benefit/danger, magic/science, life/death (in an amusing moment, the film represents the deaths of four members of a five-man research team by a trick shot in which four actors simply disappear from the shot, leaving a fifth alone, his back to the camera). The duality of light/dark is one of the film's key visual themes. Becquerel develops a photographic plate to find that a fallen piece of pitchblende has left a black circle on it; in his next photograph, between the rock and the plate he sandwiches a key, which produces a negative (white) imprint. In the scene of the demonstration before the Oriental nobleman, the Curies' uranium glows from its glass low in the frame, the only source of light in the set.

Near the end of the film, another demonstration takes place, this one staged for the movie camera: a pellet containing highly refined radium is placed on a pedestal, a gloved hand flicks a switch, the field surrounding the pellet goes dark, and the pellet immediately begins to glow. In this sequence, the film surprisingly shifts tone from seriousness to jocularity, the narrator comparing the radium pellet to a "temperamental star" that needs special treatment. To take the shot, the movie camera is placed behind a lead curtain and its operator elaborately protected with lead apron, gloves, and mask. (What about the camera taking the shot of the camera?) We get a sense of mighty technologies conjoined to produce a gratuitous spectacle for a sophisticated audience. Hyperbolizing its implication of an all-powerful modernity for which the world's wonders are transparent, the film ends with a final shot — reminiscent of *Things to Come* — of a city skyline in the future, with low-flying airships shuttling about.

"Romance of Radium" exhibits both Tourneur's themes and his visual style. The set of the Curies' laboratory is a marvelous miniature world in which lamps and laboratory flasks frame compositions, the shadows of leafy branches are projected on a translucent skylight, and windows stream with rain. Even the acting in the film is memorably Tourneurian: intense yet unspectacular.

"The King without a Crown" (1937)

MGM made this "historical mystery" to whet the public's appetite for *Marie Antoinette*. Eschewing the sentimentality of the feature, "The King without a Crown" speculates on the fate of the son of Louis XVI and Marie Antoinette. The hypothesis on which the film dwells is that the dauphin, replaced in his Paris cell by another child, was sent to America to live with a family of Indians and grew up to be a missionary named Eleazar Williams. The Prince de Joinville, son of Louis-Philippe, journeys to Green Bay, Wisconsin, to inform Williams (who has lost all memory of his childhood) of his true identity and get him to sign an abdication. Williams refuses, not because he wants power for himself but because he has no right, he says, to preempt his son's choice in the matter, although he says that he will urge his son to live and die as an American.

Perhaps the most interesting aspect of the film is the direct appeal to the audience. At the beginning, the narrator, Carey Wilson, invites the viewer to consider that the person sitting beside him or her could be "a king without a crown." The film's coda takes up this idea again: "Is there somewhere today, perhaps in this very audience, a king without a crown, a descendant of Eleazar Williams, who was, or perhaps was not, Louis XVII?" These speculations are accompanied by medium-long shots of an American movie audience. In these shots, and in the scenes involving Williams, "The King without a Crown" addresses a theme that Tourneur would persistently explore in his films: the distorted relationship between Europe and America. Williams's remarks to Joinville implicitly affirm the moral superiority of America, but by refusing to abdicate and by later writing a book setting forth his claim to the French throne, the austere missionary seems to acknowledge the attractions of monarchy and of the Old World. Wilson's suggestion that one of the members of the audience could be descended from French royalty makes explicit the family romance theme that will be a subtext of *Cat People* and *Experiment Perilous*.

"The Man in the Barn" (1937)

Is David E. George, found injured in an Enid, North Carolina, boarding-house after trying to commit suicide, John Wilkes Booth? The film flashes back from George declaring "I am Booth" and lapsing into a coma, to a torch-lit cele-bration of Robert E. Lee's surrender, to Booth fleeing Ford's Theatre; we hear the shot that kills President Abraham Lincoln as the camera waits outside the theater door through which Booth is about to emerge. In a barn in Bowling Green, Vir-ginia, the shot that kills Booth rings out as he steps behind a beam that obscures him (so we don't know, as the narrator points out, whether a trooper killed him or he killed himself). Conspiracy-theory thinking begins to take shape: since Booth "was the Clark Gable of his day," the narrator wonders why so much emphasis was placed on identifying his body.

The film flashes back again to a scene of Booth riding on the Port Tobacco Road (in the chronology of the story, this would have taken place after Ford's The-atre and before Bowling Green), to demonstrate the mysterious fact that this road was left open while all others in the vicinity were closed. A series of shots details the search for Booth. In two superb high-angle shots, searchers find the prints of a man with a crutch, evidence that the real Booth got away and that the man in the barn was a decoy. Now the film returns to the comatose David E. George in bed. As the narrator lists the traits that identify George with Booth, the camera dollies in on his face and neck, pans along his body, and even penetrates the bedcovers (by a dissolve) to show his naked legs. "And here's the MGM historian's exclusive contribution to the question, a fact that has never before been published": Booth had accidentally mangled his hand in a curtain-raising mechanism, and George's hand is similarly injured. The camera dollies back as the doctor pulls a sheet over George. We return to the earlier scene of "Booth"—his identity now made ques-tionable by the film—in the burning barn. The narrator asks, "Who was the man in the barn?"

The film's central question—whether George is Booth—is undecidable. This permanent ambiguity of the film makes it eminently Tourneurian.

"What Do *You* Think? (Number Three)" (1937)

This sequel to the first "What Do *You* Think?" (Felix Feist directed Number Two, about a mistakenly jealous husband dissuaded from murder by a ghost) unfortunately lacks the crispness and intensity of the first film and feels contrived. Again, the film uses a flashback structure and compulsively repeats a few key ele-ments, notably the "Sonata to a Kiss" with which the hero, a famous young violin-ist named John Dosier, commemorates his blissful marriage. John unexpectedly falls ill and dies shortly after the couple's first anniversary. Mary, his widow, goes into a long, obsessive mourning, declining all invitations. One night, while listen-ing to a record of the sonata and talking to her husband's photograph, she decides to rejoin him, but a high note from the record breaks the glass in which she mixes an overdose of sleeping tablets. "Not a coincidence, Mary, that was a message from

John," says John's mother, who persuades her to give up her worship of the past and marry John's brother. This conclusion has a perhaps unintended irony, since the second marriage is clearly just a repetition of the first and John's brother is just the shadow of John, so that Mary is no less trapped in her cycle than before.

The well-filmed scene of the attempted suicide uses sound effectively, with the narrator (Carey Wilson) quietly assuming Mary's thought-voice, reasonably summing up the advantages of death. As in other Tourneur films, the softness of the voice is hypnotic (cf. *I Walked with a Zombie*, *Experiment Perilous*, *Appointment in Honduras*, *Night of the Demon*) and functions as a lure.

"The Ship That Died" (1938)

Tourneur called "The Ship That Died" one of his favorite shorts.[6] Another work of permanent ambiguity, "The Ship That Died" traces the last voyage of the *Mary Celeste*, found at sea devoid of crew, passengers, and captain. At "the famed nautical court of Gibraltar," investigators propose three hypotheses, each of which is represented by the film: (1) the crew mutinied, (2) the captain, smelling alcohol fumes and fearing that a fire could break out at any moment, decided to give the order to abandon ship, (3) the crew was terrified by the apparition of a "phantom ship." The mystery remains unsolved, the narrator concludes.

With its fluid, exciting succession of dynamic compositions, "The Ship That Died" vividly demonstrates Tourneur's visual skill. The sequence in which members of the crew of another ship board the empty *Mary Celeste* marvelously renders an experience central in Tourneur's work: the encounter with absence. This sequence has a shot that crystallizes the enigma of Tourneur's cinema: from the point of view of the people exploring the deserted ship, we see shadows moving on a door; though justified by the movement of the ship on the sea, the shadow activity is uncanny.

The hypothetical phantom ship, surging forward out of a dark background, is shown as an image printed in negative, superimposed over a shot of the *Mary Celeste*— an extraordinary use in Tourneur of an optical effect to depict the supernatural (cf. Irena's implied transformation near the end of *Cat People*). The transgressiveness and weirdness of the shot suggest how we might imagine the visual ruptures that would probably have occurred in Tourneur's unfilmed *Whispering in Distant Chambers*.

"The Face Behind the Mask" (1938)

Like "The Incredible Stranger," *Cat People*, and *Anne of the Indies*, "The Face Behind the Mask" starts from ambiguity and moves into tragedy. The film is a splendid example of Tourneur's ability to show without showing. Accumulating narrative fragments while deliberately failing to tell a coherent, complete story, it creates a density of allusion and suggestion worthy of a major work.

In the first scene, we watch from behind Louis XIV's shoulder as he signs a lettre de cachet for an "unknown human being." A prisoner, his face muffled, is rowed to the island fortress of Sainte Marguerite and led past a row of soldiers (who have been commanded to turn their faces to the wall as he passes) to his cell. Alone, the prisoner slowly removes the muffle (in a slightly low medium-close shot), revealing a fitted iron mask underneath.

His desire for escape thwarted, the prisoner spends forty years at Sainte Marguerite before being moved to the Bastille, where he dies. The film now rapidly examines the three candidates that historians have proposed for the identity of the prisoner in the iron mask: Count Mattioli, a traitorous diplomat; Nicholas Fouquet, the treasurer of France; and Louis XIV's twin brother, snatched from their shared crib and hidden in order to avoid any future pretext for dispute over the succession. "Who were you?" the narrator (John Nesbitt) asks in conclusion, directly addressing the iron mask and exultantly elevating him to a symbol of all who have been condemned without open trial and who, in retrospect, can be said to have martyred themselves for the progress of justice.

The well-mounted production makes good use of lavish sets designed for more expensive films (including, probably, *Marie Antoinette*). The episode of Fouquet's visit to the king's mistress, with its high-angle long shot of Fouquet emerging from a coach and mounting the steps to her castle, crisply encapsulates the opulent costume-drama element of the film. Later in the Fouquet sequence, an elegant extreme close-up shows Fouquet's hand raising the lid of a jewel box he has placed on a table before his mistress, then lifting a cloth and revealing the jewels; at the sound of a door opening, the camera refocuses on the reflection — in the mirror inside the lid — of Louis entering the room and walking forward.

"The Face Behind the Mask" commands interest, however, not just for such polished images but also for its mystery and compassion. After we first see the iron mask, the narrator wonders, "How much despair must have been hidden beneath that curious shell of iron!" This sequence ends with a mesmerizing close-up in which the mask, shimmering against an abstract background of darkness, turns and goes out of frame as the shot dissolves. A surface on which we read various meanings or none, the iron mask, like the clown masks in *Berlin Express* and *Night of the Demon*, is also a sign of death. The prisoner dies (like the fake clown in *Berlin Express*) behind his mask, in a shot full of tenderness: starting on a medium shot with the prisoner lying in bed, his head low at the left of the frame, with light coming in through a small window at the upper right, the camera tracks in slowly and tilts down as his left hand falls slowly from his neck to his side and as his head turns — just barely — away from the camera. The scene's power comes from the slowness and delicacy of the movements of both actor and camera and from the unearthly grace with which they complement each other.

To sustain the balance between our knowledge of the purely visual conditions of the hero's imprisonment and our ignorance as to his identity, "The Face Behind the Mask" suppresses information. In an insert, the prisoner uses a knife to scratch on a silver tray the words "*JE SUIS*"; simultaneously, the narrator translates "I am." Then the film cuts to a medium shot in which the prisoner continues to write (his name, presumably) while the narrator merely breaks off. A peasant in a boat retrieves the plate, which he saw the prisoner throw from his cell window, and delivers it to the prison governor for a reward. The governor asks gravely, "Have you read this?" The question and his gaze both imply that knowing the name means death. Perhaps, like us, reading this implication, or perhaps being guileless, the peasant, after a short pause that is itself unreadable, replies, "My lord, I cannot read." The episode of the plate is Tourneur at his most elliptical and his most densely allusive. All the themes of the film converge: the equation between writing and death (with which the film begins, in the scene of the king signing the lettre du cachet); the metal surface as both medium and concealment; the need for the camera to restrain itself before reality and not tear away all its veils.

As the narrator reviews the three candidates for the prisoner's identity, the film intersperses the three mininarratives with progressively closer shots of the masked prisoner at the window of his cell. In the first two shots, he is in left profile, gazing out the window. The third shot has him in big close-up, staring fixedly past the camera (his eyes unblinking behind the small slits of the mask); the window is now behind him (still at the left of the frame). His having turned away from the window implies that, over the years, he has abandoned his hopes for escape. What great economy Tourneur shows in this progression, in which the film propounds the three variant solutions to its mystery while at the same time it reca- pitulates, in the purely visual terms of camera position, shot size, and orientation of the body, the prisoner's journey through time. This journey leads him to a state in which his former identity becomes irrelevant, since he apparently no longer hopes to assume it in the world. Thus the last section of the film is as paradoxical as it is economical. It is also thoroughly Tourneurian in its radical renunciations.

"What Do *You* Think? Tupapaoo" (1938)

"Tupapaoo" is the highlight of the "What Do *You* Think?" miniseries and one of Tourneur's best shorts. Tourneur's comments on the film are both mislead- ing and suggestive.

> The film recounted pretty much what happened to the director Murnau in Tahiti, during the shooting of *Tabu*. Murnau had wanted to use the decor of a real cemetery. The Tahitians refused, because of the phosphorescence at night in the swamps. But Murnau shot in this location all the same. The natives said it was a sacrilege. Returning to Hol- lywood to edit his film there, he was driving a car along the beach. He missed a turn, and killed himself. It's claimed that it was because he had violated the sacred cemetery. For our film, we wrote the similar story of a man who doesn't respect the Tahitian cemeteries, and who dies.[7]

Leaving aside Tourneur's error about the circumstances of Murnau's death (the driver of the car was his personal chauffeur), the statement is curious because "Tupapaoo" never mentions Murnau and isn't explicitly about filmmaking. The main character is an adventurer named Kurt Larsen—his Germanic name is a link to Murnau, but the sign on his store is in French, as are the notations in his ledger. He suggests a fusion of Murnau—who, like the character in Tourneur's film, was cursed for building his house on a former native burying ground[8]—and the evil white characters in *Tabu*. The French writing perhaps links the figure to

Maurice Tourneur, who had visited Tahiti (with Jacques as script boy) for the production of *Never the Twain Shall Meet* (1924). Larsen thus becomes a figure through which Jacques Tourneur comes to terms with the cinematic traditions of the past and his own responsibility to them.

Narrator Carey Wilson recounts his voyage on a tramp steamer in the Pacific. Aboard the ship, he says, are six passengers "beside myself," in addition to (or including?) a mysterious "seventh passenger," who keeps to himself in the saloon, declining the others' invitation to join them. While out on deck to look at the Southern Cross, the group sees a shooting star; this sight prompts one of them, "Father Harry," to recall a strange story.

To the unspoiled island paradise of Tawaynee comes "the notorious Kurt Larsen," whose right leg, three inches shorter than the left, is known far and wide as "a symbol of greed and cruelty." Larsen sets up a store to sell junk jewelry to the natives on credit, then graduates them to whiskey, which he trades for pearls. Soon rich enough to buy up the entire island, he chooses the tribal burying place to build his home. The native chief declares the ground taboo and invokes against Larsen "Tupapaoo, the terrible curse of the Polynesian gods"; the fall of a shooting star marks the occasion. One night, the wind knocks over an oil lamp in Larsen's house, starting an uncontrollable blaze that reduces the house to ashes and wipes out Larsen's fortune.

Since then, Father Harry concludes, Larsen has fled from the curse. Before they can reflect on the story, the passengers see the ship captain rush into the saloon. Bending over the mysterious seventh passenger, the captain pronounces him dead. The passenger's deformed foot identifies him as Kurt Larsen. Another shooting star falls; the camera tracks toward Father Harry, stunned, alone at the rail. Wilson sums up: "Coincidence or Tupapaoo, the curse of the Tawaynee gods? What do *you* think?"

The elaborate sequence of Larsen's downfall is beautifully done. The camera pans down from the ceiling, then left to right across the room, to end on Larsen removing his jewel box from its hiding place and bringing it to the lamp by the window to look at his pearls. Alarmed by what looks like another shooting star, Larsen goes outside to see some natives spearfishing by torchlight (the shooting star and the spearfishing are both links to *I Walked with a Zombie*). After the fire, a phonograph lies in the rubble, still playing a record of Polynesian chants — a superbly eerie touch. The last shot of the flashback starts on the group of natives looking offscreen right, then pans in the direction of their gaze to catch Larsen staggering away into the brush.

Tourneur stages Larsen's death in the saloon with characteristic discretion: he is huddled in a chair, his face blocked from the camera by the body of the waiter at the left of the frame.

"Strange Glory" (1938)

In 1862, a series of Confederate victories throws the North into despair. The turning point comes with the successful execution of "the Tennessee plan," a series of Northern attacks along the Tennessee River. President Lincoln issues a proclamation of thanksgiving for the victory but noticeably omits to credit anyone in particular for devising the Tennessee plan. Eight years later, Anna Ella Carroll (Fay Helm), a Maryland pamphleteer, appeals to a Senate committee for recognition as the plan's author. Her private meetings with Lincoln on the subject, as she describes them to the committee, are shown in flashback. Searched for corroboration of her claim, the file on Carroll turns out to contain only two pieces of paper: a list of her pamphlets and a record of payment for them. In 1894, the Senate considers the claim one last time and again finds it unproved; the film ends on a shot of Carroll's gravestone in a cemetery overgrown with brush.

"Strange Glory," though less rich than "The Man in the Barn," has interest as a drama of an individual's struggle against history and as a study in Tourneurian silence and absence. Carroll's helplessness in the face of the committee's demand for proof isn't far from the condition of Irena in *Cat People* and especially of Mrs. Rand in *I Walked with a Zombie*, both of whom also put extraordinary claims before an unbelieving world. "Strange Glory" reduces to a gender basis the problem of verisimilitude and belief, a problem that the later films will explore in other aspects. The extraordinary aspect of Carroll's case is the assertion that a woman was responsible for a military turning point.

The close-up of the empty file is a resonant moment. Much more resonant, though, is the close-up of Carroll at her final hearing before the committee: mute, she turns slightly and seems about to speak, then becomes mute again, definitively. The closing shot of the gravestone finishes her retreat into silence. This compulsive movement toward inarticulateness and the inanimate marks "Strange Glory" as Tourneurian: the same movement will be enacted, for example, in the *Twilight Zone* episode "Night Call," which returns to the central image of a gravestone.

"Think It Over" (1938)

The only Tourneur short to reach two reels, this entry in the "Crime Does Not Pay" series is fast-paced, tense, and involving. The film takes place "in a certain midwestern city," where crooks exploit poor economic conditions to persuade owners of failing businesses to hire the crooks to torch their buildings. The criminal trio is a plausible study in contrasts: a smooth, reasonable mastermind (Lester Matthews); an easygoing, all–American blackmailer (Donald Barry); and a silent, possibly deranged arsonist (Dwight Frye).

The quiet intensity of "Think It Over" stamps it as Tourneurian, especially in such touches as the expressionless, somnambulistic behavior of Frye, mechanically going about his work, and the sound of fingers rapping on the arm of a chair in a waiting room (heard quietly over a shot of an anxious conspirator). The normality of the family life of the furniture-store owner, Johnson, his gentle, discreet wife, his son, who is excited about a passing grade, and his daughter, who wants to join a dancing club, seems real, not banal. At the end of the film, Johnson's stunned resignation as he is arrested (resisting temptation for much of the film, he finally submits to it and hires the crooks to torch his store) is convincing.

"Yankee Doodle Goes to Town" (1939)

"Yankee Doodle Goes to Town" reflects the ideological, propagandistic tendency of the MGM shorts, a tendency that would culminate in the takeover of the shorts department by the Office of War Information. Interspersing new sequences with stock footage and shots borrowed from features, the film is nothing less than a history of the United States from the end of the Revolutionary War to 1939. Its main purpose is to remind viewers that pessimism about the prospects for democracy has existed at every turning point of the nation's history and to counter this pessimism with reasons to celebrate the greatness of the American achievement.

From the point of view of the history of ideology, one of the most interesting scenes is the one in which the ubiquitous central character, Nathaniel Curdleface, turns up as a uniformed, booted pro–Fascist speaker in a city park, declaring: "What we need is a modern, strong kind of government, like some of them countries in Europe. Democracy has lost its usefulness."

The film finally fails to take a stand on its great unspoken question of the role that America should take in the current world crisis. The dissolve from a shot of warships at sea to a shot of farmland, as the narrator asserts his faith in the American "way of life," could be read either as warning of an imminent threat from the sea or as advocating isolation.

For students of Tourneur, "Yankee Doodle Goes to Town" offers one excellent night scene — the mob burning King George in effigy outside the Bay Tree Tavern — and a number of other interesting moments, although the episodic narrative and the extreme reliance on montage give it a flavor that is less Tourneurian than suggestive of, for example, Don Siegel's montage sequences in Raoul Walsh's *The Roaring Twenties*, made in the same year.

After Tourneur directed his first four American features (1939–41), but before the breakthrough of *Cat People*, he returned briefly to the MGM shorts department to make two entries in "John Nesbitt's Passing Parade." Both, especially the first, are mature, elegant works that convey the definite impression that by this time, the director was overqualified for the short format.

"The Incredible Stranger" (1942)

"The Incredible Stranger" opens with a title: "As in all John Nesbitt's stories, although the events and characters portrayed in this photoplay are fictitious, they are based upon psychological truths scientifically established." The first shot is a long shot from a storefront of a dusty main street: a man walks away from the camera down the street; a superimposed title reads "Bridgewood, 1892." A scene in a store establishes Bridgewood as a small town where nothing exciting ever happens and where news of the impending arrival of a new resident causes commotion. The stranger (Paul Guilfoyle) arrives by train alone at night, talks to no one, goes inside his newly built house, and shuts the door. For five years no one else enters the house; the house remains part of the mystery of its silent inhabitant, as do also the boxes of women's and children's clothes he receives by mail. One night, the town doctor, on his way home, sees the stranger collapsed on the porch and stops to assist him. Their suspicions aroused by the doctor's empty buggy, the townspeople storm the stranger's house. They find that he has been living with life-size, dressed wooden dolls of his wife, daughter, and son, who all died years ago in a fire (in which he lost his voice as a result of smoke inhalation). The townspeople take pity on him and accept him into the community.

In linking its protagonist's obsession with the past with the portrayal of the small American town as a site of inclusion and exclusion, "The Incredible Stranger" anticipates both *Out of the Past* and *Stars in My Crown*. Like *Out of the Past*, it features a character whose muteness reflects the isolation and fear that prevail in the community. Tourneur noticeably refrains from idealizing Bridgewood: at the end of the film, the stranger's integration into the townspeople's society is shown simply as the cessation of their interest in him, as he walks out of the store ignored by men playing checkers. The stranger's fixation on the past is structurally linked to the town's obsession with him, and both are symptoms of a deeper social malaise (which is not addressed when the symptoms disappear).

Tourneur shoots the townspeople's climactic penetration of the stranger's house in high angles, as he would later shoot the attempted lynching in *Stars in My Crown* and the cowboys' "hurrahing" in *Wichita*.

"The Magic Alphabet" (1942)

The last of Tourneur's MGM shorts combines two of their main modes: the staged documentary on science and technology (cf. "The Jonker Diamond," "Romance of Radium") and the film set in an exotic locale ("Tupapaoo").

At the beginning of the film, the narrator strings together three mysterious, seemingly unrelated events: a truck driver, suddenly struck by night blindness, drives off a cliff; a typist is fired for making excessive errors; a young boy can't join his friends swimming in the lake because a weak leg keeps him on crutches. To explain the relationship between these cases, the film flashes back to Java: a few concisely magisterial lateral tracking shots of crowded activity immediately establish that Tourneur is in his element. A man in white walks slowly away from the camera on a porch, past men eating rice; suddenly he collapses, seemingly a victim of starvation. Young Dutch doctor Christian Eyckman diagnoses beriberi, a disease about which he is as ignorant as the natives.

From observing chickens, Eyckman establishes that the disease is somehow related to the native diet of rice. The accidental spoiling of his experiment by a village boy gives him the key: whole-grain rice contains some nourishment, lost in turning it into white rice, that protects against beriberi. Later, another scientist isolates the crucial amine in the husk of rice and calls it "vitamine." The "magic alphabet" of the title is the alphabet of vitamins; recapitulating, the narrator explains that each of the three victims in the opening section of the film suffers from a deficiency in some vitamin or other, correctable by changes in diet. The film, which was produced in conjunction with the Office of War Information, ends by showing an American family at dinner while the narrator declaims: "It is chiefly up to the housewives to learn their vitamins and feed their families the right foods to keep our nation strong. This is the housewife's task. We may forget to thank her for it, but if she will study the vitamins again and again, it is her gift that will keep the country healthy enough to win a victory."

"The Magic Alphabet" ties together a number of Tourneurian themes: invisible causes, displaced northerners ("Tupapaoo," *I Walked with a Zombie*, *Appointment in Honduras*), medicine. One characteristic shot shows Eyckman writing at his desk at night; the camera quickly pans to the wall behind and screen left of him while simultaneously an offscreen door opens, apparently by itself, throwing an oblong of light onto the wall, with Eyckman's shadow in it. By shifting abruptly from man to shadow, Tourneur changes a static scene into a dynamic one, a shift that belongs to the film's motif of unexpected reversals and that also logically corresponds with the shift in the narrative at this point, from Eyckman to his successors (to whom, no doubt, he will pass on important information in his writing): the next scene shows another scientist taking up the problem. The shadow also conveys a sense of the duality of science, a common theme in Tourneur's work (cf. "Romance of Radium," *Cat People*, *I Walked with a Zombie*, and *Night of the Demon*).

They All Come Out
(1939)

Sort of touches you that humanity can be so humane.

VONNIE (PAUL FIX), IN
THEY ALL COME OUT

According to Tourneur, *They All Come Out* was originally planned and made as a two-reel entry in the *Crime Does Not Pay* series and was then, on Louis B. Mayer's orders, expanded to the unusual length of four reels. On February 5, 1939, the *New York Times* reported that the film was being made as a four-reel documentary on the federal prison system, with footage shot in "hitherto unphotographed locations" at federal facilities in Atlanta, Chillicothe, Springfield, and Alcatraz. Finally lengthened to seven reels, the film became Tourneur's first American feature.[1]

Joe Cameron (Tom Neal), an out-of-work drifter, is recruited by gun moll Kitty Carson (Rita Johnson) to drive a car for a gang led by "Reno" Madigan (Bernard Nedell). After a bank robbery, all the members of the gang are caught and sent to various federal prisons, where the authorities try to rehabilitate them. Joe learns welding, and Kitty learns the trade of beautician; both are paroled. Reno, after an unsuccessful try at a prison break, is sent to Alcatraz. Reno's former cellmate, Vonnie (Paul Fix), goes after Joe, who is now working as a welder, and tries to force him to open his employer's safe, but Joe turns the tables on Vonnie. Joe and Kitty, who have fallen in love, are allowed to serve out the rest of their probation together.

The film bears traces of its successive stages of conception and production. The prologue and epilogue, in which U.S. Attorney General Homer S. Cummings (who had retired by the time the film was released) and Federal Bureau of Prisons Director James V. Bennett appear as themselves, clearly belong to the first, most ideological phase, as do many of the shots of prison activities in the film. If Tourneur's recollection that the fictional story was added for the four-reel version is correct, we must assume that a lot of material from the original two-reeler ended up unused, since little in the film does not somehow involve Neal or the other principals.

The four-reel version may have consisted of the middle section of the film — the prison sequences — much as it exists now. (Kitty may not have figured in the four-reel version at all.) The episodic narrative structure of this section would have

60

seemed less unexpected in a medium-length film than it does in a feature. Added for the feature, most probably, were the early sequences in which Joe meets Kitty, the bank robbery and its aftermath, the scenes with Reno and Vonnie in prison (setting up the last part of the film), and all of the last section of the film with Kitty and Joe on parole, threatened by Vonnie — in short, all of the most interesting parts of the film, the parts least closely tied to its ideological project and more akin to Fritz Lang's *You Only Live Once* (1937).

The documentary mode of the prologue with Cummings and Bennett gives way to the gangster film (the scene at Reno's apartment, followed by the scene of Kitty at the bank), then the social-problem film (Joe in a diner, where, unable to pay for the forty-cent meal he has just eaten, he is helped out by Kitty, to whom he complains about cops always ready to pinch a "vag"), then the film noir (Kitty and Joe pulling into a city at night, Kitty pointing out the flophouse across the street, the shot from her point of view of Joe walking away toward the flophouse).

Later, the social-problem mode returns with Kitty's account of her life: her father's physical violence toward her mother, the lousy jobs she's worked, her experience of "being kicked around." The mixing of the social-problem film with the crime thriller is reminiscent of *You Only Live Once* and also anticipates Anthony Mann's *Raw Deal* (1948), co-written by John C. Higgins, the writer of *They All Come Out*. (Higgins's other scripts for Mann, including *T-Men* [1947] and *Border Incident* [1949], also return to the semidocumentary mode of *They All Come Out*, which in the meantime became popularized through the Louis DeRochemont–Henry Hathaway films.) Even more clearly, *They All Come Out* anticipates Nicholas Ray's *They Live by Night* (1947) in its tension between the nascent romanticism of Joe and Kitty and the hard-boiled attitudes of the other criminals. "Don't fall for any dame, or you're done for," Reno advises Joe after the bank holdup; we hear the line over a soft-focus, romantically lit close-up of the wounded Kitty lying on a couch, looking screen left (toward Joe).

With the criminals' arrival in prison, where they witness a kangaroo court trial, the film enters a new mode: the prison film. The shot of the imposing front of the Atlanta U.S. penitentiary (followed by a process shot of Reno and the gang looking at the building, which they are about to enter) reintroduces the semidocumentary rehabilitation film announced at the opening of the film. This mode prevails in the long sequence in which the prison board interviews members of the gang. The scene is shown from the point of view of officialdom, the camera remaining with the board (except for brief shots of the prisoners waiting outside) as they discuss each prisoner's case before summoning him. The dominant shot is a wide establishing shot of officials sitting on two sides of a long table covered with piles of papers; at the back of the set, in the middle of the shot, is the door through which the prisoners enter and exit.

During this section of the film, the characterization of Joe changes. Previously, the film concentrated on his growing involvement with Kitty, a relationship that seemed to be leading toward a conflict with Reno. Now the film sees him, more simply, as the prison officials see him: a relatively untainted, still savable young prisoner who acts tough only because he's under Reno's influence. If the portrayal of Joe's difficulties during the depression hints at a systemic failure, especially when we learn about the wrist injury that cost him his livelihood and reduced him to vagrancy, the system redeems its failure (in spades) by repairing his injured wrist and teaching him a valued trade. The contradiction embedded within the structure of the film — society drives Joe into crime, then rehabilitates him — is echoed on the level of character by the speed with which Joe adjusts his perspective toward the system. By the time he learns that he is to move from the cell block to the dormitory, Joe is smiling.

The authorities treat the prisoners compassionately and rationally. Kitty, lodged at a women's prison that resembles a boardinghouse, is reformed through the efforts of the kindly Dr. Hollis, who (in a scene reminiscent of another Lang film, *You and Me* [1938]) proves to Kitty that she made less money as a criminal than she had made previously working at a beauty salon. The prison officials are so accommodating that they grant Reno's request of a transfer to the clothing shop even though the warden senses that "it's not for our own good" (in fact, the move is part of Reno's plan for a break).

The positive view of the prison rehabilitation system extends to the normal world to which Kitty and Joe try to belong after their parole. Unlike Eddie's boss in *You Only Live Once*, Joe's employers trust him even though he's an ex-con ("Sort of touches you that humanity can be so humane," Vonnie comments with deadpan irony on reading this detail in Joe's letter to Kitty). The film manages to hint that in spite of everything, this isn't the best of all possible worlds: the man behind the counter at the Owl Café, where Kitty goes to call the police to try to save Joe from Vonnie, is perilously slow to respond to her request for help (a detail that recalls the meanness of George Tobias's diner owner to Joe early in the film).

They All Come Out reaches the opposite conclusion from that of *You Only Live Once*: whereas in Lang's film, the lovers can be united only outside the law, in Tourneur's, they recognize the law as the condition of their unity, even to the extent of submitting to a parole regime that confines them in separate cities (a temporary separation recalling that of the lovers in Lang's previous film, *Fury* [1936]). Joe and Kitty thus fall into the pattern of the conformist outlaw couple, who can find happiness only when they go straight. "You both turned instinctively to the police," a judge tells Kitty and Joe approvingly at the end of the film.

Adhering to the standards of the MGM shorts, *They All Come Out* is an expansive production, with many different sets and much location shooting, notably in the scenes at the Birmingham bank where Kitty keeps a safe-deposit box and during the getaway after the robbery of the Memphis bank. Tourneur's direction is visually fluid. As Reno and Joe pull into an auto camp, a lengthy shot is taken from the front of the moving car, whose headlights illuminate various buildings successively until three policemen, guns raised while approaching the car, are discovered by the camera movement. This shot cuts to a shot inside the car from behind Joe and Reno, then a shot alongside the passenger window, through which Reno shoots at a cop.

Tourneur handles the scene in which the thieves leave the wounded Kitty at the hair salon in an interesting long take. It starts with a close-up of Joe behind the wheel of the parked car; he says, "Let me take her," and opens the door. The camera, panning and tilting up with Joe as he goes to help Kitty out of the back seat, reveals "Bugs" (Edward Gargan), another gang member, standing outside the car. From offscreen, Reno summons Bugs, who walks screen right, the camera following, to meet Reno in front of the salon. Reno gives him instructions, then Bugs goes back to the car, the camera following him again before picking up Joe. Now the camera follows Joe and Kitty as they pass Reno and go down the stairs into the salon. The fluid relay movement of the shot, involving four actors, creates an effect of complexity and naturalness with simple means.

The prison scenes are consistently visually interesting, with their motif of deep views of exterior spaces seen through windows behind people in offices. A strange scene in an occupational therapy clinic starts with an extended tracking shot showing patients engaged in various tasks, the camera ending on a prisoner who becomes upset while basket weaving and must be sent to the restraint ward. Despite the emphasis on rehabilitation, the film makes it clear that imprisonment is no picnic, especially in the scenes involving Reno. An expressive high-angle medium shot shows Reno being put into an isolation cell; in a harrowing tracking shot of a row of cells in Alcatraz, we see prisoners' faces (obscured by their hands and arms) as they lie on their bunks, alternating with bright white walls as the camera crosses the spaces between cells.

They All Come Out is an interesting film, as much because of the circumstances of its production and for what it reveals about the society that produced it as for its formal qualities. It is unique, and deserves to be better known.

The Nick Carter Films
Nick Carter, Master Detective (1939) and Phantom Raiders (1940)

Their characters lived in a world gone wrong, a world in which, long before the atom bomb, civilization had created the machinery for its own destruction, and was learning to use it with all the moronic delight of a gangster trying out his first machine gun.

RAYMOND CHANDLER,
INTRODUCTION TO *THE SIMPLE ART
OF MURDER*

In 1939 MGM, which owned the rights to the dime-novel stories featuring detective Nick Carter, launched a proposed series of Carter films with *Nick Carter, Master Detective*, starring Walter Pidgeon. This was Tourneur's first American feature to have been planned from the start as a feature. A sequel followed immediately: *Phantom Raiders*, also directed by Tourneur and starring Pidgeon. (For the third and last episode in the series, *Sky Murder* [1940], George B. Seitz replaced Tourneur.)

In *Master Detective*, Carter is hired to investigate the disappearance of top-secret blueprints from Radex Airplane Factory, which is developing a high-speed plane designed by Dr. John Keller (Henry Hull). The prototype plane explodes during a test flight, and Keller is murdered. Carter determines that Dr. Frankton (Stanley Ridges), the doctor at the plant infirmary, is involved with several workers in a conspiracy to steal blueprints and turn them over to foreign spies. Escaping by motorboat, the spies take stewardess Lou Farnsby (Rita Johnson) as hostage, but Carter follows them in a plane and eventually wins the day.

Phantom Raiders brings Carter and his sidekick, Bartholomew (a character introduced halfway through the previous film and played in both films by Donald Meek), to Panama for a vacation. They soon become involved in investigating the serial disappearances of British merchant ships in the region. Carter discovers that gangster Al Taurez (Joseph Schildkraut) is blowing up the ships as part of an insurance fraud scheme. Forcing Taurez aboard a ship slated for explosion, Carter terrifies him into confessing the plot.

The Nick Carter films combine detection, derring-do, and womanizing in a way that makes Tourneur's description of the character as "a little bit the James Bond of the time" not inapt.[1] As played by Walter Pidgeon, Carter is an attractive figure, easygoing and unmistakably on the side of good. An early scene in *Master*

Detective sets forth his main trait, detachment: using a gimmick later revived by Dana Andrews's detective in Otto Preminger's *Laura*, Carter keeps calm by playing a palm-held pinball game, discomfiting the person with whom he's talking.

The films preserve the boy's-adventure aspect of the Carter literature by emphasizing physical action. In *Master Detective*, Carter uses a plane to follow first a car, then a motorboat. He also strafes the motorboat with a machine gun, which he has casually picked up in a police car. With frank naïveté, both *Master Detective* and *Phantom Raiders* show Carter, apparently a private citizen with no official standing, enjoying the unquestioning obedience of local police forces.

Neither episode calls on the detective to perform great feats of intellect. In the first one, he notices in the factory logs that each time a blueprint vanished from the plant, Dr. Frankton sent an injured worker home, and he simply puts two and two together. In *Phantom Raiders*, Carter lets events confirm his hunch that Al Taurez, known to him from past acquaintance as an unscrupulous character, is behind the disappearances of the merchant ships. Also in *Phantom Raiders*, when Carter discovers Al Taurez's remote-control detonating device, he immediately activates it, not knowing what explosions it's set to trigger!

MGM's insistence on high production values for its B movies is evident throughout both films; considered just on these terms, the two Carter films surpass even Norman Foster's stylish Mr. Moto series for 20th Century–Fox. *Master Detective* is an expansive production, with much location shooting and aerial photography. The scenic range of *Phantom Raiders* is more limited, but with fewer and more modest sets to work with, Tourneur and the designers concentrated on getting the most from each, making an organic, atmospheric unity out of the completely studio-bound, B-budget Colón, Panama. (The subsequent Carter film, *Sky Murder*, seems not to have kept to the high standards of the first two. Don Miller said that it "could have been accomplished in a more professional manner by any of the low-budget units at Republic, Monogram, Universal or Columbia.")[2]

Nick Carter, Master Detective is remarkably fluid. The first sequence, in which a car chases a plane, includes a traveling shot of the two vehicles, followed by a shot from inside the plane of Carter shooting through its broken window at the window of the pursuing car. Near the end of the film, when Carter takes to the plane again to follow the spies' motorboat, the camera shoots from the window of the plane as it descends toward the boat; although there are process shots in this sequence, these setups are "live." This sequence also contains a startling low-angle shot of Lou cowering in fear in her cabin as bullets from Carter's machine gun rip through the ceiling (*Timbuktu* has a similar low-angle shot of the emir shooting holes in a ceiling with a machine gun; cf. also the shot of Gyp shooting a "W" into the saloon wall in *Wichita*).

In one of the most elaborate sequences in the film, Streeter (Addison Richards), the president of Radex Airplane Factory, introduces Carter and us to the plant. Tourneur's handling of the sequence extends the documentary-like technique he refined in his short films. The melding of studio and location shooting (the production unit went to a real factory, Lockheed Airplane Works in Burbank, California),[3] of dialogue scenes and scenes devoted to showing how a physical process takes place, is extremely adroit, using the mobility of the camera and of the two principal characters as a unifying device.

A process shot of Streeter and Carter on a catwalk overlooking the plant leads to documentary-like shots of the wing and fuselage assembly line, dissolving seamlessly to a shot, with bit players, in which the camera pans to rediscover Streeter and Carter, now on the factory floor. Carter asks, "Look, with so many men handling blueprints, how do you keep them from walking out with them?" This line serves as a sound cue (underlined by a siren) for a series of shots showing that workers leaving the factory must turn in the blueprints assigned to them. A sign reads: "YOU CAN'T come in after you go out / YOU CAN'T go out after you come in." The camera tilts down from the sign to a medium-long shot of workers leaving the plant; among them are Carter and Streeter, who resume their conversation. The scene dissolves to a shot of men going through a building with showers, then cuts to Carter and Streeter watching from a window above. This shot dissolves back to the plant: the camera pans and tracks laterally across various plane construction activities, finally picking up Streeter and Carter as they enter from behind the camera to look at a plane.

The scene of the disastrous test flight is the most striking scene in *Nick Carter, Master Detective* and one of the most unusual scenes in all Tourneur's work. It uses aggressive, Soviet-style montage, including jump cuts and extremely short shots, to create an impression of uncontrollable movement.

As the plane begins to break apart, a long shot of the plane losing part of its right wing cuts to a rapid succession of mostly very brief shots: a medium close-up of Carter; a close-up of Carter from the same angle; a "choker" of Carter still from the same angle; a two-shot of Lou and Keller; a close shot that rapidly tracks in on a choker of Keller; then a group shot of the three villainous spies, watching from another location. The ensuing shots cover the plane as it loses its left wing; the pilot struggles to free himself from the cockpit but is knocked unconscious. A montage follows:

1. High-angle shot of the nose of the plane as the plane approaches the ground
2. Medium-close shot of the unconscious pilot
3. High-angle shot as the plane approaches the ground
4. Jump cut to the same with the nose in a slightly different position and with a different background
5. Shot from in front of the plane, which hurtles toward the camera
6. Shot of the side of a rocky hill, the camera moving in
7. Same as (5)
8. Same as (6)
9. The impact
10. Shot from in front of the plane as it explodes
11. Shot that gradually tracks or zooms in toward the burning wreck; fade-out

In the context of a 1939 Hollywood film, this montage has a freakish, experimental quality (although it uses techniques that were fairly common in silent films). Its stylistic freedom recalls Tourneur's work in the short films and in the

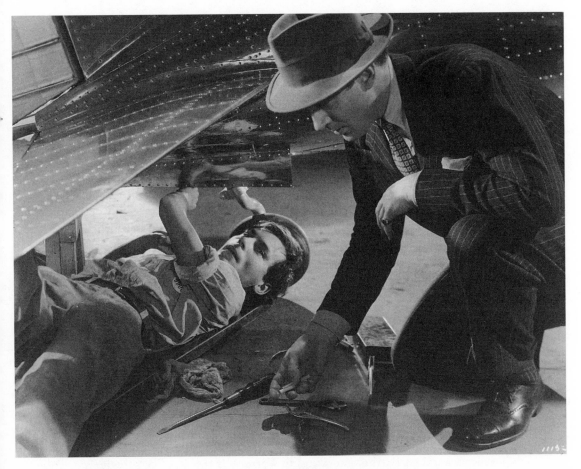

Martin Kosleck and Walter Pidgeon in *Nick Carter, Master Dective*.

discrete, montage-oriented sections of the features on which he directed second units.

Other aspects of *Master Detective* look forward to Tourneur's later films. Bartholomew "the Bee-man," the eccentric beekeeper who is a disciple of Carter, is introduced by a camera that suddenly takes overt responsibility for the narrative in a manner that anticipates the first shot of *The Leopard Man*: in long shot, Carter walks to his inn; a quick pan left reveals the house next door, and the camera tracks in on the sign, which reads: "BARTHOLOMEW THE B-MAN/HONEY." Bartholomew himself is a philosophical misfit of a type that will appear frequently in Tourneur's films. Through him, Tourneur displaces the concerns of the film. Bartholomew is given to speculations: "Do you suppose that we as humans are also victims of a gigantic hoax? That we labor in vain and nature takes away our honey in the end?" Here again, the film anticipates *The Leopard Man*, in which Galbraith's ball becomes a symbol of human futility. (Note also the weird process shot of animated bees crawling on Bartholomew's open hand; reminiscent of *Un Chien andalou*, the shot looks forward to further mysterious entomological effects work in Tourneur's *Appointment in Honduras*.)

The scenes in *Nick Carter, Master Detective* that most suggest Tourneur's later work are, predictably, those that take place at night and that put the protagonists in situations of danger and uncertainty. In the scene of Carter going to Keller's house, the camera holds on a wall on which first Carter's shadow, then Bartholomew's ("shadowing" him), are projected. Carter finds Keller dead in his car in the garage. In an effective moment, Bartholomew startles Carter, who hasn't noticed him, by suddenly exclaiming (offscreen), "Murder, sir, or I miss my guess!"

The scene in the spies' hideout starts with a close shot of a man pointing with a pencil at an overhead projection of a blueprint. At the sound of knocking, the camera pans to a two-shot of Lou (who has been kidnapped) and one of the spies, who goes to answer the door, the camera following. As another spy enters, Tourneur at last cuts to a medium-long shot of the whole room. This gradual, movement-based way of introducing a setting is characteristic of Tourneur.

The film foregrounds its theme of the misinterpretation of signs, laying bare the device, as in this dialogue at the airplane factory:

> DOCTOR: This place is plastered with signs warning
> men to be careful, but nobody reads them.
> CARTER: Maybe they're too big to be seen.
> DOCTOR: You know, you sound like that detective,
> what's his name, Dupin in the Edgar Allan Poe stories.

Through Bartholomew's obsession with Carter's detective-magazine image, the film fuses two realities: the one in which Carter is a real person and the one in which he is a fictional character. The use of Bartholomew to parody detective-story convention sometimes makes it hard to determine in which reality the film is taking place, as when Bartholomew says to Carter, "If it looks like suicide, it can't be, right?"

Phantom Raiders is both less and more than its predecessor: less expansive and exciting, more fluid and homogeneous. A brief opening montage establishes the studio version of Panama, where the film takes place: a long shot that pans right to left across a plaza, loosely following a woman carrying a basket on her head, ends on the arched doorway of La Cita Café. This dissolves to a shot that tracks right to left inside the cafe, passing dancing couples and waiters before reaching a closed door. Another dissolve takes us through the door into the office of Al Taurez, all-purpose criminal mastermind. These opening shots combine balanced, well-orchestrated movement with a feeling of hermetic enclosure. The successive dissolves open up a series of boxes, each containing the next, until we arrive at the heart of the system, Taurez's headquarters, whose decor proves to contain more boxes: the cage of Taurez's beloved bird; the safe that hides the detonating device. The last shot of the film, by returning to the plaza shown at the beginning, gives a sense of spatial completion.

Phantom Raiders relies on lighting and decor more than on physical action. The camera tracks toward the desk in Carter's empty office while a phone rings urgently, the light casting shadows of jalousies across the set. The film has a large proportion of interior night scenes. During one dialogue, Taurez and Cora (Florence Rice) are mainly lit from behind, so that the camera sides of their faces are in slight shadow;

lit lamps are strategically placed in the composition. In a cutaway, the shipping magnate Ramsell, talking on the phone, is lit by a low-placed key light: behind and above him in the medium-shot composition, closed jalousies (through which we see a palm tree) dominate the set.

A long sequence at Taurez's night club contains swift, brilliantly orchestrated action: a waiter goes from a young couple's table to deliver fortune cookies to a table of Chinese men; one of them takes a fortune, reads it, and (under the eye of the spying Bartholomew) shows it to Gunboat, the bouncer, as the latter passes by; Gunboat walks around toward the bar, where he sees Carter with Dolores (with whom Gunboat is in love). News of the latest ship-sinking prompts masses of people to crowd the frame as Taurez and the shipping executive Morris, a conscience-stricken fellow conspirator, push through the crowd to Taurez's office, followed by Carter. The blocking and direction of the crowd creates a powerful emotional impact, heightening our awareness of the guilt and panic of Morris.

Throughout *Phantom Raiders*, we find the visual style that Tourneur would develop in his subsequent films, a style marked by atmospheric schemes of decor and lighting and a subtle drawing-out of scenes of silence and expectation: the predominance of rattan chairs, screens, and jalousied doors and windows; the mosquito netting over the bed in the shot of the thug Eddie (Dwight Frye) sneaking into Carter's room at night with a blackjack; the high angle as Dolores enters Carter's dark room.

Bartholomew has more screen time in *Phantom Raiders* than in *Nick Carter, Master Detective*, with much of that time devoted to matters extraneous to the plot. At one point, as he and Carter pause to consider their next step, the film unexpectedly gives the actors a chance for a deftly played light comedy routine: Bartholomew imitates Carter's musings, then they stroll out of the shot together like vaudeville comedians. One of Bartholomew's key functions is to secure the film against the danger represented by Carter's promiscuous interest in women: three times, his disturbances break up Carter's trysts with Dolores; he also interrupts a meeting between Carter and Cora. Bartholomew constantly diverts Carter from these women and toward his duel with Taurez, Carter's perennial rival and first-name-basis enemy, an evil double with whom he is on terms of mysterious intimacy. After Taurez's defeat, the film ends with Carter declaring to Bartholomew, "Let's go some place where there aren't any women," but then changing his mind and telling the cab driver to follow a pretty girl.

Nick Carter, Master Detective is quicker and more immediately striking, but *Phantom Raiders* has more in common visually with Tourneur's later films. If *Detective* looks back to Tourneur's past with its skillful interweaving of documentary and fiction, *Phantom Raiders* anticipates his future with its sustaining of mood through rich decor and careful lighting, its low-budget exoticism, and its hints of thwarted sexuality.

Doctors Don't Tell
(1941)

Even a director has to make a living!

FRITZ LANG (ABOUT AN AMERICAN
GUERRILLA IN THE PHILIPPINES)

"I detest this film; it's my worst."[1] Some might hold out for *The Comedy of Terrors* or *War-Gods of the Deep*. For all their enormous faults, however, Tourneur's final two features aren't as stupefyingly routine and banal as *Doctors Don't Tell*, his fourth American feature.

How Tourneur became involved with the project is unknown. Don Miller observed, "MGM's B pictures took a definite turn toward family fare in 1940";[2] possibly Tourneur's track record with darker subjects — not just in his three features for MGM but also in his second-unit work and most of his shorts — put him at a disadvantage under this new policy. However explained, the leap from MGM to Republic was precipitous. The difference in quality between *Phantom Raiders* and *Doctors Don't Tell* shows in every department, especially in the writing and in the quality of the lighting.

Doctors Don't Tell is the disjointed story of two friends, Dr. Ralph Sawyer (John Beal) and Dr. Frank Blake (Edward Norris). Ralph risks his certification by operating on a critically wounded car-accident victim, Diana Wayne (Florence Rice), while he is still an intern and thus technically disqualified from performing the operation. Diana's complete recovery makes the point a moot one, and Ralph is allowed to practice as an M.D. Ralph falls in love with Diana, but she is drawn to Frank.

Frank accepts a bribe from gangster Joe Grant (Douglas Fowley) to fix up his sidekick, Barney (Ward Bond), after the latter suffers a gunshot wound. Thanks to Grant's patronage, Frank's practice begins to thrive, but both Ralph and Diana become alienated from him. In a spontaneous drive-by shooting, Barney kills the man who shot him; before dying, his victim manages to identify Grant (who drove the car). Grant persuades Frank to remove the tell-tale scar on his cheek by surgery, but Grant is arrested anyway and, thanks to Frank's decision to go straight and testify, convicted. Barney assassinates Frank on the courthouse steps; the police kill Barney; the end of the film indicates that Ralph will get Diana.

The film is so utterly un–Tourneurian and so lacking in any feature of interest

70

as to defy commentary. The halting, implausible screenplay provides only the most rudimentary delineation of character. The film suffers gratuitously from poor musical numbers. At one point, Diana and her brother, a singing duo, perform a purportedly comical Latin novelty song. It prompts Frank to say, "I'm going home and smash all my phonograph records"—a remark that, though intended as praise, is easier to understand as a revulsion from any manifestation of an art that could produce the monstrosity we've just heard. The short running time of the film is also saddled with running comedy relief from Grady Sutton as a squeamish doctor named Peter Piper. At the end of the film, Piper arrives at a house call to find that his patient is a horse. The film's willingness to spend its precious last moments on such trivia shows its lack of confidence and interest in its supposedly serious themes.

Exhibiting many of the worst traits of the B movie, *Doctors Don't Tell* is the antithesis of the richly textured, subtle work that Tourneur had already shown he could do on a small budget and of which his next film would offer a complete manifesto. The direction of *Doctors Don't Tell*, though not inept, is pedestrian and betrays a lack of conviction. Occasional felicitous shots testify to Tourneur's professionalism: the large glass windows of an office set are used well, and at one point the camera makes an interesting movement around the phone booth from which Barney takes aim at Frank. Such moments prove that Tourneur could still be sensitive to the possibilities of decor even in the most barren dramatic and visual context.

The acting is competent. Douglas Fowley and Ward Bond, as the crooks, effortlessly steal the film. Barney's reflex violence ("that guy hurt me and I just had to hurt him back, that's all," he explains after killing a druggist) makes him a crude early version of Tourneur's violent characters, including another one incarnated by Ward Bond, Bragg in *Canyon Passage*. The three leads are colorless, perhaps as an effect of the intentional underplaying in which Tourneur would later, with more success, encourage such actors as James Ellison (*I Walked with a Zombie*), George Brent (*Experiment Perilous*), Victor Mature (*Easy Living, Timbuktu*), and Glenn Ford (*Appointment in Honduras*). Edward Norris, in particular, makes little of what is potentially the most interesting part: the ambitious doctor tempted by corruption.

Doctors Don't Tell adds little to the Tourneurian study of the medical and scientific professions (cf. "Romance of Radium," *They All Come Out*, "The Magic Alphabet," *Cat People, I Walked with a Zombie, Experiment Perilous*, "Reward Unlimited"). In the film's odd universe, no middle ground exists between Ralph's socially useful but poorly paid work as assistant medical examiner and Frank's success at catering to both gangsters and Park Avenue hypochondriacs. The film implies that Frank's booming high-society trade is somehow due to the gangsters, but their drugstore-protection racket seems a bit déclassé for such a connection.

Cat People (1942)

The world of the happy man is a different one from that of the unhappy man.

LUIDWIG WITTGENSTEIN, *TRACTATUS LOGICO-PHILOSOPHICUS*

In 1942, Val Lewton, Tourneur's collaborator on the second unit of *A Tale of Two Cities*, left the Selznick organization to head a new unit at RKO devoted to B horror films. For the unit's first effort, RKO production head Charles Koerner insisted on the title *Cat People*. After considering several stories that might fit the title, Lewton hit on the basic premise of a young woman obsessed with the fear of turning into a cat.[1]

Lewton chose Tourneur to direct; writer DeWitt Bodeen and editor Mark Robson completed a four-man team that worked together closely on the development of the story. From their conferences emerged the decision to ground the story in reality and common fears. "At first, Bodeen wrote *Cat People* as a period thing but I argued against that," Tourneur recalled. "I said that if you're going to have horror, the audience must be able to identify with the characters in order to be frightened."[2] According to Bodeen, however, the modern New York setting was Lewton's inspiration. Bodeen also said that the idea for the swimming pool scene came from his once having nearly drowned while swimming alone at night in a pool; Tourneur, on the other hand, said that the scene was based on his own experience of being alone in a friend's swimming pool while one of his friend's pet cheetahs, having got out of its cage, was prowling around nearby.[3]

One of the crucial decisions was to suggest, rather than show, the heroine's transformation into a panther. This discretion characterized the film's attitude toward the fantastic and clearly distinguished the Lewton unit's approach from that of Universal, which had made two films that used makeup and lap dissolves to show men becoming monsters (*Werewolf of London* [1935] and *The Wolfman* [1941]).

Tourneur brought the film in at $141,659, slightly over its minuscule budget. To the surprise of the RKO executives who distrusted the picture (Tourneur recalled that Lew Ostrow, the executive producer, wanted to fire him after viewing the rushes from the first three days but was overruled by Koerner), *Cat People* became a huge success. It helped save the studio, which had been in financial difficulties. Tourneur was later fond of recalling that the film played at the Hawaii Theatre in Hollywood, where it had been booked for one week, for thirteen weeks — one week longer than *Citizen Kane*. According to the *New York Times*, by the end of 1943, the film was approaching a domestic gross of $4,000,000.[4]

Cat People opens with a chance meeting in the zoo between Oliver Reed (Kent Smith), a draftsman for a shipbuilding company, and Irena Dubrovna (Simone Simon), a commercial illustrator. Irena, obsessed with a legend concerning her native Serbian village, fears that she may be one of the village "cat women," who change into panthers when aroused by sexual passion or jealousy. She and Oliver fall in love and marry. Because of her fear, however, the marriage isn't consummated.

Oliver urges Irena to see a psychiatrist, Dr. Judd (Tom Conway), but Irena terminates the analysis after a single visit, convinced that Judd's rationalism is unsuited to a problem of the "soul." Meanwhile, Oliver's dissatisfaction with his marriage drives him closer to his co-worker Alice (Jane Randolph). Jealous, Irena stalks Alice, first on the sidewalk through the park and then in the swimming pool of her apartment building, both times seemingly assuming the form of a cat. When Judd, who is attracted to Irena, tries to seduce her, she turns into a panther and kills him, but before dying, he manages to wound her fatally with the concealed blade of his walking stick.

Cat People derives its situations, including its horrific ones, from the emotions of the protagonists, a tactic that sets it apart from the typical horror cinema of the time. The main tension in the film comes from Irena's fear of her own sexuality as "evil"—a daring choice of theme for 1942. The meaning of Irena's pathetic appeal to Oliver on their wedding night is hardly in doubt: "I want to be Mrs. Reed really. I want to be *everything* that name means to me. But I can't, I can't. Oliver, be kind, be patient. Let me have time, time to get over that feeling there's something evil in me."

The script links this feeling to her foreignness, building a subtext of cultural difference that becomes another, subtler source of conflict and pathos in the film. Irena's tragedy is partly a tragedy of displacement. The film prompts us to identify with her condition; her otherness defines our attitude toward the other characters' normalcy. J. P. Telotte has perceptively noted that her "deep cultural roots ... not only suggest a mysterious depth in her character, but also underscore a significant absence in the Americans here who seem quite divorced from history.... [H]er situation accentuates an unexamined rootlessness typifying the Americans around her."[5]

Hoping to naturalize Irena, Oliver explains away the legend of the cat women of the Serbian village in a speech that manifests an almost compulsive banality: "They're fairy tales, Irena, fairy tales heard in your childhood, nothing more than that. They have nothing to do with you, really. You're Irena, you're here in America. You're so normal you're even in love with me, Oliver Reed, a good plain Americano. You're so normal you're going to marry me. And those fairy tales, you can tell 'em to our children. They'll love 'em."

Oliver's Americanness takes a variety of forms. At Sally Lund's, a restaurant near his office, he eats nothing but apple pie whereas, at a meeting to discuss whether he should have Irena committed, Judd orders Roquefort and even Alice has "the Bavarian creme." Oliver has never known any artists, and he has never been unhappy. Bodeen's script has him quoting Keats to Alice in the first scene at the zoo, but this touch is eliminated from the final film,[6] in which Oliver's prosaic nature is unmitigated. His lack of imagination and his inability to believe in Irena's experience of the supernatural render him as unable to help her as is Judd and make him the inadvertent cause of her destruction.

Cat People represents Irena's problem in terms of dividing lines, barriers, traces, and absences. The first shot of the film, after the titles, tracks back from the panther cage in the zoo. The shot includes a gradually wider view of the spectators, who stand behind a low fence that surrounds the cage, then takes in Irena, her back to the camera, drawing on her sketch-pad; the camera continues to track back so that a bush becomes visible in the foreground in the lower right quadrant of the frame. Three barriers appear over the course of the shot: the bars of the cage, the protective fence, and finally the bush. These barriers represent the dividing line between human and animal, categories whose mutual exclusivity is staged by the zoo. The emphasis on repeating this line in multiple forms suggests that the prohibition against crossing it is as obsessive as Irena's temptation to cross it. Later in the film (we return with Irena to the zoo many times), a chain measures the length of the space across which Irena, imitating the panther, paces back and forth. The chain marks Irena's imprisonment, which we (and she) have come to recognize as equivalent to the panther's. In the scenes in the stairwell outside Irena's apartment, camera placement and lighting repeatedly emphasize the rail of the balustrade, which suggests a prison-like boundary; its bars are echoed in the interior of her apartment, with its jalousies and birdcage.

The bush that looms up in the foreground at the end of the opening shot illustrates a key aspect of the film's mise-en-scène: the insistent placement of shadows and dark areas in the frame. Lewton knew the importance of these zones of darkness in the house style he and his collaborators were developing: "If you make the screen dark enough, the mind's eye will read anything into it you want! We're great ones for dark patches." As Paul Willemen has observed, this strategy was also characteristic of Tourneur's style apart from Lewton. Willemen identifies the presence of a dark area in the foreground of shots as one of three main ways in which Tourneur produces a "barrier effect," along with the insertion of objects of decor between the camera and the actors and the overlaying of shadows on the actors' bodies. Willemen sees this effect as "a dramatization of the essential structure of fantasy: a scene, a subject looking at it, and the passage which separates/unites the two." J. P. Telotte also gives a psychological interpretation of the "dark patches" in the visual fields of Lewton's films. The absence they mark "signals a black hole or vacant meaning in the physical realm which, in spite of man's natural desire to fill it with consciousness and significance, persistently and troublingly remains open."[7]

In *Cat People*, these visual barriers blur the edge of the film frame, extending the space around the characters, a space that merges into, and mirrors, the darkness surrounding the film audience. In the scene in which Irena, under hypnosis, reveals her obsessions to Judd, her face is a small spotlit circle of light in the middle of an otherwise totally dark field. The celebrated sequence in which Irena follows Alice on the sidewalk—the film calls this a "transverse," a word suited to its theme of transformation—repeatedly places darkness at the edges of the frame, where it merges with a threatening offscreen space.

The transverse sequence is built on two cinematic figures: the alternation of light and dark and the breakdown of parallelism. Throughout his films, Tourneur will continue to use these figures to create suspense.

As Oliver and Alice say good-night on a street corner, they stand in a pool of light. Walking away into the background down a street that retreats from the camera

Simone Simon in *Cat People* (courtesy of the Academy of Motion Picture Arts and Sciences).

at screen right, Alice passes through a dark area and into another illuminated area, where she turns; she and Oliver wave at each other before both disappear in opposite directions (Oliver entering a dark area near the camera before leaving camera range). This shot establishes the scene's motif of alternating light and dark areas. Each of several subsequent shots shows a character (either Irena or Alice) passing from darkness in the background or at frame left into a light area in the middle of the frame and then continuing into a dark area in the foreground or at frame right. These shots are silent except for the sounds of the women's heels on the pavement: Irena's clicking loudly and rapidly, Alice's sounding more muted and more measured.

The formal breakdown breaks down precisely when Irena's heels are suddenly no longer heard. This cessation coincides with the camera's holding on an empty area of light (just vacated by Alice) for a pronounced duration. The next shot appears at first to repeat the established pattern, as Alice enters the frame at left and crosses a zone of illumination into a dark area, but this time the camera, tracking laterally, continues with her through the dark area — again, for a noticeable duration — to the next lamppost, where she slows her pace and turns to look behind her. As in the walk to the Houmfort in *I Walked with a Zombie*, the breakdown of parallelism defeats our expectations, signaling that we, along with the character on screen, have crossed into an unpredictable universe.

Here the scene cuts to a shot of the street in depth, with Alice's figure in the foreground. The next shot, inverting the established pattern, has her start in a light area, pass through a dark area, and stop again in a light area, where she turns again. We cut to a second shot of the street, a shot similar to the first one (the composition dominated by two streetlamps at a diagonal in the frame, the farther one framed underneath an arch) except that now Alice's figure is absent. The emotional movement between the two shots of the street corresponds to Alice's growing fear: in the first shot, the retreating streetlights are fixed in reference to Alice's body; in the second, her absence from the frame leaves them floating in an impersonal space of absolute otherness.

Alice continues to the next lamppost, where she stops again. A low growl is heard; the growl becomes the jarringly loud blast of a bus braking in front of her. This famous bus, which gave its name to a succession of effects in various Lewton films (and functions within quotation marks, in the critical discourse on Lewton, as the equivalent of the Hitchcockian "MacGuffin"), both actualizes and momentarily displaces the possibility of an attack from an offscreen space that we have come to read as completely hostile.

The rest of the sequence moves to a set of disconnected spaces: a low-angle shot of bushes rustled by something behind them is followed by shots of the caged panther and leopard at the zoo, then by scenes in a pasture (part of the zoo, presumably), where a watchman carrying a lamp discovers some slaughtered sheep. In an insert, his lamp shines on animal tracks in the mud. This cuts to a traveling close-up on the transverse, which follows a series of animal tracks that metamorphose into prints of high heels; at the moment of this metamorphosis, the lost sound of Irena's heels on the pavement resumes. The camera's movement over these traces is doubled by that of a spotlight, perhaps from a flashlight or from the same watchman's lamp, but the next shot, in which Irena, holding a handkerchief to her mouth, stops beside a lamppost, suggests (by the absence of any character who, following the tracks, would here catch up with Irena) that this moving light is to be read instead as a nondiegetic component of the search by the *camera*.

In the swimming pool scene, the film uses shadows to represent an unseen intruder — initially, in the shot of a shadow descending the stairs toward the pool. After the long shot of Alice plunging into the swimming pool, the annihilating absence threatening her becomes a diffusion of sourceless shadow over the whole space. The empty shots of the walls and ceiling, over which Alice's reverb-drenched screams assault us, are images of contemporary horror as bleak and disturbing as any on film. Tourneur always claimed that the shadows on the walls of the pool came from his fist moving in front of the lens. This would likely have rendered the frame completely black, something that does occur once in the scene; but the other shadows that appear are created by the momentary slight dimunition of light (suggesting something moving in front of the light source, not the lens) and, at one point, by a distinctly outlined, animated black shape that could be that of a panther.

Another overt manipulation of the light source takes place in the distinctive wipe from the shot of Irena tearing the couch with her nails to the conference in

Teresa Harris, Kent Smith, and Jane Randolph in *Cat People* (courtesy of the Academy of Motion Picture Arts and Sciences).

Sally Lund's among Oliver, Alice, and Judd. A mask seemingly moving laterally across the space progressively blacks out the shot with Irena, then continues in the same screen direction across the next shot, which it progressively leaves clear. (A similar mask-wipe occurs near the end of *I Walked with a Zombie*.) The extinguishing of light at the end of the first shot appears to have been done, unusually, by gradually shutting a single actual light source on the set, whereas the introduction to the next shot was probably done optically.

The most famous of the many ellipses in the film is the refusal to show the transformation of Irena into a cat. This refusal leaves a number of traces on the film. For example, after the scene in which a panther menaces Oliver and Alice in the drafting room, the film suggests the panther's departure by shots of the elevator door closing and of the revolving door turning by itself. Optical distortion both registers and conceals the transformation triggered by Judd's kiss: in a shot taken with a heavy diffusion filter, Irena approaches the camera, walking out of frame. After the death of Judd, we don't see Irena leave the apartment; instead, the cutting whisks us to Oliver and Alice arriving at the building and dashing upstairs, whereupon Irena is shown hiding in the landing.

The one concession the filmmakers were forced to make to the RKO front office was to include shots of a panther in the drafting room sequence. As originally written, shot, and cut, this scene used shadows and sounds to suggest the thing that threatens Oliver and Alice: "In the darkness, to one side of them, there is a sound like a snarl.... From the darkness, following them, there is a whisper of light, padded feet — a delicate tick, tick of claws scraping the floor.... Now there comes again, pursuing them, the whispering tread of soft paws."[8] Partly because of the addition of the panther (and of heavy scoring, in contrast to the transverse and swimming pool scenes, which have no music), the drafting room scene is by far the weakest and most conventional of the film's scenes of terror, although Tourneur, cinematographer Nicholas Musuraca, and Robson managed to limit our direct view of the panther.

Other effects in the film play on the withholding of information from the audience. When Irena reaches into the birdcage to play with her pet canary, for example, the close composition keeps the bird offscreen so that we can't know what Irena is doing to it. All we see is her face; the canary's death, later ascribed to fright, is registered only in Irena's change of expression and the cessation of the bird's cries.

Irena's apartment, strewn with barriers, becomes the site of a complicated play on visibility and invisibility. Bodeen's script meticulously itemized its decor:

> A nicely proportioned living room with a little fireplace set under a neat Georgian mantel. Doors at either end of the room lead off into small bedrooms. Behind a fantastic three-part screen on which is painted the long, sleek figure of a black leopard against a background of jungle foliage, is concealed the two-burner stove, tiny sink, and old-fashioned icebox which make up the kitchenette. In the other corner, under the wide window, are a drawing board and a desk, littered with crayons, brushes, bottles of discolored water, and papers. On one side of the wall, in neat frames, hang three of Grandville's amusing studies of cats dressed as humans. Over the mantel hangs a beautiful reproduction of Goya's sinister portrait of Don Manuel Osorio de Zuniga and the cats.[9]

Rarely showing much of the set at once, Tourneur breaks it into zones serving different dramatic purposes. The leopard screen, for example, twice separates Irena and Oliver: first, fleetingly, when Oliver examines the statue of King John of Serbia while Irena brings the used cups and saucers to the kitchen; second, in a striking deep-focus composition with Oliver pouring sherry in the kitchen while Irena broods alone, upset over the death of the canary. The screen also functions as a sign of Irena's obsession. It suggests Irena's identification with her animal nature (as in the scene of the bird's death, which starts with the camera tracking back from the screen), but it also suggests her ability to keep it under control by objectifying it, so that it functions in another sense of the word "screen," as a site of projection. The screen is prominent when Irena becomes a panther and attacks Judd — a scene that recapitulates all the art objects in the apartment set, including the Goya painting and Irena's fashion sketches.

Another cat sign in the apartment appears on the wall in the background of certain shots: the catlike shadow cast by an armchair. The scene that starts with Oliver sleeping on the couch and with Irena kneeling on the floor beside him is precisely staged so that when Oliver triggers Irena's fears by mentioning that they've never kissed each other, she draws away just enough to cause her head to be framed within the cat shadow. This shadow reappears when Oliver tells Irena that he is in love with Alice and wants a divorce and again when Judd, Oliver, and Alice wait for Irena.

The dark shape of the couch, which dominates many of the shots in which it figures, defines the illusion of stability in Irena's life. When Oliver shatters this illusion by announcing that he loves Alice, Irena tears the surface of the couch with her nails — a logical form of protest and a gesture rehearsed earlier in the film by similar downward movements of the hand by both Irena (at the end of the wedding-night sequence) and Alice (after her ordeal in the swimming pool, when her hand slides down the doorjamb after she sees that her robe has been "torn to ribbons").

One of the objects to which the film draws our attention most often is the statue of King John spearing a panther with a sword. In the first scene at the apartment, Oliver's curiosity about the statue prompts Irena to recount the legend of the cat people. Later, the statue comes to life in Irena's dream. Perhaps the least schematic use of the statue occurs when Irena calls Oliver's office and listens silently to Alice's voice before hanging up. Here the statue's presence in the shot comments ironically on Irena's assuming John's role as scourge of evil (now embodied in Alice's supposed adultery).

The image of the statue draws together a number of the film's themes. When Oliver suggests that he and Irena should seek help, she looks instinctively at the statue. He catches her look and says: "Not that sort of help. There's something wrong and we have to face it in an intelligent way. We don't need a King John with fire and sword. We need someone who can find the reason for your belief and cure it. That's what we need. A psychiatrist." For him, the legendary and the contemporary figures contradict each other; for her, they're fused — a fusion hinted at after the opening credits, when the film superimposes over a shot of the statue an epigraph attributed to Dr. Judd in a work called *The Anatomy of Atavism.*

Just as the statue of King John is always shown next to a lamp, Judd is introduced next to a lampstand during Irena's hypnosis session. The film draws attention to Judd's association with light by having him get up, open the curtains, and switch off the lamp. In Irena's dream, Judd wears King John's armor. But he holds the sword crossways instead of erect, as John holds it in the sculpture. This way of holding the sword recalls Judd's encounter with Irena at the zoo: there, as he says the words — "the, uh, key" — that will echo, their lapsus intact, in Irena's dream, he points with his walking stick toward the key in the lock of the panther's cage. The sword is linked with the hidden blade of Judd's walking stick, just as the key to the cage is linked with the key to the Reeds' apartment (a key that Judd later borrows on the pretext of having to retrieve his stick).

Other objects in Irena's apartment also have specific symbolic and dramatic functions. The Goya painting forms a backdrop to the shot in which Irena recounts the tortured history of her village to Oliver; the figure of Don Manuel echoes the heroic figure of King John but casts virility in a more ambiguous, "sinister" light. Before confronting Irena with the knowledge that she has stopped seeing Dr. Judd, Oliver absently touches a model of a ship that has materialized on a table beside the King John statue. The model indicates the emergence of Oliver's obsessions into the space previously defined by Irena's. It also subtly marks the couple's isolation from each other at this point in the film: she has kept secret from him her failure to see Judd, whereas he has grown closer to Alice (Oliver and Alice will use Irena's uninterest in ships to get rid of her at the museum).

The curving lines of Irena's drawings contrast with the mathematical precision of Oliver and Alice's drafting, just as the practical nature of shipbuilding contrasts with the luxury connotations of Irena's work. Although Irena's drawing is solitary (Oliver's intrusion in the first scene is strongly marked), it is virtually her only vehicle of communication with society. It combines two forms of alienation: in her drawing of a panther impaled by a sword, Irena identifies herself with the beast; later we read her drawing of an elegant female figure as representative of the women Irena envies for their "normal, happy lives." Both the panther and the female figure are alienated self-images — variations on Irena's incapacity to *be*, showing her as petrified by images of herself (as, in a different way, Allida in *Experiment Perilous* is petrified by the portrait commissioned by her husband).

The wedding party scene, one of the highpoints of the film, confronts Irena with another alienating double. The scene opens with the camera on the street outside the restaurant, tracking back from the window, through which we see, in a wide shot, the wedding group's table with Carver (Alan Napier) at its head, facing the camera. This shot cuts to one inside the restaurant, from roughly the same angle.

The Commodore (Jack Holt) makes a toast "to the bride." During the toast, the scene cuts for the first time to a woman sitting alone at another table; she turns and looks offscreen past the camera, apparently in the direction of the party. (The woman is played by Elizabeth Russell, a striking actress whom Lewton would use in bigger parts in *The Seventh Victim* and *The Curse of the Cat People*.) There follows a two-shot of the Commodore and Carver, the former pointing out the woman and the latter putting on his glasses and turning to look at her; this cuts back to the shot of the woman, still looking in the same direction past the camera, with an indefinable expression, perhaps of indignation. In a return to the two-shot of the men, Carver comments, seemingly loudly enough for her to hear, "She looks like a cat."

This line cues another cut to the woman, who rises. The cutting, and her enigmatic expression, imply that Carver's remark has offended her and that she is going to rebuke him. Therefore the next shot, a two-shot of Irena and Alice (the former thanking Alice for the party and expressing surprise at the existence of a Serbian restaurant in New York), violates our expectations. This two-shot cuts to a high-angle group shot, in which the woman walks into the right of the frame and looks down at the group, who notice her and look up. In close-up, the woman addresses Irena: "*Moja sestra?*" ("my sister" in Serbian, as Irena later explains to Oliver; Simone Simon dubbed this line). The scene cuts to a close-up of Irena looking up, frightened, and cuts back to the close-up of the woman, who now moves closer to the camera, which reframes slightly; she repeats her words, this time with a stronger suggestion of sympathy and solidarity. The shot cuts back to Irena, who crosses herself; cut back to the

Alec Craig and Simone Simon in *Cat People*.

woman, who starts to walk out of the shot. At this point the scene cuts to a group
shot of the whole table, with the camera now shooting toward the door and the window (reversing its placement in the scene's original establishing shot): the woman
walks the length of the table to the door, throws a fur over her shoulders, and leaves.

The film links the lone woman to the group entirely by means of cutting on
dialogue spoken by members of the group: the toast that seems to arouse her
attention; Carver's remark that apparently makes her indignant. But the close-up
confrontation between her and Irena abolishes the previous set of relationships and
shows that she is interested only in Irena. This structural surprise heightens the
force of her intervention.

The brief two-shot of Irena and Alice, used only once in the scene, is also
remarkable. The balancing of the two women in the frame hints at the rivalry that
will develop between them. At the same time, in conjunction with the offscreen
presence of the strange woman, the two-shot has a hint of female solidarity. A single
candle burns at the right of the frame, mirroring the composition of the stranger at
her table, in which a candle was at the left of the frame, and thus linking Irena
and Alice to her. This subtext of the scene was, according to Bodeen, not lost
on contemporary viewers: "Val got several letters after *Cat People* was released,

congratulating him for his boldness in introducing lesbiana to films in Hollywood."[10] The reversal of angle in the shot of the woman leaving (which is accompanied by a mournful tune that accentuates her mysterious solitariness) correlates
with the reversal of tone caused by her solicitation of Irena.

Cat People begins and ends with texts that underline its theme of duality.
The film's epigraph reads, "Even as fog continues to lie in the valleys, so does
ancient sin cling to the low places, the depressions in the world consciousness."
The title at the end of the film quotes one of John Donne's "Holy Sonnets": "But
black sin hath betrayed to endless night / My world, both parts, and both parts
must die." From the first title to the second, several movements take place: from
prose to poetry; from science to confession; from a totalizing, surveying view that
claims to encompass the topography and history ("*ancient* sin") of the world to a
personal, subjective view in which not the whole world but specifically "my world"
has been "betrayed" and becomes subject to time and death. This movement is
metaphorically that of the viewer of the film, from the initial state of detached
expectation that belongs to the viewer at the beginning of any film (and that finds
in the epigraph only general hints as to what it should look for in the narrative
about to unfold) to a final catharsis (if the film has worked for the viewer). The
images accompanying the two titles reverse each other: King John, in symbolic triumph over Judd's "low places," raising the panther impaled on his sword above his
head; the black, faceless figure, all that remains of Irena, lying at the foot of the
empty cage.

The sign that Oliver points out to Irena at the zoo when she drops a page from
her sketchpad on the ground — "Let no one say, and say it to your shame, / That all
was beauty here, until you came" — is another thematically central text. "Shame"
recalls Donne's "sin"; the verse also relates to Judd's invocation of "a psychic need to
loose evil upon the world." Dirt befouling beauty becomes a key theme in the film:
Irena's torn sketch blown against the wall by the wind is a piece of trash, an element
that doesn't belong and must be eliminated, like the obsession it represents. The film
repeatedly shows people getting rid of dirt: the Revelations-quoting zookeeper
sweeps the aisle between the panther's cage and the public space; twice we see the
cleaning woman in Oliver and Alice's office building compulsively flicking ashes
from her blouse. After the transverse scene, Irena's attempt to wash away the traces
of her adventure occasions one of the most startling shots of the film: the camera tilts
up from the claw ornament at the base of the bathtub to Irena's nude back as she
weeps, crouched in the tub.

A turning point in the narrative is marked by a powerful superimposition
from a close-up of Irena (after she sharply repeats the name "Alice" just uttered by
Oliver) to a medium shot of the revolving door at the entrance to the office building.
The momentary conjunction of Irena's face with the door makes us recognize the
revolving door as a sign of transformation. Hinged and multipartite like the screen
in her apartment, the door is the site of the passage from one world to another, the
passage that Irena's jealousy will drive her to take. (*Out of the Past* also uses a
revolving door symbolically; in the later film, it visualizes the verbal idea of the
"double-cross.") Threateningly, the door at first appears to turn by itself while
Oliver watches; then the cleaning woman, previously invisible because she is on
her hands and knees, comes into view.

The structural use of the revolving door is one of several symmetries in the film. Its final appearance in the film marks the end of Irena's threat to Oliver and Alice: the shot in which it again turns by itself, apparently after having been set in motion by the vanished Irena. This scene also brings to a close a separate series: Alice notices "Irena's perfume — strong, sweet," the first thing Oliver noticed when he entered Irena's apartment for the first time. Similarly, the high angle shot in which Irena, slinking away on the staircase after being mortally wounded by Judd, takes a last look at Oliver as he enters the apartment echoes (and retrospectively justifies) the use of a similar angle early in the film (when it was felt as excess), in the shots of Irena on the landing watching Oliver descend the stairs. Finally, the last shot of the film refers to the first, as the camera again retreats from the panther's cage.

Cat People is a master text in Tourneur's filmography. Most of Tourneur's later films have some connection with *Cat People*, most obviously the two next Lewton films and *Night of the Demon*, but also *Experiment Perilous*, *Out of the Past* (in which Jeff's attempt to flee from his past recalls Irena), *Berlin Express* and *Circle of Danger* (with their American heroes ill-equipped to deal with the complexities of European problems), *Anne of the Indies* (in its foregrounding of female sexuality), *Nightfall* (in which the hero is a commercial artist and the heroine a model, splitting the two aspects of Irena's profession, drawing and fashion), and even *Days of Glory* (the rivalry between Irena and Alice is repeated in that between Nina and Yelena). The recurrence of cats in Tourneur's films suggests a trademark: in *Way of a Gaucho*, *Appointment in Honduras*, *Stranger on Horseback*, and *The Comedy of Terrors*.

Cat People is so famous that it has, inevitably, suffered a backlash, and now it might even be called underrated. Charles Higham and Joel Greenberg wrote: "Careful — perhaps overcareful — the film today seems so understated that much of its intended effect is dissipated.... [I]ts total impression is distinctly tepid." For Joel E. Siegel, the film is "seriously weakened by passages of lumpy, strained dialogue, uncertain performances and uneven pacing." Tourneur himself tended to be hard on the film: "As a script, as a story progression, *Cat People* is very poor.... *Cat People* was very childish."[11]

The acting in the film is a frequent target of criticism. Siegel finds Simone Simon's "acting range ... too narrow for the film's more dramatic moments, a problem heightened by her difficulties with American pronunciation. Kent Smith is terribly stiff most of the time, and Jane Randolph, though somewhat better than Smith, is not fully convincing."[12] I disagree with these assessments. The much maligned Smith is thoughtful and natural; his unconventional modesty makes it easy to see why Lewton cast him again in two more films (*The Curse of the Cat People* and *Youth Runs Wild*). Despite Tourneur's own reservations ("I wasn't too happy with Simone Simon's performance as the cat girl"),[13] Simone Simon's performance, though not delicately nuanced, is effective in its mixture of narcissism and hesitant uncertainty. Randolph makes an ideal contrast to Simon with her superbly underplayed confidence. Tom Conway's muted performance is in the mainstream of Tourneurian acting. The most interesting aspect of his performance is the strain of his constant effort to control his reactions: note, for example, his suppressed little laugh after Alice, who is trying to convince him that "the cat form of Irena" has been stalking her, reveals that she loves Oliver.

Cat People remains, with all its flaws, a perfect film — which means that even its flaws have become classic. The "careful," "tepid," "strained," "uneven" quality that critics complain of ideally expresses the discreet involvement with which Tourneur regards his characters' dilemmas, making the viewer identify with the morbidly sensitive Irena and poignantly underlining her estrangement from Oliver. The conviction of *Cat People* is still contagious; the viewer can still share the surprise and pleasure the film evoked in audiences who discovered this unheralded B horror film on its initial release.

I Walked with a Zombie (1943)

It is a place in the world, our world; we have all lived there. Still, while open on all
sides by nature, it is strictly delimited and even closed: sacred in the ancient sense,
separate. There, it seems, before the action of the book or the film's interrogation
begins, that death — a certain way of dying — has done its work, has introduced
a mortal inertia. Everything there is empty, missing, in relation to the things of
our society: missing, in regard to the events that seem to occur there — meals,
games, feelings, language, books that are not written, are not read, and
even nights which belong, in their intensity, to an already defunct passion.

MAURICE BLANCHOT, "DESTROY"
(ON MARGUERITE DURAS'S
DÉTRUIRE, DIT-ELLE)

I Walked with a Zombie went into production only two months after the end
of production on *Cat People* (and before the earlier film was released). Again, the
title came down from Charles Koerner, who had discovered an article called "I
Met a Zombie" by Inez Wallace in *American Weekly* magazine. (Wallace is credited
in the film for the "original story," although her article, an anecdotal account of
voodoo practices, has no relation to the film plot.) With his characteristic knack
for turning around unpromising assignments, Lewton decided to use the title as a
pretext for "a West Indian version of *Jane Eyre*."[1] Although often noted, the film's
similarity to *Jane Eyre* is vague, and it has become, in a way, as much of a red her-
ring as the title.

Ardel Wray, co-writer of the script (with Curt Siodmak), later recalled Lewton's addiction to research, out of which he drew "the overall feel, mood, and
quality he wanted, as well as details for actual production."[2] The shooting script
even provides a bibliographic reference for the scene of the voodoo ceremony:
"Please see pages 28 to 31, *Life Magazine*, December 13, 1937. All the details represented are graphically illustrated."[3]

To try to synopsize *I Walked with a Zombie* is a peculiarly ridiculous task,
since the film, more systematically than any other Tourneur film, abolishes narrative verisimilitude. Betsy Connell (Frances Dee), a Canadian nurse, is sent by her
employment agency to the West Indian island of St. Sebastian to take care of Jessica (Christine Gordon), the wife of a sugar planter, Paul Holland (Tom Conway).
Betsy learns that Jessica was suddenly stricken with a fever that has left her mute

Frances Dee and Clinton Rosemond in *I Walked with a Zombie* (courtesy of the Academy of Motion Picture Arts and Sciences).

and without will. She also learns that Paul's half-brother, Wesley Rand (James Ellison), was in love with Jessica. Betsy falls in love with Paul but resolves to try to restore his wife to him. After insulin shock treatment fails to improve Jessica's condition, Betsy, under guidance from the Hollands' housemaid, Alma (Teresa Harris), takes Jessica to the Houmfort, or voodoo temple. Her experiment succeeds only in arousing the interest of the voodoo priests, who believe that Jessica is a zombie and use magic to try and call her back to the Houmfort.

Alarmed by the excitement over Jessica, the local commissioner decides to launch an official investigation into her illness. Mrs. Rand (Edith Barrett), the mother of Paul and Wesley, tries to forestall this by confessing that she cast a voodoo spell on Jessica, whom she hated for bringing trouble to her family, but her confession isn't believed. Finally, Wesley kills Jessica to free her from her condition and then walks into the sea with her body, drowning himself.

One of Tourneur's most beautiful films, *I Walked with a Zombie is* a sustained exercise in uncompromising ambiguity. Perfecting the formula that Lewton and Tourneur had developed in *Cat People*, the film carries its predecessor's elliptical, oblique narrative procedures to astonishing extremes. The dialogue is almost nothing but a commentary on past events, obsessively revising itself, finally giving up the struggle to explain and surrendering to a mute acceptance of the inexplicable. We watch the slow, atmospheric, lovingly detailed scenes with delight and fascination, realizing at the end that we have seen nothing but the traces of a conflict decided in advance.

Tourneur distances the characters from us through (1) a narrative that leaves large gaps in our understanding of their actions and motives; (2) a performance style that is restrained to an almost excessive degree; (3) a camera style that subordinates human figures to the decor and to patterns of light. (Our sense of the characters as somehow not fully present is strengthened by the relative dearth of musical cues to underline their emotions: for long passages of the film, the score consists only of low drumbeats; some scenes of dramatic tension have no music at all.) This distancing of the characters, a technique that enhances the timelessness and mystery of the film, is Tourneur's mode of humanism. We come to pity and love these people, not because we identify with them strongly (as we do with Irena in *Cat People*) or are anxious over their fates (Betsy is never put in mortal danger, unlike Alice in *Cat People*), but because we see them as lost and adrift.

Of all Tourneur's feature films, only *I Walked with a Zombie* fully meets the three conditions of "the fantastic" identified by Tzvetan Todorov in his seminal study of the genre: the reader (spectator) "hesitate[s] between a natural and a supernatural explanation of the events described"; the hesitation is inscribed within the text as shared by a character in the story; and the reader interprets the events literally, not as allegory or poetry.[4] If we accept the reality of what *Cat People* shows us, we accept that Irena turns into a cat; in *Night of the Demon* (setting aside for now the problem of Tourneur's original intentions for this film), a belief in the supernatural is imposed on us from the beginning, since we see the demon. These two films thus belong to Todorov's subgenre of "the fantastic-marvelous."

In the Tourneur films whose narratives are predominantly "realistic," an emphasis on illusion, deception, and magic creates ambiguity for both the characters and the viewer (*Berlin Express* and *Stars in My Crown* are good examples of this tendency). Although this ambiguity is not sustained long enough to propel the films wholly into the realm of the fantastic, its presence suggests that many Tourneur films — both the fantastic and the realistic ones — share an important feature of another genre, the mystery, and that the consistent element in his plots could be defined by modifying the terms of Todorov's description of the fantastic: the viewer/reader, along with one or more characters, must hesitate between several explanations of the events of the narrative (whether the explanations are natural or supernatural is, for the purposes of this definition, irrelevant).

I Walked with a Zombie never obliges the viewer to commit to either a natural or a supernatural explanation of Jessica Holland's state. By the end of the film, we may still not be convinced that a supernatural causality has determined the events of the narrative. A mystery that never reveals its solution, the film extends mysteriousness to all its levels and characters. The mute harp and diaphanous curtains in Jessica's room and the flowing gowns she wears are visual metaphors for her condition, which Dr. Maxwell (James Bell) calls that of "a sleepwalker who can never be awakened. Feeling nothing, knowing nothing." From what we later learn about her past character and actions, this description could be equally appropriate to the pre-fever

Jessica (the eulogy at the end of the film says that she was "dead in the selfishness of her spirit"). It could also apply to many of the characters who stalk somnambulistically through Tourneur's films (and even, in a sense, to all human figures in films).

The opening image of Betsy and Carrefour (the guardian of the crossroads) walking along a shoreline will prove not to have a place in the narrative, in which the "zombie" with whom Betsy walks turns out to be Jessica; there is no time in the narrative for the walk of Betsy and Carrefour to take place. Bertrand Tavernier has aptly described the strangeness of the shot:

> The photography is very beautiful, but isn't done to be noticed. In appearance, nothing is told us, and yet how is it possible not to be struck by the deep sadness of this shot, which from the beginning plunges the film into that atmosphere of melancholy evocation (and invocation) in which it will be steeped. It's possible that this poignant emotion is provoked by the tone of the commentary, the presence of the sea in the distance and the discretion of the framing, that the great force of Tourneur consists in believing in these invisible and supernatural forces that he represents and in feeling them from within.[5]

The shot comes in a sense from outside the narrative and functions as an epigraph, offering an iconic conjunction of the film's main themes: Betsy, whom we will come to know as the representative of rationalism and positivism, walking side by side with an uncanny embodiment of the gods' power over mankind; she is white and he is black; they walk along the line that divides and joins earth and sea (a dichotomy that archetypally echoes the conflict between a materialist, rationalist worldview and a supernatural, poetic one).

Over the shot, Betsy's narration begins. The film takes the earliest possible opportunity — right after the director's credit — to distance itself from the naively trashy expectations raised by its title:

> BETSY (*voice-over*): I walked with a zombie. (*Laughs.*) It does seem an odd thing to say.

Her uncomfortable disclaimer — the narrative commenting on itself — pulls the audience out of the film, just as Paul's intrusion ("It's *not* beautiful") pulls Betsy out of her reverie in the boat scene, but the disclaimer also gives the audience another, oblique way into the film by preparing us for an "odd" story, that is, one that is not strictly a horror story. The film will continue to insist on this oddness in relation to Betsy as a means of reversing the expectations she and the audience bring to the narrative. Betsy's voice-over narration says that it is "strange" to have Paul break in on her thoughts on the boat, that at her first view of Fort Holland "from the gate it seemed strangely dreamlike," that she would hear a "strange confession" at Fort Holland. Wesley, however, demystifies the "mysterious, eerie" drums by explaining their function as a code used by the sugar mill, and Paul questions Betsy's description of the tower as "an eerie sort of place, so dark," implicitly ridiculing the association between darkness and danger that is one of the basic principles of suspense in the cinema (including the cinema of Lewton and

Jieno Moxzer in I *Walked with a Zombie.*

Tourneur). Paul corrects Betsy's assumptions about voodoo — "I thought voodoo was something everyone was frightened of" — by reducing it to spectacle: "I'm afraid it's not very frightening. They sing and dance and carry on, and then as I understand it, one of the gods comes down and speaks through one of the people." Later, he refers to the voodoo priests' "cheap mummery."

After the opening shot, we enter the narrative as an interviewer at a sugar company in Ottawa asks Betsy a series of questions, culminating in one whose "irregularity" he apologizes for in advance (repeating the initial gambit of Betsy's narration): "Do you believe in witchcraft?" Until this point the scene has been played on a shot of the man at his desk; the witchcraft question prompts the cut to the reverse-shot that gives us our first distinct view of Betsy. The cut hints at Betsy's role in the film as the person whose belief and disbelief are constantly in question. In response, she laughs and makes a mild joke ("Well, they didn't teach it at Memorial Hospital, but I had my suspicions about the directress of training"), but the close-up of her softly repeating "palm trees" at the end of the scene belies her apparent levelheadedness, hinting at a romantic streak that comes to the fore in the sequences that bring her to St. Sebastian.

Betsy's voice-over, which started out criticizing the title from an implicitly worldly, rationalist perspective, comes under attack from Paul aboard the boat for idealizing the beauty of the sea and sky, which he identifies with "death and decay." (The unexpected device of an on-screen character replying to an offscreen narration may have been inspired by an RKO production of the previous year, *The Magnificent Ambersons*, on which Mark Robson, the editor for *I Walked with a Zombie*, worked.) Throughout the early scenes, Betsy is subtly but insistently identified as the subject of desire and fantasy in the narrative and as someone isolated from social reality. To the coachman's account of how the Hollands brought "the long-ago fathers and the long-ago mothers of us all" to St. Sebastian in a slave ship, she offers a response that we register as bathetically insensitive: "They brought you to a beautiful place, didn't they?" Her romanticism keeps her from seeing the legacy of oppression underneath the "beauty," just as her reaction to Paul's information that animal putrescence causes the phosphorescence of the sea is to muse that Paul has been "hurt, badly hurt." Later, the "horror" of *I Walked with a Zombie* is revealed as, partly, the product of Betsy's imagination, a faculty that she tries to disavow to Paul: "I'm not a frightened girl ...Well, I — I used to be afraid of the dark when I was a child, but I'm not afraid anymore."

During Betsy's first night at Fort Holland, after Paul frustrates her curiosity about her patient by preventing her from taking Jessica her dinner, Betsy turns out the light in her room, suddenly transforming the scene into a screen for the projection of shadows. She goes to the window and looks out, an act prompted by no visual or aural cue, motivated only by her as yet objectless desire to see. We thus register the next image, of Jessica walking across the garden, as the projection of Betsy's desire. The two women's costumes enhance the undercurrent of desire: Jessica wears a flowing white nightgown, Betsy a tight dark robe that she starts to remove at the end of the scene, revealing a white nightgown underneath. On the level of the image, Jessica is both the opposite of Betsy (light vs. dark) and that which Betsy, without avowing it, would like to be or really is (the light hidden by the dark).

Later, Betsy's waking up at night to the sound of weeping betrays an unconscious motivation (just as in *Out of the Past*, Jeff's waking up from a doze in the bar hints that Kathie's appearance, which directly follows, is summoned by his own unconscious). The shot of her waking is followed by a shot of the closed door to the tower, a shot that is not from her point of view but that her curiosity seems to invoke.

Betsy's search for the source of the sound repeats a familiar Gothic motif, but in a brilliant twist, the scene becomes one of "oddness" rather than horror. Approaching Betsy relentlessly in the tower, Jessica backs her toward a rectangle of light on a wall. Betsy screams and runs past Jessica, who turns to follow her. At Betsy's scream, Roy Webb's music reaches a climax with a chord that it sustains over the succeeding shots, creating the effect of a reverberation; it then dies inconspicuously as Paul and two servants enter the tower. Prolonged past its climax (Betsy's scream), the scene ceases to work as a horror scene, a transition enforced by the music: with Betsy, we come to regard Jessica less as a potential source of physical harm and more as a disturbing enigma. The film presents Jessica ambiguously: when she first appears to Betsy, she has frightening dark circles around her eyes and seems to be operating under her own malevolent will; in the light that Paul and the servants bring, she turns out to be completely passive, and the dark circles around her eyes have disappeared. Presumably we are now meant to assume that they were caused by the absence of light, although they were unmistakably present on her face as makeup — a contradiction between two different narrative codes, indicative of Jessica's problematic dual status in the film.

Jessica personifies the emptiness at the core of the narrative, a lack the film symbolizes in a lightly humorous register by the brioche, or "puff-up," that Alma brings Betsy the morning after her ordeal in the tower. Alma explains that Jessica "was very sick and then she went mindless" — the first of a series of varying explanations of Jessica's illness. Dr. Maxwell's similar account is scarcely more scientific: Jessica came down with "a tropical fever" that partly "burned out" her spinal cord. When Betsy, still under the spell of the incident in the tower, tactlessly expresses her surprise that Jessica is "a mental case," Paul approves of the epithet and warns her not to pay attention to "local legends." We hear one of these from the calypso singer: "The wife fell down and the evil came / And it burned her mind in the fever flame." Eventually, Paul is more forthcoming: "A woman driven mad by her own husband.... Before Jessica was taken ill, there was a scene, an ugly scene."

The sequence in which Betsy and Wesley drink at an outdoor cafe is one of the highlights of *I Walked with a Zombie*. In interviews, Tourneur exaggerated the prominence of the calypso singer (Sir Lancelot) in the film: "Whenever we were having a dramatic scene somewhere in the street at night he'd go by singing and he was observing this drama going on and telling us, just like the old Greek tragedies. This gave a wonderful *poésie* to the film." Tourneur added, "We used him as a Greek chorus, wandering in seven or eight times and explaining the plot."[6] In fact, the singer appears only in this sequence. If Tourneur is literally incorrect, however, his misrecollection underlines the structural importance of the singer's role: the "Fort Holland" song indeed functions in a choric way. It also imparts crucial information that we (and Betsy) did not previously possess: that Wesley and Jessica had an affair, that Jessica wanted to leave the island with Wesley, that Paul's opposition to this plan preceded Jessica's fever. The concluding verse makes literal the film's subtextual suggestion that the rivalry between the two brothers is being repeated, with Betsy as its object: "The brothers are lonely and the nurse is young / And now you must see that my song is sung."

Over the course of the sequence, the way the film presents the singer changes. Initially, we perceive him strictly in his public role as an entertainer, albeit one who expresses a complex function, since he belongs to the postslavery entertainer tradition of black Americans and brings out the subversive dimension of this tradition, appropriating and subtly mocking classical culture in his litany of "the world's great heroes" (this is accompanied by an ironic tracking shot that, at the word "heroes," arrives at Wesley draining a tall drink and ordering another) and indiscreetly recounting the "shame and sorrow" of the whites who are his social superiors. After the singer becomes aware of Wesley's presence (his rebuke to another musician for having failed to warn him of this shows, by the way, that he really was unaware of Wesley's presence, precluding the possibility that he has been deliberately taunting Wesley), his statement of his intention to apologize is humorously florid and consciously ironic: "Apologize, that's what I'll do. Creep in just like a little fox and warm myself in his heart." This mode prepares us to see his actual apology as the performance of another role — the contrite servant — and not as an expression of his true nature. Robin Wood points out how unexpected the singer's behavior is in the context of the cinema of the time: "There can't be many Hollywood movies of the early Forties in which a colored character is permitted to make sly, malicious fun of whites who are neither comic nor villainous — with the film's at least partial endorsement — and get away with it. One could, I think, find Tourneur's use of Sir Lancelot more acceptable, in its unobtrusive way, than the pious (hence insidiously condescending) treatment of blacks in the later Forties movies that began to handle racial issues explicitly."[7]

The singer foregrounds the racial subtext of *I Walked with a Zombie* and the way the film defines its white characters through their relations to blacks. We first see Paul, whom the film repeatedly associates with the blacks, brooding on the ship deck in a composition that balances his figure with that of the black man steering the wheel. Later, explaining to Betsy the presence of Ti-Misery (a statue of Saint Sebastian, stuck with spears) in the garden of Fort Holland, he says: "It was once the figurehead of a slave-ship. That's where *our people* came from." The "our" could be heard as a possessive, but this sense fluctuates with one in which Paul includes himself in the same group with the slaves' descendants. This sense of equality is confirmed in a later shot in which Paul is again visually equal to a black man (with whom he discusses the possibility of a drought). In contrast, Wesley's usual relationship to the blacks is one of domination (curtly giving orders to the butler and the waiter, angrily dismissing the calypso singer). Yet, Wesley finally succumbs to the "charm" of voodoo, something that Paul never ceases, apparently, to regard as "nonsense."

Tourneur said in his *Positif* interview:

> I've always refused to caricature blacks. I've never or almost never showed them as domestics. I've always tried to give them a profession, to have them speak normally without drawing any comic effect. Watch in *Out of the Past* the scene in the nightclub where there are only black people, look at the way they're dressed and filmed, the elegance of the young woman in responding to Mitchum. Several times I've been accused of being a "nigger lover" and for long months I was out of the studios for that reason. It was a sort of gray list.[8]

The Tourneur film that deals most explicitly with racism is *Stars in My Crown*; black people also figure in bits in several other Tourneur films. In *Cat People*, Teresa Harris, the superb actress who plays Alma in *I Walked* and the woman in the nightclub in *Out of the Past*, is Minnie, the waitress at Sally Lund's. (In his post–Tourneur films, Lewton also made a point of not caricaturing blacks. James Agee called Sir Lancelot's servant character in *The Curse of the Cat People* "one of the most unpretentiously sympathetic, intelligent, anti-traditional, and individualized Negro characters" he had ever "seen presented on the screen.")[9]

One of the best examples of the antitraditional treatment of blacks in *I Walked with a Zombie* is the scene in which Alma appears to be struggling with the commissioner's horse. Betsy arrives and shows her the correct way to lead a horse. Up to this point, the viewer may think that Alma's ineptitude is meant to create a conventional comic effect. We realize from the ensuing dialogue, however, that Alma has been using the horse's apparent recalcitrance as a pretext to eavesdrop on the commissioner's conversation with Paul.

The tone of the cafe sequence changes radically in its second part. In close-up, a lamp is lit — a privileged action in Tourneur's films, signifying nightfall and generating the scene's new lines of force: visual, dramatic, and psychological. The camera cranes down to the table where Betsy tries vainly to wake Wesley, who has passed out. A cut takes us to a shot from behind Betsy: against the background of the sea, the singer slowly walks toward her/us, singing a new verse of "Fort Holland." His fixed stare at Betsy and his movement toward her make explicit an aggression that was previously only implicit while the lyrics spell out an insulting suggestion: "The brothers are lonely and the nurse is young." The singer has moved out of his role as an ironic spokesman for the film to become a threatening Other; "he becomes associated," according to Wood, "with the mysterious, disturbing forces by which Betsy feels herself menaced." Wood reminds us that in perceiving him in this light, we see him from Betsy's perspective, which we cannot, Wood claims, simply share: "The fact that, previously, his dignity, intelligence and irony have engaged our sympathy serves to detach us further from Betsy." Yet I side with J. P. Telotte in reading the scene as deepening our identification with Betsy: the singer's narrative is part of an "ongoing process of revelation and incarnation, one plunging Betsy deeper into the mysteries of this world.... [T]he singer's intrusion points up the audience's similarly increasing immersion in the film's fantasy context, for we have been dislodged from our initial perspective and cast into a world where nothing is quite as we had originally expected, no appearance totally reliable."[10]

The turning point of the film is the high-angle shot of Betsy walking on the rocks above the shore at night as her voice-over declares her love for Paul and her intention to cure Jessica: "Because I loved him, I felt I had to restore her to him, to make her what she'd been before." As Sylvie Pierre has noted, the significance of this moment is that "Betsy has to admit to her definitive implication as an agent in the action, which, from then on, she will no longer be at liberty to narrate." With the breaking-off of her narration, Betsy's claim to mediate the viewer's access to the fiction evaporates; no longer in a transcendent position in relation to the narrative, she descends to the level of the other characters, mysterious to us and themselves. Even if we accept her declared rationale for wanting to cure Jessica, we also recognize her determination as masochistic, since a successful result would deprive her of the man she loves; we may also read it as an unconscious attempt (in the event, a successful one) to cause Jessica's death through dangerous, experimental treatments. (The shooting script called for Betsy's narration to continue after the scene on the rocks, having her say, for example, over a shot of a rite performed by the *sabreur*, "It had been foolish of me to take my patient to the Voodoo ceremony." Betsy's narration was also to have been heard at the end of the film.)[11]

In the absence of the first-person narration, other modes of narration take over, initially the third person; finally "we pass over into a kind of non-person beyond the actors, the narrative being entrusted to the purely musical closure of an impersonal incantation."[12] Scenes in *I Walked with a Zombie* usually show only the beginning or the result of an action, rarely the complete action, so that we are constantly trying to

Tom Conway and Frances Dee in *I Walked with a Zombie*.

catch up to the characters' state of knowledge in a scene or to resolve apparent contradictions in their actions. As Paul is still hesitating over whether to permit the use of insulin shock treatment on Jessica, the film dissolves to Betsy and Dr. Maxwell at Jessica's bedside, the treatment already concluded. Later, when Paul asks Betsy to leave the island, she refuses, but subsequently it appears that she has agreed to leave; similarly, we learn only after the fact that Paul has given in to Betsy's request (which at first he stiffly denies) to leave the whiskey decanter off the dinner table. Sequences are linked by ideas, images, or the characters' temporary preoccupations rather than by cause and effect: Betsy's obsession with curing Jessica, for example, takes us from the unsuccessful insulin shock treatment to the scene in which Alma recommends to Betsy the services of the *houngan* and Dambala ("better doctors"), which then takes us to Mrs. Rand treating a boy at the village dispensary and admonishing him, "How do you ever expect to get to heaven with one foot in the voodoo Houmfort and the other in the church?" *I Walked with a Zombie* increasingly resembles a poetic or musical development more than a dramatic narrative.

The famous sequence of Betsy and Jessica walking to the Houmfort shows more clearly than any other sequence in a Tourneur film the oneiric, aesthetic, and poetic mainsprings of his art. The traveling long shot that opens the sequence would stand out in a more comfortably budgeted production and is astonishingly expansive in a B movie. Already in motion at the beginning of the shot, after the dissolve from the previous sequence, the camera takes in the entire housefront of Fort Holland, uniting in a sweeping movement Paul writing in his room, Wesley slumped in his chair by a table on the porch, and Betsy and Jessica emerging through a door at the back of the set, crossing the garden. The shot beautifully exemplifies Tourneur's love of visual homogeneity, wholeness, and flow and his insistence on finding the simplest possible configuration of characters and themes.

Except for Betsy and Jessica's brief conference with Alma before they set out through the woods, the sequence has no dialogue. The soundtrack is a tapestry of natural sounds, predominantly the wind and the two women's clothes rustling in the sugarcanes; against this background, a number of distinct sounds become prominent: the amplified hum of the wind whistling through a gourd with holes, suspended from a kind of scaffold; the call of the conch; the voodoo drums.

The main theme of the sequence is the crossing of boundaries. Alma gives Betsy and Jessica patches to wear as signs to Carrefour to let them pass (a light one for Betsy, who wears a dark cape; a dark one for Jessica, who wears a light dress). At each stage of their journey through the cane fields, Betsy and Jessica stop before crossing a boundary marked by a sign: an animal skull, an animal carcass, the gourd, a skull in a circle of stones, the sound of the conch in the voodoo ceremony, Carrefour himself (the human being as sign, as the symbolic function his name designates, the crossroads between life and death). In the series of signs, the conch, the sign that differs in nature from the others (being aural rather than visual), signals what we initially take to be danger, since at the crossing of *this* boundary, Betsy unwittingly leaves behind her protective patch. Its loss confirms that Betsy has committed herself and Jessica to an irreversible course: she will enter the Houmfort taking less with her than she brought from Fort Holland. The loss is purely symbolic: the sign proves to have less than the practical efficacy Alma attributed to it, since Carrefour lets Betsy pass anyway — an anticlimactic development that has been criticized as a cheat[13] but that is a striking example of the film's inexplicable details and reversals of expectation. The loss of the sign is echoed later in the removal of Jessica from the Houmfort: once she has been there, the voodoo worshipers, for a reason that we don't understand, regard her absence as a lack and try to cause her to return (so that they can finish some sort of "ritual tests," we are later told). Jessica becomes, to them, a lost object, just as the patch was to Betsy; both belong to a symbology to which we are denied the key.

When Betsy and Jessica reach the Houmfort, the center of the mystery proves a hoax: the voice of the goddess Dambala, supposedly speaking through a spider-web painted on the door of a hut, turns out to belong to Mrs. Rand. As in the cafe scene earlier, her appearance is linked with the lighting of a lamp (cf. the repeated association of Dr. Judd with lamps in *Cat People*), which here symbolizes the light she proceeds to throw on the matter with her explanation. This explanation ("I should have known there's no easy way to do good") proves, however, utterly ambiguous, raising rather than answering questions. "It seems so simple to let the gods speak through me," Mrs. Rand says, characterizing her actions as those of a rationalist who condescends to use the irrational for the ends of reason. She too is, however, a "crossroads" figure: her remark to the boy in the dispensary about having "one foot in the voodoo Houmfort and the other in the church" applies to herself.

The revelation that Mrs. Rand speaks for Dambala crystallizes the problem of *I Walked with a Zombie.* Later in the film, when Mrs. Rand confesses that she asked the *houngan* to turn Jessica into a zombie, she recounts her involvement with voodoo differently: "I heard a voice speaking in the sudden silence. My voice. I was speaking to the *houngan.* I was possessed." The undecidability of these questions — whether or not Jessica is a zombie, whether Dambala speaks through Mrs. Rand or Mrs. Rand speaks for Dambala — lies at the heart of *I Walked with a Zombie.* As a satisfying, univocal explanation of events appears less likely to emerge, the narrative becomes more discontinuous and fragmented, the connections between scenes increasingly abstract and tenuous and stretching across more distant periods of screen time so that, for example, a voodoo worshiper putting a dress on a doll echoes Alma's line about dressing Jessica like a doll (spoken during Betsy's first morning at Fort Holland), just as Alma's patches recall the pin Betsy gave to Alma's newborn nephew. The shots of the sorcerer drawing the doll to him and of Jessica setting out toward the Houmfort are linked by parallel cutting in a totally abstract way (despite the parallelism of movement and gesture between them), simultaneously, as Sylvie Pierre has pointed out, imposing a causal logic and offering the viewer the means to detect (and thus escape from) the oppressiveness of this logic.[14] The same can be said of the analogy between the pin that the sorcerer draws from his sleeve and the arrow that Wesley pries loose from the figurehead of Saint Sebastian. The narrative has trained us to suspend our judgment on the efficacy of magic: we watch these sequences neither fully believing nor fully disbelieving or, perhaps, both believing and disbelieving, in the idea that what the sorcerer does in one place causes the acts of Jessica and Wesley in another. The montage sustains the film in its extraordinary dual dimension, the hesitation of the fantastic.

In its final section, dominated by the presence of the sea and the torches of the spearfishermen, the personal drama of the film recedes at last into myth and ritual — a movement that the "Fort Holland" song began but could not complete. As he carries out the murder-suicide, Wesley is constantly seen in long shot or from a high angle. These camera positions and the actor's impassiveness make his actions appear impersonal and involuntary. Responsibility for the on-screen actions of the narrative is ascribed to the offscreen voodoo priests ("They can make anybody do what they want," Wesley says) before being shifted to the fishermen, who accidentally come upon Jessica's floating body and carry it back to Fort Holland, forming a mute, unindividuated chorus of witnesses to the Holland family tragedy. Finally, the eulogy, apparently delivered by a black Christian priest at some indeterminate narrative time, identifies Jessica as the responsible party ("The woman was a wicked woman…. Her steps led him down to evil") but absolves her because "she was dead in her own life," morally and spiritually dead ("dead in the selfishness of her spirit"). The eulogy's only possible conclusion, which coincides with the close of the film on the image of Ti-Misery, the eternal sufferer, is to put everything in the hands of God: "Yea, Lord, pity them who are dead, and give peace and happiness to the living." The implication is that whereas God knows "the secret of all hearts," the living can find peace and happiness only in giving up the struggle to know, in resigning themselves to death and sorrow. *I Walked with a Zombie* rehearses the closing gesture of *Night of the Demon,* but whereas in *Demon,* Holden optimistically asserts that "it's better not to know," the people in *I Walked* hardly have a choice. The film ends with the simplest of gestures, a division between the living and the dead, intercutting a shot tracking toward Ti-Misery with a shot of Paul and Betsy.

The clumsiness of this interposition expresses the inanity of survival;[15] we may be reminded, with a shock, how little Paul and Betsy matter to us, how insignificant they and their romance are. "Empty of joy and meaning" as it was, Jessica's existence was all that held together the lives of the other main characters; the problem of this existence gave them a reason to meet under the film's limpid light and intricate shadow-work and gave matter to their slightly overformal dialogue. With Jessica gone, the film can now make good the promise of abandonment it implied in the shots of the unpopulated rooms of Fort Holland, as Betsy's voice-over introduced them to us: sets dressed, lit, and waiting to receive the actors, spaces suspended between the memory (Jessica) and the anticipation (Betsy) of love and desire.

Tourneur preferred *I Walked with a Zombie* to *Cat People* and frequently cited it as one of his favorite films. Of all Tourneur's films, *I Walked with a Zombie* goes farthest in the direction of pure cinematic poetry and the use of sounds and images purely for their "power of suggestion," a power enhanced by the film's narrative strategies, whose insistent ruptures, enigmas, and contradictions force the viewer to give up the attempt to read the narrative in a linear way. The film also expresses more directly than any other Tourneur film the essential features of his view of life: refusal of condemnation; respect for cultural difference; and the awareness of a permanent unknowability behind the lives and motives of people, their relations with each other, and their place in the cosmos.

The Leopard Man (1943)

Nothing is more fantastic than the human brain. Fear, horror, terror
are in us. Rightly or wrongly, we all carry in us a feeling of guilt.
Cruelty flows in our blood, even if we have learned to master it.... Now,
a good horror film is one that best awakens our old dormant instincts.

JACQUES TOURNEUR

Critics have generally regarded *The Leopard Man*, the last of Tourneur's three films with Lewton, as a flawed work, inferior to its predecessors. Joel E. Siegel, for example, calls it "a mixed effort, superb in its individual sequences and its general ambiance but uncertain in structure and lacking any deep thematic resonance."[1] Tourneur himself disliked the film: "It was too exotic, it was neither fish nor fowl: a series of vignettes, and it didn't hold together."[2]

Here Tourneur points out two of the problems of *The Leopard Man*, two of the ways in which the film offers an experience that is disturbing and unresolved. "Neither fish nor fowl," *The Leopard Man* fits uncomfortably in either the horror or the mystery genre. The title is misleading: its semantic analogy to *Cat People* turns out to be only apparent, the film having to do not with a man who supernaturally becomes a leopard but with one who merely pretends to be one. As a mystery, *The Leopard Man* is distinctly a failure, even though it has the required elements: murders; a killer whose identity is (nominally) concealed until the end; a hero and a heroine who play the roles of amateur detectives. Contrary to one of the unwritten laws of the genre, the film's three killings aren't all committed by the same assassin. Moreover, the killer's identity is obvious from the start, so that the film confronts us with a mystery that is no mystery (or perhaps one that is displaced). For its denouement, the plot resorts to the most worn-out device of the genre: the amateur detectives trick the killer into trying to repeat his crime and exposing himself.

The other main problem that Tourneur's criticism highlights is the episodic narrative structure ("a series of vignettes"), derived from its source novel, Cornell Woolrich's *Black Alibi*. Early in the film, a supposedly tame leopard escapes during a publicity stunt arranged by press agent Jerry Manning (Dennis O'Keefe) for an entertainer, Kiki Walker (Jean Brooks). Much of the rest of the film follows, in turn, three women, each of whom is violently killed: Teresa (Margaret Landry), a teenage girl sent by her mother on an errand at night; Consuelo (Tula Parma), a young woman from a rich family who goes to meet her lover in a cemetery; and Clo-Clo (Margo), a dancer at the hotel nightclub. Initially, the police attribute the killings to the escaped leopard, but Jerry and Kiki discover that Dr. Galbraith (James Bell), the curator of the local museum, committed the second and the third killings. Galbraith confesses to the crimes and is immediately killed by Raoul (Richard Martin), Consuelo's boyfriend.

In retrospect, *The Leopard Man* appears ahead of its time, related only loosely to earlier horror films. Tourneur's staging of self-contained mininarratives in which women are stalked and killed addresses the direct connection between the spectator's gaze and death, foregrounding the desire of the spectator in a way generally associated with later films by Hitchcock while also foreshadowing the Italian *giallo*, a baroque subgenre characterized by setpieces dealing with the sadistic killing of women (cf. Mario Bava's *Sei donne per l'assassino* [*Blood and Black Lace*, 1964] and Dario Argento's *Profondo rosso* [*Deep Red*, 1975]). The film also anticipates Michael Powell's *Peeping Tom* in making the sight of a victim's fear the factor that fascinates the killer and compels him to kill.

To paraphrase the zookeeper's description of the panther in *Cat People*, *The Leopard Man* is like a horror film but not a horror film, as the reduced role of the supernatural in the film indicates. At several points, Clo-Clo meets a fortune-teller (Isabel Jewell), whose repeated attempts to tell her fortune all yield the fatal ace of spades, marking Clo-Clo for her eventual premature death. Unlike voodoo in *I Walked with a Zombie*, the fortune-teller's power of prediction remains peripheral to the narrative. It exerts no influence on events and never attracts the scrutiny of the people investigating them. The film foregrounds this irrelevance: in one scene, leaving Clo-Clo's room, the fortune-teller nonchalantly passes Jerry, who ignores her as he goes into Kiki's room. The fortune-teller and Jerry are indifferent to each other because they exist on different levels of the story. By bringing them together, however, the film hints that such a division between people is untenable, a point that relates to the film's themes of collective responsibility and individual interchangeability.

Things turn out as the fortune-teller predicts: Clo-Clo meets a man, he gives her money, and then "something black" comes, bringing death. Her stubborn prescience links *The Leopard Man* not just to the horror film but also to the fatalism of film noir. The film's credits are superimposed over a shot of a dark, empty street — "identifiable above all as a movie street," as Bernard Eisenschitz observed[3] — which locates the film within the visual terrain of noir (already well defined by 1943, although the cycle was still a year or two short of its classic period). The script's philosophical fatalism preserves the mood of Cornell Woolrich (and looks forward to the next Lewton film, Mark Robson's despairing *The Seventh Victim*). Galbraith sounds this note early in the film: pointing out a ball on a jet of water in the cafe fountain, he comments to Jerry, "We know as little about the forces that move us and move the world around us as that empty ball does about the water that pushes it into the air, lets it fall, and catches it again." At the end of the film, Jerry interprets Galbraith's philosophy to Kiki: "That's the way it was with us, only we were too small to know it."

The film's unusual narrative structure, although it keeps us from identifying with any character for very long, ideally allows the film to generalize its theme. By

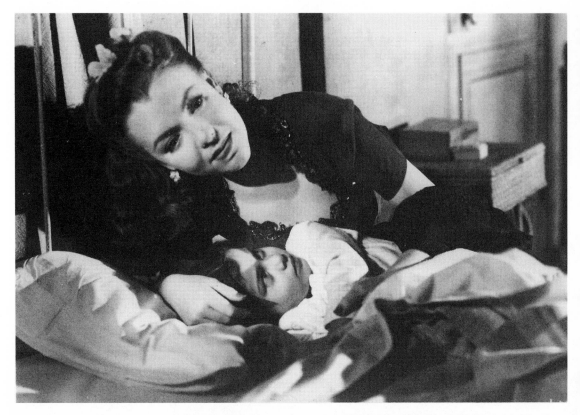

The Leopard Man: Margo and Rosa Rita Varella

shifting attention unpredictably from one character to another (as do, more systematically, such films as Max Ophuls's *La Ronde* and Buñuel's *Le Fantôme de la liberté*), *The Leopard Man* highlights the arbitrariness inherent in film narrative and makes it the structuring device that mediates the viewer's relationship to the characters, causing us to see them, perhaps, as "pawns of a bizarre and terrible destiny" (in the words of Manny Farber, who singled out *The Leopard Man* as one of the most original of Lewton's films).[4]

The first shot of the film after the credits is an exterior shot of the open door of a dressing room. We hear the sound of castanets, carried over from the main title music. The camera tracks toward the empty doorway, seemingly hunting the invisible source of the sound; the viewer's lack of knowledge coincides with the lack in the visual field represented by the empty doorway. Then Clo-Clo, rehearsing her castanet dance, enters the frame, at first as a reflection in a mirror (a frame within a frame — the doorway — within the frame). Abruptly, the camera pans right to another open door, through which we see Kiki banging on the wall for quiet. Kiki slams the door, at which point the scene cuts to a shot inside her room. The first shot proves to have been an oblique, initially misleading introduction to the dialogue scene that takes place in *this* room.

The sudden pan from Clo-Clo's room to Kiki's makes us see them as rivals for our attention and hints that they are, in some sense, equivalent. Multiple mirror images define the imaginary space of this equivalence: Clo-Clo appears in a mirror in the first shot; subsequently, we see Kiki put on her makeup in a mirror while Eloise, the cigarette girl who apparently shares Kiki's dressing room, primps in front of a third mirror. The more flamboyant Clo-Clo overshadows Kiki: later in the film, we see Clo-Clo's act, but we're only *told* that Kiki is a performer; she doesn't even begin to compete with Clo-Clo on the spectacular plane. Eloise comments on the "irony" of Kiki's having a show-business career whereas she's just a cigarette girl, implying that she is just as good as Kiki; she also offers to take Kiki's place.

The leopard, which Jerry proposes to Kiki as a gimmick to steal attention from Clo-Clo in the nightclub, comes to occupy this highly charged space of envy and rivalry. At the end of the sequence, Kiki decides to wear her black dress to escort the leopard to the nightclub: "Then I'll be just like him." This line, succeeded on the image track by a shot of the ball in the fountain (later associated with Galbraith) anticipates Galbraith's becoming a sort of "leopard man." Through her wish, the film generalizes his psychosis, proposes it as an extreme form of a general human identification with the bestial. (In the funeral parlor scene after Teresa's death, the film again links Kiki to the leopard, in a composition that balances her with a mysterious shadow, the double of the leopard shadow that Teresa's brother makes with his hands.)

The pan at the end of the opening shot sets up a distinctive motif in *The Leopard Man*: sequences at first appear to center on Clo-Clo, only to shift abruptly to follow another woman. Clo-Clo repeatedly cues the narrative's transitions between its two groups: the outsiders (Jerry, Kiki, Galbraith, the rich tourists) and the locals (the victims, their families and friends, the police captain, Charlie How-Come). As Bernard Eisenschitz observed, "Clo-Clo is characterized as the go-between, the mediator between the place where money is spent and her own place of origin, associated thus to the city with a double face, Mexican and American, like her double name: Gabriela and Clo-Clo."[5] Clo-Clo has something in common with everyone else in the film, in particular with the other two victims: she is poor like Teresa and is something of a romantic like Consuelo.

The switch from Clo-Clo to Kiki also underlines an important, though unstated, thematic point: even though she precipitates the killings by frightening the leopard into flight, Clo-Clo is never accused of being indirectly responsible for the killings and is never shown feeling remorse over them, whereas people are constantly either asserting the responsibility of Kiki and Jerry or denying it, which amounts to the same thing (in this narrative, negation has the force and meaning of affirmation; like a dream, *The Leopard Man* does not say "no").[6] The exoneration of Clo-Clo is consistent with the film's subtextual linking of her to the leopard. She has no moral responsibility because she is the object of the fatality underlying the animal's appearance: just as she was the initial target of the leopard-as-publicity-stunt, so she becomes the ultimate target of the leopard-as-killer.

The film's second sequence, set at the hotel cafe, starts with the camera craning and tilting down from the fountain to Clo-Clo's reflection in the pool, closing the loop of mirror images that we have seen (and linking them with what we will come to recognize as the image of ignorance and powerlessness). As Jerry planned, Kiki's entrance with the leopard on a leash diverts attention from Clo-Clo to her — another in the series of transferences between the two women. The series is completed when Clo-Clo scares the leopard away with her castanets. A physical mark signals the narrative's turn from its initial uncomfortable lightness to danger, death, and mystery: the slashes on the back of a waiter's hand, seen in close-up after the leopard has fled.

While the police are hunting the leopard in the streets, a boy's flashlight picks out Clo-Clo's legs in the darkness. This shot, made memorable by the briskly peremptory stamp of feet with which Clo-Clo (confident in her mastery of all situations) makes the boy turn off the flashlight, affirms the mysterious connection between Clo-Clo and the leopard. Like the ace of spades she draws from the fortune-teller's deck, the beam of the flashlight symbolically marks her. (The symbolic mark is a central feature of Tourneur's films, as also of Lang's: the strange woman's solicitation of Irena in the restaurant in *Cat People*; Betsy's lost voodoo patch in *I Walked with a Zombie*; the window-shade pull ring that dangles like a noose in the foreground of a shot of Jeff in *Out of the Past*.)

The gaze of the camera also plays the role of a mark, according to the logic of one of the principal mechanisms of cinematic suspense: if a film follows a character closely for an unknown reason, the audience assumes that something bad is going to happen to the character, especially given the narrative conventions expected to operate in a film with a title like *The Leopard Man*. The elaborate detailing of Clo-Clo's walk home leads us to think that she is about to be killed. However, after tracking with her as she passes various people on the street, including a man in a shadowy doorway and two lovers embracing in another doorway, the camera unexpectedly stops at Teresa's window, letting Clo-Clo continue out of frame. The camera transfers Clo-Clo's mark and, provisionally, her victim stigma onto Teresa, just as, later, the film passes them to Consuelo after the scene at the flower stand.

Each of the three murder sequences launches a self-contained series of substitutions, transferences, and choices. For example, Teresa is sent to the store for corn-meal because the other possible candidate for the job, her brother, is too young; she must go to a distant market because the nearer one is closed; when she gets there, the storekeeper lets her have a bag of cornmeal on credit (confident that "the poor don't cheat one another" — a detail that shows the moral and economic basis for the film's formal theme of exchange and equivalence); and on her way home, Teresa must choose between two tunnels beneath a railroad overpass: one is completely dark, and on a wall inside the other, we see a dim, watery reflection of light.

Through such doublings, the murder sequences extend the structural use of repetition and difference in the transverse sequence in *Cat People* and the walk to the Houmfort in *I Walked with a Zombie*. Tourneur fragments space, alternating between close and long shots, high and level angles, and frontal perspectives and perspectives behind or to the side of the subject. The placement of these different types of shots in relation to each other shows an ambition, scope, and mastery probably without precedent in the Hollywood B cinema, outdoing even the two previous Lewton-Tourneurs. Note, for instance, the magnificent long shot of Teresa walking toward the railroad bridge — so casually and so precisely placed in the sequence. The multiplication of perspective has a dual effect, making scenes both more concrete, because of the emphasis with which the subject is situated in her surroundings, and more abstract, because this over-situation is often bewildering and forces us to try to reconstruct the space of the scene from its visual and structural fragments.

In the cemetery sequence, the cutting produces a subtle effect of disorientation:

1. Consuelo, emerging into a clearing at the end of a corridor formed by hedges and passing the statue of a bearded man, with her figure and that of the statue juxtaposed in a medium shot from behind
2. Presumably from her point of view: a depopulated area filled with grave markers and shrubs
3. Frontal close shot of Consuelo, the statue partly visible in the background at left
4. Same as (2)
5. Same as (3): she looks screen left
6. Close shot from behind her, part of the statue visible at right, as her head turns right and looks up
7. Close shot of the statue head
8. Setup (3) again: she turns away from the statue and looks off right
9. Long shot of the moon visible through the branches above the wall

Particularly unusual is the transition from (5) to (6), which breaks the so-called 180-degree rule, disrupting spatial continuity, and subverts the classical shot-reverse-shot pattern, whose normal functioning is emphasized in this sequence at the transition from (3) to (4). In (5), when Consuelo turns her head, we expect (by analogy with the previous pair of shots) that the next shot will be from her point of view. Instead, we see Consuelo again, completely isolated in space. The cut is a dark joke on vision, visibility, and the place of the spectator in the film. We think the film is encouraging us to identify with Consuelo and share her perceptions; the cut suddenly breaks this illusion. Similar cuts — from a frontal view of a character turning to look over her shoulder to a rear view in which the character's face, having turned, again faces the camera — recur twice in the film, both times cued by sounds: when Clo-Clo hears a rustling footstep on the street and when Galbraith hears a woman call for help as he walks past the cemetery. (Compare Alice's turnaround on the transverse in *Cat People* and Holden's enigmatic experience in the hotel corridor in *Night of the Demon*.)

Sound effects take on unusual prominence throughout *The Leopard Man*. Each murder sequence contains an aural false shock or "bus," in which a sound suggesting the dreaded leopard proves to come from a train or a car. (In the third sequence, the suggestion is vestigially weak, since the car sound — even though, as usual, it precedes the car's appearance — doesn't frighten either Clo-Clo or us; the survival of the device here proves the consistency of the Lewton-Tourneur team's concern with formal elements.) The momentary deception confirms the success of the mise-en-scène in constructing an imaginary trap, for the viewer as well as for the victim. Entrusting to an aural signifier the function of springing the trap, the film preserves the elusiveness of the space around the victim. We see the train passing above Teresa's head only as the flickering of lights on the inner walls of the tunnel; we don't see the car stopping outside the cemetery (since we are on the

Dennis O'Keefe and Richard Martin in *The Leopard Man* (courtesy of the Academy of Motion Picture Arts and Sciences).

inside with Consuelo); the car that pulls up near Clo-Clo is on a trajectory whose relation to hers is unclear.

The absence of music also functions as a sound effect. The first murder-sequence has no music until the shot of the blood seeping under the door; in the second, the score fades away well before the climax of the scene (after a single organ chord sustained for an incredibly long time, repeating a device used in the scoring of the scene in the tower in *I Walked with a Zombie*); the third has no music at all. As in the transverse and swimming pool scenes in *Cat People* and the journey to the Houmfort in *I Walked with a Zombie*, the absence of music in these scenes lends gravity and naturalness, eliminating a conventional connotator of emotion and helping to impose the detached point of view implied by Tourneur's tracking shots and high-angle shots.

Each of the murder sequences ends with a shot in which offscreen space absorbs the victim. At the limit of representation, death is elided, recuperated, and represented in negative by traces: Teresa's blood oozing under the door; the branch in the cemetery shaking as if an animal has just leaped from it; the extreme close-up of Clo-Clo's discarded cigarette, over which shadows move chaotically. Over each of these paroxysmal images of absence, we hear the victim's screams. Sound serves as the transition from the unshowable to the narratable (each death is followed by a scene in which the survivors try to understand what has happened).

The film's empty spaces are visual equivalents for the disastrously missing objects in the narrative: Teresa's mother needs cornmeal; Consuelo has apparently just missed Raoul at the cemetery; Clo-Clo loses her $100 bill. These missing objects all relate to another, crucial, absence: that of the father. Teresa's father is at work (motivating Teresa's fatal journey, her mother darkly threatening the consequences if there are no tortillas on his return); Consuelo's and Clo-Clo's fathers are dead. In place of the fathers, middle-aged or elderly men figure in each sequence: the kindly storekeeper; the cemetery gatekeeper; the rich tourist who gives Clo-Clo a hundred dollars; and especially the statue of an old bearded man in the cemetery, with its enigmatic expression of warning, rebuke, or sorrow. The film's fathers are, if not missing, inadequate. The rich tourist is a figure of contempt to his daughter. Chief Robles, the figure of paternal authority for the town, seems to exercise his authority mainly by relieving others (Teresa's father, Jerry, the gatekeeper, Charlie) of responsibility and guilt, as J. P. Telotte has observed.[7] The father's symbolic role of affixing guilt and prescribing punishment is abrogated until the end of the film, when Raoul, Consuelo's boyfriend, kills Galbraith in revenge for her death and is arrested by Robles.

The gesture is a token one. Circulating from one character to another throughout *The Leopard Man* is a debt that no one owes and that is owed to no one but that nonetheless insists on being paid. The impossible nature of this debt partly accounts for the film's disturbing effect. The traditional task of the mystery narrative is to assign the generalized sense of (possible) guilt that ensues from a crime to a specific person. In *The Leopard Man*, this guilt is unassignable. Various people could have prevented the tragedies by acting differently: the woman storekeeper could have reopened for Teresa and spared her the trip across the arroyo; Señora Delgado could have left the door unbolted or opened it more quickly; Raoul could have waited for Consuelo; the gatekeeper could have looked for Consuelo in the cemetery before locking the gate. Others participate in the chain of responsibility: Charlie, because he loaned out the leopard; Jerry and Kiki, because they bring it to the club; and Clo-Clo, because she frightens it away. Charlie's readiness to believe Galbraith's subversively joking hypothesis that he killed Consuelo during an alcoholic blackout suggests that, unconsciously, he recognizes his share in the collective guilt the film exposes. (Galbraith himself is driven by larger, uncontrollable forces, like Irena in *Cat People* and the "possessed" Mrs. Rand in *I Walked with a Zombie*.)

In *Cat People*, Oliver and Alice acknowledge his obligation to take care of Irena if she is insane; in *I Walked with a Zombie*, Paul broods over his "technical responsibility, real responsibility" for his wife. *The Leopard Man* goes further than the earlier films by extending the chain of responsibility beyond the family to the whole community and beyond the community to history. Weaving through the film's final section is a procession of black-robed penitents, commemorating the massacre of a tribe of peaceful Indians by conquistadors. The procession symbolizes an ineradicable guilt that must be passed on over generations; by momentarily joining the marchers, Galbraith, Jerry, and Raoul "link the distant historical event to the modern incident to suggest a continuum of such inexplicable human horrors."[8]

The film uses the distant, uncomfortable figures of Jerry and Kiki to foreground the theme of responsibility in a schematic way that some viewers, understandably, have felt as "unconvincing"[9] and that leaves us at a loss to know what attitude we're expected to take toward the pair. The film portrays their problem in terms of the inability to display emotion. "Where I come from you had to be tough," Jerry tells Galbraith to explain his apparent unconcern over Teresa's death, but in reality, both Jerry and Kiki are "softies." Read as centering on them, the narrative is therapeutic: they become better by learning to externalize their compassion. Kiki becomes the film's "heroine" only by assuming responsibility for the holocaust and putting herself literally in the victims' places — an extension of the film's theme of interchangeability. Sitting on the bench in the cemetery where Consuelo sat, Kiki tries to identify imaginatively with Consuelo and wonders what she was thinking about before she died. Later, Kiki presents herself to Galbraith as a potential victim. Like many other Tourneur characters, including Dardo in *The Flame and the Arrow*, Douglas in *Circle of Danger*, Penalosa in *Way of a Gaucho*, Pentecost in *Great Day in the Morning*, and Holden in *Night of the Demon*, Jerry and Kiki start from a position of mastery and independence, a false position that they are eventually forced to surrender, recognizing their implication in a larger pattern over which they have no control.

In the final sequences of *The Leopard Man*, the accumulation of repetitions takes on a strangely obsessive quality, producing an atmosphere of fantasy and unreality. Jerry and Kiki turn against Galbraith the signifiers of the earlier murder sequences: the voice calling for help from the cemetery; the cigarette thrown on the street. Hunter becomes hunted; the fiction is turned inside out (we were with Consuelo inside the cemetery, now we're with Galbraith outside). The fatal lack associated with the victims reverts to the killer: alone in the museum with Kiki, who visits on the pretext of seeking a view of the procession, Galbraith cannot see her face — and thus her fear — because her back is turned to him. Later, Galbraith, whom the narrative also entrusts with explaining the historical meaning of the procession (itself an annually repeated ceremony), compulsively recounts the deaths of Teresa and Consuelo. The film's short coda refers to earlier scenes, as Jerry and Kiki recall their discomfort in the funeral parlor and as Jerry repeats Galbraith's comment about the ball in the fountain; the final shot, in which the couple walk up a street that retreats from the camera in perspective, recalls both the shot of the Delgados walking up the same street and the first shot of the film (under the opening credits). These repetitions ostensibly indicate closure, but on another level they suggest that the issues raised by the film remain open. Telotte noted, "We are left with a sense that there is no real ending in sight, certainly no true consolation here for the victims' families, and no satisfying feeling that things have at last been 'made right,' just a disturbing residue from these terrible events."[10]

Tourneur attributed the commercial success of his films with Lewton to "war psychosis.... In wartime, people want to be frightened."[11] Of the three films, *The Leopard Man* has the clearest relationship to war. Edmund Bansak calls the film "a courageous essay in the random nature of death.... Wartime audiences may not have liked *Leopard*'s downbeat message — that the young and the innocent also die — but it was an important one for them to grasp."[12] As Bansak implies, *The Leopard Man* has a therapeutic, redemptive power. We never regard the killings as *merely* chaotic and purposeless. We see them in relation to several patterns: a supernatural, metaphysical framework that appears, but isn't explained, in the linking of the victims to Clo-Clo and, through her, to the leopard and the fate predicted by the fortune-teller; the networks of families, economics, the community, and history; and a personal, biographical pattern that emerges in the way the film takes us through the life of each victim, recalling their pasts (Teresa stopping in the store to admire the toy birds, which she loved when she was a child) and detailing the temporal context of their adventures (Consuelo's impatient look at the sundial through her window, and the gatekeeper's philosophical discourse on time: "A moment can be as short as a breath or as long as eternity"). There are also the visual patterns, by which the film confers gravity, mystery, and unity: the metaphors of journey and labyrinth; the symbols of water (in the tunnel); flowers; the statue in the cemetery. By combining these perspectives, the film gives us an intuition of totality (without, however, giving us the answers that would allow us to construct this totality as an interpretative framework), a sense that the killings are a necessary part of an impersonal cycle.

The Leopard Man is a pivotal work in the careers of both Tourneur and Lewton. Pushing to extremes the experiment with narrative ambiguity undertaken in *Cat People* and *I Walked with a Zombie*, this radically unusual film has its own precise, inexhaustible poetry.

Days of Glory
(1944)

After *The Leopard Man*, RKO split the pair of Tourneur and Lewton. In Tourneur's words, "We were making so much money together that the studio said, 'We'll make twice as much money if we separate them.'" Although it meant moving up to "A" production, Tourneur regretted this development: "We complemented each other. By himself, Val might go off the deep end and I, by myself, might lose a certain poetry. We should have gone right on making bigger pictures with bigger budgets, and not necessarily horror pictures. Why put things in boxes?"[1]

RKO could scarcely have chosen a less auspicious project for Tourneur's first A assignment than *Days of Glory*. Part of the brief Hollywood vogue for pro–Soviet films, *Days of Glory* suffers from an artificial conception and a trite script (by producer Casey Robinson) that no director could be expected to surmount.

In their underground communal lair, a group of Russian guerrillas wait for orders that will dictate their role in an upcoming major offensive against the Nazi invaders. The group takes in Nina (Tamara Toumanova), a member of a theatrical group sent by Stalin to entertain soldiers on the front. Overcoming her initial dainty distaste for slaughter, Nina shoots a German soldier and participates in a raid on an ammunition train, meanwhile falling in love with Vladimir (Gregory Peck), the leader of the guerrilla band. Vladimir reluctantly sends Nina on a dangerous mission to receive and bring back the group's order from headquarters; she manages to complete the mission. Vladimir, Nina, and the rest of the guerrillas die heroically while carrying out their appointed task of drawing off the German force from the main Red Army push.

Although he disliked the film, Tourneur enjoyed working with Peck and Toumanova, both novices at film acting: Peck had come straight from Broadway, and Toumanova was a former star of the Moscow ballet. "It was a pleasure for me because I did with them everything I wanted, exactly as with clay."[2] Peck's understated, modestly effective performance bears out Tourneur's claim of manipulation (or at any rate testifies to its success); the actor later remembered Tourneur telling him to stop projecting and to "common up" his speech.[3] Toumanova's deep-eyed intensity is also effective, at least up to a point; eventually, however, the contrived conception of her character and the hackneyed development of her relationship with Vladimir render her, inevitably, an irritant. The other actors, most of them also debutants, are all fine, especially Dena Penn (Olga), a young girl who has an amazing tour-de-force scene in which she performs a complex set of tasks with various kitchen objects while giving a long monologue about her day's activities.

Days of Glory is pictorially accomplished. Exterior long shots of forests and lakes have the crisp grandeur we will later find in *Out of the Past*. The scene of Mitya leading Nina through a foggy, snowbound marsh distantly echoes the walk to the Houmfort in *I Walked with a Zombie*; they even meet a menacing guard (whom they at first take for a German but who turns out to be a Russian). Tourneur handles the scene of Mitya's hanging with great force and skill: in a low-angle shot, the truck on which Mitya is standing pulls forward; cut to Vladimir reacting with grief at the garret window from which he has been watching; in a striking dramatic contrast, this shot dissolves to Olga at the hideaway, still expecting her brother's return with the others and rushing toward the camera excitedly, calling his name.

Mordecai (Max) Gorelik's superbly detailed production design appropriately emphasizes the hermetic theatricality of the script. The set of the underground hideaway gives Tourneur plenty of opportunity to indulge his preoccupation with placing light sources within compositions. Throughout the long sequence that introduces the guerrillas, Tourneur's camera movements interweave with the movements of the actors in fluid, dramatically logical medium shots.

Unfortunately, the strengths of the film fail to overcome the absurdity and falseness of the script's attempt at a stagy poetic realism. The film has the air of a bad experimental play dreamed up (in James Agee's words) by "the more fatuous contributors to Russian War Relief" and somehow preserved on film with A-level Hollywood production values.[4] The stifling unreality of the project is alien to Tourneur's cinema, one of whose qualities is a meticulously conveyed sense of social and physical reality.

The film shows all too clearly the strain of the effort to portray modern Russians to an American audience. Even before the main title appears, the producers signal their eagerness to reduce the strangeness of the film's setting by having a narrator's voice come on over a shot in which the camera draws back from a cloudy sky: "Here is the true story which could have happened in any land of a little group of free people who lived and loved and fought to drive the invaders from their native soil."

Although the guerrillas always address each other as "comrade" and form a cooperative society, discussion of their politics is noticeably absent: the word "communist" is never used; Stalin is mentioned only once; and the word "socialist" occurs only in the last scene when Nina is inducted into the army of the "Soviet Socialist Republic." On the other hand, the film surrounds the guerrillas with Christian imagery, as Bernard F. Dick has noted.[5] Nina wears a cross throughout, the guerrillas take shelter in a ruined monastery, and Yelena receives a Christian funeral service (in which Vladimir, significantly, does not participate but merely observes noncommittally, "Few of us can choose the time of our entering or leaving this life").

Days of Glory is perhaps best viewed as an object lesson in cultural adjustment to war. The film juxtaposes two attitudes, both of which, it suggests, are inappropriate to the guerrillas' situation: Nina's aestheticism and Vladimir's destructiveness. The film criticizes these attitudes from two points of view. Nina's

Days of Glory. Facing camera: Tamara Toumanova, Gregory Peck, Maria Palmer, Edward L. Durst, Hugo Haas; backs to camera: Lowell Gilmore, Dena Penn, Glenn Vernon, Alan Reed (courtesy of the Academy of Motion Picture Arts and Sciences).

impromptu performance distracts Mitya, allowing the German to enter. After Nina protests squeamishly as Vladimir is about to smash the German's head with a rifle butt, the guerrillas decide (incredibly) to hold him prisoner instead — a concession to humanism that later allows him to endanger the group again. The moral is that culture and compassion must sometimes be put aside in war because they dangerously relax the soldier's vigilance.

On the other hand, Vladimir's destructiveness, though it makes him a good soldier, is excessive. Nina thinks he is sadistic ("as if to kill something, to destroy something gave you — forgive me — gave you happiness"), but his response suggests sadism turned inward, a bitter, perverse enthusiasm for destruction in retaliation for his frustrated desire to create. Vladimir is close to being like Petrov, the embittered, emotionally isolated guerrilla whose only interest in life is to become "a bomb to be thrown among them, to explode myself and kill one of them with every little splinter."

The optimistic message of the script is that Nina and Vladimir give each other what the other lacks: Nina teaches Vladimir "to love life again," and

Vladimir teaches her how to load his gun. Weighing against this implication of harmony, however, are the attitudes of Yelena and Mitya, revealing the tension created in the group by the Nina-Vladimir couple. When Vladimir chooses to send Yelena, rather than Nina, on the dangerous mission on which Yelena is eventually killed, Tourneur emphasizes, in turn, Yelena's resentment, Vladimir's embarrassment, and Nina's guilt. These distress signals reveal the underlying contradiction of *Days of Glory*: the discordance between desire and the needs of the group. The contradiction can be "resolved" only by the deaths of Yelena and Mitya, both of whom the formation of the romantic couple has displaced and turned into superfluous irritants.

Days of Glory is the inverse of *Cat People*. In *Cat People* Irena represents the death drive inappropriately plunked down in a country of life; in *Days of Glory* Nina is, as the Oxford–educated Semyon describes her, "a person of light and such life, out of place in this region of death." In *Days*, war has normalized the death drive, and the cultural qualities and the capacity to dream that Nina embodies render her "strange." Vladimir, formerly an engineer, like Oliver in *Cat People*, now finds "happiness in destruction" (the line is a distorted echo of Oliver's remark that he has "never been unhappy"). Alice returns as Vladimir's capable comrade Yelena, blonde to Nina's brunette; in another mysterious echo of *Cat People*, Yelena is killed by a German sniper as Nina, in the next shot, suddenly bolts upright out of a dream as if protesting the act of violence that her unconscious has willed.

Experiment Perilous (1944)

I don't like complications very much.

JACQUES TOURNEUR

With *Experiment Perilous*, we are back at the heart of Tourneur's universe. Sadly neglected and often underrated, this is one of Tourneur's most personal and beautiful films.

In adapting Margaret Carpenter's novel, screenwriter-producer Warren Duff changed the period from the present day to 1903. During production, it was reported that Hedy Lamarr pushed for this change because she wanted to wear turn-of-the-century costumes, but executive producer Robert Fellows offered a more reasonable explanation: "It was felt that the slightly archaic quality of the heroine, who appears in the book as a cloistered and frustrated orchid, would lend itself to a clearer expression on the screen if presented against a less realistic background." The period change required the filmmakers to use some imagination in transposing the events of the novel. A key scene was moved from a restaurant to a department store because in researching the period, Tourneur had learned that women never went unescorted to restaurants at the turn of the century. "Moreover," Tourneur said, "we wanted some place where there would be activity around. Something that would furnish a lively background for the meeting, not something static. Warren Duff, who wrote the finished screenplay, and I batted it around for two days. Finally we hit on the store." (Later Tourneur recalled that more of the department store was shot than remained in the finished film: "There was a very fine sequence — a wonderful sequence — that was cut out: it took place in a department store, with the old baskets with the wires for delivering money. It showed Hedy Lamarr followed by a detective: she couldn't be sure if she saw him or not." This scene does not appear in the shooting script.)[1]

Much care was spent on the design of the sinister house where much of the film takes place. The result is a superb example of the work of the RKO art department (which, under the supervision of Albert S. D'Agostino, was perhaps the most significant factor in creating the consistent look of the studio's films during the 1940s). Journalist Thornton Delehanty found the house

so faithful to the foreboding note of the original that to move about in it was like stepping directly into the concept

of the author. Mr. Tourneur was particularly proud of the
fact that nothing had been overdone. "The rooms, you see,
have been kept moderately small, as you would expect to
find in such a house. There is nothing colossal about them,
nothing that might suggest the movie mind at work. What
we are trying to do is to give the feeling of the novel without
exaggeration."

Years later, Tourneur revealed that this conception of appropriate size in set design
belonged to a general aesthetic principle: "I have a whole theory about sets and I
always have long discussions with the designer. A set should be either very small,
or very big, but I don't believe in medium-sized sets. When you have a very small
set, it's very interesting because the actors don't have room to move." The production of *Experiment Perilous* also involved two other coups for the art department:
the manufacture of a daisy field with 3,000 daisies, and "Hollywood's first real
snowstorm on a soundstage."[2]

The film begins on a train bound for New York during a downpour. Dr.
Huntington Bailey (George Brent) has a chance meeting with Cissie Bederaux
(Olive Blakeney), who says she is returning to New York after a long absence to
visit her brother, Nick Bederaux, and his wife, Allida. Later, at a party in New
York, Bailey learns that Cissie has died, apparently of a heart attack. Bailey
arranges to have himself invited to tea at the Bederaux house and meets Allida
(Hedy Lamarr) and Nick (Paul Lukas); the latter immediately confides in Bailey
his fears about his wife's mental health. Later, Nick visits Bailey to ask him to see
Allida as a patient.

In Cissie's dressing case (which the train porters have switched, apparently by
mistake, with Bailey's briefcase), Bailey finds a detailed account of Nick's life,
which is shown in flashback. After reading it, Bailey becomes convinced that Nick
is insanely possessive of Allida, and he suspects that Nick murdered Alec Gregory
(George N. Neise), a young poet infatuated with her. Bailey himself has now fallen
in love with Allida and decides to save her from her husband. Nick fakes a suicide
at sea and returns home to try to kill his wife and their young son by turning on
the gas, but he is killed in the explosion, and Bailey manages to rescue Allida and
the child.

The generic context of *Experiment Perilous* is all too familiar. Most contemporary reviewers noted a similarity with *Gaslight* (released earlier in the same year),
and the film also contains reminiscences of *Rebecca, Suspicion, Laura,* and the
then-unreleased *Notorious.* Estranging this material, Tourneur's film imperturbably
moves away from the obvious, for example by declining to use Nick's machinations
as a possible source of surprise. A central piece of this oblique strategy is that the
viewer should never be in doubt that Nick is the source of evil; only the exact
nature of his "experiment" is unknown for awhile.

The main benefit of the decision to switch the period to 1903, suggested
though not stated by Fellows's description of Allida as "a cloistered and frustrated
orchid," is the ability to tap into the subtext of Victorianism. The change strengthens the sexual motifs of the story. Nick becomes the arch–Victorian bourgeois,
obsessed with the constant danger of his wife's sexuality and driven to kill in an

effort to control it. The Bederaux family is a classic Victorian family with a dark tragic past (the suicide of Nick's father), an aunt who must be locked away for a long period, and a neurotic child.

Experiment Perilous revises the triangle of *Cat People*: a fascinating woman; a European man who tries to represent her as neurotic; and a plain, uncomplicated American. (The other interlocking triangle of *Cat People*, with Oliver positioned between Irena and Alice, is present vestigially in *Experiment Perilous* through the minor character of Bailey's friend Elaine.) Whereas *Cat People* transforms and displaces female sexuality into a monstrous becoming-animal, *Experiment Perilous* instead makes the heroine's husband into a kind of monster, motivated by his own sexual problem, at which the film hints in Nick's line, "Mentality never quite makes up for the physical, does it?" (Another detail emphasizes the role of sex in Nick's insanity. On the night of Alec's death, Allida recalls, Nick's "face was young and fresh, and for the first time, we found a moment of happiness." Nick probably owed his sudden surge of potency to the excitement of having just killed Alec; this may be why he names his son Alec — in grateful tribute to his victim.)

Although *Experiment Perilous* resembles Lewton's films in its pervasive sense of fear and anxiety, in the use of a psychiatrist as a main character, and in the other characters' insistence that there is "something fateful" about the enigmatic heroine, this film is more optimistic than Lewton's films. Correctly reading Allida's mystery as Nick's creation, Bailey manages to bring the heroine back to a normal existence, thereby succeeding where Oliver in *Cat People*, Betsy in *I Walked with a Zombie*, and the heroes of Robson's *The Seventh Victim* fail.

Experiment Perilous gives Tourneur larger scope than his previous films to treat one of his favorite themes, the relationship between Europe and America. Europe, in *Experiment Perilous*, is the storehouse of culture and the past. It is where people go to "see all of the places and treasures of history." Nick, who has even his tea especially imported, has filled the famous Bederaux house with some of these treasures, such as the statue in an alcove on the stairway (his "prize goddess," which topples over on him when the house blows up). Europe is also the storehouse of psychological complexes (tigers under the bed, to use Bailey's metaphor), "nighttime terrors," self-hypnosis, and witches. In contrast, America is a land of generosity and simplicity, a place where witches, as Bailey tells little Alec at the end of the film, are good and retrieve things that have been lost. Perhaps inevitably, *Experiment Perilous* has a war subtext. The storm clouds that gradually cover the sky above a field of daisies under the opening credits symbolize, in terms of the film, a European threat to America's pastoral calm. Bailey describes Nick as "at war — with what or with whom I don't know. Perhaps with life." Bailey's climactic rescue mission, on which he enters Nick's European home and risks being caught in the explosion that destroys it, is clearly a metaphor for the "experiment perilous" in which the United States was engaged at the time the film was made.

The film starts awkwardly, almost apologetically, and develops slowly, relying more on generic allusion and inevitability than on logic. There is no reason why Bailey should meet and fall in love with Allida, other than that he must. The film is disarmingly straightforward about omitting motivations and explanations ("Don't

Hedy Lamarr, Paul Lukas, and George Brent in *Experiment Perilous.*

ask me why, there isn't any why," Bailey impatiently tells his sculptor friend, Clag [Albert Dekker]) and is brisk and elliptical about things that it cannot, and need not (if one accepts this restriction), explain, such as Allida's background, why she agrees to marry Nick, the circumstances of Alec Gregory's death, the apparent failure of both Allida and Cissie to suspect Nick until it is too late.

Unconcerned with such problems, Tourneur patiently devotes himself to creating a dense labyrinth of images and sounds. The sets atmospherically evoke turn-of-the-century New York, a society where everybody knows, or knows about, everybody else and where restaurants have private entrances and curtained booths. To explore this hermetic universe, Tourneur adopts an almost perversely elaborate visual style. One of the most striking features of *Experiment Perilous* is its repeated use of multiple camera angles to cover a single event or movement. In the first of three scenes in which Bailey, alone, recalls things that various people have told him, each new voice on the soundtrack (except the fourth and last, that of Clag) is accompanied by a new angle on Bailey. Later, Tourneur takes three different setups simply to show Bailey carrying Cissie's dressing case out of his living room and hiding it in his bathroom; the shot of the corridor between the living room and the bathroom seems superfluous — and this shot is repeated when Bailey comes out! The arrival of Bailey and Clag at the Bederaux house for tea is an extraordinary succession of static medium shots, each taken from a new angle and revealing a separate area of the huge set. When Cissie goes downstairs to investigate Nick's and Alec's shouting, Tourneur explores various parts of the house in an elaborate series of shots that take Cissie down the spiral staircase, across a darkened room, across the hall on the second floor, and down the first flight of the big staircase.

This fastidiousness, which at first appears merely gratuitous, eventually begins to make sense. The fussiness with intermediate shots (e.g., the scene of Bailey prowling the upstairs floors of the house to find the child's room) conveys the idea of a rich private life going on in the house, behind doors, in other rooms — a life that is closed to the viewer. (Tourneur's lingering over transitions in this film interestingly contradicts his strictures, stated in his interviews, against "*temps morts*" and shots of people entering houses, of doors opening, etc.)[3] By evoking an inaccessible richness and complexity, Tourneur suggests the subjective position of Allida, a simple, young New Englander who finds herself alienated amid Nick's refined, European-style surroundings and trapped by the decor of the past (Clag calls the house "the only place in town where you're never sure what century you're living in").

The incredible profusion of bric-a-brac in the Bederaux house not only makes us aware that Allida is merely another piece — albeit the centerpiece — in Nick's collection (in Cissie's diary, Allida is called a "jewel" that Nick was determined to see "polished and mounted to perfection") but also creates a stifling atmosphere that correlates with Allida's panic. (On the train at the beginning of the film, the mention of the house is enough to cause Cissie to suffer a short vertigo.) The pedantic slowness and multiplicity of angles in *Experiment Perilous* provide an abstract visual metaphor for Nick's strategy of treating Allida as mentally fragile, reinforcing the stifling mood of oppressive care and insulting circumspection. Marc Vernet observed, "The suffocation felt by the spectator on seeing the images associates him to the feminine position at the site of the paternal figure, constructed in such a way that it assumes at once the idea of creation and that of possession."[4]

Similarly, Nick's almost nonstop talking, first when he introduces Bailey to Allida and second during the sequence in which Bailey comes for dinner, becomes tremendously unnerving. We realize that Nick is constantly speaking for Allida, depriving her of her voice. He is a master of image as well as sound: he turns Allida into the simulacrum of her image in the portrait (which shows her wearing a dress he designed for her). Bederaux resembles a film director, manipulating decor, costume, and performance to create "a speaking likeness" of reality, distressed by the collapse of his mise-en-scène during the climactic confrontation with Bailey. The film metaphor comes close to the surface at several points in *Experiment Perilous*. Since film combines elements of all the other arts, it is fitting, for example, that Alec points out that various arts are represented at Allida's birthday party: painting (Maitland), sculpture (Clag), and poetry (himself); he might also have mentioned music and dance, with only theater missing (unless we count the theatrical quality of the Nick-Allida-Alec triangle).

Bailey, who emerges as Nick's successful rival for control of image and sound, is repeatedly shown as a spectator or listener, someone who goes to see things (he goes to the museum to see Allida's portrait and then attends the Bederaux tea to get a look at Allida herself) and for whom events are staged and recounted. When Cissie first meets him on the train, she instinctively recognizes him as a doctor and comments on the ability of doctors to see "beneath the flesh." At Clag's party, Bailey is linked compositionally with Clag's Medusa bust and thus appears as a sort of Perseus, able to master reality by means of the image (the mirror next to the front door to his apartment also belongs to this thematic motif). His reading of Cissie's "Life and Times of Nicholas Bederaux" resembles a film screening, an analogy made clear when the first page of one of Cissie's notebooks becomes, by superimposition, a frame within a frame representing her narrative in flashback, the page lingering briefly in the image as a border.

Although Clag calls Bailey a "mental inquisitor" and insists on his unromantic nature ("He looks into the eyes of a beautiful woman and the only thing he can see is an inflamed cornea"), the doctor becomes subject to the "disturbing" power of the image. His fascination with Allida turns him into a kind of artist. At tea, he rhapsodizes about how he would paint her full-length, against the sky, in a field of grass and daisies. Later, revealing his suspicions about Nick to Clag, he uses a musical metaphor: "There's something out of tune with him, like a chord of music with a basic note missing."

The film repeatedly makes Bailey's subjective perception the point where sound and image separate. Bailey's opening narration (like *I Walked with a Zombie*, *Experiment Perilous* begins with a narration that never formally ends but just drops off) accompanies exterior shots of a train moving at night through rain and lightning. We cut inside the train, where Bailey wakes up from a nap and has a conversation with Cissie. Bizarrely, his voice-over continues over their inaudible dialogue, muting Cissie and putting in place of her speech a speculative diagnosis: "I wondered vaguely if she were mentally ill." The violence the voice does to the image is strongly marked: here Bailey resembles Nick, speaking for a woman, imposing his discourse on her. (Later, Bailey violates the injunction on the cover of Cissie's diary: "Cissie Bederaux — Her book — Do not dare to open.")

At Clag's studio, Elaine walks away from Bailey, leaving him alone in the shot with the Medusa bust; the background piano music fades down, and simultaneously the voice of Maitland fades up as he recounts the sudden death of Cissie. The sound mixing, suggesting artifice and fantasy, draws our attention to the fact that our knowledge of the narrative is limited to what Bailey knows. Bailey joins the group, the camera tracking and panning with him, and asks Maitland for more information. At this point the piano music resumes — as if it necessarily accompanied a contact with reality that was broken momentarily by the news of Cissie's death. The scene ends on a slow track-in to a close-up of Bailey, under the voices of Clag and Maitland; again, the voices-off enforce our identification with Bailey as the scene's central consciousness.

Scenes of Bailey thinking in his study and, toward the end of the film, walking on a sidewalk are accompanied by various characters' voice-overs, repeating dialogue he has previously heard. To familiarize himself with the history of the Bederaux family, he has his nurse read aloud a magazine article about them. The beginning of the scene, a medium close-up of Bailey at the window, dislocates the source of the nurse's voice and makes us think at first that this is another of Bailey's remembered voices. Alone in his office after his consultation with Nick,

Experiment Perilous: **Paul Lukas and Hedy Lamarr.**

Bailey walks pensively away from the camera toward the window. The light dims, the partial darkness suddenly transforming him into the double of the spectator in the dark movie theatre, as he listens to the remembered voices on the soundtrack. When the ringing of a phone breaks his reverie, the light goes on again. The nonnaturalistic lighting effect strengthens the link between Bailey's consciousness and the apparatus of film, as does the use of a sound effect as a recall to reality.

The emphasis on the voice, on stories, prepares us for the revelation that Nick is poisoning his young son's mind with stories indicting women as witches: "And the more beautiful they are when the sun is up, the blacker and uglier they are when it gets dark. And what they want are little boys like you.... Papa knows all about witches. Papa put up magic bars to keep you safe." (Without insisting on this connection, we may wonder if this scene and the motif of absent or injurious fathers throughout *Experiment Perilous* reflect Tourneur's relationship with his father.) At the end of the film, Bailey takes up Nick's theme but overturns his lesson, telling the boy about the "good witch" who flies around at night "finding all the things that were lost during the day." Bailey's appropriation of the "witch" theme completes his triumph over Nick as director.

Alec Gregory is the link between Nick and Bailey. Like Nick, Alec tries to make Allida into what he wants her to be, to proclaim and appropriate her true nature: "I want to say how you are, how I know you are, warm and simple and bright inside. You're not a great lady in a great house, you're the earth and everything that grows and breathes, and when I'm not with you, it's a blanket over it." Just as Bailey progresses from detachment to involvement, from the place of a spectator outside the frame to that of a figure within the picture, Alec tries to enter the image with his attempt to "say" Allida (his poem states: "Say the name and you'll know the person / By the way it forms upon the lips / How then shall I say 'Allida'?").

In a shot in Cissie's flashback, Alec seems to fill the spectator/reader position that Bailey has taken in relation to the flashback itself. The shot comes in the scene in the conservatory involving Nick, Allida, and Alec. Behind and above Alec, a huge mirror reflects Nick and Allida. Alec also appears in the mirror. If we read just the mirror, Nick and Allida form a simulacrum of marital concord (as in the tea scene, in which they are briefly framed in a balanced two-shot), whereas the image poses Alec (who skews the composition both horizontally and vertically by appearing in the bottom-right corner of the mirror) as the vanquished would-be seducer and the spoiler of this harmony. Because he figures both in the mirror and outside it, Alec also occupies the position of the absent Bailey, projecting himself into the Oedipal triangle while remaining in the state of exclusion that belongs to the spectator.

In its long flashback section, *Experiment Perilous* plays insistently on the ambiguities of narration. We come to read Cissie's book as revealing a truth of which she is unaware. Cissie's voice-over says that even though Nick gave no outward sign, she could tell he was proud of Allida at her coming-out party in Paris. The shot of him grimly watching Allida dance with another man suggests, however, that he is jealous. Cissie's own complete sexlessness (Bailey sums her up to Clag by stating that she "made a burnt offering of her life") apparently prevents her from seeing the significance of Nick's impotence. Later, Bailey tells Clag that Cissie "probably hated" her brother without realizing it. Nothing we've seen or heard supports this interpretation, and we may question how Bailey arrives at it.

Experiment Perilous manages to be ambiguous about Cissie's failure to grasp the truth that her book transmits to Bailey. During the fateful birthday party, Nick remains alone in the conservatory after the guests go in to dinner. We see him retrieve Allida's forgotten jade necklace from the top of the piano. How can Cissie know he does this; how is she able to report it? In the next scene, while dancing with Maitland in the aquarium hall, Cissie notices that Allida isn't wearing the necklace and signals to her warningly. This gesture suggests that Cissie thinks the necklace is merely misplaced; therefore, she didn't see Nick pocket the necklace. Cissie's warning gesture, one of only two exchanges between Cissie and Allida in the film, implies a solidarity between the two women against Nick, a solidarity that is not explicit in her text. The film nearly juxtaposes, then, two symmetrical looks by Cissie: one that her text presumably accounts for but that could not have taken place in reality (her seeing Nick pocket the necklace) and one that takes place in reality but that has no place in her text (her warning Allida that the necklace is missing). This contradiction (on one level, a trivial example of a kind of cheating with first-person flashbacks that goes on routinely in Hollywood films; Tourneur is, perhaps, merely obeying the formal requirement to put the viewer in the best-possible position to evaluate the action) is central to the narrative; it implies that Cissie knows what she is supposed not to know — that Nick is insane — and that her entire writing project may be intended to reveal what it seems to cover up: Nick's murder of Alec.

At the end of the film, Bailey consciously steps into Alec's shoes: he says he loves Allida, just as Alec did. To drive home the point, the Bederaux maid mistakenly calls Bailey "Mr. Gregory." We might read the end of the film as saying that Alec and Bailey have the same "truth" about Allida, a truth constructed out of their own desires and nostalgias. Or we could sum up *Experiment Perilous* as the story of a plain, ordinary American who saves a woman from her European husband who is trying to fill her head with complexes. Remarkably, this is indeed the story that Jacques Tourneur, a European, told. He told it, however, in a way that lets the other reading be true too, or rather in a way that makes either reading unnecessary, since the characters of the film are, like all Tourneur's other characters, "perfect strangers whose mystery does not have to be elucidated or explained."[5]

Like other Tourneur films, *Experiment Perilous* has an emotional quality that never quite becomes explicit. The film's emotion is not found in its banal sentimentality about Allida's love of daisies; the emotion comes closest to the surface in the beautiful montage, with lyrical lap dissolves, of Allida's Paris education, in the way Allida and Bailey start calling each other "dear" toward the end of the film, and in some of the close-ups of Allida, such as the dazzling shot of her profile against Bailey's dark coat in the restaurant. If *Experiment Perilous* has many points in common with *Vertigo*, Tourneur's treatment of romantic love is more humane than Hitchcock's while also more detached (from the obsessive viewpoint of the romantic subject).

Much of the intense, evanescent eroticism of the film can be attributed to Hedy Lamarr. Modern audiences may luxuriate in the camp effect of casting the Vienna-born star as a woman who retains her simple Vermont origins despite an intensive program of Europeanization by her Austrian husband, but the internal contradiction of Lamarr's casting perfectly suits the ambiguity of the film. Her strange, paradoxically triumphant performance is visibly a weird structure of compromises required for the character simultaneously to seem "insane" and be "normal." Lamarr's acting in this role (surely the most challenging she ever played) is hard to evaluate or even describe: completely natural, she somehow suggests both fragile inadequacy (the character's and the performer's) and modest assurance. Clearly, Lamarr needed and got sensitive, encouraging direction.

The other performances are successful in a more normal way. As the evil Nick, Paul Lukas is one of the quiet, relatively inexpressive villains Tourneur favors (cf. Kirk Douglas as Whit in *Out of the Past*). George Brent's Bailey is paradoxically an interesting hero precisely because he is so boring and conventional. A down-to-earth, almost self-effacing figure rather than a dashing leading man, he resembles the heroes played by Dana Andrews and Glenn Ford for Tourneur. Because he lacks glamour, he appears vulnerable, and the dangers to which he is exposed are believable. Brent's somnambulistic calmness in dealing with the gas in

Albert Dekker and George Brent in *Experiment Perilous*.

the nursery is strikingly convincing. Tourneur photographs his thought (just as he photographs Brian Donlevy's thought in *Canyon Passage* and Jane Greer's in *Out of the Past*, for example): note the close shot of Bailey visibly thinking about how he is going to handle Nick, who is covering him with a gun.

Judged only on its visual style, *Experiment Perilous* is one of Tourneur's three or four greatest achievements. Tourneur uses actors' bodies, camera position, and decor to create subtle patterns of imagery extending throughout the film. The recurrent shots of people turning, for example, define a space in flux, divided by curious angles of perspective (cf. Clag's imitation of Nick as a baboon, looking up at people with tilted head). This conception of space also determines the compositions and camera angles in the several street scenes. For example, in a high-angle shot from a window, the triangle formed by a telephone pole, a manhole cover, and a mailbox emphasizes the angle of our vision while the perfectly straight lines left by wheels in the light snow remind us of the earlier scene in which a strange man follows Bailey in the street.

The aquarium tanks on the second-floor hall of the Bederaux house are repeatedly linked with forebodings of disaster: they remind Bailey of "something out of Jules Verne"; Cissie is shown in front of them when she notices that Allida isn't wearing the necklace Nick gave her; we see them in the background through a doorway when Allida phones Bailey to ask him to observe Nick with her son; the light in the aquariums eerily silhouettes Nick as he walks crookedly toward Bailey at the film's climax. This series of shots, which builds up considerable (though understated) tension, culminates in perhaps the most inexplicable and magical shot in all of Tourneur's work: the explosion of the tanks behind Bailey — a potent image of release.

"Reward Unlimited" (1944)

This short, produced by David O. Selznick's Vanguard Films for the U.S. Public Health Service and distributed by the Government Office of War Information, was designed to support the recruiting efforts of the Cadet Nurse Corps. It succeeds admirably.

The opening credits are superimposed over a shot of a pond, in which trees are reflected; limpid, gray light dominates, evoking the constant mood of Tourneur's pastoralism. The first scene introduces two lovers, Paul (James Brown) and Peggy (Dorothy McGuire), sitting on a bench beside the pond, their backs to the camera. He is about to report for amphibious training in Florida. She wants to get married; he replies: "We'll be married, but afterwards, after we've won the war. Not now. It wouldn't be fair to you." She resolves to quit her job at the plate-glass company, saying: "I'm going to get some war work myself.... I'm going to find something that will make you proud of me. Something that means something, to bring you home quicker."

At the train station, in a cramped composition (the camera shooting the couple through metal girders), Peggy kisses Paul goodbye. Returning home on the sidewalk, she trips and falls; a friendly nurse, Mrs. Scott (Aline MacMahon), who passes by, invites her to her nearby house and treats her scraped knee. Mrs. Scott tells Peggy about the country's "desperate need for nurses," describes the new U.S. Cadet Nurse Corps, and settles Peggy's doubts about the profession, concluding, "It's the most important kind of war work." Peggy goes home to discuss her new interest in nursing with her fatuous mother (Spring Byington) and her newspaper-reading father (Tom Tully). The mother won't hear of Peggy's choice: "No daughter of mine's going to do anything so distasteful. Imagine messing around with blood and germs and disinfectants. Ugh!" Modestly and quietly, the father gets up from his newspaper chair, speaks for the first time in the scene, and encourages Peggy to fulfill her dream.

A montage of Peggy's training leads to the graduating-class ceremony. In the last sequence, Peggy and another nurse, walking down a corridor, hear weeping from the room of a child patient. Peggy enters the room, which is dark except for dim light coming through the institutional window. Switching on the light next to the boy's bed, she comforts him (he has just awakened from a nightmare about his car accident). He says he likes her best of all the nurses because she has "kind of an inside shine. It shines through your eyes." She says, "I guess that's what happens

123

when you're happy." She turns the light out, throwing the room in darkness again. The film's last shot returns to the corridor: Peggy walks toward the camera, which is slightly high and tracks back before her. Over the shot, the voice of a male narrator urges female viewers qualified by age and education to apply for the nurse corps "if you want a dignified career that you can continue after marriage and a valuable preparation for life."

Visually, only the first and the last scenes of "Reward Unlimited" suggest Tourneur's style — and that only vestigially. The set of Mrs. Scott's living room is strangely empty: the walls are largely bare, the bookshelves only partly filled. The parents' home suffers from a similar decorative impoverishment. This sparseness, which perhaps suggests an atmosphere of wartime impermanence, violates Tourneur's philosophy of decor: "A wall where there are things hanging looks solid; a wall where there is nothing looks as if it were made of cardboard, which it is, really."[1] The graduation ceremony takes place in the barest decor of all: vast empty walls; rows of nurses in seats; a long window through which we see bare trees sticking their branches in the air.

This efficiently functional film is interesting mainly as Tourneur's most explicit study of the medical profession. Putting aside the ideological message about womanhood (a nurse "has indeed achieved the richest measure of her potentialities as a woman," Peggy tells her parents, quoting the surgeon general), one notes in the film's characterization of nursing the same thematic combination of spirituality and service that informs *I Walked with a Zombie* and *Stars in My Crown*. All three films emphasize symbolic lamps beside the beds of patients; here the lamp is associated with Peggy's "inside shine."

Canyon Passage
(1946)

Think of anything, of cowboys, of movies, of detective stories, of anybody
who goes anywhere or stays at home and is an American and you will realize
that it is something strictly American to conceive a space that is filled
with moving, a space of time that is filled always filled with moving.

GERTRUDE STEIN, "THE GRADUAL
MAKING OF *THE MAKING OF
AMERICANS*"

Canyon Passage is another of Tourneur's neglected masterpieces and one of
the greatest Westerns. If the film remains underrated, perhaps this is because it
conforms to none of the standard Western models, being neither a revenge story,
nor a journey story, nor a story about an outlaw (whether real, reforming, or
falsely accused), nor a story of the cavalry, nor primarily a story in which the hero
tames the town or accomplishes some difficult feat. Atypically, *Canyon Passage* is
about the themes that underlie the whole Western genre and are usually taken for
granted in Westerns: the cohesion of the community; the conflict between its values and those of the individual; the defects of frontier justice; the psychological
and social meaning of the westward trajectory.

Several directors had been linked to the project before Tourneur. On May 6,
1945, the *New York Times* reported that Robert Siodmak would "most likely" direct
the picture for producer Walter Wanger.[1] Sometime later that month, however,
Wanger secured Stuart Heisler's services from Paramount to direct *Canyon Passage*;
then Paramount, deciding it needed Heisler for *Blue Skies*, offered George Marshall
as a substitute, but Marshall apparently bowed out for health reasons. Tourneur
must have been assigned to *Canyon Passage* by July 24, the date his name appeared
on the list of those who were to receive copies of a lengthy letter from Joseph I.
Breen to Maurice Pivar at Universal detailing concerns about the script.[2]

Shooting on *Canyon Passage* began on location in and around Diamond Lake
and Medford, Oregon, in August 1945. *Canyon Passage* was one of the few Tourneur films to use a second unit; he later said: "I've always fought second units.
Whenever I have any authority at all I just don't have them."[3] The second unit,
directed by Charles Barton, contributed to the Indian breakout sequence, the trek
sequences, and perhaps most significantly, the cabin-raising sequence.

On September 4, Wanger sent an anxious telegram to production manager

Percy Ikerd: "Am concerned about enterprise as so far first unit progressing very slowly at speed that cannot be tolerated. Want to get quality but must be on reasonable schedule." On September 7, Wanger sent a telegram to Henry Spitz, also on location, stressing the need "to bring this picture in at price" and announcing his intention to visit the location himself the following week with suggested cuts in the script. Wanger visited the set briefly and was apparently satisfied; on September 14, after returning to Hollywood, he wired Tourneur, Spitz, and Ikerd and expressed his renewed enthusiasm and optimism.

On September 20, Wanger dashed off two wires to Tourneur. The first stated: "Saw kiss scene. Liked it very much. Looks great." The second added: "Saw lots of film today. Looks very good with exception lack of closeups of leads which necessary to carry story. Without closeups technicolor looks like scenic. Have sent detailed wire to Spitz. If you correct this everything fine." A wire to Edward Cronjager, director of photography, carried the same message: "Quality excellent however very worried about lack of closeups of leads as we are losing story points."

The "detailed wire to Spitz," also dated September 20, gives Wanger's specific concerns.

> In scene of [Dana] Andrews and Bragg [the character played by Ward Bond] at Dance's cabin definitely miss closeups both men which should be shot by all means. Andrews should be really angry in this closeup.... Explain to Tourneur that in color you have to use more closeups than in black and white as characters fade into background with scenery and story points lost because we cannot see facial expressions and eyes. Also need closeups for your lily pond scene but we can get those at studio. Essential to have closeups of [Susan] Hayward, Bond, [Brian] Donlevy and Andrews in all important scenes. Otherwise picture will look like scenic.

The next day Tourneur wired a reply to Wanger: "Will have so many closeups of cast in studio interiors and street for seventy five percent of story we will all be glad of relief of medium shots in the few exteriors we do have. Aside from that I disapprove of closeups except when I reach story points." This telegram is precious for two reasons: one, it contains a statement, however laconic, of Tourneur's aesthetic principles; two, it shows Tourneur standing up for these principles to a producer who has commanded him to violate them.

Obviously dissatisfied with Tourneur's response (Tourneur also phoned Wanger on the same day that he sent the telegram), Wanger insisted again on the need for closeups in the Bragg-Logan scene, wiring Spitz that night, "I have feeling Tourneur afraid of closeups not realizing how important they are to color and regardless of how he feels about matter we want closeups which we can eliminate later if not necessary." Wanger got his way, at least regarding the close-ups of Andrews and Bond outside the cabin. The close-ups were omitted from the finished film, however; the scene appears probably just as Tourneur intended. Nor are there close-ups in the "lily pond scene" Wanger mentions.

Canyon Passage takes place in Oregon in 1856. The central character, Logan Stuart (Dana Andrews), owns a mule freight line and a general store in the small

The cabin-raising in *Canyon Passage*: Logan (Dana Andrews) and Vane (Victor Cutler).

mining town of Jacksonville. The script develops Logan's relationships with several characters: his friend George Camrose (Brian Donlevy), a banker who is secretly stealing gold dust from his customers to support his gambling habit; George's fiancée, Lucy Overmire (Susan Hayward), who is attracted to Logan; Caroline Marsh (Patricia Roc), who becomes engaged to Logan during a cabin-raising for another young couple; and Honey Bragg (Ward Bond), a brutal loner whom Logan suspects of several crimes. To conceal his embezzlement, George kills a miner, McIver (Wallace Scott), but he is caught and tried by a kangaroo court. Logan helps him escape during the confusion caused by news of an Indian break-out. Both George and Bragg are killed, and Caroline, realizing that she would be unhappy with the "restless" Logan, calls off their engagement, leaving him free to ride with Lucy to San Francisco.

A rich study of a Western community, *Canyon Passage* develops its themes through contrasting characters and situations, an approach that makes it impossible for the audience either to adopt a detached point of view from which to judge the characters or to identify wholly with any of them. *Canyon Passage* is another of the films in which Tourneur subverts filmic identification, as he also does in *I Walked with a Zombie* (fading of the narrator's voice, which is submerged into an impersonal, collective point of view), *The Leopard Man* (undercutting of the stature of the hero and the heroine, with the narrative following various characters in turn), and *Experiment Perilous* (unreliable narration). The film's emphasis on irresolvable conflicts makes it interestingly modern, anticipating certain aspects of the Westerns of Sam Peckinpah (later Tourneur's assistant on *Wichita*) and Robert Altman. In *Canyon Passage*, tangled chains of causality lead to multiple conclusions, each affirming the irreducibility of difference. Logan banishes Bragg from the town; Caroline rejects Logan because she realizes she is attached to the land; Logan pronounces George's epitaph: "There's a fine margin ... between what could be and what is.... In some other kind of country he might have made the grade."

Through the scenes at the Dances' house, the cabin-raising scene, and the character of Caroline, the film emphasizes the pioneer themes of home and rootedness. *Canyon Passage* is concerned with couples: their establishment and perpetuation and the qualities needed to make them succeed. (A repeated theme in the cabin-raising scene is Ben Dance's urging of Caroline, "You've got to give him the sign," i.e., she must in some subtle manner signify to Logan that if he should propose to her, she wouldn't turn him down.) Yet the heart of the film is the relationship between two men who embody different aspects of uprootedness and rejection of home: Logan and George. Throughout *Canyon Passage*, Logan is defined as "a restless man": he remains nowhere for very long, neither in Jacksonville nor (like Ben Dance) in some intermediate "fort" between town and wilderness. George, meanwhile, is nostalgic for the East and appears increasingly out of place in Jacksonville. Without necessarily going as far as Louis Skorecki in regarding *Canyon Passage* as "the most beautiful homosexual melodrama ever filmed,"[4] we may note that each man is obsessed with the other: Logan twice ironically criticizes George's demure way of kissing Lucy, and George twice responds automatically with the same words: "Could you do better?" The second time Logan demonstrates by taking Lucy in his arms and kissing her long and passionately in front of the heavily expressionless George. In these scenes, George turns his own lack of desire for Lucy (hinted at from another angle in his hopeless flirtation with Marta Lestrade [Rose Hobart]) into the occasion for competing with Logan. When Lucy reproaches George for his gambling, he replies: "Even Logan gambles, doesn't he, every time he sends out a pack train.... He's not responsible for his character, neither am I for mine." Although George then accuses her of making "a comparison between us that leaves me at a disadvantage," he is the one who first compares himself with Logan.

One of the film's inconspicuous epiphanies — perhaps its hidden climax — is the brief confrontation in which Logan asks George why he gambled away the money Logan had loaned him to pay off his debts. "Envy of you, Logan," George replies. "That's no answer," Logan says. "Maybe it's the only answer." (Brian Donlevy's performance in this scene shows the highest level of acting — of a certain kind of acting, anyway — possible in the cinema.) Underlining the significance of the scene, Tourneur breaks it down into medium-close shot–reverse shots when they discuss Lucy and then, after Lucy arrives, into complementary close-ups of Logan and George, each giving a look that shifts from the other to Lucy.

Ernest Pascal's script (based closely on Ernest Haycox's novel) allows the characters to reflect philosophically on the events of the narrative, on each other's natures, and on life in general. From the beginning, in the scene at the assayer's office in Portland, the film establishes this mode with Logan deprecating his own money before the practical assayer (Peter Whitney, later more prominent in *Great Day in the Morning*) and declaring as a parting shot: "A man can choose his own gods, Cornelius. What are your gods?" Later in the film, Lucy speculates on the persistence of the "primitive" in civilization, and George and Jack Lestrade (Onslow Stevens) conclude a poker game with a discussion of the definition of friendship. The dialogues between Logan and his partner, "Clench" (Halliwell Hobbes), are particularly interesting because of their relation to Tourneur's constant theme of the opposition between Europe and America: the Englishman Clench always advises caution and warns of "the trouble that always comes," but Logan refuses to heed his warnings, saying: "This is America, Clench. We sail with the tide." Clench can't dissuade Logan from helping George because Logan is motivated by "something deeper than reason."

Canyon Passage gets under way in a deliberately fragmented manner, introducing characters and themes so rapidly and bluntly that the viewer seems to have stumbled in late. The dialogue alludes mysteriously to earlier events and to characters we don't know (at the hotel in Portland, Logan inquires about Lucy Overmire and is told by the desk clerk, "She's been asking for George Camrose"; after being attacked in his room at night by a shadowy intruder who escapes through the window, Logan tells Lucy, "I have an idea it was Bragg"). The film moves from one short, enigmatic encounter to another. In most of these encounters, questions are asked. Many of them are left hanging at the ends of scenes, coloring subsequent scenes with doubt: "What are your gods?" "Would you mind having me on your hands, Logan?" "Must it always be a woman?" "Say, how long does it take to open a safe?" The film is pointedly elliptical: we don't see George killing McIver, or George getting killed.

The superbly orchestrated crisscrossing lateral movements of the early scene in which Logan and Lucy arrive at the Dances' house and meet Caroline are typical of the film's visual patterns; panning to follow the characters and cutting on their movements, Tourneur envelops them in an atmosphere of freedom while inconspicuously defining their relationships to each other. The scene ends at the dinner table: Dance asks Logan whether the Indians are likely to break out; the scene cuts from a two-shot of the two men to a final two-shot of Dance's two young boys, the older one at left concentrating on his food and the younger at right looking at his father (offscreen) and nodding intently as the latter says, "It's my fort and darned if I'm going to leave it." After all the flurries of activity, the static shots that end the scene create a contrast that subtly reinforces the ominousness of the dialogue. The scene sets up several important motifs in the film — the polite undercurrent of rivalry between Lucy and Caroline, the danger from the Indians — and establishes the Dances' house as a place of food, family, plenty, and constant movement. This contrasts with our last view of the house, after Ben and Asa Dance have been killed by Indians: in the later scene, the characters are static, the dialogue quiet.

As in *The Leopard Man*, the mise-en-scène emphasizes unexpected connections and shifting alliances between people. Characters' paths meet and diverge, the camera following now one, now another, in fluid lateral tracking shots. Jacksonville is introduced in long shots of crisscrossing activity: the camera follows Bragg for a while, only to pick up Hi Linnet (Hoagy Carmichael) on muleback. Subsequent shots rapidly introduce new characters: Jonas Overmire (Stanley Ridges), George. The surface complexity of the film is amazing: a shot of George and Lucy going into the Overmire house dissolves to the interior of Logan's store; Logan has conversations with Clench and, briefly, Vane Blazier (Victor Cutler); then Logan goes to the doorway to smoke his pipe at the same time that George and Lucy, out for a walk, arrive at the door. They discuss when Lucy will marry George ("When the leaves fall," she says enigmatically). Then off-screen voices announce that a fight is in progress; Hi turns up to report that the fight is between Vane and Bragg.

As Roger McNiven has noted, Tourneur withholds "any simple explanation of the strange interrelationships comprising the community."[5] The film emphasizes this absence of explanation through the pivotal role played in many of these relationships by Hi Linnet, who, standing apart from the other characters, embodies the figure of the artist and entertainer so crucial in Tourneur's cinema. Like the calypso singer in *I Walked with a Zombie*, if more obliquely, Hi comments with his songs on the events and images of the film. "Rogue River Valley," which accompanies our introduction to Jacksonville, matches the scene-setting intention of the sequence, and "Silver Saddle" both connotes money and conveys a romanticism ("The moon is my silver saddle ... / I'll be with my love tonight") that we impute to George, who appears on-screen while the song is heard. Later, the bright "I'm Gettin' Married in the Mornin'" is obviously appropriate to the dance that follows Gray and Liza's wedding, and "Ole Buttermilk Sky" optimistically reflects the movement of regeneration on which the film ends. Moving freely between diegetic reality and incidental musical score, Hi's songs integrate the narrative of *Canyon Passage* with the film's folk purpose, the affirmation of American myth.

The peaceful Hi, the artist and dreamer, recognizes and can express the community's need for violence, not because he shares it but because he is free from it. (Conversely, in *Great Day in the Morning*, Phil the Cannibal, an outsider within the community, reminds Pentecost of his duty to the community.) Although he sets up the fight between Logan and Bragg (ruefully commenting, "The town won't have it any other way"), Hi refuses to bet on it, and in the middle of the fight, we see him (through the thick of spectators) turn and walk away—an action that foreshadows his finally leaving Jacksonville with Logan and Lucy. Hi mediates between Logan, the individualist, and the community. During the cabin-raising sequence, Hi also mediates between the whites and the Indians, filling a conciliatory basket of apples and sacrificing his beloved mandolin to one of the Indians (who decides to take only the strings but rips off the bridge of the instrument to get them).

The beautifully directed night sequence at the bank involving George, Hi, and Johnny Steele (Lloyd Bridges) demonstrates the complexity of Hi's role in the visual and narrative patterns of the film. The sequence starts in an inner room in the bank, with the camera panning from a table with cards strewn on it to the open doorway to the main office of the bank. Through the doorway, we see George enter the frame, cross to the safe, and remove coins from a box. A knock at the door interrupts him; the scene cuts to the office as George opens the door and talks to Johnny, who has come to withdraw his gold dust from the bank to fund a night of gambling. Citing bank rules, George has Johnny wait outside, then goes back to the safe and refills Johnny's leather poke of gold dust by drawing from

Dana Andrews and Susan Hayward in *Canyon Passage*.

another miner's sack; we infer that he has been routinely siphoning off the miners' dust for his own use.

The scene cuts from George to a shot of Hi walking outside his house, finishing the song "Silver Saddle," which has accompanied the entire scene and which we now understand to have belonged to the scene's diegetic reality (i.e., having a "real" source in the scene rather than being part of the incidental score). The camera cranes up as Hi approaches Johnny, waiting on the porch outside the bank; the two chat briefly before George emerges with the poke of dust and gives it to Johnny, who leaves as George returns inside thoughtfully. Hi goes around to the side of the building and peers in curiously through a window. George flips a coin to make a decision; disappointed, he locks the safe and leaves the bank. In a shot symmetrical with the crane-up as Hi walked toward the bank, the camera cranes down as George goes down the stairs. Hi asks him if he's going to go gambling tonight; George says no, and the two men separate.

The sequence is a densely integrated network of character actions and camera placements. In the opening panning shot, the juxtaposition of cards and the safe announces that gambling will be the main motif of the scene. Watching George through the open doorway to another room, we're conscious of spying on his actions as he kneels by the safe. Therefore we read the scene as telling us (even though Donlevy's performance doesn't, at this point, suggest that the character is trying to conceal his actions) that George is stealing; further, we infer from the cards that he has a gambling problem. The camera's spying sets up a framing structure that is completed near the end of the sequence in the shot of Hi spying on George through the bank window. In the first shot, the camera isn't identified with any character (nobody is in the room where the camera is placed) or with any narrative agency other than that of the film as a source of objective information. Finally, in the shot of Hi at the window, Hi becomes the representative of our (and the community's) interest in George.

The cabin-raising sequence brings together most of the major characters and themes. The sequence is full of movement and activity: men cutting down trees, laying the foundation of the cabin (with an unexpectedly vulgar joke, for Tourneur, when Andy Devine's rear fills much of the frame as he says confidently, speaking of the doorway, "This ought to be wide enough"; later in the sequence, he can't fit through the doorway and must walk over the as-yet low wall to get inside), and building various portions of the house while women serve them refreshments. The sequence might have lent itself to Tourneur's "documentary" mode (e.g., some of the shorts, *They All Come Out*, and *Nick Carter, Master Detective*), but instead it takes on the celebratory glory of a frontier apotheosis, sealed with the talismanic sign of a horseshoe nailed over the door of the finished house.

In contrast to this activity are the scenes of George and Lucy, who avoid the work (as does Hi) and sit by a pond. George talks about his desire to go east; she suggests he take things more seriously and not gamble so much. He replies, "This is a gambling country, everybody gambles." We could hear the line as a comment on Gray and Liza, the couple whose cabin is being raised; their bet of living in an isolated place away from the town will prove later to be a losing one when they are killed, and their cabin is burned, in the Indian breakout.

After Gray and Liza's marriage ceremony, Caroline and Logan look in through the outside window of the cabin; a fire burns in the hearth. Robin Wood aptly noted that "we are not taken inside the door," seeing this as an instance of Tourneur's "detachment,"[6] but it is also an instance of his romanticism. Logan's indifference and "restlessness" link him to George: "Do you like Jacksonville, Logan?" "It's a place to do business in." Caroline talks about being conservative, about wanting her children to stay on the same land: "When I'm dead, I'd like them to stand where I stood and see the things I saw."

The film strikingly introduces the Indians by accentuating their absence from the frame and delaying their emergence. During the dance, Hi, who leads the musicians, is the first to look offscreen toward the camera; others gradually notice his consternation and look in the same direction. All this happens in a single long shot that becomes full of suspense. The film holds on this shot until all the musicians have stopped and the happy crowd noise has been entirely stifled. (The last laugh of a woman is allowed to stand out alone briefly, unbearably, at the last possible moment, accentuating the ensuing silence.) Only now does the film cut to the reverse shot of the Indians. In the world of *Canyon Passage*, the Indians come from offscreen space and return there; their home is silence and invisibility (later, we don't see the attack on the mule train, only its aftermath).

The Indians are not like the leopard in *The Leopard Man* (or the birds in

Hitchcock's *The Birds*), embodiments of tensions within the group; instead, they unite the group (as the camera placement in the cabin-raising scene makes clear). Later, their uprising causes Logan and Johnny to settle their differences provisionally in order to protect the community. (Of Tourneur's three other Westerns, only *Great Day in the Morning* involves Indians — briefly, at the very beginning of the film. Again, the Indians function to define and unite a white group, when Kirby and Masterson help Pentecost fight off an Indian attack.)

At the end of the cabin-raising sequence, the camera tracks laterally over people packing up, then passes a single candle burning (referring visually back to the hearth) and stops at Caroline and Logan, who resume their conversation from before as if there had been no break (another example of the film's deft integration of different plot strands). Logan and Caroline become engaged; in a two-shot, George and Lucy overhear Mrs. Dance congratulating the new couple. Letting George walk out of frame toward Logan, the camera reframes, surprisingly, on a two-shot of Lucy and Vane Blazier — the former in love with Logan, the latter with Caroline — both of them transfixed in shock and disappointment, looking offscreen at the newly constituted couple. We register their feelings strongly because of the sudden contrast their stillness makes with the dominant patterns of movement in the scene and also because of the incongruity of their grouping: they have no other contact with each other in the film, and in this shot, they're on different planes of the visual field (Lucy relatively close to the camera, Vane in the middleground), so that their juxtaposition, an effect of the camera movement, creates a visual shock. By emphasizing their look, the film reminds us, perhaps, that the problem threatening to divide Logan and Caroline, the incompatibility of their goals, has not been resolved but merely passed over.

The cabin-raising is the spectacle of the community as it wants to see itself and as the ennobling view of folk history and folk art would have it; it is simultaneously work, celebration, and ritual (the actual marriage ceremony performed at the end of the day strikes us as redundant, as a metaphor for what is already a metaphor). Significantly, the sequence is bracketed by two scenes that emphasize the darkness and conflicts in the community: the gambling scene at Lestrade's, in which Lestrade affirms that "the human race is a horrible mistake"; and the scene in which Logan must fight Bragg at Stutchell's saloon because, as Hi says, "the town won't have it any other way." These reminders of the forces that threaten the community don't negate or invalidate the spirit at work in the cabin-raising. The film simply balances the various forces and claims on our emotional involvement. By playing them off each other, *Canyon Passage* enriches our experience by encouraging us to see the events of the narrative from multiple points of view.

After the cabin-raising sequence, the mood of the film darkens as it moves swiftly through a succession of conflicts, separations, and upheavals. Logan's attitude toward the other characters after his victory over Bragg sets him firmly apart from the community for the first time in the film: we see this in his small but important gesture of pulling away from Johnny on the steps in front of Stutchell's. Lucy agrees, without enthusiasm, to marry George and leave Jacksonville, then decides to join Logan on his trip to San Francisco, ostensibly because she wants to buy a wedding dress but actually because she is in love with him. During their stop at the Dances' cabin, Tourneur briefly emphasizes Lucy's sadness as Logan

The kangaroo court in *Canyon Passage*: Johnny (Lloyd Bridges) pointing, Hi (Hoagy Carmichael, center with hand in vest) looking on, Overmire (Stanley Ridges), Logan (Dana Andrews), and George (Brian Donlevy) standing against the bar.

and Caroline go outside alone — the mood of the scene is utterly different from that of the earlier scene at the Dances', involving the same triangle.

The night scene in which George decides to murder McIver is a haunting example of Tourneur's use of architecture, light, and composition to create a sense of entrapment. George stops on his way up the steps to the bank, his back to the camera; hearing the drunken singing and conversation of an offscreen group of miners, he turns his head slightly left (so that we see him in quarter-face). Over this shot, we hear McIver decline an invitation to join the other miners and say that he is going home. In a long shot, McIver separates from the others; then, jarringly, the film cuts to George, from the same angle as before, his back to the camera and his face turned partly left. His impassive stare almost imperceptibly hardens. This moment, in which "an idea is *literally* born on a face," is one of the shots that inspired Louis Skorecki to write: "Tourneur doesn't exist, he is alone. Not the last cineaste: the only one."[7]

George walks downstairs; his face goes into shadow before he walks offscreen at left. The movement of his face into shadow triggers an explosion of splendidly bleak images, accompanied (as are some scenes in Welles's *Touch of Evil*) by an irrelevant honky-tonk piano that sounds distant and forlorn, suggesting a cosmic indifference to man's treacherous designs and ignoble ends. George, in shadow, stands in the far background of a shot in the middleground of which McIver lies on his belly, drinking from the river: here the mise-en-scène makes us give the scene the squint of destiny, tracing occult forces in the shadows that divide and trap hunter and prey. In the distance between George and the camera, the shot represents the distance between George and himself: he is carried away from himself, has abdicated responsibility (as when he flipped a coin to decide whether to play cards at Lestrade's). At the fade-out, George's slow, expressionless walk forward toward his victim recalls Wes following Jessica in *I Walked with a Zombie*, Doc Black climbing the hotel stairs in *Wichita*, and Jumbo before and after he kills Boston in *Great Day in the Morning*. All these murderers are dead men, already so committed to self-destruction that their strikes against others seem foredoomed and empty (there's never any glamour about murder in Tourneur; it is always tragic and horrible).

The film multiplies small but telling ironies. At the kangaroo trial for George at Stutchell's saloon, Hi warns Johnny against the dangers of quickly concluding from circumstantial evidence, yet he produces the evidence (his account of what he saw through George's window; McIver's shamrock-shaped nugget) that damns George. As Roger McNiven has pointed out, there is also irony in Logan's helping George escape after the illegal trial while, without trial, banishing Bragg into the wilderness (effectively dooming him to be slaughtered by the Indians). [8]

Bragg's attack on an Indian girl, which caused some consternation in the office of Joseph Breen,[9] is not shown; its nature can only be inferred from what comes before and after. The shot of Bragg smiling as he gazes down on his victim is another example of Tourneur showing an idea being born on someone's face (it also recalls the shot in Lang's *Rancho Notorious* in which a bandit looks down at a girl opening a safe). The scenes devoted to the Indian breakout are filmed with Tourneur's characteristic insistence that the mise-en-scène conceal the unshowable, with Indians forcing women behind a hedge and behind a wagon before butchering them; later, the Indians drag Bragg behind fallen branches for their final revenge.

After this violent sequence, *Canyon Passage* regains a certain calm — a calm of resignation, not celebration. The final section of the film reverses details from earlier in the film. The Fordian shot through the window of Caroline's room, from the inside, is the formal opposite of the shot in which Caroline and Logan look in through Gray and Liza's window. The window signifies the longing for a connection to the land, which she cites as her reason for deciding not to marry Logan: her line "I want to look out the window in the morning and see my man plowing" accompanies an insert of the plow seen through the window. This sequence ends with another shot through the window, this time showing Logan riding back to town.

Canyon Passage resolves its love story characteristically by again repeating material from earlier in the film and by pulling our attention back successively from the couple to the town to the landscape. In the ruined store, a setting that reminds us visually of the cabin-raising (there too, everything was a matter of people in medium shot, of structural boundaries neither fully real nor entirely imaginary, like the low wall that Ben Dance walked over), there is a brief shot-reverse-shot exchange between Lucy ("Logan, would you mind having a woman on your hands?") and Logan, who smile at each other. Logan turns and goes away. We cut to Hi in the window frame; he looks, then turns and also goes away. He starts singing "Ole Buttermilk Sky" in a brisk tracking shot of him walking through the devastated town. The song continues over a dissolve to a long shot of Logan and Lucy riding through the country (this time away from Jacksonville rather than toward it as in the beginning of the film), followed at a distance by Hi on his mule. Hi closes the film, remaining on a ridge after Logan and Lucy have ridden down out of the shot.

Tourneur's first color film, *Canyon Passage* has a greater emphasis on scenic beauty than any other Tourneur film, as we become aware with its opening Mizoguchian long shot from the rooftops of a town drenched with heavy rain. The early sequence of Logan and Lucy's return to Jacksonville uses the landscape as a harmonizing or, perhaps, a dissipating element, inviting us to lose ourselves in its flow. Cronjager's magnificent photography and Frank Skinner's spacious score create an atmosphere that is still emotionally involving, as it must have been in 1946. (*Canyon Passage* was one of several Westerns that were released in 1946 and that were commercially or artistically significant;[10] all must have carried a powerful message of historical continuity to postwar audiences.)

In *Canyon Passage*, Tourneur uses texture, movement, light, and shadow in the same ways as in his black-and-white films. The exteriors of the film resemble those of *Days of Glory*, *Out of the Past*, and *Berlin Express* in their emphatic scale, with human figures constantly low in compositions. The shootout between Logan and Bragg in the forest, for example, uses the height of the trees to create an impression of nature's indifference to the human conflict, of a permanent calm momentarily broken.

Shadows and dark areas function as in Tourneur's horror films. Note, for instance, the threatening shadow on the wall as Bragg invades Logan's hotel room, a shadow that is echoed (in *Canyon Passage*, everything happens twice) when Logan's shadow appears on the wall of Stutchell's saloon, where Logan has come to fight Bragg. Light sources regularly appear within the compositions of interior night scenes, for example in the scenes at Lestrade's and at the bank.

Often in *Canyon Passage*, an actor's body is oriented screen left, with only his or her face turned toward the camera, to interact with someone in the foreground or in the offscreen space behind the camera. Logan is posed and photographed in this way, for example, when he criticizes George's lukewarm good-night kiss to Lucy, when he urges George to give up poker, and when Johnny accuses him of helping George escape (in this shot, Tourneur also uses the bodies of men in the crowd as compositional elements, framing Logan within the frame). This mise-en-scène of the human figure, characteristic of Tourneur's films, enforces our sense of offscreen space and our sense that the people in the film are not fully understandable, that they have something to conceal (the sinister interpretation), or simply, and more generally, that they live in a world of which we can see only fragments, often from oblique angles.

One of the most moving effects in the film depends on the placement of camera and actor so that the actor's face is only partly visible. When Mrs. Dance talks to the Indian-fighting party after her husband and one of her sons have been killed, she is in close shot, with her back to the camera. Logan asks if Caroline (who has disappeared) was carrying a gun. Mrs. Dance turns slightly, so that her right profile is to the men (and the camera), as she tries to remember, an effort that prompts a narrative of "red beasties" who killed her husband "right off." She says, "It was him I was thinking about." As always in Tourneur, the emotion is all the more affecting for being so unwilling to reveal itself, so understated and matter-of-fact; nor do we feel that the pathos is cheaply bought. The pretext for the scene is the need, which all the characters understand, for Mrs. Dance to provide information that might help save Caroline. Her bereavement remains an unexpressed, incidental factor that nonetheless dominates the scene.

Note also, for example, the sudden cut to a low angle on Caroline after she breaks up with Logan. The low angle underlines her unexpressed emotion. It is typical of Tourneur to have the actress express very little, almost nothing, and to use the shot change to convey her feeling.

Throughout *Canyon Passage*, the direction of actors is assured. Dana Andrews, in his first of three films for Tourneur, gives one of the best performances of his career: Andrews's precise minimalism proves ideal for Tourneur, as it is also for Preminger (*Laura, Fallen Angel, Daisy Kenyon, Where the Sidewalk Ends*) and for Lang (*While the City Sleeps, Beyond a Reasonable Doubt*). All the other actors in the film are equally restrained, a restraint that creates interesting effects, such as the unexpected softness of Ward Bond's voice in the prelude to Bragg's brutal fight with Logan ("Let's have a drink"; "I left my gun home").

Fundamentally so grave, the film has lightness. Note the eloquence of Johnny's casually handing Logan's pistol back to him as they stand in the ruins of Logan's store — an act that signifies nothing less than the community's pardon of Logan, its willingness to reinstate him, its respect and need for him. Yet none of these meanings are stated, even implicitly, in the dialogue. "We were a mind to hang you" — that's it. All the key points in the film are touched on fleetingly, implicitly. Nothing is resolved between these people. Logan's "restlessness" expresses the community's need not to resolve, and his repeated back-and-forth journeys in the film are a search for perpetual life (which Caroline seeks through home and the land). The unique atmosphere of *Canyon Passage*, its integrity and mystery, have to do precisely with our sense that Logan's journey has no destination: it is only motion. Thus Logan resembles several later Tourneur heroes, especially Jeff in *Out of the Past*, Tourneur's next film.

Out of the Past
(1947)

Mysticism consists, perhaps, in rediscovering an elementary, and in some ways, primitive sensation — the sensation of pursuing life on an uncharted course which has been set through an already completed life which seems already to *have happened*.

PAUL VALÉRY, "ON PAINTING"

Out of the Past, which reunited Tourneur with producer Warren Duff, the producer of *Experiment Perilous*, was based on a novel called *Build My Gallows High*, written by Daniel Mainwaring under the pseudonym Geoffrey Homes. Although the name Homes receives sole screenplay credit in the film, Jeff Schwager has established that Frank Fenton decisively influenced the characterizations and "was responsible for the bulk of the film's best dialogue" as well as for several key plot points. (Fenton was the third writer to work on the project: James M. Cain wrote two drafts, contributing little that was used in the final film.) Mainwaring's statements in a 1972 interview minimizing Tourneur's contribution ("he did what was in the script — very much so") should be considered in light of Mainwarning's failure, in the same interview, to do more than acknowledge that "Frank Fenton had worked on it for a while." For his part, Tourneur claimed that at the stage of his career when *Out of the Past* was made, he "participated very closely in the writing of the scripts." He noted, "I made big changes, with the agreement of the writer, of course." According to Jean-Claude Biette, Tourneur said that he "had refused several times to shoot this crime film, whose script he didn't like, until all the changes he wanted had been accepted."[1]

Dick Powell was originally announced for the part of the doomed detective hero; reportedly, Humphrey Bogart also wanted the part but could not get a release from Warners.[2] Powell would have blurred the film with the insincerity he projected in Edward Dmytryk's *Murder My Sweet* and *Cornered*, overcompensating for his earlier juvenile image; Bogart would have upset the careful balance of the screenplay and would have accentuated its debt to *The Maltese Falcon*. Robert Mitchum, who eventually played the role, proved ideal for it and for Tourneur. His talent lies in total self-absorption in the scene, his ability to convey emotion and urgency with the subtlest means, by a glance, for example, or by a change in the tone of his voice. His acting, like that of Dana Andrews, has strong affinities with Tourneur's direction. The quality Tourneur particularly prized in both actors is the ability to show that they are listening:

> [Andrews] had an enormous quality, which someone like
> Mitchum has also, and which is of prime importance for
> me: he knows how to listen in a scene. There are a large
> number of players who don't know how to listen. While one
> of their partners speaks to them, they simply think: "I don't
> have anything to do during this; let's try not to let the scene
> get stolen from me." Mitchum can be silent and listen to a
> five-minute speech. You'll never lose sight of him and you'll
> understand that he takes in what is said to him, even if he
> doesn't do anything. That's how one judges good actors.[3]

Behind Rory Calhoun in *Way of a Gaucho* and Robert Stack in *Great Day in the Morning*, one can see Tourneur trying to recapture the confidence of understatement he found in Mitchum.

The plot of *Out of the Past* is notoriously complex. Jeff Bailey (Robert Mitchum) runs a gas station in the small town of Bridgeport, California. As we learn through a flashback, narrated by Jeff for the information of his girlfriend, Ann (Virginia Huston), Jeff was formerly a New York–based private detective named Jeff Markham. Hired by a powerful gambler, Whit Sterling (Kirk Douglas), to find Whit's mistress, Kathie Moffat (Jane Greer), Jeff instead fell in love with Kathie and escaped with her to California. His former partner, Jack Fisher (Steve Brodie), tracked the couple down; Kathie killed Fisher and fled.

In the present time of the narrative, Whit, now reunited with Kathie, locates Jeff and entrusts him with another mission: to steal some incriminating papers from his blackmailing lawyer, Leonard Eels (Ken Niles). When he finds Eels dead, Jeff realizes that he is to be framed for the murder, but he manages to secure the papers and offers to trade them to Whit for his freedom. Kathie kills Whit to avoid being charged with Fisher's murder (as envisioned in Whit and Jeff's bargain). She and Jeff are both killed when they're caught at a police roadblock.

The film went into production under the novel's title (which is spoken near the end of the film by Jeff to Kathie), but test responses were negative and the studio changed the title to *Out of the Past*. The film was released with little fanfare and no great expectations, apparently, on the part of anyone associated with it; according to Mainwaring, new RKO production head Dore Schary "didn't like *Out of the Past* because it had been bought before he came.... He just threw [it] out without any decent publicity." Jane Greer recalled that after the film was finished, those involved "thought *Out of the Past* was okay but really just another picture."[4]

With the surge of interest in film noir in the late sixties and early seventies, *Out of the Past* became a "cult classic"; it is now assuredly an official classic and, with *Cat People*, the most famous of Jacques Tourneur's films — although its fame is of a kind that makes its author almost irrelevant. *Out of the Past* has been tagged as the quintessential example of film noir — that nonexistent thing that could be a genre, or a "generic field," or a set of patternings that can exist in individual films regardless of genre.

Critical writing on *Out of the Past* has tended to focus on its centrality to whatever aspect of noir the writer is attending to. Tom Flinn opens his discussion of the film by locating it within what he calls the "'baroque' phase of film noir." Although Flinn is sensitive to the qualities of Tourneur's direction, his main interest is the "motherlode of noir themes and stylization" in the film. Robert Ottoson considers *Out of the Past* "quite simply the *ne plus ultra* of forties film noir." Leighton Grist examines the film as a typical example of the mythic function of genre: the film's ending "essentially articulates the ideological contradictions which inform film noir, which in turn relate to certain social and sexual tensions of forties America." In its combination of the Hammett-Chandler private-eye mode, the James M. Cain femme-fatale mode, and the Cornell Woolrich "paranoid" mode, Michael Walker finds "a clear indication of [the film's] centrality to the cycle."[5]

Most of the makers of the films that we now call "noir" would have been unfamiliar with that term. Tourneur would, however, have been aware of the historical antecedents of the usage and the sense in which the word "noir" could be applied to a film like *Out of the Past*. We might also cite the Renoir of *The Woman on the Beach* and recall the anecdote about the French journalist who garbled information about *The Southerner* over the phone, changing "*The Southerner, un film de Jean Renoir*" into "*Le Souteneur [The Pimp], un film de genre noir*."[6]

If *Out of the Past* seems in some ways like a typical film noir, this is only because Tourneur's constant preoccupations — the unreliability of appearances, the helplessness of people to resist their obsessions and avoid becoming the victims of an apparently impersonal fate — are also those of the genre. Tourneur places these concerns within a context marked by his realism, humanism, and love for aesthetic fascination and mystery.

The film beautifully captures not necessarily the existing world as we (or a 1947 audience) would recognize it but a universe that seems to possess the wholeness and the incompleteness of the existing one. Locations are used not to give the film a supposed documentary-like quality (as in the Henry Hathaway–Louis de Rochemont films) but to heighten the mood of the film. Bridgeport, consisting of a gas station, a diner, and a law-enforcement office, with mountains looming in the distance, is more like a dream or a stage than a real place. Characteristically, Tourneur stresses the coherence of the space and the relationships between its various parts. In the shot that begins under the director's credit, the camera is mounted on a car that drives off a road to stop at a gas station. The sense of a fateful approach (our being in the car suggests that the driver is stopping here for a more definite reason than to buy gas), the funneling delineation of space, could not have been achieved by the more standard back projection or fixed shot from outside the car; the traveling camera puts the car and the gas station in a dynamic relationship. The ensuing scene in which the driver, Joe Stefanos (Paul Valentine), questions the deaf-mute Kid (Dickie Moore) keeps the road and the mountains continually in the background. When Stefanos goes into Marny's diner, the gas station is visible through the window across the street.

The film constantly calls our attention to the ambiguity of external behavior, a strategy that causes us to perceive the characters as possessing greater depth and mystery than those of most films noirs; we sense that they have thoughts, feelings, and qualities that they hold in reserve. The real purpose of Stefanos's visit to Jeff lies just under the surface of a meeting of "old friends" and can be only obscurely understood by the first-time viewer. Similarly, the menace conveyed by another surprise visit, Whit's to Jeff in Acapulco, is undercut by Whit's jocularity ("I hate surprises myself. You want to just shut the door and forget it?") and by the self-consciousness of Jeff's tough pose ("Let's go down to the bar, you can cool off while we try to impress each other"). Repeatedly throughout the film, elaborately "normal" social behavior hides sinister intentions: for example, the seductiveness of Meta Carson (Rhonda Fleming) on her first meeting with Jeff and her pretense before Eels that she and Jeff are cousins. An exchange between Jeff and Petey (Wallace Scott), his cab driver pal, foregrounds the characters' constant need to wear a mask: "You look like you're in trouble." "Why?" "Because you don't act like it." (It is a congenial touch, and typical of the film, to give the bit player the punch line.) Even such a conventional scene as that of Jeff making a deal with Whit's henchmen (his freedom for the tax papers he has secreted) is subtly written and played as a study in power struggles, mistrust, and shifting alliances, all with a surprising mildness and decorum.

Characteristically for Tourneur, *Out of the Past* expands the mystery of the plot so that the protagonist himself becomes mysterious. We're constantly unsure of Jeff's feelings and intentions. The narrative is organized so that the meaning of Stefanos's arrival in Bridgeport and that of Jeff's remark to Ann about places — that he has been to "one too many" — are unknowable until the flashback. The flashback itself may be unreliable, since the narrator's point of view is subject to the dazzling fascination of Kathie (whom Jeff first sees coming toward him "out of the sun"). After the flashback, Jeff's entrapment coincides with the displacement of his point of view: the shot of Jeff through the gate in front of Whit's Lake Tahoe house marks the film's switch from a subjective to an objective viewpoint. This displacement also coincides with what appears to be a deliberate heightening of narrative confusion. (Tourneur commented, "The script was very hard to follow, and very involved; often in this type of film the audience is deliberately confused, because if your story becomes too pat then it's often dull.")[7] During the San Francisco sequence, the ellipses in the narrative make it hard to determine what Jeff knows about the other characters, what they know about him, and how they come to learn what they know. The displacement of point of view and the complexity of the plot heighten the mystery of the duality of Jeff, with his two names, two roles, and two girlfriends.

Crucial to this mystery is the quintessentially Tourneurian figure of the Kid. He is one of Tourneur's privileged outsider figures, characters who have little influence on the action but who are distinguished by their place in the films' circuit of language and information. Each of them introduces a break or gap in the circuit, either by speaking what has been repressed by the principals (the function of the "cat woman" in *Cat People*, Hi in *Canyon Passage*, Phil the Cannibal in *Great Day in the Morning*, and Mr. Meek in *Night of the Demon*) or by not speaking, thereby forcefully signifying the act of repression. The Kid marks the limit to the flow of information and conjecture that passes through *Out of the Past*. The first question addressed to him, and the first words spoken in the film — "Where's Bailey?" — might serve as a title for much of the action (these words are repeated, by the same speaker, in the San Francisco section of the film) or as a heading for the film's complicated play with locations. From the start, the Kid's "symbolic" presence reveals to the audience "that we are in a labyrinth of reciprocal false communications — the world of film noir."[8]

By general consensus, the term *film noir* refers to a group of films that were

Jane Greer and Robert Mitchum in *Out of the Past* (courtesy of the Academy of Motion Picture Arts and Sciences).

made in America from 1940 (or 1941 or 1944) to 1958 (or 1955 or 1956) and that usually, though not necessarily, share certain narrative concerns, stylistic and iconographic traits, and (for some viewers) a critical or subversive treatment of American life. Let's list the prototypically "noir" features of *Out of the Past*, without analyzing (since this task has been done exhaustively) the significance of the features to the genre or worrying whether they are rigorously described: (1) a first-person voice-over narration (for, at any rate, part of the film); (2) a sense of the inadequacy of American "normal life" and economic and social institutions to contain the threat, or compensate for the attractions, represented by the "noir" world of crime and passion; (3) a preponderance of scenes that take place at night and in cities; (4) the use of certain visual patterns, especially emphasizing the presence of dark areas in the frame; (5) a private detective as hero; (6) a femme fatale; and (7) the entrapment of the hero by a fate that finally destroys him.

Out of the Past exhibits some of these features in what might be called their classical form but uses them for particular artistic purposes. Others it turns against themselves. Regarding first-person voice-over narration, *Out of the Past* preserves the convention of having the hero recount past events — which are shown in flashback accompanied by his voice-over — to another character, in this case Ann while the two are driving from Bridgeport to Lake Tahoe. Since Ann is Jeff's girlfriend, and since the story he tells is concerned with his relationship with another woman, addressing the narration to Ann has a certain shock, which the film does not mitigate, but rather consciously underlines by returning briefly to the car in the middle of the flashback, allowing us to see Ann's reaction.

As for the second feature, the critique of normalcy, there are a number of clear ways, some of them fairly standard in film noir, in which *Out of the Past* "exposes contradictions within bourgeois society." Bridgeport is no sentimentalized idyll. Each of the short scenes in which we see the minor characters who inhabit the town (Marny, the café owner; Jim, the game warden, who loves Ann; Ann's parents; the police) reveals some aspect of the horror of small-town American life: gossip, sexual frustration, the threat or reality of fascistic violence, the abysmal idiocy to which Mrs. Miller (Adda Gleason) is reduced by fear and conformism.

The portrayal of Ann makes it impossible for us to have a merely negative attitude toward the town. Ann is, as Christian Oddos notes, one of Tourneur's strong women characters.[9] She could have been a conventional and uninteresting character, more a symbol than a person, like the wife of Glenn Ford's police lieutenant in *The Big Heat*. Instead, the positive portrayal of Ann (who recalls Betsy in *I Walked with a Zombie*) confirms Tourneur's humanism. She is given the film's most mysterious and beautiful close-up: framed in the side window of the car, serenely looking past the camera at Jeff, whom she has just dropped off in front of Whit's house at Lake Tahoe, she turns away so that her face is in profile as she drives the car out of frame.

Rather than privileging night and city scenes (the third noir feature), *Out of the Past* begins and ends with daytime rural scenes. Their sense of vast space sets the tone of the film and affects our attitude toward the story. The noir scheme of suffocating enclosure and entrapment remains, notably in the San Francisco section, but the film contrasts it with another visual scheme that allows the characters to breathe and suggests their freedom.

Fourth, of the major features of noir visual style identified by J. A. Place and L. S. Peterson in "Some Visual Motifs of *Film Noir*,"[10] *Out of the Past* exhibits several: low-key lighting; compositions that alternate light and dark areas; the use of objects as framing devices within the frame. All these elements are, however, consistent features of Tourneur's work outside the noir genre. They are present to some degree in many of Tourneur's shorts and in all ten American features that Tourneur directed before *Out of the Past*, including the Technicolor western *Canyon Passage* and even (though marginally) the Republic quickie *Doctors Don't Tell*.

It is interesting to consider how these visual elements are supposed to function in film noir and how they actually function in *Out of the Past* and other Tourneur films. The "striking and offbeat schemes of light and dark" that, according to Place and Peterson, go toward making up "the depiction of the typical noir moods of paranoia, delirium, and menace,"[11] are always used by Tourneur and cinematographer Nicholas Musuraca to create moods too subtle and specific to be encompassed by such words. In many scenes in the film, darkness is not a sign of danger: for example, the scene of Jeff picking up Ann at her house and the scene in which Jeff goes into Pablo's (the Acapulco cantina that Kathie has recommended to him as "like a little place on 56th Street"). Scenes are often lit by visible sources — the lamp on Whit's table in his first meeting with Jeff, the "one little lamp" in Kathie's Mexican bungalow, the fireplace in their California cabin — so that the shadows on the set and on the actors' faces and bodies, though frequently connoting danger or uncertainty, belong to the visual realism of the film.

Some essential features of noir style, as defined by Place and Peterson, are either absent or deemphasized in *Out of the Past*. Tourneur and Musuraca never use the wide-angle lens for grotesque close-up effects, nor do they favor close-ups in general, particularly the "obtrusive and disturbing" choker close-ups often used in films noirs.[12] Whereas many noir directors deprive the viewer of spatial orientation by avoiding establishing long shots, Tourneur (like Hawks and Walsh) almost invariably favors such shots and almost never resorts to the shock effect created by cutting between long shot and close-up. Finally, if Place and Peterson's contention that "camera movements are used sparingly in most noir films" is granted as valid, *Out of the Past* must be counted a major exception (and so must the films noirs of Preminger, Ophuls, and Welles).[13]

In the traditional hard-boiled detective story, the reader discovers the action through the perceptions of the detective (our fifth noir element), who remains an observer or "catalyst" (Chandler) of the action, uncontaminated by its nebulous equivocity. If occasionally he appears to lose this status by descending to the moral level of the other characters, this is only to reaffirm his essential apartness. Jeff in *Out of the Past* loses the privileges conferred by this detachment because he is driven by desire. When we first see him, he has already renounced his detective role, which he assumes only in a compromised manner: he betrays his client, Whit, by falling in love with Kathie and concealing her from him. On his second mission for Whit, he is the conscious object of the other characters' machinations: "All I can see is the frame. I'm going in there now to look at the picture." Embedded in the action, he lacks the freedom to move outside it. This embedding takes place not only in the plot and narrative construction but also in the image: Jeff is seen through the gate in front of the Lake Tahoe house and is "framed" in the panes of the glass door of Eels's balcony when he finds Eels dead.

This film humanizes its femme fatale (the sixth noir feature). Ann could be speaking for Tourneur when she says about Kathie: "She can't be all bad. No one is." Jeff's reply — "She comes the closest" — is characteristically hard-boiled and at the same time revealing. Kathie approaches being "all bad." The difference that remains, however small, is the measure of what in her is still human and irreducible to formulae like "femme fatale"; it is also the measure of Tourneur's permanent refusal to judge his characters. (The forbearance the film shows toward Kathie complements the way Jeff moves out of the private detective role to become compromised by events.) Jane Greer's great performance gives the character warmth, sensuality, and spontaneity, making her more significant than the rather limited beauties who luridly bring the heroes of Robert Siodmak's films to their doom. Also, Greer and Tourneur make it clear that Kathie is in love with Jeff and is not *only* using him.

Kathie is at the heart of the mystery of *Out of the Past*, not because we are in fundamental doubt about her motives (which aren't mysterious so much as ambiguous, mixed) but because she is in constant connection with the unshown: absence, repression, the negative, and traces. Kathie is initially an absent object in the film. In the scene in which Whit hires Jeff to find Kathie, Jeff at first thinks that Whit is more interested in getting back his stolen money. Whit speaks Kathie's name only at the end of the conference, almost as an afterthought. (This postponement is echoed in the scene in Pablo's, when Kathie expresses surprise that Jeff has not yet asked her name.)

When we first see Kathie, she is surrounded by an aura of illusion, reinforced from several directions: by the sunlight that silhouettes her, by the presence of the cinema across the street, and by the fact that Jeff has just awakened from a doze at his table. The Ciné Pico sign in the background is part of the chain of references to fantasy, dream, and image-production in terms of which the film presents the relationship between Jeff and Kathie (later, during their underground existence in California, they find a "movie house in North Beach" in which to pass the time).

The scene in Kathie's Acapulco bungalow during the storm, one of the film's privileged moments, is a nexus between desire and absence. Kathie and Jeff kiss; he carelessly throws away the towel with which he has been drying her hair. The towel upsets and extinguishes the room's "one little lamp" (to which Jeff's voice-over narration has called our attention); at the same time, a gust of wind blows open the front door, toward which the camera tracks. The scene then cuts to a shot that pans and tracks slowly along the edge between the house and the woods, before returning inside the bungalow as Jeff shuts the door. The epiphany has a strange effect of rupture, accentuated by the exclusion of human figures as the camera tracks toward the door and prowls along the woods.

In the next scene, of Whit and Stefanos's surprise visit, Jeff tries to obliterate the traces of Kathie, whose emergence from offscreen space is constantly expected by the viewer. Later, Kathie is repeatedly associated with absences in the image or in the narrative: Jeff's fight with Fisher (represented as traces, with sounds-off of fist blows and a shadow play on a curtain behind Kathie); Fisher's murder (a gunshot heard over a shot of Jeff); Kathie's subsequent disappearance (again, the camera is on Jeff, as we hear the sound of a car starting, but the scene then cuts to a shot of the vacated space where Kathie was standing); Kathie's refusal to explain events to Whit over the phone; Kathie's offscreen killing of Whit.

The last noir feature is the hero's entrapment by fate. "My timing was a few minutes off," Jeff says ruefully to Petey after emerging from the apartment building where he found Eels dead. The story of *Out of the Past* is less that of a man in the thrall of a malevolent destiny than that of a man whose timing is off, who suffers a discrepancy between his personal time and the time of actual events. The switch in title from *Build My Gallows High* to *Out of the Past* reflects this displacement of emphasis (with its corresponding philosophical shift). The original title denotes an irresistible destructive power. The changed title indicates an unwelcome movement across time and locates the central drama in the confrontation with the past.

Robert Mitchum, Jane Greer, and Tourneur on the set of *Out of the Past* (courtesy of the Academy of Motion Picture Arts and Sciences).

Although time is a traumatic force in *Out of the Past*, Jeff's attitude to time is relaxed. "I'm sorry he didn't die," Kathie says about Whit. "Give him time," Jeff replies. (This is echoed later in the film, when Kathie says, "You ought to have killed me for what I did a moment ago," and Jeff answers, "There's time.") In apparently dangerous situations, Jeff is in no hurry. When the phone rings in a room he is searching, he merely glances at it, then continues searching as if he can hardly be bothered to hide from the person who will inevitably come in to answer the phone. Later, before leaving Baylord's office with the briefcase containing the tax papers, Jeff pauses to examine a cigarette lighter and light a cigarette with it. Through these gestures, Jeff shows his contempt for time and tries to maintain the illusion that he is the master of time. This effort vindicates Jeff's humanity and, again, takes him out of the standard role of the noir hero. His automatic habit of putting a cigarette in his mouth at moments of crisis (whenever someone dies) has a similar function. The cigarette is a way of playing for time or playing with time, of trying to arrest the rush of time as it appears to leak out of a scene of death, to bring time back to the scene and personalize it at the apparently insignificant level of an object to which he alone has a relation.

The intricate temporal and spatial patterns of *Out of the Past* are less meaningful if viewed in the context of film noir than if seen as a further extension of the play with time, repetition, and absence characteristic of *Cat People*, *I Walked with a Zombie*, *The Leopard Man*, *Experiment Perilous*, and *Canyon Passage*. Like all Tourneur's other major works, *Out of the Past* uses repetition extensively to structure our relationship to the narrative and the characters, as becomes clear if we divide the film's narrative into four parts: section A introduces Jeff in his new life in Bridgeport; section B is the flashback; in section C, Jeff accepts a second mission from Whit and goes to San Francisco; in section D, he again escapes to Bridgeport. The two middle sections have similarities that set them apart from the two embedding parts: in B and C, Jeff ostensibly acts as Whit's agent, whereas in A and D he works for himself; B and C take place largely in cities, whereas A is set in Bridgeport and D in Bridgeport and Lake Tahoe; B and C both involve Jeff's search for lost objects (Kathie, Whit's tax papers), but in A and D, Jeff is the object of searches (by Stefanos, by the police).

Every element in the film has a contrasting or opposing element. There are two "guides," José Rodriguez (Tony Roux) in Acapulco and Petey, the cab driver, in San Francisco; both of them take Jeff to Kathie. Jeff flees after both the Acapulco and the San Francisco episodes; both times, he is followed, and the person following him (Fisher, then Stefanos) is killed. The first and the last scenes of the film are almost perfectly symmetrical:

Beginning	*Ending*
The first shot after the credits is a traveling shot (a1) of a car approaching (b1) the gas station.	The film ends on a stationary shot (a2) of a car leaving (b2) the gas station.
Stefanos, who doesn't know the Kid is deaf (c1), asks "Where's Bailey?"(d1).	Ann, knowing the Kid to be deaf (c2), asks "Was he going away with her?"(d2).
Stefanos and the Kid are filmed in shot–reverse shot (e1).	Ann and the Kid are in two-shot (e2).
After the scene (f1), Stephanos crosses the street (to enter the diner) (g1).	Before the scene (f2), Ann has crossed the street (toward the gas station) (g2).

These elaborate symmetries mark a totally closed world, "real" and yet inaccessible, sealed off from the viewer by its own completeness, much like the remote dreamworlds of *I Walked with a Zombie* and *Experiment Perilous*. Tourneur mediates the viewer's relation to this world by emphasizing the arrivals and approaches of characters and the delays and anticipations that characterize their experience of time: Stefanos's car heading for the gas station at the beginning; Jeff waiting in La Mar Azul and Pablo's; Kathie entering the two places; Jeff, Kathie, and Fisher arriving at the cabin; Kathie (in the background) approaching Jeff and Whit on Whit's balcony. The film also emphasizes certain departures. Tourneur uses no less than five shots to show Jeff and Kathie leaving the house and going to the car in which they take their final drive: two shots inside the house and three outside. This excess of shots (reminiscent of certain scenes in *Experiment Perilous*) corresponds psychologically to our awareness that Jeff is delaying the departure as long as possible: we note the apparent failure of the car to start on his first try, and we also note Kathie's suspicious look at him. (The situation echoes Jeff's meeting with Whit in Acapulco, a scene also marked by Jeff's feigned or real clumsiness — knocking over his glass — and the other's suspicion: "You've picked up a set of nerves since you've been down here.")

Tourneur uses the difference between planes of action to visualize the return of the past. The movement across time enacted by Stefanos in the opening shots of the film is repeated in the shot of Fisher walking up the driveway to the cabin — another figure who emerges "out of the past," from the background to the foreground (where Jeff and Kathie stand transfixed by this apparition). When Jeff arrives at the Lake Tahoe house, Whit strides from deep in the middleground of the shot to the foreground to greet him. Later in the scene, we first catch sight of Kathie as a shadow moving across a wall in the background, as the camera tracks right with Jeff (who doesn't yet notice her) on the patio in the foreground: his past visibly catching up with him without his knowledge.

Like other Tourneur films, *Out of the Past* emphatically uses long and medium-long shots to increase the space around the characters and to suggest social, natural, or cosmic contexts indifferent to their concerns. The many long shots in the Bridgeport scenes are the most obvious examples of this strategy. The film also uses, however, fairly distant camera positions in interior scenes, such as those in Eels's apartment building and Whit's Lake Tahoe house.

Out of the Past also uses ellipsis to create distance. In the sequence in Pablo's, the camera memorably pans from Jeff (at the bar) around the room, returning after a dissolve (which represents both a temporal and a spatial advance) to Jeff, now sitting at a table. Absence is doubly inscribed in this figure, as a circular search that fails to discover its object (Kathie fails to show up during the first night Jeff waits for her), and as the suppression of a linear segment (the quantity of space-time covered in the dissolve). The use of offscreen sound is another type of ellipsis. In the cabin scene, Jeff and Fisher's fistfight is for the most part only heard, not seen (and when it is seen, it is mostly as a shadow play). Similarly, we hear the gunshot that kills Fisher before we (and Jeff) see Kathie holding the gun. Here Tourneur uses offscreen sound for three purposes: to delay information, reinforcing for a brief moment our constant sense that the world of the film is a labyrinth; to make us identify with Jeff; and undoubtedly to avoid showing Kathie in the act of murder, in order to preserve, as much as possible, our capacity for regarding her sympathetically.

The elided, almost invisible death of Jeff is a perfect emblem of death in the cinema. Tourneur shows it with an absolute lack of emphasis. While still driving and keeping his eyes on the road — in other words, while occupied with something else — Jeff struggles with Kathie over the gun. The gun, out of frame, goes off; Jeff's body lurches forward; the scene cuts to something else. The death is "in parenthesis."[14] The moment of death marks the limit of what can be shown, just as, by necessity, it marks the limit of our capacity to identify with Jeff. Since we don't see it, this death has to be confirmed, in the eerily plain high-angle shot of the car door opening and Jeff's body tumbling out.

Within the terms of the film, the question Ann puts to the Kid at the end of the film — "Was he going away with her?" — can't be answered. In the last sequence in the Lake Tahoe house, after Kathie goes upstairs to get her bags, we see Jeff pick up the phone and dial a number. What he says on the phone is elided; the shot cuts to a shot of Kathie upstairs. This shot then dissolves to her coming down the stairs after Jeff has already finished the phone call. The film leads us to infer that he has called the police in order to prevent his and Kathie's escape; his hesitation in starting the car supports this inference, and Kathie, when she sees the road-block, immediately realizes that Jeff is responsible. Nevertheless, by eliding the phone call, the film preserves Jeff's mystery.

The film's last scene, which confuses some viewers, expresses in the most direct way possible what Tourneur thinks about the story. This scene takes place largely under the "Jeff Bailey" sign at the gas station; the beginning of the film drew our attention to this sign: "It's a small world." "Or a big sign." (This exchange between Marny, the cafe owner, and Stefanos manages to suggest, in its dry way, the capacity of language to eclipse the world, or to devour it.) At the end of the film, the sign serves as a metonymy for the dead Jeff, the Kid saluting it conspiratorially before sauntering away (with an ineffable air of bereaved confusion) toward the mountains in the far background — again, big sign, small world. The muteness of the Kid is the silence with which death covers over the meaning of Jeff's life. This meaning is now a secret between the Kid — who stands for the narrative itself, exercising through concealment its total power over revelation — and the audience. The car that disappears in the background carries Ann into a future that is of only theoretical interest to us. The movement of the car stands for the quick draining of time, of life, out of the void of death that is left for us at the gas station, where we remain.

Out of the Past is an endlessly renewable source of cinematic fascination. Although Tourneur himself only belatedly (after the film's release in France in the late sixties) acknowledged it as one of his major works, it forms, along with *I Walked with a Zombie* and *Night of the Demon*, his poetic manifesto. *Out of the Past* contains numerous signs of Tourneur's cinema: the somnambulism of the characters; the combination of detachment and tenderness with which the film views them, preserving their mystery while showing them as complex people capable of a range of emotions and responses; the muted gray tone of Musuraca's photography, filled with saturated areas of black and sprinkled with shimmering dots of light reflecting off water and the actors' pupils; the understated line readings (I think particularly of how Kirk Douglas, as Whit, threatens Kathie and of how Jane Greer, as Kathie, talks to Jeff after she has killed Whit); and the mixture of resignation and lucidity that Jeff embodies and that dominates the tone of the film.

Berlin Express
(1948)

The true picture of the past flits by. The past can be seized only as an image
which flashes up at the instant it can be recognized and is never seen again.

To articulate the past historically does not mean to recognize it "the way it really was"
(Ranke). It means to seize hold of a memory as it flashes up at a moment of danger.

WALTER BENJAMIN, "THESES ON
THE PHILOSOPHY OF HISTORY"

The germ of *Berlin Express* was a *Life* article about an army train passing
through the Russian Sector. Working first with Curt Siodmak, and then with
Harold Medford, producer Bert Granet developed a story and screenplay and
applied to the U.S. Army for assistance in making what would be the first Hollywood feature to shoot in Europe after the war. Granet chose Tourneur to direct on
the basis of his previous work. According to Granet, Tourneur "made no suggestions either about script or casting." (The two became friends, as did their wives,
who accompanied them on the trip to Europe for location shooting. Years later,
Granet gave Tourneur jobs on two TV series he was producing, *Walter Winchell
File* and *Twilight Zone*.) At the insistence of studio head Dore Schary, Merle
Oberon was cast as the female lead, against Granet's wishes. Oberon brought in
her husband, Lucien Ballard, as director of photography, creating what Granet
described as "a two against one situation" that did not, however, leave marks of
disruption on the film: the cinematography accords Oberon no special privileges
(at least no more than those that were usual in glamorizing the female stars of Hollywood films).[1]

The production team spent seven weeks shooting in Paris, Frankfurt, and
Berlin, shipping exposed footage back to Hollywood for processing as they went
along. Shooting in Germany in 1947 was an adventure. Film equipment was so
scarce that Billy Wilder had to wait until the *Berlin Express* crew was finished
before he could borrow what he needed for *A Foreign Affair*.

So that the ruins of Frankfurt would film effectively, on Ballard's recommendation "the shooting schedule was revised to take full advantage of cross-lighting
by the sun." Ballard also made sure that the process shots photographed by Harry
Perry would closely match his own master shots.[2] Although some of the process
work in *Berlin Express* is poor, especially in the final sequence, on the whole the

blending of location exteriors, studio interiors, and process shots is remarkably
smooth, testifying to Granet's intelligent planning (a former scenic designer
in the New York theater, he production-designed the picture, preparing story-
boards for the major scenes) and to Ballard's and Tourneur's concern for visual
texture.

In *Berlin Express*, Dr. Heinrich Bernhardt (Paul Lukas), a famous resistance
leader who is now "head of a fact-finding commission to unify Germany," is
traveling by train from Paris to Frankfurt under an assumed identity. During the
journey, an agent (Fritz Kortner) posing as Bernhardt is killed in an explosion.
After arriving in Frankfurt, Bernhardt is kidnapped by members of an underground neo–Nazi movement. To find him, his secretary, Lucienne Mirbeau (Merle
Oberon), enlists the aid of four of their fellow passengers on the train: Robert
Lindley (Robert Ryan), an American agricultural expert; Henri Perrot (Charles
Korvin), a Frenchman; James Sterling (Robert Coote), a British teacher; and
Lieutenant Maxim Kiroshlov (Roman Toporow), a Soviet army officer. Lindley
and Lucienne are lured to the neo–Nazis' brewery hideout, where they find Bernhardt held hostage; the arrival of MPs, who have been alerted by a spy, Hans
Schmidt (Peter Von Zerneck), dressed as a clown, narrowly saves our three heroes
from being killed. On a train bound from Frankfurt to Berlin, Perrot, who as we
now realize is actually Holtzmann, the leader of the underground, tries to kill
Bernhardt but is himself killed. The last scene shows Lindley, Kiroshlov, Sterling,
and Bernhardt and Lucienne separating in four different directions at the Brandenburg Gate.

The film's heavy-handed allegory, in which each of the main characters
stands for one of the national powers, is partly a defense of the imperialism and
chauvinism of one of these nations, namely the United States. The guileless Lindley gives the Marshall Plan a human face. He is blundering in over his head, and
we are meant to love him because his instincts are good. In any case, the other
allies are represented by duplicitousness (Perrot, who turns out not to be a real
Frenchman), bland stiffness (Sterling), and prim dutifulness without irony or
humor (Kiroshlov). When the film refers to matters outside the scope of the narrative, it is to seal an ideological message about history with the verisimilitude of
fiction. This message is today becoming less and less clear: how is a post–cold war
audience to know what it means, for example, when Lindley tells the Russian
Kiroshlov: "We've tried to understand you. Why don't you try to understand us?"
Or when the latter, having negligently dropped Lindley's calling card, changes his
mind and retrieves it?

The voice-over narration, spoken in tough-guy fashion by the actor Paul
Stewart (who would appear in Tourneur's next film, *Easy Living*), repeatedly drives
home the film's ideological message, limiting the viewer to Lindley's consciousness
and identifying his vision with that of the United States. The narration's domination of the film is felt most strongly when it spells out points that are simultaneously being made visually and through performance, for example, in the scene
in which Lindley, smoking in the train passageway, speculates on the mysterious
Hans Schmidt. "You could be wrong, though," says Stewart, addressing Lindley.
"Maybe he *is* a right guy. Then you find yourself rolling over the former enemy
border, and back comes the doubt. You're in his territory now." Bernhardt enters,

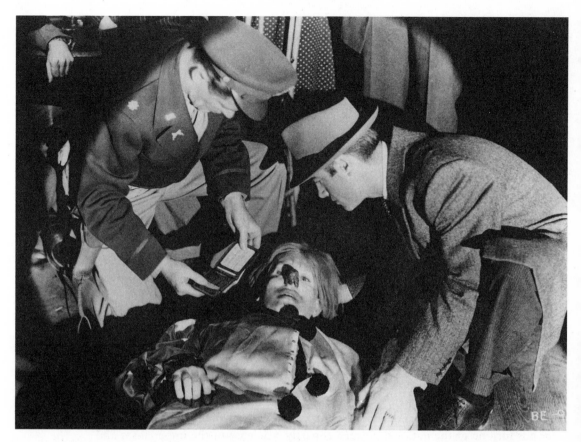

Richard Powers, Peter Von Zerneck, and Charles Korvin in *Berlin Express*: the death of the fake clown.

passes Lindley, and stands next to him at the window. Lindley looks back and forth between the two Germans, both of whom have their backs to him. "All at once the vestibule was chilly, and his own compartment seemed inviting and warm." Lindley leaves. These voice-over interventions flatten the character of Lindley into the nonentity of the second person ("you") to whom the film addresses its discourse, as though it were a training film for American bureaucrats going to assist with the Occupation.

The characterizations exist on the same clichéd level as the plot devices. Robert Ryan is good as Lindley, but it is an unimpressive part. Merle Oberon's Lucienne is perhaps the most damagingly bad performance in any Tourneur film. Her attempts at a French accent ("FAN-atics," "IM-portant," "The Col-o-nel has put you in my sharge") are dire.

The only way to make sense of *Berlin Express* is to see it as three films. The first is an improbable melodrama about a neo–Nazi group's attempt to silence Bernhardt. The second is a documentary of conditions in Germany during the early years of the Occupation, showing the ruins, the informal economy, the ubiquity of military personnel, certain technical aspects of administering the four-zone system; this film retains its importance as a historical document. The third film is a Tourneurian study in doubt, terror, failure, and impossibility; this third film, which we must mentally assemble out of fragments from the other two, is the one that mainly compels our attention.

For a scenario concerned with power, Tourneur substitutes a film about defeat. When Bernhardt's old friend Walther (Reinhold Schunzel) receives his wife's address on a piece of paper (for which he has betrayed Bernhardt to the neo–Nazis), he holds it up to a tall oil lamp on a table. He recognizes the address as that of a cemetery. In an astonishing, tersely Tourneurian shot, Walther turns his back to the camera, weeping, and walks toward the wall, on which the lamp casts his shadow: the shot is composed as a two-shot of the shadow and the man. The pathos of the shot comes from the weakness in Walther's being turned away from the camera and his being reduced as a compositional element to the equivalent of his own shadow.

The film memorably underlines the characters' helplessness: the fake clown (Schmidt) dying from a bullet wound, staggering across the cabaret while the audience, assuming that his weaving movements are part of his performance, laughs; Lindley, trapped in an empty brewery vat, realizing that Bernhardt and Lucienne are about to be killed and that he can do nothing; the horrible death of Perrot at the rear of the train, his body jerking up sharply after being hit by a bullet (that also shatters the glass in a door) and ending up draped over the railing. Tourneur refuses to give these moments any special emphasis. They take on meaning from movement (Walther turning away from the camera, Lindley turning toward it), from camera placement (Perrot dies at the back of the shot), and especially from context: what surrounds them in the narrative space, what attention to them excludes. Tourneur chooses to show not the action in the brewery but Lindley's inability to intervene in it; the clown's struggle assumes its significance from the on-screen audience's misreading of it as spectacle, which ceases only when the inversion of his body reveals his bleeding back *to the camera*.

Accompanying this negation of strong signs is an extreme fragmentation of the visual field, a correlative to the smashed buildings and rubble-filled streets where much of the film was shot. The elaborate opening montage that sets up the premise of the plot moves inexorably from calm to fear, from day to night, in a subtly disorienting way that distinguishes it sharply from typical opening montages in Hollywood films (e.g., Michael Curtiz's *Casablanca*). The possibility of the anecdote, of the realistic detail used for local color, does not exist in Tourneur's work. The shots of people carrying valises in the streets of Frankfurt (the narrator has informed us that everyone here sells things) are dispersed on the intricate surface of the film as casually and as precisely as the shots of the principals wandering through the ruined city in search of the missing Bernhardt: all the parts of the film belong to the same world of constant displacement and mystery. The homogeneity of the film's effects has nothing in common with the flashy eccentricity of Carol Reed's *The Third Man*, another thriller set amid the ruins of postwar Europe. Reed's film is more entertaining and seemingly more serious, but Tourneur's film is more deeply pessimistic and more mysterious.

Michael Henry, one of the few commentators to have focused on *Berlin Express*, rightly sees it as a characteristically Tourneurian work, distilling "the feeling of insecurity that ... derives from the *uncertainty* in which his creatures find themselves plunged as soon as they have been uprooted, placed out of their element, literally sidetracked."[3] As Henry points out, Lindley's average-Americanness qualifies him as a typical Tourneur protagonist: "His simplicity, his pragmatism are easily unsettled by the irrationality of foreign cultures, ideologies, ways of life." *Berlin Express* thrusts this Tourneurian hero (previously incarnated in Tourneur's work by Oliver in *Cat People* and Bailey in *Experiment Perilous*) into a rapidly shifting phantasmagoria that the film calls "Europe." Two dialogues between Lindley and Lucienne interpret this confrontation for us quite explicitly. In the first, aboard the train bound for Berlin, Lucienne talks about being a European: "Because we are more used to the sensation, it is easier for us to control it." "Sensation?" "Of fear, insecurity, suspicion of everyone and everything." (This dialogue echoes Lindley's discovery of "doubt" at finding himself in the territory of his former enemy.) The second dialogue is the couple's farewell: "Where will you be, Lucienne?" "Nowhere for very long. Don't you see, there is nothing one can count on. No one's address is dependable."

In Tourneur's hands, the plot device of Lindley and Lucienne going randomly into cabarets to look for clues has a lunatic appropriateness. As Lucienne points out, "We are the ones who are being looked over." The world of the night-club — with its economy of cigarettes and its tawdry entertainment of tumblers, dancing girls, clowns, and mind readers — is created as definitively and as unforgettably as in a Sternberg or Welles film. The craziness of the scene is reflected in its visual patterning, for example in the stark contrast between the bright stage (we see the light projector in the background of some shots of Lindley and Lucienne) and the dark-lit, mostly dark-clothed audience. Because the scene is basically surrealistic, we accept the coincidence that Lindley and Lucienne have in fact stumbled onto one of the centers of the neo–Nazi conspiracy, whose veil they penetrate almost instantly by spotting a blonde ("Maga the Mind Reader") smoking one of Bernhardt's monogrammed cigarettes.

Of all Tourneur's films, *Berlin Express* is the most immediate and explicit in its relation to the time of its production. He later said, "I think it had some cogent points to make about the changes that were taking place at the time."[4] Today, when the fall of the Berlin Wall has become part of our past, seeing this film made at the very dawn of the cold war is a paradoxical and affecting experience. The aspect of the film that strikes us most strongly is its urgent attempt to freeze time at the crossroads (to use a Tourneurian word) of historical strands that are about to separate, the way characters and nations separate at the end of the film. The not-yet-rebuilt ruins of Frankfurt, where the heroes wander in search of Bernhardt, are monuments of the temporary, photographed at the moment when their meaning was most agonizingly clear — a fragmentary city technically under military occupation but all too clearly uncontrolled and chaotic, under an "off limits" sign, where Germans wait to be permitted to flow back into the mainstream of "human society" and where individuals who stand for the nations that emerged from the war as its "victors" find themselves displaced and perplexed.

Berlin Express has a number of scenes that exist at the heart of Tourneur's universe. Searching through the dressing rooms of the cabaret, Lindley enters a room in extreme darkness, the only light source being an open window at left with a torn, diaphanous curtain floating listlessly (recalling the tattered shade dangling outside the smashed window of the fake Bernhardt's train compartment). A clown appears

Tourneur directing Merle Oberon in *Berlin Express*; Charles Korvin is at far left; Peter Von Zerneck is in background (in trenchcoat) (courtesy of the Academy of Motion Picture Arts and Sciences).

in the doorway, smiling obscenely, taking an ambiguously threatening step toward Lindley. The clown's apparition is an image as sinister and minatory as any in *Night of the Demon*, a film that also features a clown. Asked about the recurrence of evil clowns in his films, Tourneur said: "I must have a sort of complex about that. I don't find dwarves amusing, I don't find hunchbacks amusing, and I don't find clowns amusing. They're characters out of a nightmare.... What's sadder than a clown all made-up?"[5] Later, when the spy Schmidt disguises as the clown to try to rescue Bernhardt at the brewery, he appears beside and slightly behind Lindley; the framing of the two men in a two-shot, as Bernhardt and his captor harangue each other offscreen, is subtly jarring. The scene manages an extreme contrast between the loud voice of the Nazi brewer and the whispered instructions of the fake clown.

The use of moving objects as obstructions or screens becomes a major visual motif in *Berlin Express*. Early in the film, a peasant's horsedrawn cart, its wheel broken, blocks the Frankfurt-bound train. As the train comes to a stop, the shadows of shrubs are projected onto the shiny surfaces of the cars; the same articulation between a stable image and a moving surface of projection will recur at the film's climax. After the cart is moved off the tracks, the train gets under way again, the camera framing a sign that reads "Sulzbach" (the town designated earlier in the film by a mysterious message delivered by carrier pigeon), which the lead car gradually blocks from view. This cuts to a shot of the peasant, watching the train pass; apparently lit only by the moving train, he is gradually left in darkness. In this scene, the stopping and the starting of the train disclose to us its functioning as a metaphor for the cinematic apparatus itself, alternately revealing and concealing objects in the world.

This metaphor recurs in the scene of Bernhardt's kidnapping at the Frankfurt train station. The narration hides the kidnapping from our view by switching to the point of view of Lucienne just before it takes place: she can see nothing because a cart loaded with trunks has interposed itself between her and Bernhardt.

The scene of Perrot's attempt on Bernhardt's life on the Berlin-bound train is the film's most extended and brilliant elaboration of this metaphor. In the neighboring compartment, Lindley and Lucienne have a conversation in two-shot. Between and behind their faces, through the window, we see the struggle in Bernhardt's compartment reflected on the window of the train stopped alongside. The staging is an extraordinary example of a film's ability to create suspense purely through the manipulation of cinematic point of view. At first only the viewer can see the attack, thanks to a fortuitous arrangement of the two trains and the camera. Only when Lindley moves to the position previously occupied by the camera, to have one last word with Lucienne before leaving, does he notice the mirror image of Perrot strangling Bernhardt. Momentarily confusing image for reality, he rushes toward the window — a mistake that betrays the hold that illusion has over all the people in the film: only the disappearance of the "screen" (caused by the movement of the train) frees Lindley from this hold so that he can rush next door to save Bernhardt. (The scene recalls the disappearing writing on the train window in *The Lady Vanishes*, a film that was a recurrent source of inspiration for Tourneur or, at any rate, for the screenwriters of his films: its theme of a clue contained in a remembered melody recurs in both *Circle of Danger* and *Night of the Demon*. Collaborators of Hitchcock worked on the latter two films: Joan Harrison, Hitchcock's longtime assistant, produced *Circle of Danger*; and Charles Bennett, who wrote the scripts of several Hitchcock films, though not *The Lady Vanishes*, wrote the original script of *Night of the Demon*.)

If anything, the total aesthetic collapse of the final sequence of *Berlin Express*, a sequence that consists almost entirely of banal process shots (appropriately accompanied in the score by fragments of national anthems), confirms Tourneur's commitment to *his* film, for by making the ideological message responsible for the mise-en-scène, that is, by erasing everything but the bare form of power, he lets it sabotage itself. The one-legged man passing between the pillars of the Brandenburg Gate in the fade-out shot was perhaps intended by the writers as a symbol for a world marching onward in spite of disaster. Tourneur saves the shot from any such overdetermined reading and makes it into one of the most logical and beautiful in the film by (1) integrating the shot into the film's dominant visual theme of boundaries and partitions, which it completes; (2) putting the gateway in the middleground and shooting it so that the sun is behind it and it casts long shadows toward the camera, which is at a slightly high angle; (3) having the man enter the shot from behind a column at the edge of the frame, so that it is hard to be sure when he first appears; and (4) having him cross from right to left, that is, "backward" with respect to the direction one would expect to be used to connote progress. (Michael Henry sees the one-legged man as "the specter of that cold war falling upon a Europe more torn, more divided than ever.")[6] At the heart of ideological certainty, Tourneur finds ambivalence. This lesson can teach us how to read Tourneur's two 1950s films that have ostensibly ideological themes: *Appointment in Honduras* and *The Fearmakers*.

Easy Living
(1949)

It was incredible in my time: a married couple, not only did
they have to be in twin beds, but there was a man who would
come on the set to measure the space between the two beds.

JACQUES TOURNEUR

Tourneur's next project after *Berlin Express* was supposed to have been *A Woman's Secret*, Herman J. Mankiewicz's abysmal script about the rise of a ruthless singer. On November 19, 1947, Tourneur, who was then finishing *Berlin Express*, let Dore Schary know that he did not want to make *A Woman's Secret*. Schary assigned it to Nicholas Ray, who had recently finished his first film, *They Live by Night*.[1] Tourneur's next project, which proved to be the last under his RKO contract, was instead a football story called *Interference*, eventually released as *Easy Living*.

The history of American film would not have been much different if Nicholas Ray had directed *Easy Living* and Tourneur *A Woman's Secret*. The two 1949 RKO releases have enough in common to be in some respects interchangeable: both have a certain light, glossy, pseudo-sophisticated tone; both are indictments of ambitious women; and both are among the most minor works in their respective directors' oeuvres.

If *Easy Living* is more satisfying than *A Woman's Secret*, this is partly because it has a less pretentious script. It must also be said, at the risk of belaboring the comparison, that whereas Ray's cynical, almost contemptuous handling never gives *Secret* a chance, Tourneur makes the most of whatever opportunities *Easy Living* offers. This is not to suggest that Tourneur is in some absolute sense a greater artist than Ray but to state the obvious truth that Tourneur is more responsive to uncongenial material (from which truth one could argue, of course, that he is the lesser artist).

Tourneur must have felt the uncongeniality acutely. He called the film "a hard one" for him. He added, "I'd never been to a football game, I've never played football; I'm not interested in any sports."[2] In a different interview, he said mysteriously, "This is a very bad film for a reason that I must keep secret."[3]

Pete Wilson (Victor Mature), the star quarterback of the Chiefs, learns that he has a heart murmur and that continuing to play could kill him. He decides to keep his condition a secret so as to avoid losing the respect of his success-obsessed wife, Liza (Lizabeth Scott). Liza, meanwhile, is pursuing her career as an interior decorator with the support of the wealthy Howard Vollmer (Art Baker). Facing the ruin of both his marriage and his career as his fears about his physical condition affect his playing, the troubled Pete gets sympathy from Anne (Lucille Ball), the secretary (and former daughter-in-law) of the team's owner, Lenahan (Lloyd Nolan). Eventually he decides to quit playing and try to fix his marriage.

Like *Days of Glory*, *Easy Living* exemplifies the modest success that Tourneur could achieve with a basically flawed project. *Easy Living* suffers from holes in character development and conflict; adultery is one of the main themes of the script, yet the film is unable, because of the Production Code, to express clearly what the characters' attitudes toward adultery are and whether or not they actually commit it. One feels that the filmmakers may originally have had more to say about the degeneration of Liza, that the mysterious Billy Duane (June Bright), a fashion model who commits suicide, was at one time more fully present in the story, and that Pete's drunken night in Anne's apartment, about which so much is later said, figured at some stage as a scene rather than merely a reported event. The film plays as if scenes were shot and then omitted, which would account for the film's short running time, but an examination of the script material and the Production Code Administration files shows that the filmmakers censored themselves at the writing stage.[4]

The shooting script called for Pete, at the end of the film, to reject Liza at the stadium and join Anne in the Chiefs' office to watch the football game. The implication that Pete is now free to become involved with Anne appears not to have bothered the Breen office, whose main concern over the film was Liza and Vollmer's relationship. (A letter dated June 30, 1948, from Stephen S. Jackson, Production Code Administration, to Harold Meiniker of RKO objects to having Vollmer walk in on a negligee-clad Liza without knocking: "We feel sure that the other action and dialogue in the story conveys this point [that Liza has become Vollmer's mistress] with sufficient emphasis as to be unmistakable, and it is not necessary to paint the picture with so broad a brush.") For some reason, while the film was in production, a new ending was written showing Pete deciding to take Liza back. Their last-minute reconciliation, hastily shot by Tourneur, is utterly unconvincing. There is a tradition of Hollywood melodramas whose narratives pose unresolvable dilemmas and serve up apparently happy endings that simply violate or ignore the premises of these dilemmas, making their own contrivance the final turn of the screw — a glorious tradition from *Woman in the Window* to *Bigger Than Life*. Unfortunately, this tradition doesn't recuperate the ending of *Easy Living*, which feels tacked on, conventional, and unrealized. It is a nice touch, however, to end the film with a shot of the cynical photographer, Dave Argus (Paul Stewart), turning his back on the simulacrum of marital unity with a derisive "Yeah, yeah."

The holes and lapses of *Easy Living* are interesting for what they reveal about Production Code morality and the extent to which filmmakers could circumvent it. The sequence of Vollmer's party presents a slick, amoral view of marriage: Gilbert (Steven Flagg) tells his father, Howard, that Liza has "no talent, no taste," whereupon Howard ponders the idea of having her redo his apartment; Billy Duane flirts unsuccessfully with Pete and admits to Liza that she has been trying

Victor Mature and Lucille Ball in *Easy Living*.

to steal Liza's husband. In the next sequence, a party at the house of Pete's friends Tim (Sonny Tufts) and Penny McCarr (Jeff Donnell), Anne admits easily to Argus that she is attracted to Pete. The generally flippant attitude toward Liza and Pete's marriage is consistent with earlier small hints: Pete tells Anne he needs an advance to go out on "a date" (with Liza, as it turns out); and Pete is casually intimate with Penny in the first scene ("Jealous?" he teases Tim).

The film is so successful at conveying the pervasive social attitude as tolerant of adultery, at least as far as the Wilsons are concerned, that the film's caginess about getting down to specifics is a bit surprising. The scenes between Liza and Vollmer are written, staged, and acted to leave little doubt that she becomes his mistress in exchange for his bankrolling her business, and the certainty of her infidelity seems the only possible motive for Pete's slapping her in the last scene. Yet the script never spells out its innuendo about the relationship between Liza and Howard; nor do they ever have any physical contact.

Conversely, although Anne kisses Pete on the lips in his train compartment on the way to Chicago, the script goes out of its way to make clear that their relationship remains chaste: not only is Pete not shown drunk in Anne's apartment, but when they recount the incident, it is established that they ended up sleeping separately. Of two extramarital couples, adultery is denied in the case of one, although they're shown kissing, and assumed in the case of the other, although they're never shown touching. Given the film's handling of these relationships, and Pete and Liza's own separate-beds sleeping arrangements, Pete's joke to Penny after he learns she's pregnant—"I want to hear how it happened"—can almost be taken as a sincere expression of baffled ignorance or as a commentary on the film's inability to satisfy the curiosity it deals in arousing.

With its other main theme, the precariousness of the life of a professional athlete, the film is on surer ground. The first locker-room sequence dwells at length on the plight of "Holly" Holloran (Gordon Jones), a player whom Lenahan releases from his contract. The predicament of Holly, clearly unfit for any life outside football (he plans, without enthusiasm, to tend bar for his aunt in Hartford, Connecticut), reflects Pete's hidden dilemma. Although the script tries to establish that Pete's troubles are mainly caused by Liza's high living, economic demands, and obsession with fame, the parallel between Pete and Holly lets us infer a more convincing explanation.

The focus on Holly's problem is part of the film's underlying critique. Unlike typical Hollywood films on team sports and more like boxing films (such as Robson's *Champion* and Wise's *The Set-Up*, two other 1949 releases), *Easy Living* concentrates on professional sports as a business; it reveals that money, rather than glory, is the key motive for a team's quest for victory. Lenahan, who owns the team as well as coaches it, repeatedly emphasizes the financial importance of making the playoffs. After the Chiefs lose a game, he reminds the players in the locker room that a win in the playoffs will be worth $1,000 to each of them. During the conference on Pete's declined performance, Lenahan reveals he stands to make $100,000.

The Chiefs have a dubious team ethic. The publicity buildup masterminded by Scoop Spooner (Jack Paar), the team's press agent, apparently has Pete as its exclusive subject. The excessive attention on Pete perhaps explains the resentment that causes his teammates to call him "King Cripple" behind his back and plant a pair of crutches in his train compartment.

The football players' unpredictable life, subject to forces that are beyond their control and that cause tensions within the team to surface, relates *Easy Living* thematically to other Tourneur films. Pete's inability to articulate (or, at first, to recognize) his problem links him to Jeff in *Out of the Past*; his remark to Tim on the subway—"Maybe I'm in trouble and don't know what it is"—dimly echoes the dialogue of the earlier, greater film.

Above all, *Easy Living* is a success of mise-en-scène. After a briskly filmed but vaguely claustrophobic kitchen sequence that introduces us to Pete from the sympathetic perspective of Tim and Penny, the film quickly plunges us into the world of football—not as a release into the freedom of physical action but as a descent into confinement. Stressing the drab, oppressive nature of the Chiefs' surroundings, which he shoots generally from high angles, Tourneur turns them into a trap. The wire mesh in the locker rooms casts shadows that visually underline the scene in which Holly tells Pete he's to be canned. (The mise-en-scène and even to some extent the postures of the actors anticipate the locker-room scene in Ray's *Bigger Than Life*, another film that concerns a man stricken by a mysterious disease and in which, incidentally, a football is a prominent symbol. As unlikely as it may sound, it seems

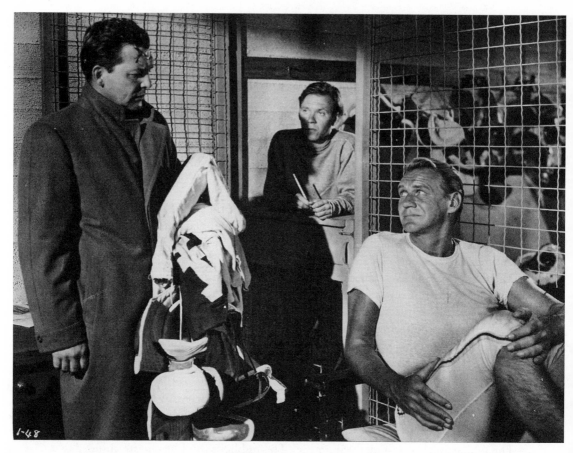

The locker room in *Easy Living*: Holly (Gordon Jones), Buddy (Dick Erdman), and Tim (Sonny Tufts).

plausible that Ray was influenced, perhaps unconsciously, by *Easy Living* in making *Bigger Than Life*: both films also have similar montages of medical examinations.)

The mesh is echoed in the metal gate against which Pete and Liza play their confrontation/reconciliation in the final sequence. At the start of the sequence, we see Liza hemmed into a narrow space between the gate and a stairway — visually, an excessive sign of her capitulation to her husband. After he smears her lipstick with his thumb and walks away, a reverse angle from her point of view shows Pete, in his Chiefs' sweat jacket, hurrying down a narrow, shadowy corridor (which the slightly wide-angle lens distorts into an erratic funnel), lit by a diagonal shaft of light that casts an oblong shape on the floor and the opposite wall. It is the film's most startling shot, placing an incomprehensible message of fatefulness, visual distortion, and fear in the center of the sequence. In a different context, the effect could have come off as directorial pompousness, but because Tourneur has already established a dark mood and texture for the whole film, and because the shot is marked as from the point of view of the distressed Liza, the shot hardly feels overstated. It is typical of Tourneur, also, that the most bravura shot in the film is of a character walking away, a "weak" subject, and is placed as the coda of a scene, as the shot to dissolve away from, a weak temporal position.

As always in Tourneur's films, transitions are the director's forte. A scene in Pete's hotel room starts on an extreme close-up of a newspaper with a headline predicting the defeat of the Chiefs. The camera tracks left to a close-up of Pete, his face diagonal in the frame, harshly lit, looking tense, as the phone rings. The camera tracks back as he lifts the receiver (it is Lenahan summoning him) and then left as his hand reaches for the lamp on the bedside table, which fills the frame as he turns it on. This shot dissolves to a close-up of a film projector in Lenahan's room: the room lights are switched off, and the projector starts running. In this sequence, the smooth gliding of the camera and the dissolve hide a complex chain of meanings and events. Pete's face appears on-screen at the nexus of two camera movements—from the paper and to the lamp—so that not only the uneasy composition of the close-up (and Mature's strained expression) but also its placement at the center of a movement comprising three close-ups combine with the assaultive rings of the phone to characterize Pete as a helpless victim, precariously inhabiting a world dominated by outsized objects. The match-dissolve from the lamp turning on in Pete's room to the lights going out in Lenahan's room continues this theme of alienated, uneasy living: Pete turns on the lamp in an attempt to control his environment, but instead of offering a clearly illuminated space, the next shot plunges us back into darkness. This darkness is immediately punctuated by bright images that enact a compulsive, inescapable return to the past: Lenahan's montage of game footage, highlighting the contrast between Pete's early-season and recent performances.

In another visually impressive scene, Anne finds Pete passed out in the back room of a bar. The scene is shot in very subdued light, coming almost entirely from a large translucent screen that provides an unearthly background to all the shots in the scene. Nor are the film's successful scenes invariably interiors: despite Tourneur's dislike of football, his compositional use of Lenahan's figure and dress (felt hat and long coat) in long and medium-long shots as he walks among his men during practice is thoroughly in his characteristic visual style.

Such scenes show that even on a project that did not engage Tourneur's interest, he was capable of creating good cinema. *Easy Living* is not just an example of a mediocre script competently directed; it is a film that—without, admittedly, entirely overcoming the limitations imposed by the script (and by self-censorship)—exists in its own right as an uneven but imaginative and often compelling work.

Stars in My Crown (1950)

[A]t once it struck me, what quality went to form a Man of Achievement especially in Literature & which Shakespeare possessed so enormously — I mean *Negative Capability*, that is when man is capable of being in uncertainties, Mysteries, doubts, without any irritable reaching after fact & reason.

JOHN KEATS, LETTER TO GEORGE
AND THOMAS KEATS, DECEMBER
1817

Tourneur invariably referred to *Stars in My Crown*, the first film of the post-RKO stage of his career, as his favorite, or at any rate one of his favorites, among his films. He accorded it a special place in his personal myth: the only film that he fought to do, *Stars in My Crown* was also the one that almost ruined his career.

His involvement in the project began when his friend Joel McCrea, who had been cast in the film, gave him the novel (by Joe David Brown) on which it was based. Tourneur "fell in love" with the book and set about trying to get the assignment to direct it.

> I went to see the producer [William H. Wright] at MGM and I said, "I want to make this picture." He said, "Jacques, I'm sorry, it's a B picture, a quickie, and we're going to put a contract director on it." So I went to see Eddie Mannix who was the boss. He said the same thing: "It's a little B picture. We can't pay your price." To which I said to Eddie, "I'll do this picture for nothing." He said, "Do you mean it?" "Yes. Now that's cheaper than your contract director." He said, "I'll call you Monday." Well, he called me Monday and he said, "We're not allowed to pay you nothing because there's a Guild and we'll have to pay you the minimum." So I said, "Fine. Pay me the minimum."[1]

Tourneur's willingness to cut his own rate in order to get the assignment cost him heavily in the long run, he said. Subsequently, studios interested in hiring him checked with MGM to find out how much he had been paid. "Thus it happened that my salary decreased by two thirds. That's how I paid for my desire to shoot this film."[2]

In *Stars in My Crown* Tourneur, who claimed that he worked closely on the script with the screenwriter, Margaret Fitts,[3] dedicates himself to an exercise in an area that at first seems peculiarly remote not only from his personal experience but also from the themes of his other films. Set in a southern town called Walesburg in the late 19th century, the story consists of episodes centered on the figure of Josiah Doziah Gray (McCrea), a Protestant parson, and narrated by his adopted son, John Kenyon (Dean Stockwell). The dramatic highpoints of the narrative are created by two forces. One is a typhoid epidemic, for which the town doctor, "Young Doc" Daniel Kalbert Harris (James Mitchell), initially suspects the parson to be the carrier but which is eventually traced to the well near the schoolhouse. The other is the attempt by a local mine owner, Lon Backett (Ed Begley), and his workers to frighten a black man, Uncle Famous Prill (Juano Hernandez), off his land. Forming a band of "Night Riders," similar to the Klu Klux Klan, Famous's harassers try to lynch him, but the parson shames them into dispersing by reading Famous's supposed will, containing bequests that remind them of the benevolent role he has played in their lives.

Tourneur's enthusiasm for this material may seem surprising to viewers who associate the director primarily with the Lewton films and *Out of the Past*. Once we get past the trivializing view of the film as a "successful" work in its "genre," however, it is clear that *Stars in My Crown* contains not just the same visual qualities (which we would expect) as his previous films but also the same way of organizing narrative and the same point of view toward human dilemmas. Far from being an aberration in Tourneur's career, *Stars in My Crown* bears directly on his main concerns. To show this, I shall discuss the film's relationship to some of Tourneur's previous films, in particular *Cat People*, *I Walked with a Zombie*, and *Canyon Passage*.

Both *Cat People* and *I Walked with a Zombie* touch on the inadequacy of Western medicine (if we stretch the term to include the kind of psychoanalysis practiced by Dr. Judd). In *Cat People*, psychoanalysis is contrasted with Irena's belief in the totemic power of Serbia's good King John. "Not that kind of help," Oliver protests when, after musing that they need help, he catches Irena's look at the statuette of the king spearing a panther. Yet the kind of help Oliver has in mind eventually triggers Irena's destruction, so that both modern science and medieval superstition play the same, annihilating role in Irena's story (as her dream of Judd in armor makes clear). So the film tends toward a merging of the two forms of therapy into something that is not therapy, but a violent exorcism or, as when Oliver invokes "the name of God" while brandishing a T-square, a warding-off.

I Walked with a Zombie tells a story of science and magic in conflict. Magic wins out not because it can offer a better interpretation of phenomena, or because it has greater curative powers, but because two of the film's advocates of science, Betsy and Mrs. Rand, turn to it. Mrs. Rand at first believes she uses the native religion merely to coat the pills she gives her patients, but she finally realizes that she is "possessed" by it. Betsy turns to voodoo after science has failed the test of Jessica's insulin shock treatment. For a while the film seems to present the rival worldviews (or disciplines) as alternatives, in balance, but it eventually shows voodoo engulfing science, just as the ceremonial drums engulf the film's sound track in a siege of the whites' fort of reason.

In *Stars in My Crown*, interestingly, the situation is similar. The parson's religion and Young Doc Harris's science appear to be in balance, a theme announced in the scene of the Widow Smith's death, in which the parson, kneeling at one side of the bed at the left of the frame, balances Harris, standing at right, whereupon the two men are shown separately in contrasting one-shots. Outside the house, the parson tries to conciliate: "You and I are going to be meeting each other like this right along, so you'd might as well get used to it."

The relationship between the two forces proves to be not what it first appears, that of two seeming adversaries symmetrically opposed, balancing and in the long run complementing each other. Young Doc Harris secures a temporary victory over the parson by quarantining him within his house, checking the spread of the spiritual solace he offers the town (though not that of typhoid, the "slow fever" of which the doctor accuses the parson, wrongly, of being the carrier). "This unhappy time was Young Doc's real homecoming," the narrator says over a shot of the doctor's buggy passing the parson's church. The doctor eventually recognizes his helplessness, however, and finds himself in need of the parson. The miraculous recovery of Faith Samuels (Amanda Blake), the schoolteacher whom the doctor loves, ends a conflict whose issue may be said never to have been in doubt. The doctor's science is inadequate because it is based on desire. Young Doc Harris resents the parson with an implicitly sexual envy and compulsively seeks to exclude him. The parson embraces everything and seeks to build an ever larger unity. The last scene of the film shows Young Doc Harris sitting with the rest of the towns-people in church.

Noting that both *I Walked with a Zombie* and *Stars in My Crown* deal with the conflict between the rational and the irrational, Paul Willemen argues that in *Stars*, "the contradiction between the two systems of cause and effect is no longer the traumatic one because there is no longer a relation of antagonism between the two." Willemen adds: "The conflict can appear to be solved within the social order.... [A]s Christianity itself has already (or at any rate is supposed to do this in popular mythology) defused the nature of the conflict, the doctor is able to over-come what Betsy couldn't 'cure,' and to establish his position alongside that of the parson."[4] The film shows, however, the parson, not the doctor, triumphing over the disease when his son establishes that the well is infected; and far from showing the two men side by side, the film's conclusion puts the doctor among the parishioners, merely a member of the community of which the parson is indisputably the leader.

Because of the absence of such a unifying figure in *Canyon Passage*, the community of Jacksonville shown in that film appears in a much less positive light than does Walesburg. Throughout *Canyon Passage*, centrifugal forces dominate: Logan and George both feel driven to leave the town, whereas the tendency of towns to grow more prosperous and more populated is a source of fear and displeasure for several of the characters. The main forces in *Stars in My Crown* are centripetal: Walesburg attracts to it first the parson and then Young Doc Harris; the parson's effort to build community pays off in the end when his service is attended by not only the doctor but also Jed Isbell (Alan Hale), whose refusal to go to church has been a mild running joke throughout the film. The parson manages to prevent the lynching of Uncle Famous by appealing to community ties in the form of concrete objects that have linked Famous to his persecutors. In *Canyon*

Passage, nothing links the members of the kangaroo court to George except money, and his defenders can adduce nothing in his favor except the abstraction of law (which fails to save him).

If *Canyon Passage* is built partly on a set of conflicts between inside and outside, *Stars in My Crown* has virtually no sense of an outside: the film has no scene set outside the town and almost no reference to any activities taking place outside the town except for the parson's and Jed's running reminiscences of the Civil War; the medicine show comes from somewhere else and is presumably going somewhere else after Walesburg, but we know nothing of its past and possible future course. The basic lack of conflict in *Stars in My Crown*, what Willemen describes as "an impression of a more or less timeless, fixed community in near total repose,"[5] explains why the church-building scene in this film is so brief (three shots, which barely show us the construction activity) compared with the cabin-raising in *Canyon Passage*: the film doesn't need to embody "community" in this symbolic activity, since the idea of community is already present in every scene. The joyousness of the scene in *Canyon Passage* is louder and more vividly exciting than the community rituals in *Stars in My Crown*, just as the songs of Hoagy Carmichael are livelier than the hymns the parson favors; but the primitive urge to destruction is close to the surface throughout *Canyon Passage*, constantly threatening, like the Indians in the film, to "break out," whereas the destructive forces in *Stars* ultimately fall under the parson's control.

The opening of *Stars in My Crown* defines these issues in terms of a relationship between narration, memory, and community. Under the opening credits, the camera cranes back from the church over horses and buggies waiting in the main street of Walesburg. The shot, which will be repeated at the end of the film, establishes a closed universe (bounded at the top of the frame by the branches of trees the camera nearly grazes). Most of the people who will occupy our attention during the film are inside the church, hidden from us. It is remarkable that the camera cranes *back*. The beginnings of films are usually meant to take us *toward* some subject, like the beginning of *Citizen Kane,* in which the camera gradually approaches, then enters, Kane's bedroom window, or the beginning of *Out of the Past,* in which the camera, mounted on Stefanos's car, approaches Bridgeport. Realizing a metaphor or model of film viewing, such beginnings inscribe within the film the spectator's initial ignorance about the film's narrative, point of view, and procedures and enact a movement from ignorance to insight that parallels the experience of the viewer.

The backward movement at the beginning of *Stars in My Crown* implies something else. Watching the film is not going to be a progressive enlightenment; one might even say that to begin the film with this shot precludes the possibility of progress. We are simply meant to perceive our own separateness from a unique, whole, and "timeless" (Willemen's word) experience, which can take on these qualities for us only if we perceive this separateness, since our own world is multiple, divided, and transitory. This perception precedes any "introduction" to the world of the characters. Included in this experience of separateness is our recognition of the gatherers presumably inside the church as potentially standing in for us, the audience gathered in the theater to see the film *Stars in My Crown*. Outside the theater there may be cars waiting for us, just as the empty buggies wait for their

Alan Hale, Dean Stockwell, and Joel McCrea in *Stars in My Crown*.

owners outside the church. (This connection is obviously more resonant when the shot reappears at the end of the film, when we are preparing to leave the theater.)

The voice-over narration identifies various characters as they emerge from the church: Faith, her aunt, Lon Backett, Chloroform Wiggins. The narrator concludes: "Walesburg people. Gone now, most of them. And yet as close to me still as people in a favorite story. A story that had its beginning before I was born, on the day the parson arrived in our town." After the narrator repeats the word "story," the film dissolves from one long shot of Main Street to another. In the first, churchgoers on their way home walk away from the camera in couples or groups on the sidewalk or drive away in carriages, passing rows of pleasant-looking houses. After the dissolve, a second, farther long shot shows an older, ramshackle town with few buildings; a carriage is driving, and people are walking, *toward* the camera, and at the far back of the street, we perceive the train that has brought the parson to Walesburg.

This way of leading the viewer into the story has a number of ramifications. We expect that the story will metaphorically reverse the dissolve from an orderly, well-established town to a sparse set of woodframes and that this reversal, the progress we have just seen melt away in the film's reversion to flashback, is due to the parson.

Not only is the story placed under the sign of the past, but this sign is doubled. In fact, we see a flashback within a flashback, the adult John's narration having already established that the first shots of the film take place in a past possibly more distant from the time of the narration than Walesburg at the "beginning" of the story is distant from the Walesburg seen in those first shots. Only the earliest of the three times of the film is clearly situated in history (the parson's arrival took place "in those first hard years that followed the War between the States"). Instead of an irresistible forward drive, time in *Stars in My Crown* is a surface strewn with mythical, emblematic incidents in unpredictable succession.

The marks of forward movement in the film are dispersed erratically over the story, sometimes taking the form of interruptions of narrative events. For example, the subplot of Uncle Famous's refusing to sell his property and the increasing persecution he suffers is introduced in the middle of a scene of Famous and John fishing, when Lon Backett comes upon them; subsequently, the attacks on Famous and his property come as unpredictable, terrifying intrusions into the narrative (e.g., the dissolve after Faith's recovery from typhoid to the "Night Riders" bursting into Famous's house). The film subtly weaves the subplot of the typhoid epidemic into its other concerns, so that John's fateful drink from the schoolhouse well is linked, in narrative time and space, to the Isbells' assistance to Famous, to Young Doc Harris's courtship of Faith, and to the arrival of Professor Jones's medicine show.

Stars in My Crown has a double narrative. In what should be, if we believe Tourneur himself, the most personal of Tourneur's films, he effaces himself even more than in his other films in favor of the point of view of another—in this case, a child. Tourneur said: "I had to efface myself before him. Maybe I effaced myself too much."[6] John's point of view dominates the film only sporadically, however. In the early scene in the kitchen, in which John imitates all the parson's actions, the child is repeatedly tucked into corners of frames that have been composed for adults, and he moves constantly without ever finding a fixed place that would associate him with a definite visual perspective. Sometimes Tourneur introduces a scene from John's point of view so that he can expand from it. Before the attack on Famous's farm, there is a long scene in which John and Chase Isbell (Norman Ollestad, Jr.) lie in the grass and John interprets the sounds made by hounds as they chase a fox. Unexpectedly, gunfire is heard, and the boys go to investigate; the sequence then breaks down into a series of fragmented perspectives on violent, chaotic actions. This fragmentation corresponds partly to the boys' ignorance, so that Tourneur makes us feel the attack as inexplicable and irrational, even though its economic motives have been stated already (in Lon's warning to Famous). In other words, John's innocence is a device that allows Tourneur to slant and underline the narrative. He freely dispenses with the device at other points in the film; for example, the camera adopts a long-shot view to show the aftermath of the attack, a view associated with the adults—Famous, Jed, and the parson—who are surveying the wreckage.

The medicine show sequence is dominated by John's bewildered, uncomfortable point of view, especially in the close shot that tracks back with John as he walks off the stage and collapses beneath it. (The shot is echoed in the sequence of the aborted lynching, when a single close tracking shot follows John as he emerges from his hiding place next to the house and runs headlong into the crowd of Night Riders, one of whom—still in the same shot—picks him up and deposits him against the parson's leg.) The limiting of perspective causes us to see the performance as a mysterious, magical spectacle of deafening noise and inexplicable transformations. As Professor Jones (Charles Kemper) mixes up his "pudding," the camera pans right to left across the awed faces of children all in big close-up, at the edge of the stage, behind the footlights. The camera pans back in the reverse direction after the professor takes the lid off the pudding and reveals a goose. The scene marvelously demonstrates Tourneur's career-long belief in the power of suggestion. Jean-Claude Biette wrote, "The child is poisoned *objectively* by the well water he has drunk and *subjectively* by being called on by the magician."[7] The child's perspective is once again a formal device that enables Tourneur to suspend the viewer's ability to give the scene a univocal reading.

Children figure constantly in Tourneur's films ("Killer-Dog," "The Rainbow Pass," *Experiment Perilous, Canyon Passage, The Flame and the Arrow, Wichita, Great Day in the Morning, Night of the Demon*) and in Tourneur's stated definition of cinema: "The cinema, it's like when you were a kid and you wanted to know the end of the story, it's: one day, in such a place, there was...."[8] In Tourneur's films, children occupy the role of the audience and have stories told to them (in *Experiment Perilous,* little Alec listens to his father's horror stories of witches), or they are the awe-struck spectators of shows that are incomprehensible and sometimes fatal (Karswell's magic show at the children's party in *Night of the Demon,* the cowboys' "hurrahing" in *Wichita*).

The scene of the fox hunt is a kind of metaphor for Tourneur's cinema in its foregrounding of the audience function of children, its separation of sound from image, and its insistence on putting the audience in a position of not knowing. The scene is a variant on the classic Tourneur situation in which a character is placed where he or she can only hear, and not see, something (usually threatening): Alice in the swimming pool in *Cat People*; Señora Delgado listening to her daughter's screams in *The Leopard Man*; Lindley inside the vat in *Berlin Express*. Throughout the scene in *Stars in My Crown*, John keeps up a running commentary on what the noises of the hounds mean, annoying Chase, who repeatedly protests that he can tell for himself what is going on and doesn't have to have it explained to him. Chase is the viewer/hearer who doesn't need to be told because he already knows, but the viewer/hearer in the theater can't know because the signs that need to be interpreted in order to produce knowledge all depend on the placement of sounds in three-dimensional space. A stereo remix of the sound track that approximated this placement would destroy the point of the scene, which is that the audience is not supposed to know and that our ignorance is both represented and recuperated on screen in the person of Chase. This relationship between the viewer's ignorance and the on-screen characters' knowledge undergoes a further development when the Night Riders' guns disturb the field of sounds in a way that John can't interpret, so that John and Chase must get up and run to see. At this point, Tourneur frees the viewer from their point of view.

John's bout with typhoid fever gives the film another opportunity to depart from the perspective of childhood. The parson persuades Harriet, his wife, to get some rest and takes her to her room, which adjoins John's. In a moving scene, beautifully acted by Ellen Drew and Joel McCrea, the film suddenly privileges us to an intimate confession, unlikely to have been made in John's presence. Harriet,

Stars in My Crown: **Juano Hernandez, Joel McCrea.**

exhausted, expresses remorse for having at times in the past spoken sharply to John, and she tries to account for the roles they have played in each other's lives: "He's always been just the same as my own to me. Just exactly the same. Maybe it hasn't been the same for him; I suppose it was foolish of me to think it could ever be the same." As she talks, the pastor tenderly removes the pins from her hair. ("It's almost his only gesture of love in the whole film," Gérard Legrand has commented. This is the closest to an expression of physical, erotic love that the film shows us.)[9]

The sequence is a great example of the importance of lighting in Tourneur. A dim lamp on a low table next to John's bed provides the only light in his room, starkly illuminating the faces of Harriet and the parson and casting their shadows on the walls above and behind them. Everything is oriented toward this lamp — a directionality emphasized by the shadows radiating from it, not only those of the actors but also those of the furniture — and derives from it meaning and on-screen existence itself. Harriet's room too is lit by a single low-placed lamp, which casts the parson's shadow on the canopy that slants over the bed. At the end of the scene, the pastor turns out both lamps, leaving Harriet's room to return to John's; Tourneur insists on showing both actions in the same shot, by having the camera remain in Harriet's room and dolly slightly to show John's room through the door-way. The camera movement links the three characters in an imaginary triangle—with the pastor at the apex above and between the two lights that stand for Harriet and John—just as it joins the two rooms into a single partitioned space.

Although Harriet's lament regarding John takes place out of his presence, it has its echo and answer in a subsequent scene *with* John, becoming integrated into the story that John as narrator is able to tell. After John's recovery, she tells him the story of the "straight stick," her mother's symbol for the "perfect man" whom Harriet despaired of finding among her suitors (and whom she recognized in the parson at first sight); John impulsively replies that he's glad he lives with Harriet and the parson rather than with his real parents. In this scene, Tourneur sets up a group of visual patterns that reinforce its limpid central meaning of family unity. The window in John's room mirrors the window in the parson's room, which we can see through the doorway (in a shot that reverses our view of John's room through the doorway in the scene discussed above). John plays with a wooden puppet that refers visually to Harriet's "straight stick"; swinging on a beam back and forth between two diagonal positions, it repeats, in miniature, the diagonal dynamics of the composition. The entire scene is framed between two identical shots of the church belfry—an architectural confirmation of the triangular struc-ture set up in the scene with the two lamps.

The care evident in the lighting and visual patterning in these scenes is sus-tained throughout the film. Visually, *Stars in My Crown* is one of Tourneur's mas-terpieces, not because it contains many scenes that are outstanding for their pictorial beauty (although the lyrical scene of John and Chase's hayride, with its low-angle traveling shots of tree branches hanging over their heads, is certainly one that would qualify) but because throughout the film camera placement and move-ment, lighting, and the placement and movement of characters in the frame are so sensitively judged, so appropriate, and so eloquent.

Tourneur's tendency to place light sources within the frame is especially marked in the sequences dealing with the typhoid epidemic. The narrator offers a pretext for this stylistic feature near the beginning of this section of the film when he says, "Lights were burning till daylight all over town as the sickness spread and kept on spreading." He speaks this line over an exterior long shot of a street at night, lights visible in many of the house windows. This shot dissolves to a shot of Harriet sitting at a table in the kitchen, coring apples. Two lit lamps, one in the foreground at the right of the frame and the other mounted on the wall by a door at left, form a diagonal that organizes the composition. The parson enters through the door, having returned from the Isbells', where Chase is sick with "slow fever." The parson says that Jed Isbell is scared and adds, "To tell you the truth, I'm scared myself." The parson's fear, which leads him to doubt himself and to submit to Young Doc Harris's quarantine, is the major emotional motif of this section of the film.

The scene cuts to another angle, approximately 90 degrees from the first, as Harriet brings a plate to the dinner table, the camera panning to reframe on her arm movement as she reaches screen right for the lamp. As she picks it up, puts it on the table, and sits down, the camera tracks left with her to reframe her in a two-shot with the parson at screen left, a reframing that discloses the wall-mounted lamp at the upper left of the frame. This shot thus maintains from the previous shot the diagonal relationship of the two lamps in the frame, even though both the camera and one of the lamps are in new positions.

The parson begins, and Harriet takes up, the litany of names of Walesbur-gites who have been stricken with typhoid. He crosses right and turns his back to the camera, saying: "Tomorrow someone else. Unless we find the source." His turning his back to the camera has great force—here Tourneur uses inexpressive-ness (the invisibility of the actor's face) as an expressive device (cf. the scene in *Canyon Passage* in which Mrs. Dance's back is to the camera after her husband's death). The parson's back, in his dark coat, becomes a powerful image of doubt and anxiety, its significance underlined by the camera's tracking forward after him as he walks away.

When Harriet goes to answer a knock at the door, the camera pans left with her to show the doorway, framing the wall lamp in the background at the upper left of the composition. This shot cuts to one in the hall, the camera panning with Harriet (past a lamp in the middleground). Again, the camera movement ends on a shot of a doorway: Harriet opens the door to admit a distraught father who wants the parson to come and see his sick child; but this time the light source is at the bottom right of the frame. Thus the top-left-to-bottom-right diagonal characteris-tic of individual compositions in the scene in the kitchen is repeated across the cut from kitchen to hall.

In the next scene, on the porch of the father's house, the father and the par-son meet Young Doc Harris as he comes out, having failed to save the child; the father runs inside. The doctor tries to stop the parson from going in, accuses him of being the carrier of the epidemic, then brushes past him to his carriage and dri-ves off. Once again, the parson's back is to the camera. Up to this point, the scene has been filmed in a high medium-long shot. Now it cuts to a closer shot of the parson, from the same high angle, his back still to the camera, his body not cen-tered in the frame but toward the left of it, the edge of a plantation house visible in the background. The parson waits for a moment, then walks away from the camera up the street. This scene expresses the parson's self-doubt in purely cine-matic terms: a large, dark figure, face hidden from the camera; the heavy pause before he walks away; finally, the resigned movement with which he becomes smaller in the inexpressively empty frame.

The subsequent scene in his parlor renders the parson's despondency by hav-ing him twice walk out of the frame, first as he tells Harriet that the doctor has "pretty near got me believing" that he is the carrier and finally at the closing shot of the scene, when he announces his decision not to hold services for the dead child (so that he can avoid going out among the townspeople and risking infecting them). In the first shot, after he walks out of frame, the camera reframes a two-shot by following on Harriet's movement, finding the parson again with his back to the camera. In the last shot, the camera reframes laterally (tilting down on Har-riet) but not horizontally, so that the parson's exit leaves the composition precari-ously imbalanced, with Harriet at left and her shadow on the wall in the center background (another example of Tourneur's tendency to use shadows as strong compositional elements).

The climax of the typhoid section, and in some ways the climax of the whole film, is the scene at the sickbed of Faith Samuels. The parson asks Harris to wait outside: "Once you asked me to leave a sick room. Now I'm asking you." Harris, exhausted by despair, obeys, and the parson closes the door. The camera remains with Harris, tracking forward as he walks slowly to the stairway and lowers his head (the shot is symmetrical with the one that begins the sequence, in which the parson enters the house and mounts the stairs). We penetrate the closed door by means of a dissolve. Tourneur puts the camera at the farthest possible distance to show the parson kneeling by Faith's bed. The tableau is unified by the diagonals that are characteristic of the film: the two faces, the parson's turned down toward Faith's as he prays, forming a diagonal that is crossed by that between the two light sources — a lamp at her bedside and a candle burning on a desk at the left of the frame in the middleground. After Faith revives and turns toward the parson, he gets up and goes to the door, the camera tracking forward; he calls Harris, who enters, looks past the camera at Faith, looks gratefully at the parson, and walks out of frame toward her. The parson turns and goes out, shutting the door.

The sequence is based on a pair of symmetrical exclusions. Only one of the two men, who have been presented throughout the film as rivals (for the custody of the town's welfare), may remain in Faith's room at one time. Faith herself is seen only briefly in the scene; for the most part she is a coveted, contested area of offscreen space. The viewer feels not only the doctor's exclusion, when he is outside the door, but also the parson's, at the end of the scene when he moves forward as if to follow Harris toward Faith but merely retrieves his hat before turning and walking out. (This moment, hinging on the parson's recognition that he is no longer needed, has almost the meaning, if not the force, of the famous one in Buñuel's *Nazarin* of the dying woman rejecting the priest's help and asking to be alone with her lover: "Not God — Juan.")

Tourneur handles Faith's recovery in a way that discourages the viewer from reading it as a divine intervention in response to the parson's prayer. One may think of Dreyer's *Ordet* to see how secular Tourneur's vision is. Whereas in *Ordet* the characters are constantly looking away from each other, as if into a space where might appear the God who undertakes, at Johannes's call, to bring the dead Inger back to life, Tourneur's scene is a relay of looks: the parson's at Faith, Faith's at the parson, the parson's at Harris and vice versa, Harris's at Faith, and finally the parson's at the other two. There is no place in the circle of looks where the look of God can be inserted. The scene does not pretend to reconcile a religious and a rationalist interpretation of phenomena but, like the scenes dealing with John's sickness and recovery, is built entirely on the visual patterns among the people involved.

The sequence in which the parson prevents the Night Riders from lynching Famous, another highpoint of the film, is a uniquely Tourneurian cinematic event with an unforgettable sense of bodies dispersed in space, suspended in stillness. To read the "will" (which is in fact, as we discover only at the end of the sequence, only blank sheets of paper), the parson puts his left foot on a lower step of Famous's porch and turns his body slightly to his right so that the paper catches the light coming from the house. This angling of the parson's body in space is, we are aware, the deliberate assumption of a definitive posture, just as in great, historical actions the postures of the actors' bodies take on defining importance. The shots of Famous during the scene are filmed from roughly the opposite perspective, that of the parson (although we don't identify the perspective with him but with, if anything, the house itself, the source of light). Famous stands caught between two hooded men holding him, the three bodies forming a diagonal in the frame; his head lowered, he has his body turned toward the left of the frame, like the parson.

Apart from, and between, these two camera positions that define the space of the scene, the camera picks out the Night Riders in close shots and medium shots without necessarily establishing them in terms of the total space. This is to underline the fleeting, suspended quality of the Night Riders' presence. The parson's voice-off, reading the will, pins the name of each beneficiary to one of these hooded listeners. (This identifying function of the name links the scene back to the one at the beginning, in which the narrator's voice-off pins a name on each of several people emerging from the church.) The camera has the power to penetrate behind the hoods: it knows who the men are and where they are in space, and it can find them as the parson reads out their names. The camera's knowledge is confirmed by various details: eyes lowering, a body shifting, a neighbor turning slightly to look at someone.

When the Night Riders leave, the camera takes up a high angle to show their mass exodus as a single movement, then cuts back to Famous, now seen from the camera perspective *toward* the house, as he turns and walks toward it. The blank pages that John retrieves from the ground as the wind blows them away (cf. papers blown by the wind in *Cat People* and *Night of the Demon*) are what the parson calls "the will of God," an invisible text that yet has a readable meaning (just as the viewer reads recognition and shame on the blank hoods of the Night Riders).

In the final scene Tourneur, ostensibly sealing the perfection of both his film and its fictional community with an image of ultimate unity and harmony, in fact raises a question about the meaning of this unity, through a shot in depth that takes in both Backett in the foreground, grinning with imbecilic beatitude as he joins in singing the parson's favorite hymn, and Uncle Famous, seen through a window in the background as he walks outside past the church. Tourneur chooses the most unexpected moment in the film to underline the historical fact that a black man would not be allowed to attend the services of a white church in a southern town (not only in the era in which the film is set but also in 1950, when the film was released). At the same time that the church excludes Famous, however, it also includes him, by framing him in its window: he too appears to be a part of its unity. On the other hand, the "outside" in which Famous circulates is a larger space that encompasses the church: the "excluded" Famous thus belongs to a space that includes even the locus from which he is excluded. The scene constructs an exclusion that can only ambiguously be called one and that is also a dual inclusion, in which what is framed is part of a more total frame.

This ambiguity is part of Tourneur's contribution to *Stars in My Crown*; the quasi-hallucinatory closure characteristic of Tourneur's films reaches its apotheosis here. Famous's appearance in the window is related to those unaccountable moments, like the hand on the balustrade in *Night of the Demon*, that turn Tourneur's films inside out and open them to an alternate reality. The presence of such a moment in Tourneur's most optimistic film should not surprise us: the parson's complete victory over the forces of chaos is also just a moment, one that the film celebrates but that, as the concluding shot retreating from the church suggests, can never be repeated despite the narrative's effort to freeze it in time.

The Flame and
the Arrow (1950)

You can engross yourself in the *Morte d'Arthur*, if your tastes lie in the least in Malory's direction and, except that finally you may arrive at the conclusion that he was a modest and pleasant gentleman, you need never give the author a thought.

FORD MADOX FORD,
THE ENGLISH NOVEL

Of all Tourneur's films, *The Flame and the Arrow* is certainly the one that conforms most limitingly to the pattern of a successful Hollywood entertainment. The film takes place in 12th-century Lombardy, where the peasants are chafing under the tyranny of the local German ruler, Count Ulrich of Hesse (Frank Allenby). Ulrich's mistress is Francesca (Lynne Baggett), formerly the wife of Dardo (Burt Lancaster), a peasant huntsman. After Ulrich seizes Dardo's son, Rudi (Gordon Gerbert), Dardo becomes the leader of a band of outlaws who lead a Robin Hood type of existence in the mountains, robbing and humiliating Ulrich's soldiers. Dardo kidnaps Anne (Virginia Mayo), Ulrich's niece, and intends to use her as ransom for Rudi but instead falls in love with her; he also takes prisoner a Lombard marchese (Robert Douglas) who at first joins the outlaws, only to turn against them. Dardo leads the rebels in a successful sneak attack on Ulrich's castle, kills the marchese and Ulrich, and retrieves Rudi.

More than any other Tourneur film, *The Flame and the Arrow* is a star vehicle. The film is largely dominated by Burt Lancaster's aggressive, self-confident personality, his toothy smile, and above all, his extraordinary athletic ability. According to James Hill (of Hecht-Hill-Lancaster), Lancaster staged all his own action scenes in the film.[1] Many scenes are merely showcases for the gymnastics of Lancaster and his former circus acrobatic partner Nick Cravat (playing Piccolo, Dardo's mute sidekick); the two men did most, if not all, of their own stunts, and it can't be denied that they put on quite a show. The last section of the film, in which the rebels take advantage of a carnival to enter Ulrich's castle disguised as clowns, is brilliantly filmed. In excitement, contrast, and integration of a wealth of incidents into large, sweeping movements, these scenes are certainly on a par with the swashbuckling setpieces of such films as *The Adventures of Robin Hood* and *The Sea Hawk*.

Tourneur's chief contribution to the film, however, is the highly aestheti-cized, somewhat precious visual quality he gives it. Unlike Raoul Walsh in his adventure films of the early fifties, Tourneur seems to accept action in *The Flame and the Arrow* simply as spectacle and fun rather than as revelation or testing of character, applying himself mainly to creating scenic and atmospheric effects. Wherever he turns his attention in the film, Tourneur finds beauty: the tenebrism of the film's many night scenes, with torches and lanterns invariably placed within the frame; the use of architecture and of the forest as architecture, to create frames within the frame and direct the eye; the romantic portrait of the communal existence of the rebels in their ruined Roman temple in the forest; Anne bathing her legs in a stream. In this film (unlike in *Canyon Passage*, *Anne of the Indies*, and *Way of a Gaucho*), his eye for beauty is a detached, appreciative view rather than one that infuses life and inner purpose into what it perceives.

Interestingly, *The Flame and the Arrow* foregrounds this purposelessness, adopting as one of its explicit themes "the vanity of art" (the title of Jean-Louis Comolli's double review of *The Flame and the Arrow* and *Great Day in the Morning* in *Cahiers du cinéma*). One of Dardo's rebels is a skinner who holds his knife with his foot while he works. Asked why he does this, he explains, "The art of civilization is doing natural things in an unnatural way." The gratuitous, excessive character of culture suggested by this remark is strongly marked in the film, especially in the scenes involving Rudi's dancing lessons and in the decor of Ulrich's castle, decorated with ornamental screens, curtains, and tapestries. The line is also a prospective gloss on the film's last scene, in which Dardo elaborately leaps, spins, and tumbles his way from the top of a parapet to join Rudi in the courtyard below.

The marchese's troubadour (Norman Lloyd) is a marginal yet central character who, like Hi in *Canyon Passage*, plainly interests Tourneur for his charm, linguistic skill, and social freedom, all of which allow him in a sense to transcend the narrative and highlight the importance of art in the film. The troubadour resembles the medieval fools and clowns, of whom Mikhail Bakhtin has written: "They represented a certain form of life, which was real and ideal at the same time. They stood on the borderline between life and art, in a peculiar midzone."[2] Perhaps the chief interest of the film is that it takes place largely in this "peculiar midzone." The troubadour describes Piccolo's unchanging grin, which disturbs Dardo, as "the very essence of the quintessence of the clown's art," stating a theme that we know to be close to Tourneur; the unreadability of invariable appearances (cf. the scenes in which characters dress as clowns in *Berlin Express* and *Night of the Demon*). The uprising against Ulrich's men in the last section of the film, in which the troubadour plays a key role, is hidden by, but becomes indistinguishable from, the ongoing carnival. The rebels' choice of weapons — pots, pans, chairs, a cushion, logs — clearly establishes the popular nature of the revolt.

If the main impulse of *The Flame and the Arrow* is escapist, Waldo Salt's script (the last for which he received credit before the blacklist kept his name off Hollywood screens) is at least intelligent escapism. The story is identical in some respects to that of *Great Day in the Morning*. Each film traces how the hero comes to renounce his extreme individualism to associate himself with a minority rebel movement (in a similar progression, in *Way of a Gaucho*, Martín eventually realizes the harm that his refusal to compromise has done to those close to him). "I don't depend on anyone, why should anyone depend on me?" Dardo asks near the beginning of the film. The action repeatedly belies his claim to independence — early in the film,

Nick Cravat, Virginia Mayo, Robert Douglas, and Burt Lancaster in *The Flame and the Arrow.*

he is shot in the back by an arrow, which the apothecary must remove — and Dardo has little difficulty in renouncing it. In a series of double entendres as he is about to fake his own hanging (e.g., "A man who knows what he's dying for only *seems* to die"), he passes on to his son, Rudi, the lesson of the importance of the greater good.

The relationship between Dardo and Rudi is central to *The Flame and the Arrow* (this is clear at the end of the film, when the reuniting of the two is an emotional climax, in comparison with which Dardo's embrace of Anne seems an afterthought). Similarly, *Great Day in the Morning* focuses on Owen Pentecost's relationship with a boy whom he takes under his wing after killing the boy's father. In *The Flame and the Arrow*, the themes of the boy's upbringing and of the man's renunciation of false independence are smoothly woven into the action: early in the film, for example, Dardo interrupts Ulrich's procession to edify Rudi with a look at his mother (who left Dardo for Ulrich); the fake hanging is a climactic moment in the plot, as well as a turning point in Dardo's character development and another educational opportunity for Rudi. The same two themes in *Great Day in the Morning* throw the film off balance because they are unintegrated and unmotivated. This disjointed, unresolved aspect gives, however, an interesting undercurrent of obsession to Pentecost's relationships with the boy, with the southern cause, and with the two women in the film. *The Flame and the Arrow* suffers from

The Flame and the Arrow: Nick Cravat and Burt Lancaster.

the absence of such an undercurrent: Dardo's difficulties are virtually all external, and the film never requires him to face challenges other than physical ones.

The film comes closest to an exception to this overall lightness in the night-time love scene in the forest between Dardo and Anne. After striking the iron collar from her neck, signifying that she will soon be free to go, Dardo walks away to a ruined parapet in the background and looks out pensively at the view of mountains and forest. Anne follows him. The dialogue concerns the uncertain state of affairs at this point in the story (Piccolo hasn't returned from a mission) and gradually bears down on Dardo's conflict over his attraction to and his distrust of Anne (a conflict that is both class-based and misogynist). A close-up of Dardo shows him in profile, backlit, so that the camera side of his face is dark. This simple shot disturbs the amiable flow of the film and suddenly changes our view of Dardo, prompting us to see him as troubled — divided, in the literal sense of the image (which splits him into light and dark sides) — by his love for Anne. Immediately the character struggles to reassert his mastery over desire and the narrative: there is a frontal close-up of Dardo as he rejects Anne's love as "a lie" and accuses her of trying to seduce him in order to improve her position (as she tried to do in an earlier scene). The staging, lighting, and narrative situation recall a scene between Jeff and Kathie in the San Francisco section of *Out of the Past* and will basically be repeated in love scenes in *Appointment in Honduras* and *Great Day in the Morning*. In all these films, Tourneur represents the disturbing effect of eroticism by moving the characters through alternately light and dark areas of the screen, creating a visual imbalance that registers the insecurity of the characters.

The Flame and the Arrow brings together several of Tourneur's visual preoccupations. In a startling shot, the camera tracks forward on the back of a soldier as he walks past a wall in the village square on which are projected the shadows of Papa Pietro (trussed up by his hands on a gallows) and a dangling noose. The noose recalls the shade pull ring in the shot of Jeff through the balcony window in *Out of the Past*, while the framing, in which a man's back and a shadow are equally balanced, is reminiscent of the shot in *Berlin Express* of Walther turning toward the wall where his shadow is projected.

The opening sequence of the film is a lesson in Tourneurian cinema: the first shot after the credits cranes slowly up toward a group of peasants meeting clandestinely under an arch in the forest at night. This shot dissolves to a closer medium shot that uses the arch as a frame within the frame, the camera tracking back slightly in a circular manner that subtly reflects the shape of the arch. The dissolve causes the torch burning at the right of the frame in the second shot to seem to burst into flame before our eyes as it is superimposed over the dark space at the right of the first shot. The third shot is a closer two-shot that dollies back from Nonna Bartoli (Alice MacMahon) and Papa Pietro; in the background, a man picks up a torch and lowers it out of frame, extinguishing it. The three shots enact a movement, from dark to light to dark again, that is an emblem of the entire film; the camera movements subtly declare the world we see as one of surprise and mystery (note how the group suddenly comes into view in the first shot and how the dollying in the last shot seems to form, with the extinguishing of the light, a single movement).

Probably the most striking scene is the climactic duel between Dardo and the marchese in Ulrich's castle. A superior swordsman, the marchese has Dardo overmastered until Dardo cuts down a chandelier and slams a door, throwing the corridor into darkness. Vibrant up to now with the clash of swords and tense tracking shots, the scene suddenly becomes hushed and full of doubt. Over a high angle on the marchese, on his guard and silhouetted against an oblong of light on the floor, we hear Dardo whispering: "Now, Marchese, we're in the dark, where a sword is just a long knife. And hunters know all about knives. You can't see me, Alessandro, but I can see you." Adopting the marchese's point of view, the camera slowly pans the dark, empty space of the corridor and retreats slightly. The scene cuts back to the marchese just before Dardo leaps into the shot and pushes him out of frame. The camera tilts down to the oblong of light on the floor, crossed by a fallen torchère. At the sound of an offscreen blow, the scene cuts to a different high angle on the same area: the marchese falls, dead, into the oblong of light. It is a brief scene of four shots, but four shots that affirm the rigor and invention of Tourneur's cinema.

The Flame and the Arrow marks a turning point in Tourneur's career. His previous feature films were all in black-and-white except for *Canyon Passage*; all but *Experiment Perilous*, *Canyon Passage*, and *Stars in My Crown* had contemporary settings. *Flame* is the first of the films that would make up the preponderance of the rest of Tourneur's filmography: color films set in the more or less distant past. The switch to escapist fare obviously reflects trends in Hollywood production and cannot reasonably be attributed to Tourneur's choice or interests, especially since we have it on his own testimony that he never turned down a script (except *Devil's Doorway*, made by Anthony Mann in 1950, the year of *The Flame and the Arrow*). A similar movement from contemporary to period subjects marks the fifties films of (for example) Raoul Walsh, Henry Hathaway, Delmer Daves, and Allan Dwan — all directors who, like Tourneur, were not specialists in any particular genre but who tackled virtually everything and who, again like Tourneur, give the impression of having been willing to do anything assigned to them rather than imposing a pattern on their careers through choice of subject or through the projection of a distinct directorial personality (as did John Ford, Alfred Hitchcock, and George Cukor, as well as writer-directors such as Joseph L. Mankiewicz and Billy Wilder).

Apart from *Night of the Demon*, Tourneur's fifties work has attracted little attention, at least in the United States. This neglect is due in part to the relative critical disrepute and commercial insignificance of the categories in which most of this work was done: the exotic "adventure" film (*Anne of the Indies, Way of a Gaucho, Appointment in Honduras, Timbuktu*); the low- to medium-budget Western (*Stranger on Horseback, Wichita, Great Day in the Morning*). It is also due in part to the understated, somewhat paradoxical manner in which Tourneur approaches these genres. *The Flame and the Arrow*, although the most popular of Tourneur's "escapist" films, is not a good representative of them because its mise-en-scène puts itself at the service of escapism and does not seek to elicit a complex response. The film contains, however, themes and devices that anticipate the later films: as in *Anne of the Indies*, the main character dictates a message to the enemy; like *Way of a Gaucho*, the film orients itself on both country-city and class oppositions; its similarities to *Great Day in the Morning* have been noted. In the overall course of Tourneur's work, *The Flame and the Arrow* is the first of a pair of transitional films: it looks forward to Tourneur's future, whereas the next film in the pair, *Circle of Danger*, looks back to his past.

Circle of Danger
(1951)

There are immense and flagrant dangers that are but sordid and squalid ones, as we feel, tainting with their quality the very defiances they provoke; while there are common and covert ones, that "look like nothing" and that can be but inwardly and occultly dealt with, which involve the sharpest hazards to life and honor and the highest instant decisions and intrepidities of action.

HENRY JAMES, PREFACE TO
THE AMERICAN

Circle of Danger, Tourneur's first foray into the world of independent production, was made by a British company, David E. Rose's Coronado Productions, under a distribution setup with Eagle-Lion. Joan Harrison, formerly an assistant to Alfred Hitchcock, was the producer; her previous film, also for Coronado, was Robert Montgomery's *Eye Witness* (1950). Mystery writer Philip McDonald wrote the script, which was based on his own novel, *White Heather* (under which title the film went into production); it is curious to note that Maurice Tourneur had made a film called *The White Heather* in 1919, on an unrelated subject.

Clay Douglas (Ray Milland) sells his share of a Florida tungsten-salvage operation to finance a trip to England. His goal is to investigate the death of his brother, Hank, who died under mysterious circumstances while taking part in a British Army commando mission in Brittany in 1944. Douglas tracks down and interviews former members of Hank's commando unit and meanwhile becomes involved with Elspeth Graham (Patricia Roc), a writer and illustrator of children's books. Douglas eventually determines that Hank was killed by the commando leader, Major Hamish McArran (Hugh Sinclair). Confronting Hamish with his knowledge, Douglas learns that Hamish was forced to kill Hank to keep the latter from endangering the mission through his recklessness and disobedience.

Circle of Danger has received infrequent and mostly dismissive notice. However much goodwill one brings to viewing the film, one's interest in its leisurely development undergoes some strain, especially in its second half. The motif of Douglas's arriving late for dates with Elspeth becomes tiresome (as scenes begin repetitively on dissolves to Elspeth drinking tea on the sofa or reading a newspaper). Too bland and lacking in suspense to reward the casual viewer, *Circle of Danger* is nonetheless fascinating to anyone interested in Tourneur. It has that strangely anticipatory atmosphere characteristic of his films — a quality underlined early in the film when Elspeth stops Douglas, during their walk to her house at dusk, to have him *listen to* the landscape. Douglas comments, "It's almost as if everything was waiting." This sequence is one of several in the film in which characters are shown full-figure and backlit, a representational strategy that assures us of being in the Tourneur universe: Douglas's dark figure entering the hallway of the McArran house and lit from the open door in the background; the identical shot a little later of Hamish; Douglas and Elspeth's first kiss in a doorway in her London flat. The least that can be said for *Circle of Danger* is that it *looks* a lot better than the average British film of the period: the lighting, camera movements, decor, and compositions all show great care.

In *Circle of Danger*, Tourneur meditates on the sources of his art: on the power of the cinema to evoke an atmosphere of reality with light, with the turns and looks of people, with sound. Early in the film, we join Douglas, Elspeth, Hamish, and Hamish's mother in the parlor as they listen to the end of a recording of Wagner (apparently a preoccupation of Hamish's). The music and the pause of silence following it punctuate, and therefore heighten our awareness of, the quietness with which the actors speak to each other throughout the film. As in *Out of the Past*, the understated delivery of dialogue in *Circle of Danger* sets a socially normal context for a story concerned with hidden motives and unavowable actions. The troubled mood palpable in much of the film comes partly from our sense of the possible duplicity of the people Douglas encounters but also from our sense that this duplicity is a reflection of his own hidden trouble. Tourneur suggests this by repeatedly showing people looking emphatically offscreen at Douglas: his partner, Sammy, in the first sequence; the children in Mrs. McArran's choir; Mrs. McArran and Hamish in the scene preceding the denouement.

From the outset of *Circle of Danger*, Tourneur is clearly as much concerned with the mystery of his protagonist as with that of the event the protagonist is investigating. The beginning of the film is characteristic in that nothing begins — Douglas's initial search (for tungsten) is simply diverted toward a new, unnamed object. As in *I Walked with a Zombie*, *Out of the Past*, and *Appointment in Honduras*, we have the feeling of having arrived late to witness a process already about to be concluded. The early scenes of *Circle of Danger* set up Douglas as wrapping himself and his motives in a mystery that he only reluctantly allows others to penetrate. In the first sequence (set on a ship), Sammy wonders why Douglas has decided to sell out of their business just after they've made their first big strike: "You're not gonna tell me it's a dame!" Turning away from the mirror that has been reflecting his image to us, Douglas replies, "Sammy, I ain't gonna tell you anything." When he arrives in England, Douglas reluctantly shares parts of his personal history and motives with others (the colonel, Pape Llewellyn [John Bailey]) to persuade them to give him information. Later, Douglas discloses part of the truth, but not all of it, to Elspeth, confiding in her his guilt over having instilled in his younger brother an excessive ambitiousness. She recognizes, however, that "there's something else" he hasn't told her — a "horrible" secret that's making him "cheap" and "low."

The film's detached, ambiguous view of Douglas disconcerts us. Such a character — a suave entrepreneur who exploits everyone he meets for his own unrevealed purposes — could be played as likable but weak (and, like Jerry in *The*

Marjorie Fielding, Ray Milland, and Patricia Roc in *Circle of Danger*.

Leopard Man, in need of getting over his need to hide himself), or as selfish and unscrupulous (like Pentecost in *Great Day in the Morning*), or as simply carrying out a mission (like Corbett in *Appointment in Honduras*). By taking the third approach, the most open-ended and ambivalent of all, Tourneur enables himself to show the character in different aspects, from various distances, without having to explain to the audience (as he would have to in a "psychological" film) what these shifts and changes mean. For example, Ray Milland is sometimes allowed to be too aggressive or smug, as in the scene in which he first meets Sholto Lewis (Marius Goring) and is instantly, visibly, put off by the fey mannerisms of the commando-turned-ballet-director. The film never resolves its view of Douglas, never makes it clear how the viewer is supposed to look at him.

　　Circle of Danger never establishes whether it addresses an English or an American viewer. This question hardly arises in watching *Berlin Express*, the other Tourneur film that defines itself as belonging to the immediate postwar period and that constantly refers to the war. The running joke (if it can be called that) of Douglas's confusion over cab fares would seem implicitly to address a viewer familiar with British currency, but the film's hint that Elspeth is drawn to Douglas partly because he is American would seem designed to flatter an American audience. Elspeth's nostalgia for American voices (like the actress Patricia Roc — *Canyon Passage*'s Caroline — Elspeth spent some time in America) is complex, since Milland, born in Wales but Americanized, still has a trace of the British Isles in his accent. A certain irony can be seen here (could Elspeth be nostalgic for *his* nostalgia?), but we aren't sure where it comes from and how much the film takes responsibility for it.

Regardless of a superficial Hitchcockian-Langian flavor doubtless due to Milland's presence, the film that *Circle of Danger* is closest to in spirit is Renoir's *The River*. Douglas's search for the truth about his brother's death is, like the Indian sojourn of Renoir's Captain John, unconsciously a search for serenity. *Circle of Danger* further resembles *The River* in its concern with the confrontation of cultures. Of the various Tourneur films that treat the dualism of Europe and America, *Circle of Danger* does so in the most dialectical way. Douglas's ancestry is Scottish, as Angus the coachman reminds him when he first comes to Scotland: "You may think you're an American but you're not. You're a black Douglas man if ever I saw one." In his feelings toward Scotland, Douglas oscillates between the familiar and the strange: "I keep thinking this country's like some place I've been before. Then I find it isn't." His relationship with Elspeth is both an opportune flirtation and a longing to reclaim continuity with the past, with history. (Uncannily sensitive, perhaps, to Douglas's dark, enigmatic side, Elspeth is obsessed with researching and recounting the historical perfidies committed by members of the Douglas family toward Mary, Queen of Scots.)

Drifting with Douglas from one encounter to the next, the narrative devotes an unusual amount of time not only to investigations that lead nowhere but also to idle conversations on subjects peripheral to the ostensible purpose of his quest. The drifting (also a characteristic of the mise-en-scène, for example in the elegant long-take camera movements in the scene at the canal lock) tells us what we might have inferred from the delay and difficulty the narrative and Douglas have shown in articulating their purpose: that the object of Douglas's search isn't an external one and can't be located. *Circle of Danger* is unusually clear in reducing the quest for truth that explicitly preoccupies most mystery stories to an implicitly endless seeking after a succession of lost objects (tungsten, the members of the commando unit, Elspeth) and to an acquisitive impulse seemingly capable of functioning regardless of object: Hank's fatal passion for "souvenirs" (e.g., the wristwatch that Bert Oakshott [Michael Brennan] displays to Douglas at the Covent Garden lunch stand), echoed in Clay's asking Hamish about "mementoes."

The folk tune that, from its use in Sholto Lewis's ballet, leads Douglas to the truth is also a souvenir, one that extends the problem of possession into a problem of origin and authorship. (The scene of the cast party after the ballet refers to the psychoanalytical dimension of this question: Sholto, asked how he came to think of a certain effect, replies, "That I dare not tell, not even to my psychiatrist.") Unconvincing as a plot gimmick, the tune interestingly hints at the way guilt in the film proves to be problematized and dispersed. The tune is apparently part of a collective cultural memory: various characters find themselves humming it. Hamish is neither the author/originator of the tune nor simply — that is, without impersonal justification — Hank's murderer; nor can Clay be blamed simply for his brother's reckless ambition and individualism.

In the film's magnificent final section, in which Douglas returns to Scotland to confront Hamish, all the ambiguity that has been dispersed over the film suddenly becomes concentrated: in the looks exchanged between the two men in the

Douglas (Ray Milland) makes a point to his tungsten-salvage partner in *Circle of Danger*.

house; in Elspeth's look as she witnesses this exchange; and in the beautiful figures-in-a-landscape mise-en-scène of Douglas's encounter with Hamish and Sholto — one of Tourneur's finest and most unheralded visual triumphs. Douglas and Hamish, sitting on the heath, where they have gone on Douglas's suggestion to settle their quarrel in private, are joined by Sholto, who after sizing up the situation takes Douglas's rifle and walks away screen right. The scene cuts from Sholto walking with the rifle to a reverse angle on Hamish and Douglas: Hamish has his rifle across his knee, and Douglas, screen right, is unarmed. The camera angle translates Douglas's vulnerability into the instantly readable terms of an implacable spatial logic: by aiming at the two men from the direction in which Sholto has moved, the camera implicitly closes off the space available to Douglas on the right side, and he is bounded on the left by Hamish. This angle cuts to a shot that expresses the same concept in a single composition: from over Hamish's shoulder, the camera frames Douglas between Hamish in the foreground and Sholto, in the far background, calling for Douglas to join him. Douglas walks toward Sholto, the camera tracking laterally alongside him.

Sholto's account of the "execution" of Hank forces Douglas to acknowledge the impossibility of avenging his brother's death. Douglas, who throughout the film has been reluctant to articulate his desire, finds his reluctance vindicated in an unexpected sense: what he thought he desired all along — the truth of his brother's death — turns out to be something he can possess only at the cost of his previous certainty. So Douglas walks away without speaking, just as Holden does at the end of *Night of the Demon*, another prisoner of a knowledge that can't be articulated.[1] The end of the film leaves us with a sadness (which also recalls the ending of *I Walked with a Zombie*) all the more profound for being covert. It is hard to think of another film, or another style of cinema, in which so much can be expressed simply in a character's walking away.

This is not, in fact, the final image of *Circle of Danger*, although it should be; there follows Douglas's last-minute reconciliation with the estranged Elspeth and their departure together in Douglas's car. Like another final sequence that shows Ray Milland and a woman drive off together, that of Lang's *Ministry of Fear*, the conclusion of *Circle of Danger* hangs so limply at the end of the film that it seems about to drop off by itself. We must be satisfied to infer the ideal film from the flawed film that exists. Along with *Berlin Express* and *Great Day in the Morning*, *Circle of Danger* is one of those imperfect works whose imperfections aren't so much transcended as ignored by the director, who patiently dedicates himself to realizing *another* film.

Anne of the Indies (1951)

There is a sort of mysterious and aristocratic pleasure for him who no longer has either curiosity or ambition, to contemplate, lying in the gazebo or leaning on his elbows over the pier, all these movements of those who leave and those who return, of those who still have the force to want, the desire to voyage or to enrich themselves.

CHARLES BAUDELAIRE, "LE PORT"

Tourneur's next assignments were two films in a row for 20th Century–Fox, *Anne of the Indies* and *Way of a Gaucho*. Both films are in Technicolor and have unusual themes: *Anne* is a pirate film in which the pirate captain is a woman; *Gaucho* is a 19th-century story of the Argentine pampas. Neither film has received its due from critics, and neither, as of this writing, is available on video in the United States (nor are *Canyon Passage* and *Wichita*). Andrew Sarris belittlingly calls them "two misguided Fox projects made in the last hectic days before Cinemascope," acknowledging that they "come off much better than anyone had any right to expect despite their intransigent exoticism."[1] Sarris is perceptive in situating the two films at the end of an era, but Cinemascope itself is a sign of the end of the era in which *Anne* and *Gaucho* arrive so late, unheralded and slated for oblivion. This is the era of the classical Hollywood genre film. We are in 1951-52. Ten years later, a major studio like Fox wouldn't have backed such projects. If *Anne* and *Gaucho* could have been made at all in the sixties, they would have been independent productions, probably shot in Spain or Italy and directed by Andre De Toth or Hugo Fregonese (or by Riccardo Freda or Domenico Paolella).

Tourneur deserves at least two places in film history. He has a certain renown as the master of subtle, Lewtonian terror and the related genre of film noir. But he is also the (largely unrecognized) master of genre cinema *in general,* master of all genres that can be identified and exploited commercially (as well as of some that can't: *Way of a Gaucho* is no Western, although it has been called one, nor does it fit in any other category — it really requires its own category). He assumed this role in the period when Hollywood devoted itself for the last time to satisfying the public's demand for these genres, before turning the job over to TV and the European coproduction.

Tourneur's willingness to take on various genres was one of his main principles; it was, one might say, the political part of his aesthetic:

> In Hollywood, I always systematically accepted all the scripts
> that were offered me, whatever they were.... [H]ow can one
> know what one is going to get out of a script? One could
> very well make a mistake and judge oneself incapable of
> handling such a type of story well or, on the other hand,
> [capable] of succeeding with some other type. Do you really
> know your sensibility so well that you can affirm that it will
> cause you to succeed with this scene rather than another?
> You must be more modest, try to handle as well as possible
> what you are given and let your subconscious work. It could
> well be that unconsciously you have an affinity with a cer-
> tain type of narratives and stories, while you think the oppo-
> site.... [I] succeeded with certain things of which I would
> have believed myself incapable. This attitude forces you to
> be open, receptive to all genres, to all forms of narration. It's
> a way of refusing to specialize.[2]

Of the films of the nonspecialist Tourneur, *Anne of the Indies* is perhaps the most powerful. Viewers who know Tourneur only from the Lewton films and *Out of the Past* may have difficulty finding the director's personality in *Anne of the Indies* (as in *Stars in My Crown*). It is unimportant, however, to link *Anne of the Indies* thematically to the rest of Tourneur's films (although this is easily done), just as it is trivializing to see the film only as a modestly successful exercise in the adventure genre. I prefer to see in *Anne of the Indies* a definition of Tourneurian mise-en-scène, a choreography of movements that annul each other, a passionate and bleak study of disappearance and impermanence.

Based on a *Saturday Evening Post* story by Herbert Ravenel Sass, *Anne of the Indies* was originally a Walter Wanger project.[3] Having failed to develop a satisfactory treatment, Wanger sold his rights in the story to 20th Century–Fox. In August 1950, Arthur Caesar wrote a new script, around which a production was mounted with George Jessel producing. Darryl F. Zanuck tested Patricia Neal and Valentina Cortese for the main part (for which he also considered Susan Hayward and Linda Darnell) before deciding on Jean Peters. In late 1950, dissatisfied with the script as the start date for the production was approaching, Zanuck assigned Philip Dunne to rewrite it — a task that the writer claimed to have completed in one week.[4] Tourneur was hired in January 1951; on January 17, he took part in a script conference with Zanuck, Jessel, and Dunne (who discussed, among other subjects, the question of how to hold off revealing at first that the pirate captain is a woman). Tourneur's contract contained an option for Fox to employ Tourneur for another year after the fifteen weeks of filming *Anne of the Indies*; the studio eventually exercised this option for *Way of a Gaucho*.

An anecdote of Dunne's suggests that Jessel (whose most worthwhile previous credit as a Fox producer was on Edmund Goulding's *Nightmare Alley* [1947]) must have been an amiable producer: "On the first day of shooting, Georgie marched briskly onto the set, saluted director Jacques Tourneur and the rest of the crew, said, 'Okay, fellas, see you at the preview,' and marched briskly out again."[5]

Around the turn of the 18th century, the dreaded pirate Captain Provi-dence — in reality, Anne Providence (Jean Peters), a protégée of Blackbeard (Thomas Gomez) — preys on British merchant ships in the West Indies. Aboard one such prize, the *Gemini*, her men retrieve a prisoner in irons, Pierre François La Rochelle (Louis Jourdan), who claims to be a French privateersman captured by the English. Anne makes Pierre her sailing master and falls in love with him, to the consternation of her protective first mate, Dougall (James Robertson Justice). On the pretext of searching for a fabled lost treasure, Pierre persuades Anne to approach Port Royal, the English headquarters in Jamaica. Dougall follows Pierre ashore there and ascertains that he is both married and secretly working for the English to help capture Anne. Anne escapes Pierre's trap and, in revenge, kidnaps Pierre's wife, Molly (Debra Paget). Pierre pursues Anne, only to get his ship sunk and himself taken prisoner. Anne at first leaves Pierre and Molly to die on a small desert island called Dead Man's Cay, but she changes her mind out of remorse and sends a longboat for them — at the same time that Blackbeard's sail appears on the horizon. Anne dies while engaging Blackbeard in battle to cover Pierre and Molly's escape.

The motive for Anne's final decision was a key point in preparing the picture. Philip Dunne's "continuity outline" dated January 2, 1951, states the motive that would eventually emerge in the final film: "Anne deliberately interposes her ship between Blackbeard and the longboat.... Her real reason is to protect Pierre, but she *gives* as her reason the fact that she will not avoid a fight." In a story conference on January 13, however, Zanuck said: "We complicate it too much by having Anne risk her life and her ship in order to divert the attack of Blackbeard from the longboat. This isn't necessary. We know that Anne's defiance of Blackbeard has angered and humiliated him; we know that he has been searching for her; therefore, when his ship comes in sight we know he is after Anne, and the fact that Pierre is there in the longboat will mean nothing to him. It is Anne he is after." In a memo to Dunne on January 24, Zanuck added, "The real reason Anne goes off to fight is because her whole life has been a fight and now she has nothing further to fight for."

Accordingly, Dunne's shooting script omits her concern with saving Pierre from Blackbeard and has her engage Blackbeard in fight simply on general principles: "We've never run from a fight yet — when it was ship to ship." On January 25, Dunne suggested shooting the ending both ways: with and without a line from Dr. Jameson (Herbert Marshall) explaining that Anne is attacking Blackbeard to cover the escape of the longboat. As initially shot, the film had Jameson, Pierre, and Molly watch the battle between Anne's and Blackbeard's ships while sailing around the cay in the longboat. After Anne's ship, the *Sheba Queen*, is destroyed, Jameson speaks the last line of the film: "She's home at last. Let the sea keep her. It was her one real love." The last shot would have been a full shot of the longboat sailing away into the sun.

After the film was finished, Zanuck was dissatisfied with the ending and sent a memo on May 1 to Dunne, Jessel, and Tourneur: "We have got to find some way of involving the boy and the girl in some sort of danger. It is essential that we find the proper last act. We are on the verge of having a splendid adventure film but I am positive that the present ending will be unsatisfactory to an audience — and it is the last act that counts." Consequently, Dunne wrote dialogue for new shots aboard the *Sheba Queen* and on Dead Man's Cay, making it clear that Anne is deliberately sacrificing herself to save Pierre. A May 4 memo from R. A. Klune to Zanuck indicated that Herbert Marshall's hospitalization would prevent him from

Herbert Marshall, Louis Jourdan, and Jean Peters in *Anne of the Indies*.

being available for the added scenes before May 17, by which time Tourneur was supposed to be in Argentina setting up *Way of a Gaucho*, and recommends that another director be assigned to the *Anne of the Indies* retakes. The final film suggests, however, that the retakes were done without Marshall (who has his back to the camera while his key line about Anne's action is heard); thus, it seems probable that Tourneur did the added scenes (which in any case are brief).

Although Zanuck's story conference memos don't preserve Tourneur's contributions, a memo from Dunne to Tourneur on February 23, 1951, shows that the director called for script revisions: "Here is a try at the three scenes you mentioned to me. Call me if you think they can be improved." These may have included the scene of Anne leaving Pierre and Molly on the cay and the subsequent scene in which Jameson hears Anne raving in her sleep and goes down to her cabin, both scenes that appeared in "blue pages" on March 14.

Anne of the Indies begins and ends with symbolic gestures of cancellation. We see a register with entries for several ships, giving for each, to the right of the ship name, its tonnage, its captain's name, and the name of a place. At the beginning of the film, a hand draws a line in red ink across an entry while a voice-off reads the information about the ship and declares that it has been sunk by Captain Providence; the line-crossing and the accompanying recitation are repeated for another ship. At the end of the film, the *Sheba Queen* is crossed off the same register, which now appears to be a narrative agency belonging to some imaginary realm rather than an account book maintained somewhere in the film's diegetic universe.

Pirates, the film informs us, are bound to each other by another kind of register, their "articles." The articles are partly a parody of the mercantilist-militarist system with which the pirates are at war and partly an emulation of the legislative efficiency of that system, but their main function is as a symbolic pact binding the individual to the pirate society. The film constantly reiterates the importance of being bound by the articles, the captain as much as "his" men, as Anne says.

Anne's identity takes shape around an accumulation of scars. Early in the film, Dr. Jameson treats the wound Anne receives in capturing the *Gemini*:

> ANNE: It's a scratch, no more.
>
> JAMESON: Oh, you'll bear a scar.
>
> ANNE: I bear many scars from the English.
>
> JAMESON: This one will mar your beauty.
>
> ANNE: Save that for the wenches.

This dialogue establishes Anne's implacable bitterness against the English, who hanged her brother, and her rejection of femininity. A later scene confirms that sexual identity is subject to choice: when Anne invites Pierre to choose something from the booty from the *Gemini*, Pierre briefly weighs the sword before choosing a golden dress, whereupon Anne claims the sword. The "treasure" (a word that circulates throughout the film) is a storehouse of sexual options and signs of identity; later, the word will be used to designate Molly, whereas Anne herself, we learn, is a "treasure" that Blackbeard has delegated Dougall to safeguard.

Anne's scars are the mark of her refusal of sexual identity, which returns symbolically in another mark. Questioning Pierre, whom her crew has found in irons aboard the *Gemini*, Anne slaps him for addressing her as "mademoiselle" rather than as "captain." In the next shot, a close-up of him, blood has suddenly appeared on his lip. The suddenness of this apparition underlines the magical nature of the exchange between Anne and Pierre. It is as if she has transferred her "scar" to him in punishment for treating her implicitly as a wench, for trying to make her aware of the nature of desire; it also suggests how quickly and arbitrarily this awareness can be produced. The blood on Pierre's lip functions as what Pascal Bonitzer, writing about Hitchcock, calls a "stain which precipitates a gaze," an element that sticks out and calls attention to itself, "the perverse or inverted element ... which serves to overturn our sense of reality."[6]

The wenches that Anne despises evidently constitute the lowest of categories: at the beginning of the first scene at the Black Anchor, the camera follows a woman sashaying through the tavern, visibly expecting admiration; the camera loses her and switches its attention to two other women engaged in a scuffle that, from the casual way the camera picks it up and then drops it, is clearly a fight over nothing, an insignificant activity. Later in the scene, Anne's duel with Blackbeard (to test her new sword) is in contrast a supremely serious kind of play, showcasing the skill, ingenuity, and grace of two opponents who respect each other.

Anne of the Indies: Anne (Jean Peters) doesn't appreciate Pierre's (Louis Jourdan's) attempt to be suave.

The torn map that is found in Pierre's possession and that gives Anne an illogical pretext for sparing Pierre's life is a message about sexuality that she cannot read. Its discovery coincides with the revelation that Anne is illiterate (Jameson, previously associated with writing and culture by his choice of a book from the booty of the *Gemini*, must decipher the writing on the map). With her rejection of sexuality comes a rejection of the sign as power and of the power of the sign. A platonic message about the separation of the sexes, Pierre's half-map figures the lack to which Anne becomes subject, as we see when she places a tracing of the map over her ship chart, reintegrating the geographic fragment into the whole (a gesture that will be undone near the beginning of *Appointment in Honduras*). The map tempts Anne fatally to proceed into the realm of signs, of postponed satisfactions and deferred presences. (Is it by accident that Port Royal, where Pierre intends to lead Anne into the hands of the English, bears the name of a monastery associated with a classic work of linguistics?)

Initially the film seems preoccupied with its sexual inversion and the shock this is presumed to carry (cf. the script conference memo, mentioned earlier, that contemplated delaying the revelation of Anne's sex). Eventually we come to understand the emotional stakes of the narrative, but we have to make the leap that makes the film powerful. Learning that Pierre slipped out of the tavern during her duel with Blackbeard (in a typically Tourneurian shot that has her first address the empty space where she expects Pierre to be and then realize his absence), Anne looks down with a puzzled, exasperated expression, signifying a regret that doesn't know its own cause. She looks down again when Dougall, her first mate, takes Pierre out of her cabin and hits him. These looks convey the instability of Anne's position. Later, a mood of relaxation prevails briefly as Anne and Pierre walk along a beach, passing members of the crew, who are performing maintenance on the ship. When Pierre's words come closest to seduction (asked for whom he chose the dress, he replies, "Perhaps for a woman I hope someday to meet"), Anne, angry with herself for having let her guard down, switches abruptly from an intimate to a commanding tone. Tourneur underlines the importance of this switch with a subtle change in shot size: previously, Anne was in medium close-up in three-quarter face; when her manner changes, the shot of her is slightly wider and from a slightly different angle, between three quarters and full face. The next shot of her (after another shot of Pierre) is from the same angle but is still wider, as she glares at him, turns, and walks away.

This shot dissolves to a night scene: the camera tilts down from a dim lamp, hanging from the ceiling of the tent, to Anne, lying in bed and wearing a white nightgown (this is the first time we have seen her in clothes that could be called "feminine"). In a single shot, the camera follows her as she gets up and goes outside the tent to stand, backlit, on the shore, gazing away from us at the glittering sea. (This beautiful shot recalls the shot in *I Walked with a Zombie* in which Betsy, standing perhaps on the same Caribbean shore, avows her love, just as the "*nuits de folie*" of which Jameson speaks later are undoubtedly similar to the barometric conditions that make Wesley Rand restless.) Anne has denied her femininity, we are told and shown; she doesn't know what it means to be a woman, to be desired. She finds herself in the process of discovering this, and she resists. For the first time, she experiences the temptation of narcissistically loving herself, of identifying with the desire of the other — it is secondary that the film hesitates to attribute this desire *actually* to the other (Pierre visibly resists when Anne first offers herself to him, and later he talks about her with disgust). The important thing is the unfolding of the internal drama; our uncertainty about Pierre's attitude is merely the projection onto another narrative plane of the conflict going on within Anne. At this point, *Anne of the Indies* becomes tragic, but we must give ourselves to the film to realize this, because the tragedy is not communicated and consists, in part, in this failure of communication. The issues in *Anne of the Indies* seem straightforward, but the film leaves the essential unexpressed.

In the next scene, Pierre surprises her as she is trying on the dress he chose from the booty of the *Gemini*. His presence is needed to complete her transformation into a "woman," just as Blackbeard supposedly made her what she has been hitherto, neither woman nor man. The mise-en-scène of this transformation underscores its artificial aspect. Jean Peters wearing the dress inside the tent (because it is an interior, a home, it has associations with femininity) and playing a love scene with Louis Jourdan — all this appears natural to us, until Anne emerges from the tent. At this point, the incongruity of the dress is underlined by Dougall's suppressed outrage as he looks from the dress to Pierre (in a superb take by James Robertson Justice, helping to make *Anne of the Indies* perhaps Tourneur's best-acted film). The dress itself becomes another stain, which initially discomfits Pierre as much as it does Dougall: Pierre's embarrassed hesitations make it clear that he is unprepared for this eruption of the desire he has manipulated.

Through Dougall, Dr. Jameson, and Blackbeard, Anne's surrogate fathers, the film highlights her crisis of identity. By becoming a "woman" for Pierre, Anne breaks her defining pact with herself. The wider consequences of this violation immediately become apparent when she slaps Blackbeard's face after he strikes Pierre with his sword. Purely symbolic, this defiance carries a greater force of outrage than her attack on the English ship in the first sequence. The discovery of Pierre's treachery drives Anne to a further self-betrayal, which she acts out against Molly, her sacrificial double. Jameson appears here as the figure who impotently observes her inability to see herself (as he does also earlier, in the cutaway to him as he watches Anne watch Pierre get into the longboat to go to Port Royal). His depressed look at Anne as she forces Molly to change into Pierre's dress suggests his recognition that in violating Molly, Anne is violating herself (Claire Johnston has noted a "remarkable resemblance between the two women").[7] In the slave market scene, Tourneur reinforces this point almost subliminally by panning down from the platform, where the auctioneer is displaying three sisters "born in the same hour and perfectly matched in beauty," to show Anne waiting her turn beside Molly. The cutaway to Dougall, looking down as Anne vaunts Molly's "smooth flesh," further strengthens our sense of the equivalence between the two women.

Neither man nor woman (Pierre describes her as "the vilest-hearted she-monster that ever came out of the sea"), Anne appears constitutively incapable of performing an act that is not outrageous. After abandoning Pierre and Molly on Dead Man's Cay (an act that the other characters perceive as the ultimate in moral degeneration), she cries out in her sleep and demands light as soon as Jameson wakes her. This scene complements the earlier scene of her waking up in her tent: then, she was awakening to her femininity; now, in her nightmare, she confronts herself as an expelled thing, with no sexuality and no place in symbolic exchange (she has violated even the law of the slave market). The word she cries out in her sleep is "No!"—which we can interpret at this point only as a (protest against the) negation of the symbolic pact that constitutes her own identity, the equivalent of striking her own name from her articles.

In this scene, Jameson calls her "Anne" for the first time. The use of this name (repeated by Jameson when she sends him in a longboat to save Pierre and Molly and then even by Dougall when they prepare to confront Blackbeard's ship) is a sign that Anne is near her origin, near death. By becoming "Anne," she finally assumes the symbolic place of Woman (the final stage of her self-betrayal), which the film represents literally as a place where women are displayed as lures and sacrificial objects: Anne challenges Blackbeard by waving her sword at him from the left (in the frame) of the foreshrouds of the *Sheba Queen*, the same place where she tied Molly in defiance of the pursuing Pierre. Sacrificing herself to save Pierre and Molly, she dares Blackbeard to kill her, just as she used Molly to dare Pierre to fire on the *Sheba Queen*.

Tourneur surprises us with the suddenness of Anne's eclipse. At one moment we see her standing beside the rigging, then there is a cut to Blackbeard, who turns to call to his men, "Hold your fire, you swabs." The camera tracks along the side of the *Revenge*, cannons firing, then shows Blackbeard again as he turns to look back at the *Sheba Queen*, and the next shot is of the destroyed bow of the ship, Anne simply not there, the broken mast falling. (Death in Tourneur's films is usually sudden and without ceremony. Characters are pushed aside, trampled, or mangled by some unstoppable inhuman force: Dougall in *Anne*, Miguel in *Way of a Gaucho*, Red in *Nightfall*, Harrington and Karswell in *Night of the Demon*; cf. Kathie's abrupt, almost automatic dispatching of Jeff in *Out of the Past*; the elided, obscured deaths in *I Walked with a Zombie*, and *The Leopard Man*; the accidental ones in *Appointment in Honduras*, *Wichita*, and *Great Day in the Morning*.) Anne is "impossible" (Molly's reaction when Pierre tells her that Captain Providence is a woman), a kind of hallucination, as we see from the final image of the film, in which an image of Anne lustily commanding her ship is superimposed over the register of ships: a conjunction of life and death. She is a phantasmic object, one that finally simply disappears from the film in a blink, just as at the beginning of the film she suddenly appeared out of nowhere (in the background of a medium shot of pirates boarding the *Gemini*).

The sophisticated use of movement and offscreen space in the film translates this central fantasy. *Anne of the Indies* often gives the impression of a perpetual-motion machine: characters appear and disappear in flurries of back-and-forth activity. At the beginning of the Black Anchor scene, the camera tracks from left to right, following several "wenches" in succession before arriving at the table where Blackbeard is holding court; then a complementary shot cranes from right to left as a bear is brought in and a bench overturned (in the same direction, from right to left) to make way for it. In a later scene in the tavern, the camera tracks backward at the same time as (1) someone throws a cup at the door at the back of the set (through which Pierre has just gone) and (2) Blackbeard walks up a short flight of steps toward the door, only to stop and turn around. These reversals — examples of which can be found throughout the film — create a constant surface impression of restless movements that, instead of clashing in an Eisensteinian way, cancel each other out.

Scenes end in weakness, surrender, inconclusion: the English captain crying out for quarter; Jameson sighing and taking a drink after Anne explains that she will spare Pierre's life because she gave him her "word"; Jameson leaving the frame, unable to address her, after Pierre's treachery has come out; Pierre's small figure in medium-long shot as he joins an English gentleman at a table in the tavern (signifying that he will turn pirate for him in order to regain his ship). Or scenes end in a jarring and unsatisfying shift: Anne turning and walking offscreen after learning that Pierre slipped out during her duel with Blackbeard; the ending of the scene on the beach between Anne and Pierre, when Anne's mood and tone suddenly change and they walk away from each other. Through these hesitations and shifts, the film suggests the avoidance of something inexpressible, acknowledging that the narrative is based on a lack that can be filled only by fantasy.

This awareness defines Tourneur's main contribution to the adventure genre: to twist the genre's surfaces in order to show their other side, which faces desolation. Barely apparent in *The Flame and the Arrow*, this negativity underlies *Anne of the Indies* and emerges as the dominant force in Tourneur's next two films, both of them also "adventures": *Way of a Gaucho* and *Appointment in Honduras*.

Way of a Gaucho
(1952)

That's really what interested me the most, in all my films: dignity.

JACQUES TOURNEUR

Way of a Gaucho was intended as a way for 20th Century–Fox to use up the profits that the Perón government had frozen in Argentina. Philip Dunne was assigned to write the script and produce, and Henry King was assigned to direct. On March 16, 1951, Dunne informed Darryl F. Zanuck:

> Henry King has told me that, owing to his wife's serious illness, he may not be able to make the trip to the Argentine. This means that he may not be able to make the preliminary trip and/or the final trip to shoot the picture.
>
> It would be, of course, a great disappointment not to have him, but I think that now is the time to be thinking of a possible replacement if we have to make one …The man I want to suggest for director is Jacques Tourneur. I am absolutely delighted with the job he is doing with *Anne of the Indies*. In my opinion, he is a much better director than many who have made big reputations for themselves and draw down huge salaries. He is quick, sure and economical and he is getting flawless performances out of his cast.
>
> I would have no worries about *Way of a Gaucho* if I knew Tourneur would direct it. I think it would mean an enormous saving in money without sacrificing quality. I am asking Lew Schreiber quietly to check his availability so that if Mrs. King does not improve, you will be able to decide whether or not to send him down.[1]

On April 25, Zanuck wrote to Dunne: "We are definitely going to use Jacques Tourneur as the director." On May 14, Tourneur arrived in Argentina; he and Dunne visited locations at Santa Catalina (Córdoba), Rio Cuarto (Córdoba), Uspallata (Mendoza), Desaguadero (San Luis), and Concordia (Entre Ríos) and interviewed English–speaking Argentine actors. Eventually, they decided to cast all but the major parts in Argentina.

On June 4, Dunne reported to Zanuck that the Argentine government's "interest tends to become a little too overwhelming. They want to have a hand in every phase of our production." Government officials were very insistent, for example, on having big stars in the picture. "No reasonable government would behave in this way, but we must remember that we are dealing with incredibly stupid, provincial people." Dunne said that he was going to do some rewriting on the script to make better use of the locations and to incorporate on-the-spot research, advice from Argentine experts, and "suggestions from Jacques Tourneur." He added, "I am sure that what Jacques and I have in mind will make for a vast improvement."

Tourneur recalled spending six weeks traveling up and down Argentina in a plane and another six weeks back in the United States taking Spanish lessons before the start of production. Dunne wrote in his autobiography that he spent nearly a year in Argentina: "first on a scouting trip with the unit manager; then with director Jacques Tourneur, the art director, cameraman, and assistant director to pick locations and make final plans; finally for the actual production.... Operating in a strange land, and in its hinterland at that — for the picture was shot on locations ranging from the high Andes to the subtropical pampas of northern Argentina — we had more than our share of production problems."[2]

Spies monitored every move the Americans made. The script, which Dunne had already rewritten after his arrival in the country, had to be rewritten again "to reflect the mystique of the gaucho as it had been recreated by official decree." Despite all the problems, the *Way of a Gaucho* unit, which was feted by government dignitaries, ended up serving as an unofficial goodwill embassy from the United States to Argentina. It did so well at this that the U.S. ambassador, Ellsworth Bunker, told Dunne that the good impression created by the production "had provided the one bright spot in what otherwise had been, for him, a difficult and unproductive diplomatic assignment."[3]

Set in Argentina in the last part of the 19th century, *Way of a Gaucho* recounts the adventures of Martín Penalosa (Rory Calhoun), a gaucho who is imprisoned after killing a man in a duel of honor. Allowed to serve in the militia instead of doing time in prison, Martín chafes under the discipline of Major Salinas (Richard Boone) and deserts. He saves Teresa Chavez (Gene Tierney), a noblewoman, from kidnap by an Indian and is captured by Salinas's men while returning her to her home. Martín escapes again and, under the assumed name of Valverde, leads a band of gauchos in resistance against the encroachments of the railroad and foreign customs on the pampas. Teresa seeks him out to warn him against Salinas, who implacably hunts him down. Martín and Teresa fall in love, and she becomes pregnant. Giving up a grueling attempt to escape with her into Chile, Martín accepts a government offer of amnesty and surrenders to Salinas.

Dunne was left with vivid impressions of Argentina but a dim impression of the film, which he considered "eminently forgettable." Tourneur, on the other hand, thought it a "very interesting, very good film."[4] One is obliged to infer a wider basis for the disagreement between the two men. In the part of Dunne's autobiography devoted to the Hollywood screenwriter's obligatory complaint against the auteur theory, he concedes, "As I writer, I have worked with many directors whom I admire and respect: William Wyler, John Ford, Henry King, Henry Hathaway, Elia Kazan, John Cromwell, Clarence Brown, Henry Koster, Carol Reed, Joe Mankiewicz, and ... Rowland V. Lee."[5] Tourneur's absence from this list (others omitted include Allan Dwan, Otto Preminger, Delmer Daves, and Michael Curtiz) is striking, considering that, as both producer and writer of *Way of a Gaucho*, Dunne must have worked more closely with Tourneur than he usually did with a director (not to mention their previous association on *Anne of the Indies*). For so deliberate a writer to omit a name from this honor roll by accident seems out of character; moreover, Dunne's memo to Zanuck recommending Tourneur for *Gaucho* shows that at the time he greatly respected his talent.

One infers that Dunne was unhappy with his experience with Tourneur on *Gaucho*. The likely source of this displeasure can be found in the testimony obtained by Argentine critic Diego Curubeto from members of the Argentine cast and crew of the film. After praising Dunne as an excellent producer, actor Raúl Astor observed that Tourneur "limited himself to doing his work without worrying much. He had made very good films, but it seems to me that he was entering into his decline. He didn't worry much about the film, he would get drunk a lot." Translator Enrique Grounauer recalled: "For my job I saw Tourneur only four or five times and he was always tremendously drunk. I remember once he was so drunk that he tried to talk and his pipe fell from his mouth. Somebody remarked that he was like that because he had just kept going from the night before." Eleodoro Marenco, an adviser on the production, added, "No wonder he was like that, since he would start with a beer before ten in the morning."

Tourneur was not alone in on-the-set alcoholism: according to Grounauer, the crew members "were divided into those who drank and those who didn't drink. The ones who didn't drink, didn't drink a single drop, but the ones who did, drank like worms."

(A dissenting voice comes from actor Nestor Yóan: "Tourneur was a very serious man, but he was very kind in the way he treated people. The work atmosphere was totally different from that of Argentine shoots. Only Tourneur's voice would be heard; there was never a technician asking for silence the way it always happened here.")

In the absence of testimony from Dunne or Tourneur, one can only speculate about this, but the following scenario seems plausible. Though disapproving of Tourneur's drinking, Dunne wanted to avoid adding to his own problems by firing the director in mid-production, and thus permitted him to finish the location shooting. No doubt, he also considered the quality of Tourneur's work at least adequate. After the unit returned to Hollywood, however, the damage to the director's reputation caused by his behavior in Argentina probably weighed in Fox's decision not to pick up its option on Tourneur's further services and led to the irreversible decline of his Hollywood career.

In any case, Tourneur wasn't called on to direct several scenes added by Zanuck and Dunne after the completion of the Argentine production. A memo on a February 13, 1952, script conference with Zanuck, Dunne, and Henry Levin, the director hired to do the new scenes, shows that Zanuck's main concern was with strengthening the heroic stature of Martín, who he apparently felt came off as somewhat wishy-washy in the film Tourneur had made. Zanuck also wanted to elaborate on the issues involved in Martín's decision to surrender to Salinas. The major additions were the jail scene in which Miguel (Hugh Marlowe) tells Martín that he will be allowed to join the militia, the scene in which Martín deliberately spills hot soup on Salinas, the scene in which Miguel visits Teresa and she tells him where Martín is, and the scene in Teresa's room that starts with her in silhouette kneeling before a prie-dieu and continues as Martín comes to announce the death of Miguel and his own change of heart. Also shot were a number of brief additions to Tourneur-directed sequences, notably in the sequence of Teresa and Martín on their way to Chile and the scene between Martín and Miguel before the stampede. Levin's additions (shot in the studio and on locations near Hollywood) are static, routine scenes that slow the pace of the film, especially in its last third, but don't disturb its tonality.

A poignant meditation on freedom and desire, *Way of a Gaucho* is, along with *Anne of the Indies*, perhaps the most beautiful of Tourneur's films. The film opens with long shots of a pampa. Gauchos on horseback meet their leader, Miguel, returning from the city in a carriage, and escort him to a fiesta. These opening scenes have a buoyancy and splash that recall *The Flame and the Arrow*. Leading off with this mode only for purposes of dramatic contrast, the film quickly turns away from it. As in other Tourneur movies, we are in the narrative before we have enough information to evaluate the importance of what we see. Precisely because of this ignorance, we interpret the relationship between Martín and Miguel in a way that gives it its full mythical value. Since they address each other as "brother," we see them as a pair of brothers in a fable, the elder of whom has inherited the father's name and wealth while the younger stands — for the time being, loyally — in his shadow. We sense that Martín, though not the biological son of Miguel's father, is a truer son to him than Miguel and that Martín's actions carry on the "way of a gaucho" whereas Miguel's betray it.

Already, the freedom that Martín will search for throughout the rest of the film exists in the world of the film only as a myth of the past. Even though Miguel's father died only a month before the start of the film, the conjunction of law and will he represents is already mythical. Later in the film, Martín assumes the revolutionary role of Valverde while recognizing that objectively, he is already defeated. "Our time has passed, Falcón," he says. The film's "revolutionary" movement thus starts off with exhaustion, under the sign of a death (that of the real Valverde) that has already happened and that lies in wait for those who go on struggling in Valverde's name. This sense of futility survives the producers' pointless attempt to highlight Martín's courage in the post–Tourneur scenes.

More than in any of his other color films, Tourneur uses extreme darkness systematically in *Way of a Gaucho*. In the magnificently shot night sequence of Martín's escape and the attack on Salinas, Salinas turns out the lamp in his room, rendering it completely dark, so that when he later collapses, wounded, while ordering his men to get Martín, the scene is in almost total darkness. Such theatrical, painterly effects (in which one might discern the influence of the silent films of Maurice Tourneur) interest Tourneur more than what is traditionally called action. The duel between Martín and Brutos (Chuck Roberson) during the fiesta erupts suddenly and is quickly, almost inexplicably, over — a typical, and distinctive, example of the way Tourneur prefers to handle action. What Tourneur shows us is ambiguously compatible with Martín's later commentary on the duel: "I fought to mark him, not to kill. He made me kill him."

Later, Tourneur presents the skirmish between Salinas's troops and a band of

Rory Calhoun in *Way of a Gaucho*.

Indians with an understated grandeur and realism that are far from John Ford's handling of such scenes. Tourneur's mise-en-scène is at the limits of the classical tradition; everything is staged and photographed with perfect clarity, but we see only fragments of actions, not enough to reconstruct their totality, so that the scene comes across as impressionistic. Martín's saving Salinas's life is staged, filmed, and edited with a lack of emphasis so complete that the act is almost unnoticeable. Shots of an Indian slinging a bola and of the Indians retreating into the hills have a similar stamp of casualness.

The film contains several scenes that function in a symbolic or atmospheric rather than dramatic way and that encapsulate a situation visually without advancing the drama. In one such scene early in the film, Teresa, who has been traveling with Martín, wakes up in the grass beside a river. As she leans forward and looks offscreen, the camera tracks back. We cut to what she sees: Martín standing on his horse, looking out over the pampa. As in other Tourneur films, the character's waking sets a surrealist atmosphere that lingers over the ensuing scene (e.g., *Cat People, I Walked with a Zombie, Experiment Perilous, Out of the Past*). We experience the shot of Martín on the horse as a vision of absolute strangeness.

Later in the film, we again see Teresa waking up, this time in a shady bower. She lifts her head slightly and looks; the scene cuts to a reverse-shot of Martín silhouetted against the sky, next to a tree. This shot cuts back to Teresa, still looking up. His shadow moves over her face, partly obscuring it, then leaves it as he apparently goes past. We cut again to the space where he was — he's not there — and then back to Teresa, who closes her eyes and turns her head back to the ground. The shot lingers on her face before the fadeout, as if reluctant to part from it.

Here Tourneur manages to photograph the desire of the characters, to make that desire into the overt subject of the scene. He does this not through the performances, but through composition, lighting, and color and by using Martín's shadow on Teresa's face less as a symbol of desire than as the legible proof of the forming of an emotion. The shot of the space from which Martín is absent sets the seal on this mysterious conjunction of images: Teresa looks not at Martín but at the space he has left. Tourneur shows that her desire is not merely physical desire for him but is an effect of the alternation of plenitude and lack enacted in the presence/absence of his figure in the shot, just as, previously, we saw her falling in love not with Martín but with Martín's love (the scene in which she sees him standing on his horse surveying the pampa). Like *Anne of the Indies*, *Way of a Gaucho* is about the cause of desire.

By handling the love story in largely visual and abstract terms, Tourneur also compensates for the inadequacy of Gene Tierney as Teresa. The mildly condescending tenderness that Teresa displays toward Martín early in the film — "You love the pampa, don't you?" — is sufficient explanation of why Tourneur wanted Jean Peters in the part. Tierney is incongruously coquettish — Tourneur thought her "very New England" — whereas Peters would have been more colorful. "I wanted Jean Peters because she was the ideal actress for the role, that of a young girl filled with vitality, with Spanish blood, not at all the Gene Tierney type, but once again it was too late." Tierney's casting made it impossible for Tourneur to carry out his intention of filming "a series of violent quarrels between the heroine and the gaucho."[6]

At other points in the film, Tourneur lingers over scenes of stalemate, stasis, or relaxation. In a night scene, the camera tracks slowly from the stockade (where Salinas, obsessed with the idea of making a soldier out of Martín, has had him spreadeagled on the ground) to a group of men sitting around. Over the shot, we hear Martín's friend Falcón (Everett Sloane) singing:

> On the trail, on the trail
> My window is the sky
> But for one look through yours
> I would lay down and die.

The lyric recapitulates an important theme of the film. "My window is the sky" expresses a sense of being inside while being outside, the sense of nature as a metaphor for architecture, which infuses the scene of Teresa waking up within the bower of trees to see Martín framed against the sky. The referential ambiguity of the line "But for one look through yours" invokes the undecidable nature of the relationship between inside and outside (cf. the shot of Uncle Famous passing outside the church window at the end of *Stars in My Crown*). The line could mean that the singer would like to gaze in from outside at his object of desire, presumably through her bedroom window, or that he would like to be inside, gazing out. The whole metaphor offers an outside-inside relation longing to be transformed into another outside-inside relation and declares longing to be a perpetual state of being either inside looking out or outside looking in. The lyric foreshadows the conclusion of the film, in which Martín "lays down" his rebellion to enter the cathedral with Teresa.

The expressive role of music in the film links *Way of a Gaucho* to *Canyon Passage*: late in the film, Falcón's broken guitar, which Martín places on the singer's grave, recalls Hi's broken mandolin in *Canyon Passage*. Music figures prominently in another scene of respite that starts with a high-angle tracking shot of Martín walking past women rinsing clothes in a stream while a flutist plays, leaning against a hut. After a short dialogue between Martín and Falcón, the latter leaves. There follows a remarkable short sequence of beautifully composed shots using a single human figure against the landscape:

1. Medium shot of Martín looking offscreen right, his head occupying a place in the composition near the valley between two hills in the background
2. Medium shot from behind Martín, showing the vast, mostly flat landscape he is looking at
3. Close shot of Martín as he touches the medallion of Saint Teresa that Teresa gave him
4. Extreme close-up of the medallion
5. Close shot of Martín again

The flute solo that has gone on throughout the sequence continues over these shots; it reaches a single sustained note when Martín touches the medallion (shot 3) and then dies in the last shot. The last shot dissolves to a shot of a city street. The dissolve gives Martín's communion the sense of a farewell, foreshadowing his decision to surrender to Salinas at the end of the film. Similarly, the medallion represents the combined forces of woman and Catholicism — the forces that will make Martín capitulate.

Another moment of respite is a short vignette. Martín and Teresa, escaping from the law, ride against a Technicolor yellow sky: Martín dismounts, looks around, helps her from her horse, says "You are my wife," and embraces her tenderly.

As *Way of a Gaucho* becomes increasingly contemplative, it becomes impossible to note such moments as unusual because Tourneur does not treat them as privileged. He integrates them into the flow of the film, dramatically, rhythmically, and thematically. The moments in which "nothing happens" are the crucial moments of the film, the moments that crystallize the nothing that happens throughout the film, its repetitive spiraling motion.

Tourneur's concentration on mood accounts for another of the strangest and most beautiful scenes, the scene at the rebels' camp, where the gauchos celebrate their victory over the police. At the beginning of the scene, we see Martín full-figure, in left profile, framed in the entrance to a shack (both inside and outside it: again the film plays on the uncertainty of this relation). We cut to Teresa in medium shot standing under some trees. At first we assume that this shot is located in the imaginary reverse field of the previous shot. It cuts, however, to a shot that places Martín for the first time in relation to the revelers. He turns away and looks over his shoulder, evidently (now) at Teresa. This shot "disproves" the earlier shot of him, in which we thought he was looking at Teresa already — a typical example of Tourneur's violation of expected spatial relations. The spatial disjunction prepares us to see Martín's desire for Teresa as, logically, tearing him in two.

Martín at first treats Teresa indifferently; they both watch couples dancing. Then Teresa walks away from him, and he catches her, turns her, and kisses her passionately (sudden close-up). This shot cuts away to Falcón, playing guitar; he says to a companion: "As for me, give me one of these Indian women. They ask nothing more than to be beaten three times a day." We cut back to a two-shot of Martín and Teresa, still kissing. The cynical Falcón may have the last word, but the image of passion negates it.

The scene in which Martín and Teresa arrive at a cathedral during a funeral to try to get married is a splendid example of Tourneur's use of architectural space. In a situation reminiscent of the climax of *The Leopard Man*, a funeral procession prevents Teresa from warning Martín, who is inside the church, about the presence of policemen. She then goes around to enter the church from the back and asks two nuns whether they've seen a gaucho; one of them merely puts her finger to her lips for quiet.

Teresa looks off: we cut to an angled shot of two men's shadows moving along a wall. Trying to avoid the approaching police, Teresa runs down a corridor toward the camera. The camera pans as she approaches, reframing her in profile against another corridor, at a right angle to the first; she stops to look around, then runs on ahead. In the next shot, she enters from behind camera left and is framed against another corridor, presumably the one she was facing in the previous shot; it is confusingly identical in appearance to the one against which that shot framed her. She pauses, then turns and runs right, the camera panning with her, down a shorter corridor with a double wooden door at the end. Unable to open the door, she turns and runs back toward the camera; as she reaches the intersection of corridors, the camera pans to show the police converging on her from the background. Architectural space becomes a source of disorientation and finally a trap for both the character and the audience. Tourneur immerses the viewer in Teresa's psychological experience of the space.

Way of a Gaucho is Tourneur's most extensive treatment of the opposition between the country and the city (cf. *Experiment Perilous, Canyon Passage, Out of the Past, Wichita, Nightfall*) because it relates both country and city to the human need for order and the alternation of landscapes to a structuring of experience that it shows to be historically and existentially indispensable. "That's what makes the force of things, their opposition," Tourneur said.[7] The script establishes this theme in the first scene, in which the gauchos comment on the luxury of Miguel's carriage, which contrasts with the gauchos' preferred style of traveling, on horseback. This is a light hint at the conflict over the perception of Miguel as a "running dog for the city men," an agent of corruption and a traitor to the gauchos' way of life. Falcón later sneers, "Foreign clothes, foreign ideas out of the gutters of Europe."

The country/city dualism becomes an important visual motif as the film dissolves back and forth between the vanishing horizons of the vast pampas and an

Not reconciled: Salinas (Richard Boone), Teresa (Gene Tierney), and Martín (Rory Calhoun) in *Way of a Gaucho.*

urban environment characterized by baroque architecture, ornamental gates, and beautiful landscape design. During the film, the movement between country and city feels less like a narrative progression and more like a deepening of intensity, as if the importance of this movement lay not in the physical displacement of the characters but in the dissolve itself: the fleeting, entirely imaginary moment that contains both places and both movements (that from inside to outside and that from outside to inside), encapsulating the longing and mystery of Falcón's lyric. After Martín finds the dying gaucho Valverde, for example, the film dissolves from Martín riding in long shot on the right side of the screen to a long shot of a little church, occupying the left side of the screen, as Teresa emerges through a door, removing a shawl from over her head. Reversing the previous dissolve's movement from country to city, a subsequent shot of Teresa (talking to Tia María, her maid) dissolves to a long shot of a range next to a hill, along which Teresa rides with Tia María (Lidia Campos) and a packhorse to warn Martín about Salinas.

The country/city theme relates to other dualisms in the film. Like Jeff Markham in *Out of the Past*, Martín assumes a new name; but unlike Jeff, he does so not to conceal himself but to wage war against the social order. He must choose a new name to be reborn under: it is part of the code of the rebel to deny birth and baptism. The gaucho friar who raised both Martín and Miguel is a central figure in the last part of the film; like Miguel, he embodies the transition between the gauchos' semiwild existence and a modern civilization. If the rebel gauchos are, by implication, close to the Indians, the friar stands for an alien, conquering religion, which Martín, through Teresa's influence, comes to accept. The friar is also the antithesis to Miguel's real father; he is a rival father-figure who translates the laws of the church rather than dictates his own.

During the last third of the film, after Teresa and Martín have become lovers, Teresa's hairstyle and costume reflect the change in her status: she has two long braids and wears colorful clothes — blue vest, patterned blouse, red skirt, orange-brown shawl — that contrast with the white or off-white clothes in which we have seen her previously. At the end of the film, when Martín and Teresa approach the cathedral to get married, they are dressed in black, and his bandanna is now white. These costume changes reflect the film's complex world, in which the dichotomies between Catholicism and primitivism, city and pampa, and foreigners and gauchos are never clear-cut; the two terms of each duality interpenetrate on every level.

The film leaves us in doubt about the exact nature of the economic exploitation of the pampas that Martín and the gauchos are fighting and about their political program. This vagueness causes us to see Martín's revolt in more or less purely existential terms. We see him as simply fighting against the world's apolitical encroachments on individual liberty, fighting against the way things are. Since Martín's responsibilities toward his group and theirs to him are unclear, we don't question Martín's decision to abandon the group to flee with Teresa into Chile. Eventually, the responsibilities of family life lead Martín to give up his rebellion and accept the new political system in Argentina, an acceptance that, in a reversal of values, he now sees as "freedom."

Martín's adventures have no specific political significance; they could be a metaphor for a bourgeois male's transition from adolescence to adulthood. Adolescence is a quasi-mythical condition in which the individual perceives himself as bound by no laws; in which the manifestations of a contrary state of things (a new economic regime, compulsory military service) appear to threaten an intolerable confinement; in which women are as plentiful and virtually as indistinguishable as stars (the comparison is Martín's). Adulthood consists in submitting to law, paying the obeisances required by society, and picking a wife to worship, marry, and settle down with.

Seen in these terms, *Way of a Gaucho* is an unusually clear example of the Hollywood adventure film as conformist parable. The film contrasts interestingly with *Anne of the Indies*: at the end of *Gaucho*, Martín lays down his rebellion for the sake of his wife and his unborn child, his family with whom, thanks to the beneficence of the government, he can expect to enjoy a peaceful life; Anne, on the other hand, plunges further into rebellion, rebelling against the rebels (Blackbeard) at the cost of her own certain death to save Pierre who, she knows, loves another woman.

Left over at the end of *Way of a Gaucho*, toughening a reading of the ending that would otherwise be merely passive, is Salinas, the most interesting character in the film. We first see him reviewing his new recruits, greeting Martín sardonically as "a barbarian from the pampa." Later, in his quarters (in a scene directed by Henry Levin), Salinas, a self-described "student of history," discusses with Martín the gauchos who crossed the Andes with General San Martín, "the father of our country." Martín, pointing out that those gauchos voluntarily chose military service, implicitly links honor with freedom; for Salinas, honor is a matter of "discipline." After Martín mock-accidentally spills hot soup on him, Salinas sentences Martín to ten lashes on a charge of "willful misunderstanding of history."

The two men have an ambiguous relationship. Salinas praises Martín to Teresa and tells her, "You and I both have reasons, if different ones, for wishing him alive." (This is as close as the film comes to articulating its homosexual subtext.) Captured by Martín, Salinas "humbly begs" Martín for his life. Martín asks enigmatically, "You have something to do with your life?" Salinas asks Martín to spare him so that he can kill him; Martín, paradoxically, agrees. Martín's decision to save Salinas has two possible interpretations: (1) Martín respects Salinas as a man ("He's more of a man with one arm than some of us with two," he declares to his men), and above all as an adversary; (2) Martín, perhaps unconsciously, wishes for his own death, wants to be made to succumb to the historical inevitability that Salinas stands for.

If Martín gets out of the adventure with a whole skin, the same can't be said of Salinas, whose arm is permanently maimed and who has been forced to change from soldier to policeman. Salinas's behavior at the end of the film is ambiguous. Perhaps he spares Martín's life because he realizes that Martín, having accepted the world, is no longer worthy of being killed. And perhaps he turns away from Teresa when she tries to speak to him not just because he scorns her thanks but because he scorns her for having transformed and emasculated Martín.

The importance of the last shot is that, like the last shot of *Berlin Express* (the one-legged man at the Brandenburg Gate), it leaves everything open: as Martín and Teresa enter the church, Salinas remains outside, unreconciled, the "student of history" who has become more a victim of history than even the dispossessed gaucho. (Originally, the film ended with Salinas walking away; it was recut to strengthen the implication that Martín would have to do prison time for his crimes.) Also left outside, leaning against the wall of the church, is the tiny figure of another victim of history, a woman pauper. Her presence hints at the failure of the social order and the eventual resurgence of revolution, just as Salinas embodies the masochism of that order, which is reduced to taking vengeance on itself when it can no longer exact it from the bodies of its opponents.

Appointment in Honduras (1953)

At the extreme limit of distress, there is in fact nothing
left but the conditions of time and space.

FRIEDRICH HÖLDERLIN,
REMARKS ON OEDIPUS

Appointment in Honduras was the second of a remarkable group of films produced by Benedict Bogeaus for RKO. The first was Don Siegel's *Count the Hours*
(1953); after Tourneur's, the subsequent films in the series were all directed by
Allan Dwan. These include three that, with *Appointment in Honduras*, are the
highpoints of the series: *Silver Lode* (1954), *Tennessee's Partner* (1955), and *Slightly
Scarlet* (1956). The Bogeaus-RKO films have certain aspects in common: they're all
entries in American action genres, with formulaic, even ritualized plots; and their
stars were all, at least at this point in their careers, of the second or third rank,
commercially. (Glenn Ford, whose only film for Bogeaus was *Appointment in Honduras*, would later see his star rise again. *Appointment in Honduras* was one of Ann
Sheridan's last films; RKO cast her in it to settle a suit she had brought over being
dropped from Robert Stevenson's *My Forbidden Past* [1951].)[1]

The homogeneity of the series also comes from consistent use of the same
production team: cinematographer John Alton, art director Van Nest Polglase, editor James Leicester, and composer Louis Forbes. *Appointment in Honduras*, anomalously, was shot by Joseph Biroc and designed by Charles D. Hall; nevertheless, it
is recognizably Bogeausian in its atmosphere and concerns.

According to Dwan, Bogeaus's budgets were never more than around
$800,000 to $850,000, and the schedules were about fifteen days. RKO picked
Dwan, he said, for his ability to act as a "policeman" in Bogeaus's unit:

> Ben Bogeaus had lost his shirt on a bunch of pictures that he
> produced, and for a long time he did nothing. But he had
> been friendly with a fellow who became the general manager
> for RKO Studios under Howard Hughes, and when they
> decided to encourage independent producers to come in and
> make pictures, they also let Bogeaus in because of that previ
> ous relationship with the studio manager. The president of
> the company was ... my old friend, Jim Grainger. Now
> Bogeaus was notoriously extravagant in the early days, and

> they weren't too confident that he could safely handle the
> kind of budget he'd have to use, so to give himself some
> security, Grainger reached out for someone with experience
> to go in and work with Bogeaus.[2]

Tourneur, who preceded Dwan, would also have been a logical choice for the role of "policeman" to Bogeaus because of his track record with resourceful low-budget filmmaking (the same could be said of Don Siegel).

Both Dwan and Siegel cited instances of Bogeaus's penury and trickery. The *Count the Hours* unit got kicked off a set that Bogeaus had "borrowed"; the crew became recalcitrant on the last day of shooting because they hadn't been paid, and Siegel could finish shooting only by promising to hide the last day's dailies from Bogeaus until everyone was paid in full.[3] On *Most Dangerous Man Alive* (1961), which turned out to be the last film Dwan made, Bogeaus hired the cast and crew at the lower rates appropriate to a two-part television pilot. He was forced to raise their salaries when it became apparent that the film had been designed as a feature all along: "He had just cut the script in half and was making the two parts."[4]

Despite such problems, Dwan recalled his relationship with Bogeaus as one of perfect understanding:

> With Bogeaus, we always straightened out difficulties (of
> script, casting, etc.) together and by mutual agreement. The
> films I shot with him are combinations of both our sensibili-
> ties. During shooting, he watched the crew on the set and if
> he saw a flaw or room for improvement, he gave me his
> opinion and we found a solution in complete harmony. That
> type of stories, those sets that were similar in all our films,
> were Bogeaus's doing as well as mine.[5]

Dwan's films for Bogeaus emphasize the romantic, mystical side of their genres; he created works that transform escapism into encounters with memory and conscience (*Pearl of the South Pacific, Tennessee's Partner* [both 1955]) or that raise cynicism and brutality to a high level of abstraction (*Slightly Scarlet*). Tourneur's achievement in *Appointment in Honduras* is related to Dwan's but is basically different: he fabricates a self-contained, jewel-like, malignant world in which characters' motives and relationships appear enigmatic and ultimately meaningless, in which political causes and issues of survival and redemption become purely formal. The result is at once one of the most minor of Tourneur's films and one of the most profound: a mysteriously perfect film.

In 1910, Jim Corbett (Glenn Ford), an American rancher, goes to Honduras to bring money to the ex-president of Honduras, who has been ousted by a military coup. With the aid of a group of convicts, Corbett hijacks a boat; for protection, they bring along a rich American couple, Harry and Sylvia Sheppard (Zachary Scott and Ann Sheridan), as hostages. The group's journey upriver and through the jungle is complicated by predatory animals, pursuing soldiers, Harry Sheppard's escape attempts, and Corbett and Sylvia's falling in love. Corbett comes down with a fever, which allows one of the convicts, Reyes (Rodolfo Acosta), to take the money from him and escape. Recovering, Corbett follows and kills Reyes;

Harry Sheppard is also killed, leaving Sylvia free to make plans to meet Corbett
later and return with him to the United States.

Appointment in Honduras, with its homogeneity of tone and its preoccupation
with death, the inhuman, and loss, is a rare example of a Hollywood film that
offers a formal experience comparable to contemporary avant-garde art. Bertrand
Tavernier was one of the first to have this insight: writing of this film, *Way of a
Gaucho*, and *Wichita*, he remarked on their "dedramatized chronicles, which, by
erasing the extraordinary and unifying situations, strangely approximate the most
modern dramaturgical investigations." [6] Throughout the film, Tourneur deliberately effaces dramatic contrast, smoothing the gradations of the narrative to a near
level, for the sake of a purely cinematic unity of tone. After a while, the film, which
at under 80 minutes is fairly brief but which could potentially go on at any length,
almost ceases to tell a story. Instead, it becomes a study of color and movement,
vegetation as decor, sudden death and love; with no story, it is a film of purposes
and projects, promises and dreams (the last line spoken in the film, at last justifying
its title, is Corbett's promise to Sylvia: "I'll be in Port Honduras in two weeks").

The film sustains a muted tonality through Hall's art direction, Karen De
Wolf's charmingly minimal dialogue, and the flat performances. Tourneur thought
he had encouraged Glenn Ford to underplay too much:

> In the script, there was a contrast between the character of a
> very sober, very cold American, who had only one goal in
> mind and who managed to reach it, and four or five other
> characters, very picturesque, very colorful. Seeing the film
> again the other day after so many years, I had the impression
> that Glenn Ford was so devoted to his task that it made him
> become very dull. I exaggerated that side.[7]

These comments suggest the diffidence to which a commercial artist may be prone
in reconsidering an experiment that, because of the circumstances of the distribution and reception of his work, has gone unrecognized. In fact, in *Appointment in
Honduras*, not only Ford but all the actors — particularly the excellent Rodolfo
Acosta — are "dull": they speak quietly and normally throughout the film; their
reactions are precise and controlled; their facial expressions are usually minimal.

The detachment that Tourneur forces on the viewer of *Appointment in Honduras* implies neither intellectual and ethical rigor (cf. Lang) nor a critique of
voyeurism (Hitchcock): it is more like the detachment that comes with immersion
in a dream world that is utterly unconvincing and thus does not compel total
commitment. From its outset, Tourneur's film has the glamour of an object made
by no one, for no one. In the first image, of a ship in calm waters, seen from far
away, the camera adopts the point of view of a narrative agency, impersonally
establishing that we're somewhere at sea. Louis Forbes's music has already suggested an exotic atmosphere full of exciting anticipation: this boat will carry *us*
away, along with the characters.

The film's second shot is a medium shot in depth of the ship deck, with a
couple of sailors at the back of the set. In the middleground, a door opens at left,
and a man emerges. It is Glenn Ford, but we can't see his face: he comes through
the door sideways, with his back to the camera, so that, awkwardly, his face is

Zachary Scott, Ann Sheridan, and Rodolfo Acosta in *Appointment in Honduras*.

turned toward the door he opens. The camera follows his back as he walks down the deck. The next shot shows him entering the radio cabin to receive a message; again, his back is toward the camera. Only when he walks left in the same shot to look at a calendar do we see his face.

Delaying the first view of the star's face is not an uncommon device in Hollywood films (one example that comes readily to mind is the party scene near the beginning of *Notorious*, a scene throughout which Cary Grant is pointedly shown only from the back), but here it seems peculiarly unmotivated. The delay is so brief that some viewers may not feel it as such or notice it as odd. The apparent arbitrariness of the directorial choice is characteristic of the film and is in fact the perfect device for introducing us to its totally closed world. It suggests the mystery surrounding Corbett, whose refusal to communicate with the other characters (and thus with us) will be a source of tension throughout most of the film. Moreover, the opening shots define our relation to him and to the film by privileging the moment of his trying to *know* something (his turning toward the calendar — a sign of thinking), announcing that knowledge will be important to the film. By asking us to pay attention to the unfolding of an enterprise that is at first utterly meaningless to us, the film sets up the relation between Corbett's knowing and our not knowing, a relationship that it will continue to maintain.

Later, Corbett traces the outline of the Honduran coast, and the river that he must travel, from a ship map onto a sheet of tracing paper. The map comes to symbolize his knowledge of the jungle, knowledge that Corbett constantly asserts before the other characters. Because it is on paper, it can be betrayed: in fact, it exists (in the plot) only so that Sheppard can find it and claim that it gives him power over Corbett, whom he threatens to "kill with a piece of paper." Sheppard's discovery of the map reveals its fatal power (which it shares with the Runic text in *Night of the Demon*), which he can't invoke, since doing so would also cause his own death. Corbett's money belt, on which the name "Lisa" is stenciled, similarly gives physical form to the mystery surrounding him and allows his secret knowledge to enter the circle of objects that can be detached and betrayed and that are matters of life and death. Near the end of the film, when Corbett is helpless with malaria, Sylvia saves his life by giving the money belt to Reyes. (The malaria brings Corbett to the vulnerable position in which most of Tourneur's heroes and heroines eventually find themselves and through which they find themselves saved: cf. *Circle of Danger* and *Way of a Gaucho*.)

The early scenes of *Appointment in Honduras* show us only fragments of situations and relationships. The Sheppards are introduced in a bland way that immediately tells us all we need to know about them — he's a snob, she doesn't love him, both are bored — and yet tells us, in a sense, nothing. The scene in which Sylvia sees Corbett leaving the captain's cabin exemplifies the film's clipped, enigmatic way of presenting the characters and setting them up for their adventure. Sylvia dryly asks him if he found what he was looking for; Corbett merely opens the door to her stateroom for her and says, "Good night, Mrs. Sheppard." (The partly opened doorway perfectly frames, in the background, Sylvia's yellow nightgown draped over her bed. This detail of the mise-en-scène is present, no doubt, only because she will be wearing the nightgown for much of the film.)

Blocking simple scenes in patterns of automatic, overlapping back-and-forth movement, Tourneur achieves a beautifully stylized monotony. After the convicts, under Corbett's orders, take over the ship, Tourneur stages a long take of about one and a half minutes (interrupted briefly by an insert of a close shot of the captain) that is amazing not because of any Ophulsian virtuosity (apart from panning and tilting slightly, the camera moves only on the axis perpendicular to the camera plane) but because of its atmosphere of automatism. The shot begins as one of the convicts shoots the radio operator through the open doorway to the radio cabin. (Note that the preceding shot of the radio operator isn't from the point of view of the killer but is from the same establishing-shot angle that was used previously in Corbett's visits to the radio cabin. Cutting from this shot to the shot of the assassin on the deck produces the jarring, incongruous effect characteristic of Tourneur's death scenes: the two spaces fail to intersect, are irrelevant to each other; death strikes as a spatial illogicality.) The camera pans with the killer, who walks away; Corbett enters the shot and casually slaps him and guns him down (for disobeying his order against shooting). Reyes, entering the shot, ruefully observes that the dead convict was his cousin, but (as he will continue to do for most of the narrative) he declines to confront Corbett. Now the background and the foreground of the frame fill up with activity as the convicts prepare to cast off in the dinghy. Sylvia emerges from her stateroom at the back of the shot and demands that Corbett release her husband (whom he has put in the dinghy as a hostage); Sheppard gets up in the foreground, then at Corbett's order immediately sits down again out of camera range. Sylvia insults Corbett, who wordlessly lifts her and hands her over to Sheppard in the dinghy, the camera tracking back.

With so much going on, the shot is remarkable for its complete lack of emphasis: the two killings at the beginning of the shot are brutally casual, and the camera quickly moves away from them; Reyes briefly stands up to Corbett, then backs down from him without the basic neutrality of his personality undergoing any change; Corbett barely acknowledges any of the other characters; Sheppard appears briefly in the frame in mechanical response to the voices of Corbett and Sylvia. The overall impression is of a flurry of movements that could be accidents or purposeful actions but to which, in either case, the camera remains essentially indifferent — an indifference it confers on the characters, who appear remote not just from us and from each other but, strangely, from themselves; they seem, while they are present on screen, as if they're about to be abandoned.

Appointment in Honduras continues to explore the malignant, inhuman space of this abandonment. In the scenes showing Corbett and his band making their way upriver, this absolute otherness is manifested in cutaways to carnivorous animals such as alligators and piranhas ("tigerfish") and in peculiar animations of insects: the ants that swarm over Sheppard's white shirt and Sylvia's yellow nightgown; the mysterious cloud of bees (?) that swoops toward the dinghy in the sky, in shots that anticipate the airborne menaces of *Night of the Demon*.

In *Appointment in Honduras*, Tourneur's seeming indifference toward the characters and their destinies harbors a kind of compassion. He shows their deaths abruptly and unsentimentally, always distancing them from us, sometimes by camera angle, for example the precisely placed high-angle shot of Jiminez's body draped over the side of the dinghy as it is carried away down the river. The film isn't purely negative: a strong positive value is attached to Sylvia's love for Corbett and possibly to the unexpected flare-up of Corbett's idealism after Reyes and his men kill the two counterrevolutionaries masquerading as villagers. Even these expressions of passion, however, remain muted and fail to overcome the dominant uncertainty of the film.

Although vicissitudes of politics supposedly determine the action, at least in a formal sense, the film gives us no information that would allow us to evaluate the claims and positions of the two rival forces. Nor is such information necessary. It is not accidental that for most of the film, most of the characters think they're in Guatemala when actually they're in Honduras: the confusion is part not just of Corbett's strategy but of the film's strategy, by which it makes clear that the film is not about Guatemala or Honduras but "Honduras."[8]

Considering the abstract nature of its preoccupations, and considering that, like many of Tourneur's other films, *Appointment in Honduras* gives the impression of being somewhat slow, it is surprising to realize the extent to which Tourneur strives to compress actions and events, creating an American action cinema at its extreme of economy and ellipsis. After Reyes decides to keep the Sheppards as hostages rather than allow them to signal the ship to pick them up, as originally planned, there is a short pause, marked by Sylvia's taking a swing at Corbett, after which, in the same unstable shot (its lines of force shifting in the shallow visual field), all the characters wordlessly turn and proceed into the jungle. Later, at

Sylvia (Ann Sheridan) kneels by her husband (Zachary Scott) in *Appointment in Honduras*.

camp, Harry Sheppard looks offscreen, ostensibly at Corbett, on whose behavior he comments to Sylvia. Without a pause, Harry gets up and goes in the direction of his look, but the next shot shows him joining not Corbett but the convicts, whom he tries to tempt with another of his inept schemes. Tourneur eliminates the time, which most directors would probably have chosen to indicate, of the change in Sheppard's attention from Corbett to the convicts.

As the film progresses, the characters' increasing exhaustion causes their abrupt movements to take on a peculiarly numbed, pointless quality. One remarkable sequence begins with a shot of Corbett, followed by Reyes, cutting a passage through the brush: they enter from behind camera right and proceed diagonally across the frame. In the next shot, Sylvia enters the frame, also from behind camera right, catches up with the others, and asks them to wait. Corbett stops and asks, "What for?" "My husband," she says. Corbett turns again and continues on his way. Sylvia turns and leaves the frame where she entered it, behind camera right. Reyes, stepping into the spot she has vacated, gestures to Castro (Jack Elam), and the two follow her off right.

The next shot has Harry enter from behind camera right and Sylvia, in the middleground, from off left. He begins, "Sylvia, listen —," but she cuts him off by turning and going off left, again reversing direction and leaving the frame within moments of entering it. Harry follows her, the camera tracking left with him: "Sylvia, please, wait a minute." She stops and turns to face him; the camera stops too. In the left background, Reyes and Castro approach. Seeing them, Harry says, "Maybe we should thank Mr. Corbett for sending help." "No, señor, you have to thank me," says Reyes, who turns and walks out of frame at left. Castro waits for Sylvia and Harry to cross off left after Reyes before bringing up the rear.

The pointlessness of these shots exhausts their dramatic interest. By speeding up the characters' movements and having them occur simultaneously, Tourneur renders them nearly incomprehensible. Harry's plight, Sylvia's becoming aware of it, what Harry wants to tell Sylvia — the beginnings of all the impulses and gestures that make up the situation have been cut off, so that we see the total only in fragments.

As Jonathan Rosenbaum has noted, the film's jungle scenes are lit and photographed as if they were interiors;[9] their fluidity reflects the total control characteristic of studio filmmaking. The rainstorm sequence, for example, emphasizes the characters' chaotic dispersion in space, subordinating them to the decor; on being shot, a soldier appears not so much to fall as to be instantly absorbed into the flora. The evenness of tone in the jungle scenes is disrupted only briefly, but with great impact. In the episode of Harry's attempted escape to join the federal police party chasing Corbett, the film uses long shots to show the space between the two groups, space that Harry tries to traverse. This sudden widening of perspective, and the relatively rare sight of a real exterior in the film, give both relief from the oppressive beauty of the rest of the film and a sense of destiny (like the long shots in *The Leopard Man*, *Way of a Gaucho*, *Stranger on Horseback*, and *Wichita*). The changes in shot scale and light quality produce the quasi-hallucination of a sudden hollowing-out of space, bringing the obscure to light and making it appear small.

The village where the last sequence of the film takes place is a timeless, abstract site, where ordinary life does not go on or has been forced into hiding. Merely a setting for the violence the foreign visitors commit against each other, the village has the air of remaining undisturbed by it (this is also true of rural or communal settings in *The Leopard Man*, *Days of Glory*, *Out of the Past*, *Circle of Danger*, *Nightfall*, and *Timbuktu*). It is an extension of the country, its houses made of materials little distanced by processing from their natural state.

The film introduces the village in a high-angle long shot. Over a shot of Reyes in a thatch hut, we hear Corbett call him out. The sequence breaks down into a series of shots whose relationship is confusing: spaces viewed from between huts or from inside them, through their entrances. Harry gets killed accidentally, absurdly, like the priest in *Great Day in the Morning*.

The final showdown between Corbett and Reyes is preceded by a portentous backward tracking shot that starts on two rifles leaning against each other, crossed, in a clearing. Corbett's victory over Reyes is so improbable as to be miraculous: he kills Reyes with an underhand machete throw before Reyes can get a shot off with the pistol pointed at Corbett steadily — but this is precisely the film's point. In this context, appearances ("Well, Reyes, looks like you win," Corbett concedes while drawing closer with the hidden machete) are absolutely unreliable. The urge to show everything at the height of provocation (as in the protracted episode of Corbett and Sylvia kissing while Harry watches, a scene that recalls Logan kissing Lucy in front of George in *Canyon Passage*) reaches a paroxysm here.

Appointment in Honduras has a happy ending, but one in which the function of the happy ending is not so much subverted as transcended in the glistening close-up of Ann Sheridan. Somehow, it is definitely Sheridan we see here (in almost the same way that it is Marina Vlady or Anna Karina we see in certain shots in Godard's work) — an actress, looking offscreen and thinking about her future, or her past, or perhaps nothing. Her "character" has already ceased to exist or has become part of the film's overall texture of appearances, in a shot that holds us for one last time before it releases us from the dream of the film.

Stranger on Horseback (1955)

Narrative sense, narrative power can survive ANY truncation.... An author
having a very small amount of true contents can make it the basis of formal
and durable mastery, provided he neither inflates nor falsifies.

EZRA POUND, *ABC OF READING*

Continuing the downward commercial spiral of his career, Tourneur's next
film, *Stranger on Horseback*, was a three-week, $380,000 Western produced for the
independent company Leonard Goldstein Productions and starring Tourneur's old
friend Joel McCrea. In the same category of commercial production as Randolph
Scott's films for Joseph H. Lewis and Budd Boetticher, *Stranger on Horseback* holds
up well next to these works. Though more conventional than Lewis's *A Lawless
Street* or most of the Boetticher-Scott films, it is no less marked by its director's
personality.

Circuit judge Richard Thorne (Joel McCrea) arrives in the frontier town of
Bannerman, which he finds to be entirely dominated by Josiah Bannerman (John
McIntire) and his clan. Thorne learns that Bannerman's son, Tom (Kevin
McCarthy), has killed a man, Morrison, whose wife Tom had been chasing.
Thorne arrests Tom and, with the aid of the local marshal, Nat Bell (Emile
Meyer), prepares to try him for murder. Fearing a raid on the jail by some of Ban-
nerman's men, Thorne and the marshal sneak Tom out of town at night, along
with two witnesses. Bannerman's men surround the small group in open country.
Thorne apparently surrenders Tom to them, only to take cover and start shooting
unexpectedly. Bannerman calls off the ensuing gunfight and relinquishes Tom to
the judge. The film ends with Thorne calling Tom's trial to order.

The force of the script lies in the conflict between the primordial law of the
clan, blood, and the earth, embodied in Josiah Bannerman, and Judge Thorne's
conjunction of legal and moral authority ("Could be a preacher in that getup,"
Colonel Buck Streeter [John Carradine], Bannerman's legal adviser, remarks on
seeing Thorne for the first time — a possible reference to McCrea's role in *Stars in
My Crown*). The conflict develops strangely, with Thorne winning over his opponents neither by reason nor by force but by a combination of inner conviction and
sexual magnetism, the latter working on Amy Lee, Bannerman's niece. Amy Lee is
one of the strangest Tourneur heroines. Introduced shooting at targets that Tom
holds up from behind a table turned on its side ("a couple of bear cubs playing

Miroslava and Joel McCrea in *Stranger on Horseback*.

around," says Josiah), she habitually carries a riding crop; the dominatrix effect this creates is accentuated by her scorn for her weak, despised fiancé and by the Slavic accent of the actress (Miroslava, who as Miroslava Stern next appeared in Buñuel's *Ensayo de un crimen* [*The Criminal Life of Archibaldo de la Cruz*, 1955]).

As in Tourneur's next film, *Wichita* (which has several similarities, mostly superficial, to *Stranger on Horseback*), the characters come in three kinds: those who are instinctively good; those who are instinctively bad; and those who occupy a gray area in between and are capable of switching immediately from one side to the other. At the end of *Stranger on Horseback*, Bannerman guns down one of his own men to spare the apparently helpless Thorne. Like Amy Lee's conversion, his own occurs without any preaching or appeals to morality, civic duty, or the progress of civilization. Tourneur is less interested in exploring a moral theme than in showing the inevitable triumph of law over the actions, consciences, and destinies of people.

Stranger on Horseback is one of the hardest of Tourneur's films to see. At the time of writing, the only copy I have had access to is a videotape of a poor black-and-white TV dupe. Its abysmal quality makes it impossible to assess the film's visual impact — and pointless to discuss the film in any but the most general terms. (Nevertheless, it may not be far-fetched to claim that this version of the film approximates its authoritative state. Tourneur saw the rushes and workprint in

black-and-white and repudiated the color version when he saw it for the first time
at the film's preview, saying that the Anscocolor process had ruined the film: "It
was quite ugly; a flat color, with no relief, a kind of grisaille.")[1]

In any case, even a bad print makes it clear that *Stranger on Horseback* is a
visually accomplished work that mobilizes high angles, long shots, tracking shots,
and frames within the frame with Tourneur's customary intelligence, giving a certain dry grandeur to the story and its low-budget trappings. In the first scene,
Tourneur uses a slow tracking shot from Thorne's point of view to show Morrison's funeral taking place alongside a trail. The subjective tracking shot conveys
both mystery and a sense of inevitability. When Thorne arrives in town and dismounts in front of the hotel, Tourneur shows him from the vantage point of the
doorway of a saloon across the street. Here we become aware of Thorne as an
intruder in a space bounded by narrow perspectival limits. This happens again
later in the shot of Thorne through a window as he approaches a house.

The prevalence of night scenes marks *Stranger on Horseback* as Tourneurian,
as does the quiet, intimate tone of the actors' line readings. Tourneur's racial tolerance is expressed in Thorne's kindly treatment of a family of illegal Mexican aliens.
The marshal's pet cat strikes me as a particularly Tourneurian detail, especially in
the scene in which Bannerman's men break into the jail: sleeping on a table in the
middleground, the cat wakes up and runs away when the men break in.

The scenes in the open range in the last quarter of the film are notable for
the architectural rigor of the compositions, reminiscent of *Way of a Gaucho*. The
film's most powerful image is the long shot of Thorne apparently giving up the
attempt to resist Bannerman's men: walking away from the camera, his figure gets
smaller and smaller in the frame. As in the shot of Clay Douglas walking away on
the heath in *Circle of Danger*, this gesture of resignation and apparent helplessness
conceals, in a Tao-like manner, renewed strength. (Similarly, the heroes of *Way of a
Gaucho*, *Great Day in the Morning*, and *Nightfall* are all spared and released at the
bottom of their own circles of danger.)

Wichita (1955)

Two things fill the mind with ever new and increasing awe and admiration
the more frequently and continuously reflection is occupied with them;
the starred heaven above me and the moral law within me.

IMMANUEL KANT, *CRITIQUE OF
PRACTICAL REASON*

More concentrated than *Canyon Passage*, more expansive than *Stranger on
Horseback*, and less neurotic than *Great Day in the Morning*, *Wichita* realizes the
golden mean among Tourneur's Westerns. It is an ideal medium-budget Western,
whose precisely judged details of performance, decor, and composition fall unerr-
ingly into place; it has no pomposity but also none of the abject baldness and
predigested triteness of the merely routine Western.

Wyatt Earp (Joel McCrea), an unknown yet to establish his fame in law
enforcement, arrives in Wichita with the intention of opening a business. On his
first day in town, his quick draw and accurate aim foil a bank holdup. The mayor,
Andrew Hope (Carl Benton Reid), a witness to the incident, offers him the job of
marshal, but Earp turns it down. Later, however, when a little boy is killed in the
indiscriminate gunfire of a bunch of drunken cowboys, Earp has himself sworn in
as marshal and arrests the troublemakers, with the help of Bat Masterson (Keith
Larsen), a reporter and apprentice printer he has befriended.

Earp's rigorous law enforcement alarms the town's leading citizens, including
Sam McCoy (Walter Coy) and Doc Black (Edgar Buchanan), who fear that Earp
will ruin business in Wichita by alienating the cattlemen. Now aided by his brothers, Morgan (Peter Graves) and Jim (John Smith), Earp catches Doc Black in a plot
against his life and runs Black out of town. Doc Black hires two cowboys to gun
down Wyatt, but the gunmen succeed only in accidentally killing McCoy's wife,
Mary (Mae Clarke), before being chased and killed by the Earps. In a final showdown, both Doc Black and Gyp Clements (Lloyd Bridges), the brother of one of
the slain gunmen, are killed. At the fade-out, Wyatt and his bride, Laurie McCoy
(Vera Miles), set out for Dodge City, where Wyatt has taken a job as marshal.

Of the major directorial approaches to the Western — those of Ford, Hawks,
Walsh, Mann, Boetticher, Peckinpah, Eastwood — that of Tourneur is the hardest
to discuss in terms of the rhetoric of themes, character types, and narrative construction, a rhetoric that is fundamental to an oeuvre as schematically compact and
consistent as, say, Boetticher's. *Wichita* crystallizes this difficulty, because it is at
once the purest of Westerns and a film that is absolutely alien. The film's concerns,

which it doesn't hesitate to spell out, are those of the genre: the difference between
gunmen and gunfighters; the danger of the marshal's job. By forcing our attention
on these issues, *Wichita* makes us see them in a new way.

   Wichita is less a film of action than one of grandeur and terror, whose mise-
en-scène is as implacable as Wyatt Earp himself. Behind the calm lies a darkness
that displaces the familiarity of the film's good-vs.-evil Western morality play. The
film shows the cowboys' degeneration into random violence as irresistible and
inevitable, whereas Wyatt's goodness and skill become signs of death, a fateful
power that the villains of the film feel compelled to test themselves against and
that destroys them with mechanical, chilling predictability.

   Many Tourneur films draw their tension from an interior conflict involving
the protagonist or from a mystery regarding his actions and motivations. *Wichita*
continues this tendency to some extent. Wyatt embodies the transition from
archaic to modern society, from coercive authority to the internalization of ethical
principles. He is thus a contradictory figure, as his initial refusal to take the job of
marshal reveals. The film displaces this tension, however, to an external conflict
between civilizing forces and forces of chaos. It also locates this conflict in the
wavering morality of the cowboys, showing them as normal men capable of generosity and reason but exacerbated by extreme physical conditions — the depriva-
tion of the trail followed suddenly by access to liquor and prostitutes. (This bias
toward moral realism is one of several key ways in which Tourneur's film differs
from Ford's *My Darling Clementine*, the classic version of the Wyatt Earp myth.)

   Dr. Judd said in *Cat People*, "There is a psychic need to loose evil on the
world." *Wichita* shares this awareness of the tenuousness of the bonds of civilization, of the permanent danger of violence and cruelty, with other Tourneur films,
notably *Canyon Passage*, in which the people of Jacksonville release their pent-up
tendencies in rituals of violence and destruction and in which the outbreak of the
Indians is not only a response to white violence but also the symbolic expression of
the whites' nostalgia for disorder.

   Wichita is built on the opposition between inside and outside, as Paul Willemen notes.[1] The film repeatedly shows violence in terms of the crossing of a line
between two spaces: the shootings of the boy and of Mrs. McCoy; the cowboys'
return across the town line in violation of Wyatt's order; Doc Black's sniping at
Wyatt from a second-story window. The law surges up out of these border viola-
tions; the town line is marked not by a gate or other obstacle but by a printed text
on a signpost: "The carrying of firearms on the streets of Wichita is prohibited."

   Wichita deals more explicitly than *Canyon Passage* with the origin of morality.
Morality begins in a reaction to the personal consequences of crime: if Arthur
Whiteside (Wallace Ford), the alcoholic newspaper publisher, is now moral, perhaps it is only because his wife was murdered, just as with McCoy at the end of
the film. In *Wichita*, everything remains still in the future: Wyatt Earp hasn't yet
made his reputation as a lawman (at the end of the film we see him head off to
Dodge City), and Wichita's brief age of prosperity is just about to begin. The pure
time when nothing yet has happened, when people are not yet judged, when they
seem to have no past and to come from nowhere — this is the time of *Wichita*.

   The opening sequences of the cattle drive crystallize the strangeness in the
familiar that Tourneur leads us to find. Because the film opens before we know

Wyatt (Joel McCrea) keeping the peace in *Wichita*.

what is at stake in the narrative or can distinguish between what is "important" and what is merely "ornament" or "atmosphere," and because there are at first no stars but only character actors (some of the most familiar ones, with faces worn smooth from exposure like stones on a beach: Walter Sande, Robert J. Wilke, Jack Elam), we read the sequence with detachment; we skim over it. The scene has an unusual freshness and the indescribable air of an event taking place for the first and the last time, of a present in the process of disappearing.

A source of potential conflict disturbs the calm of the scene: the mysterious lone stranger on the horizon, seen in an extreme long shot that is one of the most resonant and powerful images of the film. The mild consternation that this vision causes in the cowboys, and the dispatching of one of them, Al Mann (Elam), to check whether the stranger is traveling alone, evoke a danger with which we are all familiar, but the mood is of curiosity rather than alarm.

The stranger turns out to be Wyatt Earp, who joins the cowboys for supper. The underlying tension breaks out at night when Earp, apparently asleep, is robbed by Gyp and Hal Clements. Earp is, however, awake — a fact the film discloses to the audience in a cutaway, disrupting our relationship with the group. Shortly afterward, there is an almost subliminal cutaway to Ben Thompson (Wilke) nudging

Clint Wallace (Sande) awake when Earp confronts his robbers. All the moments when characters are isolated from the group in their perception of events (including the discreet dialogue between Gyp and Hal about the stranger's presumed wealth) are triggered by and center on Earp as a figure of mystery, endowed with real or speculative concealed resources. The film emphasizes Earp's emergences from offscreen, first when he arrives at the camp and second when he surprises Gyp and Hal as they count the money they've stolen from him.

Wichita visually underlines the doubling of the figure of the criminal into *two* brothers when they move apart slightly to prepare to deal with the approaching Earp. Jean-Claude Biette has identified the theme of two brothers as "the invisible thread that ties the story together."[2] The brothers represent the kernel of tribal solidarity, a fraternal unit outside the law. This idea surfaces again when two men who prove to be Wyatt Earp's brothers ride into Wichita wearing their guns, in defiance of the law posted at the town line. The ominous music and the two men's manner and dress (Morgan all in black, with a black hat) prompt us to take them for bad guys — the same mistake that Doc Black makes in assuming that they are the hired guns he has sent for to assassinate Wyatt. In *Wichita*, the fraternal relation is the ultimate in deadly violence, not because of a rivalry between the brothers but because the tension that could erupt in that rivalry, the tension of being two, is constantly ready to unleash itself on the world. Tourneur makes this clear in Gyp and Hal's play-fight that precedes the cowboys' "hurrahing" of the town.

After the opening sequences on the plain, we go to the town border, marked by a signpost, a place to which the film will return again, repeatedly emphasizing it as a site of inclusion/exclusion. Two coaches filled with laughing women pass Wyatt as he waits with his horse near the signpost; at the end of the film, Wyatt and Laurie will ride out of town in a coach amid similar high spirits and celebration.

Wichita is a crowded site of bustle and confusion. The film evokes the skepticism about civilization and growth expressed in *Canyon Passage* and develops this attitude more fully. We share Earp's disorientation in the town (he has been in the wilderness, buffalo hunting) and Whiteside's pessimism about the source of the town's economic development ("Here come the history-makers," he says disgustedly as the Big W cowboys ride into town firing their guns). McCoy's speech at the dedication of the railroad, although surrounded by signs of celebration, is subtly menacing in its blunt statement of the economic imperative: "Never forget that, folks, this is a cattle town and a cattlemen's town.... Let's get back to work!"

The sequence in which the cowboys become increasingly drunk and riotous and shoot up the town is, like the whole of *Wichita*, elemental in its simplicity, yet it is one of the most impressive sequences in all of Tourneur's films. The slow, meticulous, ominous buildup to violence recalls the mob scenes in Lang's *Fury*. Tourneur constantly shoots the cowboys from high angles, notably when they mass in the street under Earp's window and fire their guns at random. The high angles simultaneously register the film's (and Wyatt's) moral disapproval and the sense that the cowboys' violence is part of an unstoppable process that has gone beyond their freedom to choose.

The killing of the little boy in the upstairs window is a shocking event, not shown in the script, which merely has the mother carrying the boy's dead body downstairs to the hotel lobby.[3] One of the remarkable aspects of the scene is the boy's sense of wonder: to him, the cowboys' guns, their sounds, are part of a magical spectacle, perhaps the continuation of the dream from which he has just awakened. We "see" the boy's death only as his reaction to being shot, the child actor's pantomime creating the event that punctuates the flow of the medium shot, just as the window through which he looks punctuates the flow of the Cinemascope frame.

The boy's killing leads Wyatt to assume his predestined role of lawman, a moment that the film ritualizes: the mayor insists on swearing him in before he goes out into the street with a shotgun to face the cowboys. After this point, the themes of the film crystallize: Wyatt comes into conflict not only with the cattlemen but also with the pillars of the community, who, fearful for their economic interests, try to have him removed; at the same time, Wyatt courts Laurie. Their relationship is marked, strangely, by the pressure of time. "Obviously our new Marshal is not a man who believes in wasting time," observes one of the McCoys' dinner guests when Earp invites Laurie to a picnic. At the picnic, Earp says: "Time never seemed very important to me before, Laurie. Now it is. I don't want to waste a minute of it." Later, when Laurie asks him to explain the conflict between him and her father, he says: "It would take a very long time to explain it, Laurie, and I don't have much time…. I wish I did." The "time" mentioned in these lines — short, hurrying, haunting — is different from the time of the total commitment to the role of lawman; the latter is an endless time, the time of myth, "as long as it takes," as Earp tells Whiteside.

The arrival of Morgan and James Earp creates a suspense that the viewer may find gratuitous but that in fact pushes to an extreme the film's implacable, arbitrary terror. When Wyatt enters the saloon to confront the two men he has been told are wearing guns in town, the film cuts to a shot of Morgan standing at the bar, apparently ready for a showdown. He holds his flat stare, and the camera holds its impassive medium-shot gaze, for a duration that we perceive as extremely long, before he breaks into a smile of recognition. As in the films of Murnau and Lang, the delay of the look equals the delay of the shot. Both are aggressions against the viewer.

The final showdown follows Mrs. McCoy's funeral; the mourners, with Wyatt and his brothers at the head of the group, round a corner and see the cowboys, led by Wallace, approaching down the main street. (Before this confrontation, two shots show Doc Black, his head down, enter the hotel with a rifle and start up the stairs. His automatism and the shots' complete lack of comment or explanation remind us of Wes before the murder of Jessica in *I Walked with a Zombie*, of George about to kill McIver in *Canyon Passage*, and of Jumbo after he kills Boston in *Great Day in the Morning*.) The showdown is staged simply, impassively. We hear birds singing; there is hardly any dialogue, and until guns are fired, there is no music. Staging the scene right after a funeral gives it an extraordinary ambience: one might recall *Johnny Guitar*, although in that film, Ray uses the funeral clothes of the posse for ironic contrast, whereas Tourneur uses the funeral atmosphere simply to highlight the calm of the scene and to accentuate its ritual inevitability.

Gyp's death is almost tragic. As played by Lloyd Bridges, Gyp is no stock heavy, but someone who is simply unthinking and selfish rather than vicious and perverse. Wyatt's reply after Gyp declares that one or the other of them must die is

Wichita: Robert J. Wilke (on table).

simple and memorable: "I know, Gyp. I'm sorry." Finally, Tourneur underlines the importance of Gyp's death by putting his Cinemascope camera close to the ground to record it. This is not envisioned by the final shooting script, which calls for the camera to hold on a close shot of Wyatt while Gyp dies offscreen; then, after Wyatt "slowly returns the gun to its holster and starts to turn away," the script has a cut to Gyp's body lying near McCoy as the latter shoots Doc Black. As Tourneur shot the scene, Gyp dies in his own desolate, stretched-out, definitive shot, and McCoy's killing of Doc Black takes place as an unrelated miracle. The scene ends with a low shot in the street: Gyp's body is splayed in the foreground, and the futile, despondent band of Wallace and the cowboys rides away deep in the background — a quietly devastating image of waste. Immediately negating this image, the coda, in which Wyatt and Laurie, newly wed, set off for Dodge City, reaffirms the ritual aspect of the film. Like *Canyon Passage*, the film ends with a song.

This unpretentious film is a visual triumph. The interiors, especially those of the McCoy home, where several scenes take place, show the care with detail characteristic of *Cat People*, *Experiment Perilous*, and *Circle of Danger* (to name three Tourneur films in which the interior design is outstanding). We find the same compositional and dramaturgical emphasis on doorways, passages, and transitions. The set design of the film is extremely effective, creating, along with the warm lighting, a dimension of unexplored reality and organic coherence.

Wichita was Tourneur's first film in Cinemascope. Unlike some veteran directors, Tourneur embraced the new process.

> For a director, Cinemascope is the ideal for several reasons. It reproduces approximately our field of vision.... Cinemascope also obliges the director to work harder. With the small screen, it's very easy to exclude extraneous elements, certain extras for example. With Cinemascope, on the contrary, you need an enormous amount of rehearsal work because each extra is constantly in view and doesn't leave the frame. Thus, it's necessary to rehearse them separately and individually. But, on the other hand, you gain time because there are fewer cuts, less montage.... This format also makes it possible to create interesting relationships between characters in the foreground and those in the background. Since the end of the silent era, we've had a tendency to forget about pictorial composition: all the effort has been concentrated on the dialogue, on speech. Cinemascope makes it necessary to compose.[4]

Unfortunately, *Wichita* was Tourneur's only major work in Cinemascope, although he also used the format interestingly in portions of *La Battaglia di Maratona* and in a few shots in *War-Gods of the Deep*. (*Great Day in the Morning* is in Superscope, a process that involved shooting with a nonanamorphic lens and normal camera on regular 35mm film stock but composing shots so that anamorphic prints at various widescreen ratios could be made optically, cropping the top and bottom of the frame.) It is also unfortunate that Scope prints of *Wichita* aren't widely available. The sense of the town as a community and as a place is incomparably stronger in the film as Tourneur made it, in Cinemascope, than in the flat version shown on TV. Street scenes have constant activity and movement: in a shot of Wyatt entering the bank, workers at screen left are busy putting up a new building. Cowboys spill across the screen as they arrive in town ("There she is, she's all yours"). After the shooting of Mrs. McCoy, the night-to-day dissolve from the McCoy housefront to the open range has a power and beauty that the flat version barely suggests; after so many intimate scenes and shots in interiors and streets, the sudden expansiveness of the open-range horseback chase is breathtaking.

In *Wichita*, Tourneur uses Cinemascope to create visual imbalance. In the sequence at the cowboys' camp early in the film, three men's bodies fill the foreground while Wyatt, in the background, rides toward the camera on the right side of the screen. Later, at the Wichita town line, Wyatt, alone on horseback in the right of the screen, is passed by a stagecoach that fills up its left and center. The sequence of the cowboys shooting up the town includes numerous off-balance compositions: in a high-angle shot, a cowboy's rifle butt shatters a streetlamp at the left of the frame; there's a superb shot in the hotel lobby in which Wyatt's white-shirted figure at the right of the screen is precariously balanced with the dark staircase (down which the mother comes carrying her dead child) at left.

Tourneur uses the full width of the screen. In the shot of the two Clements brothers preparing to rob the sleeping Wyatt, they are at left and he is at right, the wide space between them tensely empty. Leaving Wichita, the cowboys form a procession across the screen from left background to right middleground; a sign-post at right marks the limits both of the town and of the frame. Later, Gyp shoots at a wall in a saloon, writing the letter "W" (after the ranch he works for, the Big W) in bullet holes: his figure, in the foreground at left, leaning back in a chair, is balanced by another man leaning back in his chair at right; the "W" shape on the wall in the background echoes the composition's bilateral symmetry. After the end of the gunfight in open country, a high-angle medium shot shows Morgan and Bat on the ground in the left half of the frame, with Wyatt standing in the right half, his body partly turned left. In the background, the obtrusive white shape of a salt patch thins out as it crosses the screen from left to right, creating a sense of increased space behind and around Wyatt, in contrast to the visually crowded area at left.

Despite the visual expansiveness of the film, *Wichita* remains true to Tour-neur's career-long preoccupation with the imperceptible. In *Wichita*, Tourneur films the fleeting present — not the present that is frozen in its flight, as in the films of Nicholas Ray and Rossellini, but the present that belongs to the flow of time and that cannot be taken out of it, the nonexistent present of the impossible, impenetrable event. Or as Louis Skorecki put it, Tourneur's "is a cinema of the instant, and yet that instant always exists in parenthesis."[5] The most haunting events in *Wichita* can almost not be shown, and yet the film shows them: the shooting, through a window, of the boy, a shooting that is seen by no one but us, the viewers; and the drive-by shooting, through a door, of Mrs. McCoy, a shoot-ing that we see as bullets splintering the door.

Great Day in the Morning (1956)

I no longer know whether the events I am about to relate are effects or causes.

JORGE LUIS BORGES,
"THE END OF THE DUEL"

Andrew Sarris singles out *Great Day in the Morning* among Tourneur's Westerns as a successful case of the director's "gentility" raising the genre "to a new, unaccustomed level of subdued, pastel-colored sensibility." Sarris's preference of *Great Day* to *Stranger on Horseback* and *Wichita*, films that he claims "lack both excitement and the compensating sensibility of *Great Day in the Morning*" (he doesn't comment on *Canyon Passage*), no doubt reflects not only his appreciation of a certain visual sophistication that *Great Day* possesses more obviously than do the other two films (in particular, the film's muted color schemes) but also his refusal to credit Tourneur with a genre attitude that might be expressed through other means.[1] More than Tourneur's other Westerns, *Great Day in the Morning* offers "a tension between a director's personality and his material," the tension that interests Sarris.[2] In some ways the film, which is perhaps the most puzzling and disturbing item in Tourneur's filmography, makes an ideal test case for the relevance of auteurism and Tourneur to each other.

The film takes place in 1861 in Denver, where Owen Pentecost (Robert Stack), a Southern adventurer, is lured by rumors of a $2 million gold cache intended to help the South in the event of war. The action of *Great Day in the Morning* charts the rise and fall of Pentecost's control of events. His dominance starts at a low point, where he has to be rescued from an Indian attack by three strangers: Ann Merry Alain (Virginia Mayo), Stephen Kirby (Alex Nicol), and Zeff Masterson (Leo Gordon). Pentecost's fortunes take a sharp upswing when, on his first night in Denver, he wins a saloon from its proprietor, Jumbo Means (Raymond Burr), in a poker game. Even this victory depends, however, on the intervention of the dealer, Boston (Ruth Roman), who cheats on his behalf because she is attracted to him. Subsequently, he imposes his will on the town and defends his right to do so in a duel with Lawford, a duplicitous miner, while enjoying the affections of both Boston and Ann. The outbreak of the Civil War marks the beginning of Pentecost's decline. To make the best of a bad situation, he undertakes, for a fee, to escort the Confederate gold out of the range of the Union

229

Army. During this action, he has a mysterious change of heart and renounces his fee. Back at low point, alone and hiding from the Union Army, he again benefits from the assistance of Kirby, who allows him to escape.

This outline makes the irony of the action apparent. Throughout the film, Pentecost's mastery of situations depends on the unstable complicity of other people and on the delay of the inevitable war. Only by acknowledging his dependence does he gain a certain realism. Yet Pentecost's attempts at mastery are frustrated not only by external events but also by his own actions. His renunciations at the end of the film are foreshadowed throughout, for example in his relationship with Gary (Donald MacDonald), Lawford's young son. Pentecost befriends the boy, who doesn't know that the man killed his father, and teaches him how to shoot. Pentecost's motives in pursuing this relationship are never made clear, but the other characters unequivocally mistrust them. Even the loyal Boston has the intuition that Pentecost's kindness to the boy is "wrong," and Ann complains to Kirby that Pentecost is "trying to make that boy into what he is himself." It seems impossible to avoid the interpretation, which Pentecost himself states, though attributing it to Ann's unspoken thoughts, that in teaching Gary to shoot, he is seeking his own death: "When the boy learns to shoot straight he'll fill me full of lead and save me the trouble of committing suicide. Isn't that what you're thinking?"

The film's other conflicts are also enigmatic. Pentecost and Jumbo's poker game could be "honest or dishonest." We don't know whether cheating is involved until after each hand is over. The same hand that consolidates Pentecost's position in Denver also determines his relationship with Boston, since at the crucial deal she cheats on his behalf, instead of on Jumbo's, as planned (again, we are not made aware of this until after the fact, although we might infer the truth from Jumbo's reaction). Everything depends on an action that is invisible, a point of divergence between the narrative and the mise-en-scène.

We can trace this divergence further in the two love rivalries, between Pentecost and Kirby over Ann and between Boston and Ann over Pentecost. Both the film and to some extent the characters themselves treat these affairs with remarkable indifference. The relationships are entirely arbitrary, as arbitrary as the fall of cards and Boston's "decision" that secretly determines their fall, or at any rate are subject to motives not apparent. We can read them only as renunciations. For example, Pentecost is drunk when he breaks into Ann's room to pay her his compliments; shortly afterward, when Boston puts him to bed and evidently expects to stay, he falls asleep. For the rest of the film, he treats Boston as he would any sidekick while he diligently pursues Ann, only to walk out on her just after she succumbs. In the final scene, however, Pentecost tells Kirby that he loved Boston all along without having known it.

The film may have lost some scenes that would have given these entanglements more coherence (Tourneur, who disliked the film, told *Cahiers du cinéma* that the material of the source novel had to be drastically reduced to fit the film's running time, but he didn't say whether more scenes were shot than ended up in the final cut).[3] Thus it is safest to try to deduce Tourneur's intentions from the mise-en-scène of individual scenes, examining, for example, his use of light and shadow. Two of the key stages of Pentecost's story — his kiss with Ann and his confession to Kirby in the cave — take place in partial darkness. In the scene with Ann, the two pass from a relatively light room to a relatively dark one, so that as the dialogue becomes more intense, their faces become less visible, until at the embrace, they're in complete shadow against a dimly lit wall. At first she resists, then she puts her arms around his neck, whereupon he pushes her away, both from him and from the camera, suddenly and drastically changing the composition of the static two-shot. Previously the two were in profile; now she is in full face and farther from the camera, precariously isolated on a deeper plane of the visual field. Then, as he goes out camera right and she turns to follow him with her eyes, her face goes fully into shadow.

Darkness signifies a barrier between what can and what cannot be known about the characters. At the paroxysm of the action, when, after so many equivocations, we want to see the characters' real nature exposed, Tourneur conceals them behind this barrier. Hampering the denotative or representative function of the image, darkness marks its powerlessness, or its refusal, to "speak" the action. Nor does the sound track carry the burden of meaning: the critical actions in the scene with Ann are gestural, not verbal; the dialogue between Pentecost and Kirby in the cave seems merely a formality: we're surprised by Pentecost's confession of love for Boston and by Kirby's offer to let Pentecost escape, but these last-minute peripetia have less force than Kirby's silent gesture of giving Pentecost a canteen of water, Pentecost's grateful expression as he takes it, and the camera's rising slightly as he lifts the canteen to take a drink (one of the film's few lyrical moments).

In the love scene, we might take the darkness to signify the eruption of the characters' repressed instincts. Rather than the return of the repressed, however, the scene exemplifies repression at work: embracing Pentecost, Ann turns away from the camera, toward darkness; her passage into darkness signifies not desire but her rejection of it as foreign. Pentecost's sudden exit completes the effacing of Ann's image, leaving her visible only as an outline. In the scene in the cave, the darkness is intrusive and paradoxical. We expect the final scene to solve mysteries, and the dialogue partly fulfills this expectation, but darkness conventionally does the opposite. The lighting of the cave reduces the physical difference between the two men. The darkness, the flask of water, Kirby's generosity, Pentecost's ambivalent confession — these are the scene's symbolic pretexts, by which the narrative suggests a resolution without reaching it. The imbalance that gave the story its momentum has not been reduced but merely shifted. The most striking unresolved point (among so many, such as the interrupted affairs of Ann, the fate of Gary, whether the Confederate gold reaches its destination) is that when Pentecost leaves the film, he is still ignorant of Boston's death. One would expect him, as the hero of a Hollywood film, to be apprised of such an important event as the death of the woman he loves, and a viewer who has followed the film so far would presumably be interested in observing his reaction. There is no reason Kirby should not have known of it and reported it to Pentecost. (Other Tourneur films also end with the surviving characters left unaware of some important aspect of the action. At the end of *Night of the Demon*, the whole world is to be left uninformed about the magical forces disclosed to the hero.)

Great Day in the Morning is two films. One tells the story of a man who tries to turn circumstances to his personal advantage but is forced to renounce self-interest in favor of impersonal commitments. The other takes place on the plane of the mise-en-scène, where it ceases to support the scenario and elaborates its own system of meaning, heightening the arbitrary, aleatory elements in the scenario and hinting that the actions it portrays issue from unrepresentable conflicts. This reference to the invisible renders the characters transparent and unreal (even as they remain as dangerous or as sympathetic as the script intends); their motives and destinies are determined by forces that surpass them and that can't be known.

Tourneur stages Boston's murder to give us an abstract idea of the event rather than a distinct picture of violence, submerging it in spatial relationships. Searching for Gary, who has fled, Boston hears from Jumbo, standing in the doorway of his saloon, that the boy is inside, which we know to be untrue. At first Boston doesn't believe him, but she is persuaded to see for herself after Jumbo makes a show of going to the back of the saloon and calling to an imaginary boy offscreen. The arrangement of space in the scene determines its logic. The doorway to the saloon where Boston hesitates is one of the thresholds between the certain and the unknown that take on such significance in Tourneur's horror films (cf. the two tunnels that confront Teresa in *The Leopard Man*). The center of the scene, the room in which Gary is supposedly hiding, is never shown, not even when Boston goes to look. If Lang had shot the sequence, the empty room would have appeared in all its starkness, but in Tourneur's film, absence itself is absent. The camera records the ensuing cat-and-mouse game between Jumbo and Boston in a placid medium shot, declining the offer of vicarious excitement. The murder occurs behind an upset table that conceals all but the actors' hands. Tourneur displaces the scene's brutality by highlighting its schematic and structural elements: the threshold that Boston hesitates to cross; the mysterious room that attracts her; the use of the table as a kind of curtain.

After killing Boston, Jumbo carries her body across the street in medium-long shot and lays it sacrificially on the porch of the Circus Tent saloon. This action is inserted incongruously within a sequence about the imminent showdown of the Union platoon and the Confederate band. Raymond Burr's lack of expression, the shadowy lighting, and the imbalanced composition give the event a fateful, ritualistic character reminiscent of Wesley carrying Jessica's body into the sea in *I Walked with a Zombie*.

The transitions between shots in *Great Day in the Morning* are often confusing and abrupt, reflecting the breakdown of the characters' relationships as it parallels the breakdown between the North and the South. For example, there is a straight cut from the close-up of Boston's hand falling on the saloon floor at her death to a long shot of the Union soldiers waiting outside the warehouse where the Southerners are ensconced with the gold. Earlier in the film, after the confrontation between Boston and Ann in the upstairs hall of the Circus Tent, the film cuts to a shot of Masterson outside the saloon across the street, waiting to put up his sign announcing the lying-in-state of three men killed in a shootout. Tourneur handles these transitions in a way completely different from the linking of characters and events in *The Leopard Man*, *Canyon Passage*, and *Wichita*: those films use camera movement and the circulation of characters in a public space to coordinate their various mininarratives; in *Great Day*, the use of cutting to link situations increases their discontinuity.

Tourneur also creates discontinuity even within individual sequences. In the scene at the Circus Tent in which Owen announces that he will stake the gold miners, shots are angled alternately toward the stairs, where Owen stands, and toward the front door, where Jumbo stands; the camera in both setups is behind

Great Day in the Morning: Owen (Robert Stack) teaches Gary (Donald MacDonald) how to shoot (courtesy of the Academy of Motion Picture Arts and Sciences).

the bar. Alternating between the two setups, the scene deploys progressively closer shots of Owen and Jumbo, shots that do not function as standard shot–reverse shots because neither shot is associated with the point of view of the absent member of the pair — an effect disorienting in a way difficult to analyze. Later in the same scene, when Owen asks Kirby if he wants a claim, there is a cutaway to Colonel Gibson (Carleton Young), whom we haven't yet met. Sitting at a desk with a gold scale, Gibson appears to be just the assayer, but the cutaway implies a secret connection, later confirmed, between him and Kirby (they're both incognito U.S. Army officers). Meanwhile, the sudden emergence of the shot of Gibson remains another spatially disturbing element.

The sequence of the shootout in the Circus Tent, after shots that establish the opponents in space, breaks down into spatially confusing shots as they choose various hiding places. We see Owen and Boston behind the bar, Gary through the balustrade on the stairs, Masterson and another Northerner behind a table. Only with the intervention of Father Murphy (Regis Toomey), and his accidental death, does the scene's spatial unity reassert itself in a medium shot.

Belying its title (which has no evident relation to the story), *Great Day in the*

Morning is one of Tourneur's bleakest, most pessimistic films, its tone set by the bitter hatred with which Masterson addresses Pentecost in the opening sequence after realizing that he's a Southerner. The death drive is all that unifies the film's loosely connected incidents: Pentecost's air of passivity; his ambiguous gestures toward and away from the other characters; his final renunciation of the self-interest he has ostensibly followed throughout; the obsessiveness of Masterson's and Jumbo's baleful antagonism; the low-angle shots of grim-faced men marching against a dark sky to avenge the surrender of Fort Sumter. Death occurs, as in *Wichita*, by accident: Father Murphy is shot down when he tries to stop the gun battle; Jumbo is blown up in the explosion that the Southerners set off to cover their escape. These accidents aren't "absurd" but arise logically and geometrically out of unstable situations.

The darkness that dominates *Great Day in the Morning* (virtually the entire last fourth of the film takes place at night) evokes the threat and the attraction of the void, which the lamps constantly blazing in the film's interiors try weakly to ward off. The compositions delineate spaces that are too wide for the people who inhabit them and that ultimately engulf the inhabitants. Against a visual background of brooding peace and calm — the mountains and sky looming behind the newly constructed town in Tourneur's characteristic long shots — the events of the film form an unfathomable, inevitable pattern of hostility to man.

As in *Cat People*, *Experiment Perilous*, and *Anne of the Indies*, this hostility, this seeming Ate implacably devastating human lives, is traced to a neurotic, perverted hatred of sex. Pentecost rejects Ann as soon as he proves her desire; he falls asleep while Boston puts on Ann's ribbon for him. We might read here a repressed homosexuality, a theme elsewhere present in the film: the portrayal of Masterson's sadism, which finds an appropriate channel in the masquerade of military discipline, and the bond that Pentecost and Kirby form. I see Pentecost's refusal rather as evidence of the character's total nihilism, his commitment to nothing but negative and destructive gestures. This commitment extends to the other main thematic area of the script: gold (the French distributor acknowledged this equivalence by titling the film *L'or et l'amour*). Just as Pentecost refuses to make love, he refuses to mine for gold; he has others do it for him. Then he must kill Lawford *because* he has both procreated and found gold. Lawford is the intolerable sign of phallic productivity.

The film presents Pentecost as an object to be analyzed and interpreted, rather than as an identification-figure. What more do we know about him at the end of the film than we knew at the beginning? We've witnessed only a series of contradictory gestures that, taken together, give the impression less of a single action rehearsed, elaborated, and completed than of a fitful and eventually frustrated will not to act. Pentecost remains consistent only in his negativity, even at the end: his commitment to the Confederate cause takes the form of a renunciation (giving up his payment for services); he avows the importance of Gary and Boston to him only after giving them up for good.

Instead of an attempt to represent a consistent action and the reality surrounding it, the film becomes a mirror of the process by which the action is made into a mystery. Tourneur's direction of *Great Day in the Morning* is less a triumph of form over content than a meditation on the relations of form and content and on the possibility of mise-en-scène.

Nightfall (1957)

A life without trust is a night without stars.

HÉLÈNE CIXOUS, *MANNE*

One night in Los Angeles, two strangers meet in a bar and decide to have dinner together: Jim Vanning (Aldo Ray), a commercial artist, and Marie Gardner (Anne Bancroft), a model. Leaving the restaurant, Vanning is forced into a car by two men, John (Brian Keith) and Red (Rudy Bond). They drive him to a beach, where they intend to torture him into revealing the location of a satchel containing $350,000. In a series of flashbacks interspersed with the present-time action, we learn that John and Red stole this money from a bank the previous winter. Escaping through rural Wyoming (in the flashback), the thieves had a car wreck near the campsite of Vanning and his friend, Doc Gurston (Frank Albertson). Red killed Gurston, left Vanning for dead, and mistakenly picked up the doctor's bag instead of the satchel containing the money. Since then, Vanning has been hiding from both the thieves and the police (who believe that he killed Gurston).

Vanning escapes from John and Red at the beach and goes to Marie, whom he suspects of having set him up for them. Realizing that she is innocent and now in danger herself, Vanning confides his story to her. They go together to Wyoming and, accompanied by Ben Fraser (James Gregory), an insurance investigator who has come to believe in Vanning's innocence, retrace the steps of Vanning's flight. John and Red have got there first, however, and recovered the satchel. In the action that ensues, both John and Red are killed.

Nightfall is a compact, entertaining thriller. The film has striking similarities to *Out of the Past*: the mapping of the dualism of past and present onto that of country and city; the hero's flight from destiny by relocating and changing his name; his attempt to overcome his destiny by reentering an earlier situation. Unlike Jeff in *Out of the Past*, however, Vanning vindicates himself and survives his ordeal.

Offbeat casting and naturalistic acting enhance the film. Aldo Ray is straightforward and touching in one of the handful of roles in the 1950s that used his talent and personality interestingly (cf. *The Marrying Kind, Pat and Mike, Battle Cry, Men in War, God's Little Acre, The Naked and the Dead*). Anne Bancroft's resourceful Marie is one of Tourneur's most distinctive heroines. One of the most successful aspects of the film is the interplay between Brian Keith's John and Rudy Bond's Red, with the former's quiet reasonableness, which allies him by nature with Vanning (an affinity that the acting registers subtly), contrasting with Red's casual sadism and quirky humor. Red has the funniest line in any Tourneur film: asked

Two strangers: Fraser (James Gregory) and Vanning (Aldo Ray) at the beginning of *Nightfall*.

by Fraser what he plans to do with his share of the holdup money, he deadpans, "I'm going to set up a scholarship at Harvard."

The intimacy and the warmth of the opening scene, beautifully shot by Burnett Guffey, dispel expectations of the "urban hell" type of film noir and herald a subdued, delicate film. When we first see Vanning, he could be anybody; in fact, the setting, a newsstand on a crowded city sidewalk at dusk, suggests that he *is* "anybody." Stressing his anonymity, Tourneur goes as far as to photograph him against rows of newspapers, shelved according to their cities of origin (a metonymy for the United States). Vanning becomes an individual only when he asks for a particular city (Evanston, Illinois), a request that marks him as a stranger in the city where he is. When a row of lights goes on over his head, he flinches and hides his face, a reaction that suggests that he is on the lam or has suffered a trauma. This emphasis on the physical impact of light on his body motivates the ensuing series of shots of electric signs going on in the dark, which lead by a visual analogy to the titles going on over a wide shot of the now dark street.

Before we know his name or his story, the film establishes Vanning as a stranger extremely sensitive to the transition between dark and light, no doubt because he himself is in some sort of transition (later, he speaks with anguish to Marie about the internal changes he has undergone since changing his identity). Throughout the film, Vanning continues to serve as a kind of medium between dark and light: his consciousness, for example, triggers the subjective flashback from the dark beach where John and Red threaten him to the bright snow of the camping-trip flashback.

The script for *Nightfall* came from a David Goodis novel; thus the film resembles François Truffaut's *Tirez sur le pianiste* (drawn from Goodis's *Down There*) even more than it does *Out of the Past*. One recognizes here the undercurrent of longing and unease, the vulnerable protagonist, and the solace and dread of urban anonymity of Truffaut's film, with which it also shares a journey into and a violent climax in a snowy country. Tourneur's *Nightfall* preserves the tenderness and humanity of Goodis's worldview, its combination of despair, melancholy, and a humorous tenaciousness.

Nor is Goodis's surrealism, his love of moments that push to an extreme the irrationality inherent in the fatalism of his plots, totally lacking in the film. (The film that has done the most justice to this aspect of Goodis's work is undoubtedly Delmer Daves's *Dark Passage*.) Tourneur makes no attempt to conceal the role played by coincidences and the arbitrary in the plot of *Nightfall*; he even highlights this role. The flashbacks propose a succession of events driven by pure chance: the car wreck; Vanning and Gurston's presence nearby; Red's amazing failure to kill Vanning; Red's mistakenly picking up Gurston's bag instead of the satchel with the money (an exchange that repeats the accidental switching of Cissie's dressing case with Bailey's writing case in *Experiment Perilous*); Vanning's losing the satchel in his flight. In the climactic scene, when Vanning arrives at the shack to find John and Red already there, Red's dialogue amusingly bares the film's device of building the plot out of one coincidence after another: "You're unlucky, fella. You're not lucky at all.... One more minute, two maybe at the most, we'd have been gone. Oh, yeah. You got a bad sense of timing." (Vanning shares this flaw with Jeff in *Out of the Past*.)

Throughout *Nightfall*, chance and unconscious processes determine key events. Tourneur's standard procedure of showing the effect before the cause underlines the inexplicability of these events, their fantastic nature. In the scene in the bar, we see Marie's empty place at the bar before we see her; on appearing, she quickly asks Vanning for a loan, only belatedly explaining that she has accidentally mislaid her purse. In the world of the film, happenings are always accidents: the characters are under the spell of what André Breton called "objective chance," the congruence between fate and desire.

The script links Vanning and Marie's relationship with mental processes that he can't explain. At the bar, she shows him her driver's license, and he reads her name and address aloud. Later, she writes down her address for him on a piece of paper, but John takes it from him while he is unconscious. Nevertheless, Vanning remembers the address from his brief look at the license, his memory working in an involuntary manner to direct him to her: "I didn't even look up your address. I must have remembered it from the bar." Later, he tells her that "it's important" that she believe that he never had an affair with Doc Gurston's wife, but he *doesn't know why* it's important; that is, he can't avow his love for her because it is still unconscious. The word "important" echoes the earlier scene in which she gives him her address. He asks her to write it down, saying, "I forget things." She replies, "Not important things, I hope."

Aldo Ray and Anne Bancroft in *Nightfall*.

Tourneur shows seemingly insignificant events so as to suggest that they have a hidden meaning, without stating the meaning. Looking at the sign in front of the nightclub in the first postcredits scene, Vanning, whose back is to the camera, inexplicably starts to look over his shoulder. This shot cuts to a very long shot from across the street: Vanning and the nightclub are in the background; in the middleground, on the to-camera side of the street, Fraser crosses the frame; Fraser then crosses the street, approaching Vanning. The cutting links Vanning's gesture, which suggests his habitual intuition of being watched, directly to the introduction of Fraser, who, as we later learn, has in fact been watching Vanning for weeks in the hope that Vanning will lead him to the stolen money. Fraser asks Vanning for a light; they exchange desultory small talk; Fraser boards a bus that takes him away. The staging and the acting of the scene emphasize its insignificance. Only the long shot from across the street (which would be gratuitous if Fraser were not interested in Vanning) and Vanning's slight turn at the end of the preceding shot make us aware that their encounter is fateful.

Later, the film develops the two men's relationship by match-cutting. A shot of Vanning and Marie going from the bar to the table cuts to a shot of Fraser getting off the bus in front of his apartment building (in the background, two men walk away from the camera on the sidewalk, in a subliminal anticipation of John and Red's emergence to accost Vanning in front of the restaurant). A shot of Laura (Jocelyn Brando), Fraser's wife, going into the kitchen to make him a drink cuts to a big close-up of coffee being poured at Vanning and Marie's table. A shot of Vanning, John, and Red walking up the steps of a platform on the beach cuts to a shot of Fraser in the living room, pacing. Finally, Laura's statement — "look at the time" — prompts a cut to an extreme close-up of John's watch as he times the movement of a derrick. Although this cutting, which is uncharacteristic of Tourneur, feels more like an expedient visual shorthand than a thoroughly worked-out design (which is part of the reason why *Nightfall*, despite its excellence, remains a minor work), it underlines Vanning's lack of control over his destiny, which is subject to forces of which he is unaware (cf. the intercutting between the sorcerer and Jessica in *I Walked with a Zombie*).

The relationship between Vanning and Fraser dramatizes the movement from distrust to alliance. Resigning himself to what he believes to be an implacably malevolent fate, Vanning surrenders to Fraser: "I'm tired, more tired than you know, Mr. Fraser. To tell you the truth, I'm glad you finally caught up with me. Now will you please just take me in." The winning of trust is also the subject of the scene in Marie's apartment: Vanning reasons that despite appearances, Marie must be innocent, and he tries to convince her that he is too. In these scenes, Tourneur is concerned with the same process that interests Frank Borzage in *Moonrise* and Nicholas Ray in *In a Lonely Place*: how a person comes to represent to himself the subjectivity of another. (*Nightfall* also shows us the fatal failure of the process to work. Gurston mistakenly thinks that he can arouse the thieves' sympathy by recounting the banal circumstances surrounding their encounter and making them see the situation from his point of view: "I was about to have my second cup of coffee.") In *Nightfall*, this process always takes place without the encouragement of the other, who resists and has to be surprised into accepting this gift of recognition. Vanning, for Fraser, acts guilty and hands himself over to Fraser, without protest or cynicism, as a condemned object. Similarly, Marie refuses to defend herself from Vanning's charge of betrayal and, in effect, challenges him to think her guilty.

Vanning's confrontation with Fraser takes place at a wire fence outside a church. We might read the scene in terms of grace and redemption (as we read the spiritual awakening of the hero of Bresson's *Pickpocket*, for example). The visual emphasis on Vanning's weakness — his back is turned to us, and his figure, in long shot, is dwarfed by the white landscape of plains and mountains in the background — seems to suggest his smallness before God. The church is, however, less important for its connotation as a place of worship than for the fact that Vanning is *outside* it. The setting visually represents Vanning's exclusion from a society that Fraser's trust will allow him to reenter. Like the churches in *Stars in My Crown* and *Way of a Gaucho*, the church in *Nightfall* is less a religious symbol than a site, and a sign, of exclusion/inclusion.

Nightfall shares with *Out of the Past* a narrative structure in which the motives and circumstances of the protagonist are revealed in flashback. Whereas *Out of the Past* has a single flashback section, *Nightfall* distributes its flashbacks over the course of the film, so that the issues underlying Vanning's predicament are revealed progressively and become clear only fairly late in the film. This delay permits

Nightfall: **Rudy Bond, Frank Albertson, Brian Keith, and Aldo Ray.**

Tourneur to expand on the narrative ambiguity so crucial to his cinema. It also gives him a pretext to disperse space and time. By interrupting the sequence at the beach with a subjective flashback and a scene at Fraser's apartment, for example, the film seems to prolong the real time of Vanning's ordeal. The film thus uses screen time as a metaphor for subjective time, just as it uses spatial metaphors for phenomena of consciousness, such as the fence in the country, which subtly marks Vanning's lapse of memory concerning the satchel.

The visual patterns of the film are elegant and expressive. Like other Tourneur films, *Nightfall* makes offscreen space the source of danger: John and Red emerge from behind a street corner; Red moves out of frame to hit Vanning. The film also creates uncertainty by showing vacant on-screen spaces, for example Marie's empty place at the bar, Marie's dark apartment after she and Vanning abandon it, and John and Red's empty chairs at the fashion show. In the Wyoming scenes, the snow provides a constant background of whiteness and absence, in which the characters and their preoccupations appear as violent intrusions. The film's last shot is a wide-angle long shot, devoid of people, with the camera low to the ground; the dark satchel is in the foreground, a "lonely" object of abstract contemplation.

Tourneur's skill with camera movement is evident throughout *Nightfall*. The fashion show sequence is a splendidly constructed tour de force of repeated lateral tracking shots (alongside the runway) and reverse medium shots from Marie's point of view. After she deserts the runway to join Vanning, still wearing the fancy dress she is modeling (an act of protest equivalent to Thornhill's disruption of the auction in *North by Northwest*), the sequence is capped by a breathtaking upward crane shot (one of Tourneur's infrequent flourishes of camera virtuosity) showing Vanning and Marie running up an exterior staircase; in the background we see the startled audience watching them from the ground. When Vanning arrives at the shack in the final sequence, the window of the shack is at first hidden from his (and our) perspective. He notices a fresh footprint in the snow, then starts to walk around the shack to investigate; as he does so, the camera tracks laterally, revealing John and Red framed in the window of the shack. Highlighting the use of perspective to withhold and then disclose information, this austere camera movement has great force. (Later in the scene, Tourneur echoes this movement by having John shift the angle of his rifle to aim it through the window at Red.)

Despite its several moments of violence threatened or performed, *Nightfall* is one of the most optimistic of Tourneur's films, combining a happy ending with a pervasive sense of a generally benign reality. A brief, seemingly trivial scene projects this optimism most strongly: Vanning and Marie wake up on the bus as it passes the Utah state line, while another passenger switches channels on his portable radio before settling on an instrumental version of "Red River Valley." The music gives a nostalgic, utopian tinge to the vastness of the American landscape; altogether, the scene provides a reassuring sense of relief from Vanning's traumatic experience.

Night of the Demon (1957)

> There are no conclusive indications by which
> waking life can be distinguished from sleep.
>
> RENÉ DESCARTES, *FIRST MEDITATION*

Night of the Demon sealed Tourneur's identification with the horror genre. If *The Leopard Man* had been his last horror film, he would no more be considered mainly a horror film director than Mark Robson and Robert Wise, both of whom also went on from their work with Val Lewton to careers that ranged widely in subject and theme and neither of whom is now identified with horror. Because of its stylistic similarities to Tourneur's three Lewton films, *Night of the Demon* has, moreover, assumed a central role in the Tourneur-Lewton authorship problem. The director's partisans have understandably seen it as confirming the originality of his contribution to the Lewton pictures, whereas writers concerned with establishing Lewton as an auteur have described it as Tourneur's "homage" to Lewton, treating the film as an example of the posthumous power of Lewton's vision. [1]

That *Night of the Demon* is a highly personal film for its director is impossible to doubt. "I detest the expression 'horror film,'" Tourneur told *Positif*. "I make films on the supernatural and I make them because I believe in it."[2] The personal conviction that Tourneur conveys through the film makes *Night of the Demon* in some ways the most impressive of his masterpieces (of which it is also the last). Its central conception is so strong that it withstands the notorious interference of the film's producers.

Charles Bennett, who had written or co-written most of the best prewar Hitchcock films, owned the rights to "Casting the Runes," a story by the urbane and subtle writer Montague R. James, and adapted it into a script, originally called *The Haunted*. Various people, including Robert Taylor and Dick Powell, were interested, but Hal E. Chester, an independent producer associated with Columbia, was the first to put together a deal. Bennett later regretted signing with Chester and bitterly complained about Chester's handling of the script, which, as Tourneur confirms, "was rewritten many times." (The film titles credit both Bennett and Chester for the screenplay.)[3]

According to Tourneur, he became involved in the project thanks to a recommendation to Chester from Ted Richmond, the producer of *Nightfall*. Tourneur in turn showed the script to his friend Dana Andrews, who agreed to play the main part.[4] Andrews was at this point a somewhat tarnished figure, his career blighted by an alcoholism that reputedly affected his work (there is one scene in *Night of the Demon*, a process shot of Andrews getting out of a car in front of a hotel, in which his delivery is noticeably slurred and unsteady). Nevertheless, Andrews could still be an ideal actor (as he had proved recently in Fritz Lang's last two American films, *While the City Sleeps* and *Beyond a Reasonable Doubt*); his Holden in *Night of the Demon* was one of his last major performances. It belongs to the type of role for which he was best suited: one in which his customary impassivity betrays a moral weakness, a fatal flaw (as in *Fallen Angel*, *Where the Sidewalk Ends*, and *Beyond a Reasonable Doubt*), and in which his self-control is the telltale sign of narcissism (as in *Daisy Kenyon* and *While the City Sleeps*).

The premise of both the James story and the film is that a black magician, Dr. Julian Karswell (played in the film by Niall MacGinnis), has the power to kill his enemies by passing them parchments bearing runic symbols. Near the beginning of the film, Professor Henry Harrington (Maurice Denham), whom Karswell has cursed in this manner in order to deter investigations of Karswell and his cult, is killed by a giant demon. Harrington's colleague, Dr. John Holden (Dana Andrews), arrives from America to pursue his research, aimed at debunking the supernatural. Karswell slips him a parchment and predicts his death in three days. A series of strange events undermines Holden's skepticism, and he becomes convinced of Karswell's powers. Having learned from one of Karswell's followers, Rand Hobart (Brian Wilde), that the only way to avoid his fate is to pass the parchment back to Karswell, Holden succeeds in doing just that aboard a train, within minutes of the deadline, whereupon the demon materializes and kills Karswell.

Some of the most important changes Bennett made to James's story relate to the characterizations of the two central characters. The story's Karswell is boorish, unpleasant, and given to traumatizing the village children with a scary magic-lantern show. The children's party in the film takes off from the latter idea but uses it in the opposite way: to show that Karswell has a humane side as well as an evil one. Moreover, James's Karswell, motivated by vanity and petty revenge, gives no indication of being reluctant to use his powers to cause his enemies' deaths, unlike the Karswell of the film, who tries to persuade Holden to call off the investigation (which, apparently, he is afraid will turn up something that would hurt him) before resorting to passing Holden the parchment. Bennett also introduced the Hitchcockian figure of Karswell's mother (Athene Seyler). She functions both as a confidante to whom Karswell can express his insecurities and as an externalization of his desire for death, which she indirectly brings about by informing Holden of her son's train travel plans.[5]

The character of Holden has so little in common with the equivalent figure in James's story as to be a completely new creation. Holden's skepticism, which he brandishes from the start as self-definition and existential defiance, is original — and central — to the film. The script highlights the perversity of Holden's attitude by introducing other characters, including Harrington's niece, Joanna (Peggy Cummins), all of whom are rational and intelligent but willing to believe in the supernatural.

An American in England, Holden is out of place in the same way Robert Lindley is in *Berlin Express* and Clay Douglas is in *Circle of Danger*. Each of these three films examines its protagonist's displacement in a different light. Lindley is the prototypical "average American": straightforward, without complexes, forced to adjust to the perspectives of a world of shadows and reflections. The journey of Douglas, an American of Scottish descent, leads him to acknowledge his own past, including the guilt buried in it. Of the three, Holden offers the richest study in displacement because his alienation, which expresses what Dr. Louis Judd would call a "psychic need," leads dialectically to its own cure.

Holden has come on a mission to provoke and offend people, as one of the reporters who meet him at the airport recognizes. "Take it kind of easy on our ghosts," he begs. "We English are sort of fond of them." (To which Holden, the flippant American, replies, "Sure, some of my best friends are ghosts.") Holden's amused, contemptuous attitude toward the beliefs of others quickly puts him into conflict with people, including his potential allies. Professor Mark O'Brien (Liam Redmond), a colleague, sharply defends himself when Holden dismisses his demonological theories: "I'm a scientist also, Dr. Holden. I know the value of the cold light of reason. But I also know the deep shadows that light can cast. The shadows that can blind men to truth." Later, Joanna bristles when Holden suggests that her distress over her uncle's death has made her irrational: "Please don't treat me like a mental patient who has to be humored. I also majored in psychology." Holden's ironic remarks to Karswell as the two of them stroll over Karswell's grounds during the children's party provoke the magician into summoning a windstorm.

Like John Dough in "What Do *You* Think?" Holden constantly looks for, articulates, and clings to easy explanations of mysterious phenomena, a habit on which Karswell ironizes in advising Holden to take their simultaneous presence in the reading room at the British Museum as a "coincidence." Seeing Karswell in clown makeup performing magic tricks for children, Holden automatically thinks he has found the answer to his "chemistry problem" of the vanishing writing on the visiting card. (The viewer may note that this "answer" is itself irrational, since Holden has been told that the chemist's tests of the card found no ink traces and ruled out any tampering.) Although he insists that he can be persuaded only by "logic — the reality of the seeable and the touchable," Holden is unthinkingly swayed by the closest superficial appearances to hand, even by what merely has the sound of the rational. For example, when O'Brien and Kumar (Peter Elliott) identify the tune that has been going through his head as both an Irish and a North Indian melody associated with magic spells, Holden is ready to dismiss the subject: "Well, that takes care of that. I — I guess I must have heard it somewhere."

A turning point occurs in the candlelit after-dinner scene at the Harrington house, when he and Joanna discover the parchment that Karswell has "passed" to him. Twice in rapid succession, Holden explains away what looks like (to Joanna and to us) a deliberate attempt by the parchment to immolate itself in Joanna's fireplace. When it suddenly falls to the floor, Joanna asks, "What made them stop?" (The plural pronoun refers to the runic symbols, which the characters in the film invariably speak of as if they had a life of their own.) Holden looks around him, then at her, before admitting, "I don't know." After the next day's experiences — a visit to the Hobart farm, where he learns that "he has been chosen," and then a trip to Stonehenge — Holden is ready to go even further in his admission to Joanna: "Well, after this afternoon, I must confess there are a few things I don't know."

Holden's aggressive behavior and his compulsive superficiality in the name of rationalism are part of a psychological profile that, stung by the contact with a rationalism (that of a police inspector) even more obstinate than his own, he outlines to Joanna. As a child, he went out of his way to prove he was unafraid of the objects of his friends' superstitions. This childhood activity became the model of his professional career, which he built out of proving that he was "not a superstitious sucker like about 90 percent of humanity." These lines hint at a neurotic, narcissistic basis for Holden's science and link Holden with Karswell, who is also vain about his accomplishments and who appears to have a close relationship with no one but his mother and thus has never left the childhood position of dependence, just as Holden remains stuck in a position adopted in childhood.

Karswell's closeness to childhood and children is strongly marked. "If only we grown-ups could preserve their capacity for simple joys and simple beliefs," he tells Holden during the children's party. This line echoes Joanna's angry warning to Holden: "You could learn a lot from children. They believe in things in the dark, although we tell them it's not so. Maybe we've been fooling them."

At several points, the film establishes visually that Karswell is Holden's double. In the scene in which Holden receives a phone call from Karswell ("Speak of the devil!"), the shots of the two men are elaborately complementary: a low-angle medium-close shot of Holden, lit by a lamp at the left of the frame; a high-angle medium-close shot of Karswell, lit by a fireplace at right. The lighting schemes of these shots echo O'Brien's speech to Holden, earlier in the scene, about "the deep shadows ... that can blind men to truth." At the children's party, Tourneur breaks down the scene of Karswell and Holden's stroll together into complementary close-ups of their profiles.

The script of *Night of the Demon* is so tightly knit (as this discussion of the characters and their relationships has perhaps indicated) that it is difficult to detect Hal E. Chester's revisions. During the production, however, the producer continued to interfere with the film. On at least one point, Tourneur successfully battled Chester: he fought to upgrade "the two electric fans" the producer offered him for the windstorm at the children's party to a team of airplane engines.[6] Dana Andrews, who considered Chester "a real little schmuck," recalled his unwelcome presence on the set:

> He would come up and start telling Jacques how to direct
> the picture. Jacques would say, "Now, now, Hal," and try to
> be nice. But I just said, "Look, you little son-of-a-bitch! You
> want me to walk off this picture? I didn't come all the way
> over here to have the producer tell me what he thinks about
> directing the picture. I came because Mr. Tourneur asked
> me. Let the director direct the picture!"[7]

After the completion of principal shooting, Chester exercised his power over the film in two decisive ways. Ultimately, the cutting of about thirteen minutes of footage for the American release (as *Curse of the Demon*) constituted the less important of these, since all or almost all this footage has since been restored to film and video copies now available in the United States.[8] The more significant piece of tampering, which has entered into film legend, was Chester's insistence on

showing the demon at the beginning and at the end of the film. In various interviews and published texts, Tourneur made it clear that he was opposed to showing
the demon distinctly. In his *Films and Filming* interview, Tourneur said: "The
monster was taken right out of a book on demonology — 3,400-year-old prints
copied exactly — and it looked great, I must say, in a drawing so I said, 'Fine, go
ahead.' Then they put this thing on a man. I thought it was going to be suggested
and fuzzy and drawn, in and out, appearing and disappearing, like a cartoon, animated."[9] (In the same interview, Tourneur also complained about the botched
editing of the scene in which Karswell's cat turns into a panther; he said that
"miles and miles of an ambulance" — the one that brings Hobart to the scientific
demonstration — were added after he left.)

Tourneur gave his most complete statement of his original intentions, and of
how the film deviated from them, to *Midi-minuit fantastique*:

> The scenes in which you really see the demon were shot
> without me. All except one. I shot the sequence in the
> woods where Dana Andrews is chased by this sort of cloud.
> This technique should have been used for the other
> sequences. The audience should never have been completely
> certain of having seen the demon. They should have just
> unveiled it little by little, without ever really showing it.
> They ruined the film by showing it from the very beginning
> with a guy we don't know opening his garage, who doesn't
> interest us in the least.[10]

Tourneur told Joel E. Siegel more or less the same thing and added:

> I wanted, at the very end, when the train goes by, to include
> only four frames of the monster coming up with the guy and
> throwing him down. Boom, boom — did I see it or didn't I?
> People would have to sit through it a second time to be sure
> of what they saw. But after I had finished and returned to
> the United States, the English producer [Frank Bevis] made
> this horrible thing, cheapened it. It was like a different film.
> But everything after that opening was as I had intended.[11]

Perhaps influenced by such statements, most commentators on the film have
condemned the demon. The best way to approach the problem of the demon's
presence in the film is to attend to the letter of Tourneur's objections. *Night of the
Demon*, as he says he wanted it, would have been a film in which the objective
reality of demonic forces remains, to the very end, undemonstrated. The "clouds"
seen by Harrington, Holden, and finally Karswell might be hallucinations caused
by suggestion; Harrington's and Karswell's deaths might be accidents brought on
by their own panic. Yet other details in the film, and the logic of its narrative
development, make it impossible to imagine even this "would-have-been" film as
belonging to the same order of total hesitation as *I Walked with a Zombie*. As V. F.
Perkins has noted, the film leads the spectator along with Holden from an initial
position of rational skepticism "to a state of panic in which the reality of occult
power is recognized." In other words, the success of the film depends on getting

Holden (Dana Andrews) at Stonehenge in *Night of the Demon.*

the spectator to believe, at least provisionally, that there *is* a demon. Jean-André Fieschi considers the monster's early appearance necessary because it renders Holden's skepticism suspect from the beginning and reduces the viewer "to the uncomfortable role of the incompetent witness, muzzled by the evidence of horror and the absence of logical reference points that presides over its unveiling."[12]

The demon must be considered, however, not only as an element affecting the film's structure of knowledge and belief but also as an image of horror. Tourneur understood that the early and prolonged exposure to the monster turned *Night of the Demon* into a horror film, rather than the film of psychological terror he wanted to create. This is clear from the *Films and Filming* interview: "The one-fourth of the film which had to do with the delineation of that monster belonged to another type of film which is the teenager horror film."[13] What interested Tourneur was not horror but fear. In the portion of the *Présence du cinéma* interview dealing with *Night of the Demon*, Tourneur rejected the horror cinema of the time: "A horror film, it shouldn't be a story of a mad surgeon who removes the brain from a man in order to put it in the head of another man." (Perhaps Tourneur had in mind Terence Fisher's *The Revenge of Frankenstein*, Columbia's co-feature for *Night of the Demon* on its initial release.) He goes on to offer a theory of fear, in which we can find a manifesto of his cinema:

> The real horror is to show that we all live unconsciously in
> fear. Many people suffer today from a fear that they don't
> begin to analyze and which is constant. When the audience
> is in the dark and recognizes its own insecurity in that of the
> characters of the film, then you can show unbelievable situa-
> tions and be sure that the audience will follow. For another
> thing, people love to be afraid. It's strange, when we're chil-
> dren, we say to our nurse or to our parents: "Frighten us,"
> and we love that. These fears stay in us all our life: we're
> afraid of thunder, we're afraid of darkness, of the unknown,
> of death. The horror film, if it's well done, awakens in the
> mind of the audience this fear that it didn't know it had in
> it, and this discovery makes it shiver.[14]

Making the demon clearly visible fixes in a specific thing the generalized
dread that is Tourneur's professed concern. The demon thus creates a kind of disruption that is not, however, totally foreign to Tourneur's cinema, which sometimes invokes the monstrous either by effects work simulating nonexistent objects
or simply by the standard photography of an actually existing object whose nature
is outrageous: the matte shot of Miguel trampled by cattle in *Way of a Gaucho*; the
shots of insects in *Appointment in Honduras*; the snowplow in *Nightfall*. The
demon becomes, moreover, what Slavoj Žižek has discussed, in relation to certain
films by Hitchcock, as "a kind of stain which from outside — more precisely: from
an intermediate space between diegetic reality and our 'true' reality — invades the
diegetic reality." These intrusions exploit "the feeling of threat which sets in when
the distance separating the viewer — his/her safe position of pure gaze — from the
diegetic reality is lost: the stains blur the frontier outside/inside which provides
our sense of security."[15]

If the demon upsets the visual tonality of Tourneur's film, it fits into the
film's structural play with ambiguity of point of view. The film uses several more
subtle techniques to create this ambiguity:

1. An apparently normal shot corresponding to a character's point of view
   contains what may be an unreal element (the demon that appears to
   Harrington at the beginning; the visiting card, with the mysterious
   handwriting, that Karswell gives Holden).
2. A shot corresponding to Holden's point of view is optically distorted,
   wavering, so that we interpret it as seeing into another reality (Karswell
   walking away from Holden in the British Museum; the Hobart family
   looking at him in the farmhouse).
3. In a variation on (1), a shot from one angle contains an element — the
   hand on the banister — that is missing when the same space is photographed from other angles; here the mysterious element does not
   belong to the point of view of Holden, who is oblivious to it.
4. A shot and its reverse shot — designated as such by Holden's looks and his
   presence/absence in the shots — are confusingly similar (the scene in the
   hotel corridor in which Holden hears the mysterious noise associated
   with the demon).

These ambiguities are all related to Karswell's dark powers. To the extent that the film implicitly assumes that the viewer (at least in the viewer's daily life, outside the movie theater) shares Holden's point of view, these devices attack the stability of the viewer's position as a place of knowledge about the world.

The first shots after the credits are at night: a long shot of a car passing on a road, seen through a row of trees that intermittently block from us the stream of its headlights; then a shot of the driver, Harrington, in profile; then a subjective shot, taken from the front of a moving car, of the dark road with the light from the headlights moving over it. Despite Tourneur's self-criticism in *Midi-minuit*— "a guy we don't know ... who doesn't interest us in the least"—it is precisely because we don't know the person whose point of view the film forces us to adopt and because we have a lack of "interest" (which is not, in any case, total) that the opening shots embody the hypnotic power of cinema in its pure form. In an interesting study of the film, Raymond Bellour identifies the headlights of the car in the first shot with the cinematic apparatus: "Before any development of the story, the force of this shot suggests what is at stake: this intermittent light has the effect of life and death on the spectator. It is the spectator's 'truth.' Without light, there is no image; and a naked light produces only a blinding. Between the two, there is a blinking: the cinema."[16]

Harrington is the subject of the apparatus, the film viewer who is put on-screen, for whom the image appears, and toward whom (in the subjective shot of the road) the image unscrolls. Moreover, we bring to the scene and to the unknown figure of Harrington certain expectations from the brief pre-credits narration (accompanying a long shot of Stonehenge): "It has been written ... that evil, supernatural creatures exist in a world of darkness. And it is also said, man using the magic power of the ancient runic symbols can call forth these powers of darkness, the demons of hell." When we see Harrington—distraught, "driven"—we immediately realize that he has already entered this world of darkness. The subjectivized image by which we identify with his point of view is the vehicle for exploring this world, as is the car itself, a moving projectile that brings light before it and leaves darkness behind it. The shots of the road and the trees, illuminated by the moving headlights, recall scenes in other Tourneur films ("Romance of Radium," *Nick Carter, Master Detective, Cat People, I Walked with a Zombie, The Leopard Man*) of flashlights sweeping over dark fields: at these moments, which force the viewer to identify with the formal idea of the search, the image becomes the field where the thing sought may appear and the beam of light itself becomes a "thing" that is out of place and does not belong.

After Harrington's encounter with Karswell, who seemingly agrees to lift the curse from him, Harrington drives home. The high-pitched sound that accompanies the presence of the fantastic in the film occurs for the first time over a medium-close shot of Harrington outside his garage. The scene cuts to a long shot from Harrington's point of view of a cloud moving between two rows of trees; blending with the strange sound effect, music starts over this shot. We cut back to the medium-close shot of Harrington, transfixed. The film cuts again to a long shot of the cloud approaching, but this time Harrington is in the foreground of the shot, his back to the camera.

Here, the shot-reverse-shot pattern leaves open the possibility that the cloud is Harrington's hallucination, a possibility reinforced by starting the sound effect over the shot of Harrington (as if it were "in his head"). When the "reverse shot" suddenly includes Harrington, whose point of view we supposed it to represent, the cloud can only be the "hallucination" of the film itself, and it is Harrington, as a "real person," who does not belong. His presence in the frame splits the viewer's gaze into two — one that identifies with Harrington's look and one that frames Harrington himself and the image constructed by this other gaze.

Like Harrington in the opening sequence, Holden is a surrogate for the viewer, but a different viewer. Harrington is the viewer who already believes in the world of darkness and has become engulfed by it. Holden, on the other hand, enters the fiction from a space outside the cinema, a social space that has banished ghosts and demons, and he tries to cling to the logic of this space even as the narrative repeatedly proves that this logic is inapplicable to the world he has entered. In Bellour's formulation of the relationship between Holden and the audience, Holden's "problem is trying not to believe in the devil, while ours is trying to accept belief in the cinema."[17]

The price of no longer believing in the image, in the trance, is life itself. Mrs. Meek, the medium's wife (Rosamund Greenwood), rebukes Holden for switching on the light in the middle of the seance: "Don't you know that to wake a medium out of a trance is to risk his life?" This seance is itself a kind of cinema, which disgusts Holden, perhaps because the manipulation of image and sound is too blatant, perhaps because the scene represented — Harrington's death — is too strong, perhaps because the solicitation of the viewer, Holden, is too evident, and also perhaps because an aura of pornography is attached to it, expressed perfectly in the weird Sadean machine formed by the two women, who have to wind up a Victrola and sing along to it a silly Victorian-era hymn, and Mr. Meek (Reginald Beckwith), who meanwhile shudders as if in preorgasmic excitement before finally "going off."

Through optical distortions, the film repeatedly undermines Holden's point of view. After his meeting with Karswell in the British Museum, Holden looks up in the direction of Karswell's exit. This shot cuts to a shot of Karswell walking away quickly down a corridor; optically distorted, the shot is blurred and wavering, with extremely high contrast (Karswell's figure is silhouetted). The shot is accompanied by an eerie statement by solo violin (or theremin?) of the theme that Holden later says has been running through his head. The corridor, whose existence has not been implied by the establishing shots of the reading room, appears to be more modern in style than the rest of the environment. Holden's attack of vertigo is not, then, a disturbed vision of a real space; it is an access of vision (whether the vision is "disturbed" or not, we can't evaluate) into another space, into a "parallel world" where Karswell has vanished.

The scene of Holden's visit to the Hobart farm is an inversion of the scene at the British Museum. The museum is a vast space that absorbs Holden and in which, as a scholar, he feels comfortable. At the farm, Holden is out of his element. The first shot of the sequence is a long shot in which Holden's square white sedan and his modern, urban overcoat and hat stick out as alien against the rural landscape with its dilapidated wood fence (much as urban visitors stick out visually in rural settings in *Out of the Past*, *Way of a Gaucho*, and *Nightfall*). Holden's mere presence is enough to arouse the hostility of one of the Hobarts, who shouts at him to get off the property.

When Holden accidentally exposes the parchment, which he is carrying in his wallet, the film again represents his distorted vision, this time of a scene — the Hobart family at the farmhouse table, staring at him — that clearly belongs to the real world: the camera angle, and the people and things in the shot, are the same as in previous "normal" shots in the scene. The parchment is "the stain that produces the gaze"; it causes Mrs. Hobart, on catching sight of it, to get up from the table and point at him — that is, at us, since we occupy Holden's point of view. When the shot wavers, we suddenly become aware that what sticks out isn't just the parchment or Holden's physical presence but his look: vision itself is the element that intrudes and doesn't belong.

Another example of this stain or intrusive element is the mysterious hand that twice appears on the banister in the foreground of shots as Holden explores the Karswell house. This hand appears in the film as the explicit intervention of the director: in his interview with *Positif*, Tourneur referred to the hand as an example of his obsession with "suddenly bringing inexplicable things into a shot." He noted, "I took a very long time choosing this hand and I finally used that of an old man very close to death."[18] We first see the hand grip the banister in a high-angle shot of Holden going down the staircase. Holden has just stopped and turned to look behind him, so he couldn't have missed seeing its owner if the owner were "really" there; furthermore, this owner is absent from the next shot, an overhead view of the whole staircase, a shot that logically should include him. Nor is he present in the next shot, which is taken from the downstairs hall, and which shows Holden walking offscreen; the balustrade is visible in the background. The hand appears again, however, in the following reverse shot from the staircase showing Holden walking away from the camera down the hall.

In this scene, when the camera shares Holden's (not literal but cognitive) point of view (a moving center of the universe of information about the world), the hand is absent. The camera sees the hand only at the option of the director and only precisely when the scene has established the impossibility that the hand is there in the world constructed by this point of view. The hand thus symbolizes the lack at the heart of the universe, a lack that condemns Holden's efforts to futility: what he is searching for in Karswell's house (the original text of *On the True Discoveries of Witches and Demons*) is already laid out on the desk for him to see and is useless (since only Karswell can read it).

The alternate presence/absence of the hand perfectly articulates the splitting between knowledge and belief— one of the film's great themes. We, the spectators, "know" with Holden that no one is on the staircase, but at the same time we "believe" in the purely vibratory existence of this hand that belongs to no character in the film, that plays no part in Holden's adventure as he experiences it, and that is perhaps the hand of someone in an alternate universe that happens to intersect Holden's and ours, at the nexus of the staircase.

The scene of Holden alone in the corridors of the Savoy Hotel is another "inexplicable" moment. Constructed out of eight ruthlessly logical shots, the scene is a model of Tourneurian cinema:

1. Holden emerges from the elevator at left and walks down the corridor away from the camera. Music starts low over the end of the shot (and becomes progressively louder over the rest of the sequence).

2. The camera is now closer to Holden, who is at left of frame, and at a more pronounced angle with respect to the corridor, which recedes into the background in the right part of the frame. We hear the weird high-pitched sound effect first heard when the demon appeared to Harrington. (It grows progressively louder over the rest of the sequence.) Holden stops and turns to look past the camera offscreen left.

3. In reverse shot, the empty corridor recedes in the *left* part of the frame.

4. In a similar composition, Holden is now *in* the shot, in the right part of the frame. At first looking away from the camera into the background, he turns to look past the camera offscreen right.

5. A reverse shot of the empty corridor is again angled so that it recedes in the left part of the frame.

6. This shot is the same as (4). The camera pans right and dollies back with Holden as he walks around a corner and stops.

7. The corridor recedes at the left of the frame; Holden, his back to the camera, is at right. The shot is at a higher angle than the previous shots, so that the corridor appears to fall away from the camera. Holden turns.

8. This shot is the same as (6). The camera dollies back with Holden as he walks forward down the corridor into a dark area. He stops and looks around. Behind his back, a door opens, startling him; O'Brien and Kumar, his colleagues, emerge from a room.

Everything in this scene combines to produce an effect of fear: most obviously, the sound track and Holden's cautious movements; more subtly and most powerfully, the disorienting camera placement and mise-en-scène. The corridors are lit so that they appear to recede infinitely into the background of each shot, making it appear that Holden has entered an infinite labyrinth. The cut from (2) to (3) is disorienting because (3) is not a true reverse angle from Holden's point of view: the angle of the corridor proves that the shot is taken from a point across the corridor from Holden. Shot (4), in which Holden suddenly appears in the foreground of a shot approximately the same as (3), further disconcerts us (just as we were disconcerted when Harrington was suddenly included in the foreground of the long shot of the approaching cloud). Conventionally, the "reverse shot," (3), should be followed by a return to shot (2), the same setup of Holden's look. But the camera has crossed to the other side of his look — and simply doing so has thrown the scene into spatial confusion because it unmoors the space from Holden's look.

The space of the scene is now organized around two mirror images, shots (2) and (4). If shot (4) is the sudden arbitrary addition of the human figure into a pre-existing spatial setup, shot (5) is the equally sudden and arbitrary subtraction of this figure, leaving the setup as it was, with the corridor still receding at the left of the frame. It is as if Holden were merely an accidental, transitory intruder in the space rather than the observer from whose central perspective the space radiates outward. Shot (7), in which Holden looks down another corridor logically at right angles to the first but which appears identical to the first, reinforces the sense that Holden is in a labyrinth without identifying marks. The slightly increased high

Dana Andrews and Niall McGinnis in *Night of the Demon.*

angle of this shot emphasizes the feeling of doom and helplessness that permeates the scene.

   Holden's experience in this scene is an encounter with the basic powers of cinema: camera position and angle, cutting, sound, and music. The corridor scene is similar to scenes in *Cat People* and *The Leopard Man*; using only such basic devices, and familiar objects and sets, the scenes entrap a character on-screen in an unstable situation and instill fear in the audience. In *Night of the Demon*, Tourneur goes further than in his previous films in abstracting from the scene all visual elements except for the human figure and the architecture. The corridor functions not merely as a funnel for the action but as a compositional element equal in importance to the figure. After shot (1), in which Holden is absorbed into the depth of the corridor, the shots show Holden and the corridor next to each other, balancing each other in the frame. The bleak hotel decor — with its archways, undecorated gray walls, and alternating areas of light and dark — and Holden's total isolation give the scene the desolate quality of an Antonioni film (Tourneur had already anticipated some of Antonioni's key themes in *Cat People*).

   Holden's problem is that he refuses to submit to the fascination that, for

Tourneur, the cinema represents: its power to go beyond "the reality of the seeable and the touchable." The experience for which "he has been chosen" is that of being forced to acknowledge this power and the lack that founds it, a lack that lies at the heart of Holden's "reality." Karswell's problem, on the other hand, is that he believes in "things in the dark" too much, to the point that his life depends on it. After the party, he confesses his insecurities to his mother, who urges him to renounce magic: "If it makes you unhappy, stop it. Give it back." Leaning down toward her (she is sitting in an armchair, and he is standing; the camera, from over his shoulder, looks down at her), he replies, "How can you give back life?" This moment sets forth with paralyzing clarity the issues involved in the film and, incidentally, the profundity of which the popular cinema was capable (at any rate during, to quote Bellour again, "the last nights wherein the cinema really pretended to believe in its demons").[19] What director of the "art" cinema of the period would have dared show a son asking his mother this question?

The narrative draws an implicit parallel between the specialized knowledge of psychologists and the arcane knowledge of Karswell: both are deeply concerned with control. The link between the two is Hobart, who functions as object/victim of both disciplines. Aptly, he is portrayed as having lost all knowledge, yet under hypnosis, he reveals to Holden the way to stay alive: by giving the parchment back to Karswell *without the latter's knowledge*.

The hypnosis scene is simply the mise-en-scène of the gaze, in which the compositions constantly mobilize light as delegate or agency of the gaze, as link from representation to reality. (It is interesting to view this scene in the light of Tourneur's project of a film about Charcot; such a film would undoubtedly have contained similar scenes of scientists staging their patients' psychological afflictions for an on-screen audience.) The scene begins with Hobart wheeled onstage on a stretcher as Holden introduces him to the audience as "Mr. Rand Hobart, who through an experience related to devil worship has lost all contact with reality." After the word "reality," an attendant switches on a lamp on a tall stand at the right of the frame, over Hobart's head. Then the other stage lights go out as Holden yields the platform to O'Brien. In a long shot from the back, the auditorium becomes a vast area of darkness surrounding two small areas of light onstage: one at the right of the frame containing O'Brien, an attendant, and Hobart on the stretcher, and a more dimly lit area at screen left with Holden and other scientists at a table.

O'Brien uses a penlight to examine Hobart, whose dead eye is shown in extreme close-up. The tall lamp that the editing tells us *is* the "contact with reality" that Hobart has lost looms over all the shots involving O'Brien's attempt to revive Hobart: it appears at the upper left edge of the frame over O'Brien's shoulder as he discusses the "therapeutic shock" that will be required to jolt Hobart's mind "out of the womb of darkness into which it has retreated to protect itself"; the lamp also appears, huge in the frame, in the medium-close two-shot of the attendant and O'Brien.

Revived from his catatonia, Hobart leaps at the camera (in a shock effect unusual for Tourneur) and flees into the darkness at the back of the auditorium. He is caught, brought back onstage, and held down in a chair. In the two-shot of Holden hypnotizing him with a small mirror, a small crane lamp looms in the middle of the frame; its thin ellipse of bright light is on the imaginary line between Holden's eyes and Hobart's and thus serves as a visual metaphor for the hypnotic contact between the two men. The crane lamp also appears in a close-up of Hobart and a two-shot of Hobart and O'Brien; cutaways to Holden alone repeatedly show him in relation to the tall standing lamp on the other side of the stage.

There are two scenes here: the scene that Holden and O'Brien stage for the on-screen audience, their attempted mise-en-scène of Hobart's belief in the supernatural; and the scene they produce in the mind of their hypnotic subject, Hobart ("You see only the light ... only this" and "You hear nothing but my voice")— finally forcing him to relive the intolerable scene that drove him into "the womb of darkness." The pervasive irony of the film marks the sequence: the spectator for whom the demonstration produces its intended effect of knowledge is not the on-screen audience but Holden, who receives from Hobart the secret of the parchment and the key to his own survival. In his excitement at coming closer to this truth, Holden crosses from the definite, detached area staked out by the tall lamp to the more intimate, lower (in height) area of the small crane lamp and then tries to violate the rules of hypnosis by addressing Hobart, forgetting that Hobart has been told to hear only O'Brien's voice. Another irony is that the "therapeutic shock" leads Hobart to throw himself out a window, presumably to his death.

The connection between knowledge and death is further marked in the film by the prevalence of written texts that have a fatal meaning (writings occupy the narrative and the visual space of *Night of the Demon* to a degree of near-saturation). Among these texts are the parchment; the visiting card; the book in which Harrington underlined the passage from "The Rime of the Ancient Mariner"; the stones of Stonehenge, whose message the narrator translates at the beginning of the film; Harrington's diary; Holden's calendar, from which the pages after the 28th (the date appointed for his death) have been torn out; the document, aptly termed a "release," that Mrs. Hobart signs to permit Holden to conduct his experiment on Hobart (which leads to Hobart's killing himself, i.e., to his "release," but also to Holden's learning the way to release himself from the curse); the original of *On the True Discoveries of Witches and Demons*; and Karswell's translation of *The True Discoveries*, the master-key from which the parchment is generated and from which pages are missing, as they are from Harrington's diary and from Holden's calendar—as if the suitability of these texts to serve as metaphors for life consisted in the potential for pages to be removed. This abridgability in turn reflects back on the fragmentary nature of all the film's texts. They tend to fall away, to escape and burn up, like the parchment that Karswell hopelessly chases along the train tracks in the final sequence.

Standing on the train-station platform after Karswell's death, Holden concedes to Joanna that "it's better not to know." This line comes just before a passing train erases both of them from view; the shot is held until after the train has passed, leaving the platform empty. The disappearance of the characters signals the final triumph of Tourneur's cinema, its absolute control over the conditions of visibility used to create a space in which there is, at the end, nothing to see.

The Fearmakers
(1958)

A minimum of unconsciousness is necessary if one wants to stay inside history.

E. M. CIORAN,
THE TEMPTATION TO EXIST

The five theatrical features Tourneur directed after *Night of the Demon* make an unsatisfying coda to his career. As much as one would like to find them interesting, one is forced to admit that they fall short of the standard of his prior work. Since the films suffer variously from factors likely to have been outside Tourneur's control (including straitened production conditions and, in some cases, inadequate screenplays and bad casting), it is hard to know what share of blame for this decline should be assigned to Tourneur himself. At any rate, all five films, except possibly *The Comedy of Terrors*, contain at least moments that show that Tourneur had not given up the ghost.

The Fearmakers isn't a failure — most viewers would probably find it the most acceptable of the five late films — but neither is it a film strongly marked by the director's personality. Tourneur directed the film at the request of Dana Andrews, who told the producer that he would act in it only under Tourneur's direction.[1]

The Darwin Teilhet novel on which *The Fearmakers* is based was published in 1945. The script updates the story to have its protagonist, Allen Eaton (Dana Andrews), return from a Chinese POW camp after the Korean War. Eaton comes back to his Washington public-relations office to find that his partner, Clark Baker, has died in an apparent car accident after having sold the business to Jim McGinnis (Dick Foran). Meeting with his friend, Senator Walder (Roy Gordon), who chairs a Senate committee investigating lobbying groups, Eaton learns that McGinnis is suspected of being a foreign agent.

Eaton decides to accept a job from McGinnis so that he can check up on him. From talking with Barney Bond (Mel Torme), the firm's statistician, about a poll the firm conducted for lobbyist Fred Fletcher, Eaton comes to suspect that the results were deliberately skewed to favor Fletcher's agenda. With the aid of McGinnis's secretary, Lorraine Dennis (Marilee Earle), Eaton gains access to the master-card index file used for the poll. McGinnis and his accomplice, Harold Loder (Kelly Thordsen), capture Eaton and Lorraine and attempt to stage another

Dick Foran, Mel Torme, Marilee Earle, and Dana Andrews in *The Fearmakers* (courtesy of the Academy of Motion Picture Arts and Sciences).

fatal "accident" (like the one that eliminated Baker), but Eaton overpowers them, killing Harold and delivering McGinnis to the police.

The Fearmakers is a curiosity, a film in which sophisticated techniques of mass persuasion are in the hands of a B-movie criminal group: a PR executive who talks in Fuller–ese (as in Samuel, not Buckminster), a sexually frustrated milque-toast (Barney, constantly wiping his face with a handkerchief), a printer who doubles as brutish thug (Harold), and a combination forger and would-be femme fatale, Vivian Loder (Veda Ann Borg). Meanwhile, the defense of democracy is entrusted to a senator running a McCarthy–esque committee and a war veteran subject to blackouts and nightmares, with the vet being played by a faded movie star. Where is Tourneur in all this? He thought the film was a failure, having been made too quickly to take advantage of "such an admirable subject: the power of people who control our ideas."[2] The least that can be said is that Tourneur's direction brings out the contradictions inherent in the project.

With *Stranger on Horseback*, *The Fearmakers* is one of the most minimal of Tourneur's films. It takes place mostly in a few interiors. The impersonal, neutral decor of the Eaton & Baker offices dominates the tone of the film so much that when the action bursts outdoors at the end, the viewer feels shock (not that the deserted streets of Capitol Hill at night provide any sense of an ongoing social reality).

The mise-en-scène is competent but rather flat. The long dialogue between Eaton and Senator Walder in the Senate dining room is filmed in alternating close shots in a very conventional manner that doesn't feel at all like Tourneur: usually, he prefers to break down dialogue into two-shots and group shots, and when he resorts to the shot-reverse-shot form, he generally adopts the over-the-shoulder version of it (as he does a few moments later in *The Fearmakers*, when Eaton has a conversation with a reporter). Tourneur even uses a zoom at one point to show Eaton's disorientation—a device so out of keeping with his usual practice as to seem a kind of shorthand, although not ineffective in context. (Tourneur will also use zooms in his last two films and in several of his television series episodes, including "Night Call" [1963].)

One of the more successful aspects of the film is the relationship between Eaton and Lorraine (played effectively by Marilee Earle). Eaton is drawn to her because he notices her sympathy for him and her distaste for McGinnnis. When he first tries to get her to confide in him, however, she withdraws from him, fearing, as she later explains, that he is in league with McGinnis to test her loyalty. Eventually, his outspokenness wins her over. Like Vanning and Marie in *Nightfall*, Eaton and Lorraine acknowledge that their need to trust each other is more powerful than the claims of reason. "Now are you on my team?" he asks. She replies, "How do you know I'm not on theirs?" He answers, "That's a chance I've got to take."

The Fearmakers is one of only two Tourneur films that refer explicitly to the ideological crises of the postwar period; the other is *Berlin Express*, probably the last Hollywood film for several years to portray a Russian communist in a positive light. Ten years later, the world peace that the protagonists of *Berlin Express* intuitively sought has become a subversive goal that sounds dirty. The scene in the Senate dining room, the point at which Tourneur's lack of involvement in the film becomes total, straightforwardly sets forth the problem:

> WALDER: ...and in particular Jim McGinnis's connection with certain groups in this country that are out to sell us peace at any price.
>
> EATON: From the things I've seen, Senator, it's hard to believe that there could be too high a price.
>
> WALDER: There are few things worth buying with your life, Allen, and you of all people know that slavery isn't one of them.

In short, Eaton, having seen firsthand the horrors of war, is in a position to recommend peace, but Walder prefers death to an enslaved peace (and appeals implicitly to Eaton's experience as a prisoner of the communists for his justification). Although Eaton makes a principled stand here, we're already aware of his limitations as a spokesman for peace. Early in the film, on a plane to Washington, Eaton sits next to Dr. Gregory Jessop (Oliver Blake), a nuclear physicist

Kelly Thordsen, Dick Foran, and Marilee Earle in *The Fearmakers*.

who belongs to a group called the Committee for the Abolition of Nuclear War-
fare. Eaton is startled to hear Jessop express regret over the subservience of the sciences to the military; Jessop's claim that "science has brought us to the brink of
world extermination" causes Eaton to raise his eyes in annoyance. (Eaton's distaste
for Jessop proves justified, since the physicist turns out to be a "fellow traveler" in
league with Fletcher and McGinnis.)

As the dialogue repeatedly suggests, the activities of Fletcher, McGinnis, and
Jessop have far-reaching consequences for millions. One of the film's limitations,
however, is that it is unable to represent these millions, or the effects of Fletcher's
campaigns, in any concrete way. The film feels abstract and hermetic. We could see
this as part of the point of the film: McGinnis and his world of Washington power
brokers are utterly divorced from the people whose beliefs and opinions he manip-
ulates. On the other hand, the sense that the drama is taking place in a void somewhat undercuts Eaton's moral outrage, which the audience is expected to share.

The film hardly lets us glimpse what the techniques of mass persuasion are
and how they're used. At one point, a confused Eaton opens the wrong door,
interrupting the leader of a group planning session in mid-sentence: "All right
then, so much for the Jews. The way we handle the labor unions…" The Fletcher-
McGinnis-Jessop program remains extremely vague to the viewer, just as the film

never says that the conspirators are working for China or Russia (the closest the film comes to stating this is McGinnis's remark about the "4,000-mile one-way trip" that he and Barney will have to take if the Fletcher campaign fails). The vagueness allows the film to avoid the logical consequences of its premises: that the existence of mass media destroys the distinction (which Eaton thinks he is fighting for) between "selling a package of cigarettes or soap or cereal" and "selling a mayor or a governor or a package of candidates for public office"; and that the manufactured image of public opinion has become (in a society already "postmodern" by 1958) the equivalent of, or a substitute for, opinion.

The abstraction and isolation from reality make the film more comfortless, more hopeless, more modern. The strength of the best movies overtly influenced by cold war ideology and sociopsychology generally lies in the sense of a primary, all-pervading paranoia, which the plot resolution all too clearly fails to dispel: *Kiss Me Deadly, Invasion of the Body Snatchers, The Manchurian Candidate*. On a more modest plane, *The Fearmakers* shares this strength. The world that Eaton returns to after two years in the hell of the Chinese communists is an incomprehensible nightmare. As if trying to force itself awake from this nightmare, the film resorts — in a manner reminiscent of Fuller — to the most extreme symbols of reason and democracy: the Lincoln Memorial and the Washington Monument. The freakish excess of this effort is itself a mark of failure, just as the film is marked from the beginning by signs of excess: short, barely legible shots of Eaton's Chinese ordeal under the block letters of the credits.

Eaton's vulnerability recalls the emphasis on weakness and physical affliction or restriction in other Tourneur films (*Easy Living, Nightfall*). His recurrent headaches put the narrative under a constant threat of fading — of falling back, perhaps, into the fragmented, assaultive state of the opening montage. Eaton is present almost continuously throughout the film. Our comprehension of events evolves along with his; thus, we feel his stabbing headaches and losses of consciousness or control as threats. Eaton's vulnerability makes the status of the narrative wobble, just as McGinnis, by constantly questioning Eaton's sanity (at one point McGinnis calls him a "brainwashed psycho"), reminds us that our view of events is affected substantially by gaps in Eaton's knowledge and even raises the possibility that Eaton is fantasizing part of the narrative. The film never capitalizes on this uncertainty, but its latency colors the narrative.

The script seems to imply that Eaton recovers his strength by identifying with moral, patriotic principles — a movement that culminates in his beating up McGinnis on the steps of the Lincoln Memorial — but the general bleakness and airlessness of the film undercut this theme. Nor does Tourneur attempt to signal that Eaton's triumph over McGinnis means an end to his problems. As in the other films in which Tourneur directed Dana Andrews, the actor's neutral, impassive personality is made an important feature of the mise-en-scène. Because Andrews is so ambiguous a hero, our attitude to the outcome of the story remains uneasy, and the film's sense of potential disaster lingers even at the end (especially since it gives no indication that Fletcher, apparently the Mabuse of the conspiracy, will be arrested).

The Fearmakers has a number of connections to previous Tourneur films. In some ways, Eaton is a typical Tourneurian hero. His pride in his "decent, useful business" recalls Oliver in *Cat People* or Jeff explaining the concept of "earning a living" to Whit in *Out of the Past*. In a sense, *The Fearmakers* is a sequel to *Night of the Demon*. Both start by assaulting the audience with images of horror, and both have huge close-ups of eyes: Hobart's eye in the hypnosis scene in *Night of the Demon*, and Eaton's eye in the medical-examination scene after the credits of *The Fearmakers*. In each film, furthermore, the character played by Dana Andrews is disturbed on a plane by an annoying chance encounter: in *Night of the Demon*, Joanna's reading light keeps him awake; in *The Fearmakers*, he is bored and irritated by Jessop (a person so obnoxious that he quotes *Macbeth* when Eaton says he's tired). Later, a night scene of Eaton's anguished, haunted sleep anticipates a shot in "Night Call": the camera pans from a window (on which backlighting projects the shadows of branches and of the window frame) across a dark room to arrive on Eaton in bed, lit by a dim light mottled with shadows.

Timbuktu
(1959)

He prefers to show that action has its dead times, that it has its own
contrasts, notably that contrast of lassitude and terror that he knows how
to paint admirably; for the cycle of action — fear, fatigue, suffering, and
death — which is a terrifying cycle, is also a monotonous cycle.

JACQUES LOURCELLES,
"NOTE SUR JACQUES TOURNEUR"

After *The Fearmakers*, Tourneur became involved in an even zanier project:
"the last of the desert movies, ... so far out of its time as to be high camp rather
than high adventure," as Ian Cameron notes.[1] *Timbuktu* is an absurd film but one
that glows with a special, dismal negative splendor.

Timbuktu takes place in 1940 in the French Sudan, where rebellious Tuareg
tribes, taking advantage of France's troubles at home, step up their attacks against
colonial troops. Arriving to take charge of the garrison at Timbuktu, Colonel
Dufort (George Dolenz) learns that his late predecessor had been dealing with an
American arms merchant, Mike Conway (Victor Mature), to get information
about the rebellion and locate the holy man said to be backing it, the Mohammed
Adani (Leonard Mudie). Conway delivers machine guns to the rebels' camp near
Bou Djeheba and finds that their leader, the emir Ibn-Bahai (John Dehner), is
holding Adani hostage, hoping to force him to sanction the rebellion.

Conway uses the fact that he has been observed making a pass at Colonel
Dufort's wife, Natalie (Yvonne DeCarlo), to gain the emir's trust. After a dinner
party at the emir's palace, Conway fools the emir's men into thinking that he is
making love with Natalie in her room, but instead he follows the emir to the secret
camp. Conway frees Adani, stashes him in one of the emir's wagons, and returns to
Natalie. Seeing through the ruse, the emir captures Conway and threatens to kill
him unless he turns over the holy man. Colonel Dufort frees Conway, and the two
men take off in the wagon with Adani. They arrive at Timbuktu to find that the
emir's men have taken over the city, but the two manage to smuggle Adani into the
great mosque. The emir kills Dufort and is killed by Conway. Adani makes a
speech denouncing the emir and exhorting his followers to lay down their arms.

Timbuktu repeats the basic movement of *Great Day in the Morning*: a cynical,
egotistical adventurer reaches the point where he is willing to sacrifice his self-
interest and even his life for an impersonal cause. Both narratives culminate in the

Victor Mature in *Timbuktu* (courtesy of the Academy of Motion Picture Arts and Sciences).

irony that the hero's life is saved through his rival's intervention. The other Tourneur film that *Timbuktu* most resembles is *Appointment in Honduras*, in which the heroine, filled with contempt for her husband, gives herself to another man and in which an American becomes involved in a Third World revolution. Of these three related films, *Timbuktu* is the most schematic, the most abstract, and in a way the most opaque.

Edward Small, the producer of *Timbuktu*, took his name off the credits, but not before providing Tourneur with another example of the destructiveness of producers. Tourneur recalled:

> I had shot *Timbuktu* with Victor Mature, who isn't a great actor, and the film wasn't terrible. But the producer, feeling that the film wasn't long enough, decided to shoot close-ups of extras with various expressions, which he inserted in certain sequences. So, suddenly, right in the middle of a battle, you saw more or less bewildered faces for long minutes. People must have said to themselves, "Tourneur has gone completely gaga."[2]

The viewer can easily distinguish the added shots by their flat lighting, crude

framing, and obvious studio-sky backgrounds. The shots are jarring, but they
don't exactly destroy the film; they merely accentuate an unreality already marked
in the footage that Tourneur shot and become part of its overall emptiness: the
void of the overbright desert; the moral emptiness of the cynical Mike Conway;
the stereotyped nullity of Conway and the other principal characters, the stiffly
patriotic Colonel Dufort and his bored, neglected wife, Natalie.

In the middle of this ridiculous, hypnotic barrenness appear occasional flashes
of something more than resourcefulness, less than a richly imagined reality: low-
angle shots of a muezzin on a minaret; cheap but richly textured scenes of city
streets. The film has two bewitching camera movements, both at moments when
thresholds are crossed or dispersed. When Conway enters a room in a building
that the rebels are using as their hideout, the camera, which starts close on Conway, rapidly dollies back before him to reveal that the room is filled with rebels.
Later, in the emir's tent, curtains are pulled back, revealing Adani sitting on the
floor, reading; the camera tracks back while at the same time the emir walks into
the shot from offscreen right; the camera's continued tracking reveals Conway sitting in the foreground. (This shot is central to the film. The realization that the
whole plot of the emir depends on a pro–French Islamic "holy man" whom he has
kidnapped epitomizes the lunacy of the film, but it also functions as the film's
heart of darkness.)

Frequently in the film the camera is slightly high. We first notice this tendency in the scene of the officers' meeting in the colonel's office, a scene marked by
smooth blocking of actors' movements in and out of the shot. It becomes more pronounced as the film progresses, so that we sometimes have the impression of gazing
down loftily at a humbled, flattened universe (e.g., the recurrent scenes in which
men prostrate themselves in prayer or stretch out on the sand — dead, tied to stakes,
or firing at the enemy). This tendency culminates in the final sequence, whose overhead shots of the steps leading to the minaret recall the shots in the tower in *Vertigo*
and which also contains a vertiginous high-angle shot from over and behind Adani
as he denounces the emir to the faithful assembled in the street below.

Intelligent direction manages to compensate for the schematic, unreal conception of the characters' relationships: in the scenes between the Duforts, Tourneur uses the actors' impassiveness to create a strong sense of repressed emotion.
The negativity of the film reaches its epiphany in the scenes devoted to the emir's
tortures, which include some of the most startling of the images of horror that
punctuate Tourneur's cinema: the extreme close-ups of tarantulas crawling on the
hands of Lieutenant Marat (James Foxx).

Of all Tourneur's films, *Timbuktu* is, along with "What Do *You* Think?" (in
which the hero goes over the past with a stopwatch) and *Night of the Demon* (in
which Holden attempts to pass the parchment back to Karswell before ten o'clock,
when the demon is due to appear), the most obsessed with time, possibly reflecting
some awareness on Tourneur's part that he had reached the twilight of his career.
The characters are perpetually rushing to beat some deadline: Conway hurries back
from the emir's secret camp to Natalie's room to fool the emir into thinking that
they have spent the night together; in the last movement of the film, the two
adversary parties race each other to Timbuktu. And the emir makes a point of
remarking that it takes three minutes for a tarantula's bite to kill a man.

Victor Mature and Tourneur during the shooting of *Timbuktu*. Is Mature unhappy with Tourneur's direction? (courtesy of the Academy of Motion Pictures Arts and Sciences).

Conway's unique alarm wristwatch, which he throws on the ground to distract a guard at the emir's camp and which the emir later finds, is the most direct image of this preoccupation with time. The inscription, "To Conway from Conway," describes a minimal cycle, suggestive of the metaphor of time as a circle. The watch is also part of a series of round metal objects that the film compulsively shows in inserts: the rebels' medallion (which appears in close-up at least five times in the film, an unreasonable excess that may indicate more padding by Edward Small); Colonel Dufort's wedding ring. The narrative follows a circle; the back-and-forth movements of most of the major characters between Timbuktu and Bou Djeheba plot on the space of the desert the hastening of the narrative after its lost objects: Natalie; the machine guns that Conway is to deliver to the rebels.

To thwart the rebels during one of these desert crossings, Conway substitutes sewing machines for the machine guns, invoking a surrealist metaphor that might have pleased Ado Kyrou or Luis Buñuel. The two items have a complex relationship, from the simple homophony of "sew" and "sow," machines that sew fabric and machines that sow death, to the reversal of effect, the one making holes and the other repairing them. The association of death with the sewing machine inevitably suggests another metaphor of time, that of the tapestry. This metaphor emerges again in the unspooling of the thread suspending the tarantula over Conway's bound body.

Another form of tapestry, writing, is prominent in *Timbuktu*. This emphasis links it to Tourneur's two previous films: the power of writing, best symbolized in the parchment in *Night of the Demon*, is closely linked to death; *The Fearmakers* is a storm of texts, from the forged transfer of ownership of the company to the putative letter that Eaton's partner may have written shortly before his death. An interesting motif in the script of *Timbuktu* involves the effect that written texts have on whether people trust each other: the French administration's testimonial to Adani; the general's letter that Conway carries in his shoe; the letter that Conway sends to the colonel by riderless horse; the letter that the colonel writes to his wife before leaving on his last mission. All these texts speak the truth, and all the characters have an almost superstitious belief in the force and veracity of the written word.

Timbuktu marks the logical end of Tourneur's Hollywood career, not because it is a summation (the material is too thin for that, to say nothing of the budget) but because it continues in a terminal (perhaps, as Ian Cameron hinted, posthumous) context both the generic traditions of Hollywood cinema and Tourneur's characteristically dry, disenchanted, and aestheticized way of approaching them. (*The Comedy of Terrors*, the last film Tourneur shot in Hollywood, is more of an epilogue or postscript.) For all its faults, *Timbuktu* remains a Tourneur work.

La Battaglia di Maratona (1959)

That Tourneur made *La Battaglia di Maratona* at all is a symptom of the period. The late 1950s saw the decline of the Hollywood system and the rise of international coproduction. Directors at Tourneur's commercial level either did TV, became inactive, or went to Italy. The film that Fritz Lang is making in Italy in Godard's *Le Mépris* is supposedly nothing less than *The Odyssey*, but more typical were projects such as *La Battaglia di Maratona* (which MGM released in the United States as *The Giant of Marathon*)—a script fashioned out of scraps of history and filled out with stock elements, an Italo-French coproduction with an American "Mr. Muscle" (Steve Reeves) in the lead role, with a French starlet for romantic interest (Mylène Demongeot, looking great but giving little hint of the exuberance she lent Preminger's *Bonjour Tristesse*), and with a supporting cast of familiar Italian faces.

The script is a loose transposition of the events of the First Persian War (Herodotus, *The Persian Wars*, Book VI). Philippides (Reeves), champion of the Olympic games, is appointed to the sacred guard of Athena. Hoping to win the hero's support for his conspiracy to seize political power in Athens, Theocritus (Sergio Fantoni) orders his mistress, Karis (the magnificent Daniela Rocca) to seduce Philippides, who is, however, smitten with Andromeda (Demongeot), the daughter of Creusus (Ivo Garrani), a coconspirator with Theocritus. The Persians, led by Darius (Daniele Varga), land at Marathon. Philippides goes to Sparta to persuade the city leaders to join with Athens in fighting the invader, then returns to help the Athenians beat the Persians at Marathon. Learning of the imminent landing of the Persian fleet at Piraeus, Philippides runs to Athens to warn the city, then leads the sacred guard in repelling the sea attack, killing the traitorous Theocritus.

According to Tourneur, he was hired for the film at the request of Steve Reeves, who had admired *The Flame and the Arrow*. Tourneur's contract was for ten weeks, at the end of which, he said, he had shot all the principal dialogue sequences but not certain action sequences, in particular the scenes of Philippides running, the underwater scenes, and the final battle at sea. Rather than keep Tourneur at his relatively high rate, producer Bruno Vailati decided to direct the run and the sea battle himself while entrusting the underwater scenes to the brilliant Mario Bava, the film's cinematographer, who also served on the film as designer of its special effects (glass shots).[1]

Certain situations in *La Battaglia di Maratona* echo other Tourneur films:

La Battaglia di Maratona: Sergio Fantoni and Daniela Rocca.

Philippides' disillusioned retirement from Athens to the country recalls Jeff's withdrawal to Bridgeport in *Out of the Past*; Karis is functionally the same character as Boston in *Great Day in the Morning*; the jaws of the Persian ship inexorably bear down on the camera like the teeth of the snowplow in *Nightfall*; like Molly in *Anne of the Indies*, Andromeda is tied to the prow of the ship.

The Tourneurian qualities of the film reside less in such structural resemblances, however, than in the mise-en-scène and in the moral attitude it implies. The film takes place in an atmosphere of faraway eroticism and stillness that enables the viewer to excuse a certain lack of dramatic force. Philippides declares his love to Andromeda on a promontory lined with statues and columns, overlooking the sea. The proximity of interior to exterior, of architecture to nature, determines the texture and significance of scenes: Philippides, surprised to see Andromeda in Creusus's house, is framed in a doorway against a background of trees and sky. Night scenes, typically involving Karis, the film's dark woman, are scattered with blazing torches that testify obliquely to the reality of the emotions being declaimed unbelievably in dubbed dialogue. The characteristic action of *La Battaglia di Maratona* is someone gazing into the space beyond the frame, contemplating personal failure (Creusus) or staring with love or envy at the embodiment of purity, Philippides. In a shot whose orchestration of movement recalls *Appointment in Honduras*, Theocritus strides past Andromeda and stops without looking at her; she asks him a question but turns and runs without waiting for an answer, leaving Theocritus looking in the opposite direction, where Philippides has just gone.

The film values aesthetics over athletics. To Philippides, "an Athenian who is above all suspicion," the ideal of Athenian democracy is more important than physical accomplishments; a pacifist, he reacts with disgust to the wrestling match that Karis presents to him, and he later says, "It would be better if weapons didn't exist." A musician at Creusus's house praises the pleasures of wine and company, "the beauty of life," while the camera shows that he speaks for Tourneur by tilting gracefully above the musician's head to frame a mural depicting a feast. Throughout the film one feels that what matters most to Tourneur is the beauty and mystery of this abstract, imaginary young world and the idealized love of hero and heroine. Some of the most memorable moments of *La Battaglia di Maratona* are those in which Tourneur conveys an aching nostalgia for this world: for example, the long shot at dusk of the virgins praying, to Venus, that Andromeda will see Philippides again.

In the last half of the film, its furtive beauty gives way to impressively filmed physical spectacle. The battle of Marathon itself is an excellent sequence that one would like to be able to attribute to Tourneur (whose remarks to Joel E. Siegel indicate that he indeed shot it on location in Yugoslavia),[2] if only for the remarkable shot that tilts up from a skull dropped in a field to reveal the Athenian troops lined up for battle. Bava's underwater scenes are, strangely enough, among the most powerful images in the film, anticipating the director's perverse masterpiece *Ecologia del delitto* (*Twitch of the Death Nerve*, 1971) in their abstract contemplation of carnage.

Despite its obvious insufficiencies on every plane except the visual, *La Battaglia di Maratona* is not unworthy of Tourneur. Sadly, it is the last of his features of which this can be said.

The AIP Films
The Comedy of Terrors (1963)
and War-Gods of the Deep (1965)

The Comedy of Terrors (1963)

After three years without a theatrical film credit, Tourneur signed with American-International Pictures in 1963 to do a film that was eventually released as *The Comedy of Terrors*. A sort of follow-up to AIP's successful *The Raven*, released earlier that year, *The Comedy of Terrors* reunited that film's three stars — Vincent Price, Peter Lorre, and Boris Karloff — and added Basil Rathbone (who had appeared with Price and Lorre in *Tales of Terror* [1962], which preceded *The Raven* in AIP's Edgar Allan Poe series). Richard Matheson, who had written all the Poe films to that point except *The Premature Burial* (1961), provided the script. Despite the cast and writer, AIP made no attempt to link *The Comedy of Terrors* to the Poe series; nor was Roger Corman, the regular director-producer of the series, assigned to the project. He may have been busy preparing *The Masque of the Red Death* (1964), or he may have been uninterested in doing another comedy-horror in period costumes and sets so soon after *The Raven*.

In interviews Tourneur gave while he was in Britain working on what was to be his last film, *War-Gods of the Deep*, the director defended *The Comedy of Terrors*, which by then had been released without much success in the United States, and distanced himself from Corman. "Roger Corman — his films, as far as I'm concerned, are adapted to young people, children — they're not for adults. Ours was extremely adult…. [O]ur film was deliberately aimed at the mature thinking people who appreciate satire, who appreciate cynical humor — therefore it was completely lost on the kids who were looking for horror and they didn't get it." Neither, admittedly, did the director's own intimates, according to Tourneur's comments in the same interview: "My wife and my friends say 'We don't like this film at all.' They say 'It's not you! Why did you do it?'" Tourneur went on to explain that he saw the film as "a cynical, cynical comedy, a little bit in the old René Clair tradition."[1]

The director's comments to *Présence du cinéma* have a sinister sound: "I don't want to detail all the things that happened on this film, but all I can tell you is that the first script of this film was a little masterpiece, a jewel. For the first time in my life, I read a script and said, 'It's perfect, let's shoot it without changing anything.'" Years later, when he was involuntarily retired, Tourneur told Charles

Higham and Joel Greenberg, "I wasn't too happy with *The Comedy of Terrors*, and don't want to talk about it, not on record, anyway."[2]

The contradiction between Tourneur's statements in 1964, when he was on his second film for AIP and expecting to do a third, and his comments in 1969, when he was finished in Hollywood, suggests that something went wrong with the production of *The Comedy of Terrors* from Tourneur's point of view. What this was is difficult to determine. Richard Matheson, who served on the film as associate producer, affirmed that the script that Tourneur so admired "was shot word for word." He added, "I can only assume that Tourneur was not satisfied with some of the performances."[3]

The film takes place in a small New England town in the late 19th century. A misanthropic undertaker, Waldo Trumbull (Vincent Price), and his inept assistant, Felix Gillie (Peter Lorre), drum up business during a slow period by killing people. One of their intended victims, John Black (Basil Rathbone), keeps emerging from his coffin to terrorize them. At the end of the film, Trumbull kills his wife (Joyce Jameson) and Gillie and also dispatches Black, seemingly for the last time, before dying from poison he had intended for his senile father-in-law, Amos Hinchley (Boris Karloff).

The Comedy of Terrors is a disturbingly broad farce, sometimes funny but for the most part crudely handled and grotesquely overacted. One of the characteristically schizophrenic scores that Les Baxter composed for AIP films in the sixties plays almost constantly through the film, exacerbating the irritating effect of most of what transpires on screen.

Tourneur's visual authority is barely in evidence. (Admittedly, the visual quality of the film is now hard to judge: the one Scope print I viewed is red, and versions of the film released on video are flat.) The film begins promisingly with a stately crane shot toward a funeral group in a graveyard. Suddenly, after the mourners have all gone, the film switches to fast motion as Trumbull and Gillie dump the corpse out of the coffin into the grave and cover the grave. (They have only one good casket, which they use over and over again.) This visual gimmick is the first sign that something is radically wrong with this film. By Tourneur's standards, the film relies heavily on montage, particularly in the (initially rather good) scene of Gillie and Trumbull's wife dancing while her father fiddles off-key, intercut with Trumbull in another room counting his money; the sequence builds to a series of increasingly short intercut shots. The occasional zooms are gratuitous and uncharacteristic of Tourneur (for example, the zoom-in on the coffin through the lattice door of the vault).

The film comes to life in its last fifteen minutes or so, along with Mr. Black, who, spouting random lines from *Macbeth*, rises from his tomb and comes after the undertakers with an axe ("The devil damn thee black, you cream-faced loon"). In one funny scene, Trumbull and Gillie, seeking respite from being chased by Black, shut themselves in a room. "It's a little better in the dark," says Gillie. Trumbull asks, "What is, decapitation?" Later, Black, after being shot, recites the "Tomorrow and tomorrow" speech, intermittently falling, seemingly dead, and then getting up, with Trumbull mugging away in disbelief in cutaways all the while. When Black gets to "And then is heard no more," Trumbull quips, "That I'll believe when I see it." By the standards of the film, this is a very good scene.

Of the stars, Rathbone comes off best. His recitation of the Macbeth-Macduff swordfight scene in his bedroom is one of the film's better moments, even though he deliberately overplays, trying to be funny, and the scene is marred by having him charge the camera with a sword. Lorre (replaced in many shots by a stunt double with Lorre-esque features that remain disquietingly immobile) is sometimes funny, as when Trumbull accuses him of being "a confessed bank robber," and he says: "I've never confessed. They just proved it." Price also has a few good moments (such as the line "He bit me, the son of a bit me"), but otherwise his performance is overbearingly over the top. Karloff has almost nothing to do but also manages to be somewhat irritating.

War-Gods of the Deep (1965)

As depressing as it is to have to contemplate *War-Gods of the Deep*, Tourneur's last feature film finds him a little more in his element than *The Comedy of Terrors*. Although perhaps not conceived as such, the film emerged as another entry in AIP's Poe series — the first without the participation of Roger Corman, who, after eight films, was tired of the series, to which he had just contributed his masterpiece, *The Tomb of Ligeia* (1964). None of the post–Corman Poe films have much relationship to Poe; in this they take off from Corman's *The Raven* and *The Haunted Palace* (1963), which justified their titles only by having Vincent Price recite lines from the poems on which the films are ostensibly "based." *War-Gods of the Deep* uses the same device, although by releasing the film under this title rather than that of the poem ("City in the Sea"), AIP elected not to publicize the connection to Poe — a decision that may reflect an awareness that the value of the Poe name had depreciated over eight films in four years. (In Great Britain the film was released as *City under the Sea*.)

War-Gods of the Deep was a coproduction between AIP and Anglo-Amalgamated in England. Charles Bennett (*Night of the Demon*), who wrote the original script, was well qualified to do a Jules Verne–like fantasy-adventure, having recently written *Voyage to the Bottom of the Sea* and *Five Weeks in a Balloon* for Irwin Allen. Original plans to reteam Vincent Price with Boris Karloff had to be scrapped because of the latter's health; presumably Karloff would have played the role of Reverend Jonathan Ives, a part that went to John LeMesurier.

During production, while the film was still being called *City in the Sea*, Tourneur put the best face on things in his encounters with interviewers. "It's in the Disney tradition in the sense that it's completely fanciful," he said hopefully to *Films and Filming*. To *Midi-minuit fantastique*, he went further: "It's above all an adventure film in the spirit of Jules Verne ...Personally, I like this *City in the Sea*."[4]

According to Louis M. Heyward, the film was already in production when the English producer, George Willoughby, began raising objections to the script and feuding with the American coproducer, art director Daniel Haller. Heyward, a former TV comedy writer whose previous feature film credits were Don Weis's *Pajama Party* and Norman Taurog's *Sergeant Deadhead*, was sent to England to

Vincent Price and Susan Hart in *War-Gods of the Deep*.

troubleshoot the production. He immediately set about rewriting the script with a view toward lightening it up, adding the character of Harold Tufnell-Jones (David Tomlinson) and his pet rooster, Herbert. "At the point when the English producer saw that I had written in a chicken, and knew that whatever I wrote was going in, he quit — he said, 'I don't do chicken pictures!'" Willoughby's departure left Haller as sole producer; Heyward stayed on to back Haller up in the face of possible resistance from the English crew and to continue his tinkering with the script.[5]

While making *War-Gods of the Deep*, Tourneur was still expecting to do a third picture for AIP, an adaptation of H. G. Wells's *When the Sleeper Wakes*. Susan Hart, the wife of company executive James H. Nicholson and ingenue in *War-Gods of the Deep*, remembered Tourneur as "happy to be working." His position in *War-Gods of the Deep* was all too clearly described by Heyward:

> Poor Jacques! Jacques was, again, at the nadir of his career,
> but he wanted to direct another picture or two. He was
> overly agreeable, and there was a sadness to that. At AIP, it
> was the same with directors as with actors. If you were a
> young director, AIP was giving you a chance; if you were an
> old director, your career was on its way down when we
> inherited you. You were usually afraid to fight because it
> would influence the next picture.

Tourneur summed up the film: "I had a producer who took himself for a screen-writer, who constantly changed the script and completely ruined the film."[6]

In *War-Gods of the Deep*, Jill Tregellis (Susan Hart) is kidnapped from her hotel on the Cornish coast by a strange gill-man. Following the trail of seaweed left by the creature, Ben Harris (Tab Hunter), an American engineer, and Harold Tufnell-Jones (David Tomlinson), an artist, discover a passage to an underwater city. The city, whose inhabitants are immortal because of the lack of ultraviolet light, is ruled by a person known as "the Captain" (Vincent Price), who had Jill kidnapped because he believes her to be the reincarnation of his dead wife. After Ben, Jill, and Harold escape, the city is destroyed by erupting volcanoes, and the Captain dies from exposure to the sun.

The opening scenes of *War-Gods of the Deep* are uneven but contain moments that feel more like Tourneur than anything in *The Comedy of Terrors*: the discovery of a body washed up on the shore; the arrival, at the inn, of Ben (the last in the line of Tourneur's Americans in Europe), greeted by suspicious looks from the old residents in the lounge. Our first view of one of the gill-men is handled in a man-ner that is delicate by AIP standards: Ben enters a dark room; wind blows in through an open window; a hunched figure crosses the space in shadow.

The long shots of Harold and Ben in the cave have a faintly Lovecraftian air. As the men continue exploring, they hear strange sounds as if from a group of people whispering. The sourceless whispering, which continues intermittently throughout the picture, is another potentially Tourneurian element, but it is han-dled crudely by the sound department and falls short of the atmospheric effect it could have had. Tourneur introduces the Captain in a characteristic manner: in semi-shadow in an open doorway, he pauses to deliver his first line before entering the room.

The mute guard, Simon (Ray Patrick), has some potential as a Tourneurian outsider figure, but it is squandered, and the character is uninteresting. More notable is the senile Reverend Ives (John LeMesurier), who mutters things like, "There's some good in everybody, don't you think?" Later in the film, as he moves, in the tradition of the Kid in *Out of the Past*, from a marginal to a central position in the plot, he remembers the way out and shows the heroes how to escape. (Amusingly, he apologizes on the way to the prostrate guard who apparently has been either knocked out or killed.)

That's about it for the credit side of the ledger. Watching *War-Gods of the Deep* is, on the whole, a numbing experience. Early in the film, Ben advises Harold: "Why don't you leave that chicken behind? He'll only get in our way." Alas, this advice isn't followed. The rooster ends up being one of the more promi-nent, and annoying, elements in a script that includes a little of everything — including the Captain's dead wife, whose portrait he keeps behind a curtain in his room in an apparent sign of solidarity with Price's characters in the Corman-Poe films.

The performances are little better than the script. Though more subdued than in *The Comedy of Terrors*, Price gives one of the performances that earned him a somewhat unfair reputation as a ham rather than a serious actor. Tab Hunter and Susan Hart seem not to know or care what sort of movie they've been cast in, and it's not easy to blame them.

Near the end of the film, any flickering tolerance one might have is extinguished by an underwater sequence that goes on interminably and is more a triumph for the music orchestrator than for anyone else. Tourneur said he refused to go underwater to direct these scenes,[7] which are credited to John Lamb. It is difficult to imagine how any director could have saved these scenes of men in diving suits and gill-man costumes.

War-Gods of the Deep doomed Tourneur's hopes of reviving his career. Charles Bennett noted, "Jacques, the poor devil, got the blame for it, but actually he was not to blame at all."[8]

Television Films

From 1954 to 1966, Tourneur worked extensively in television, joining the ranks of other veteran directors who found it increasingly difficult to earn their living from feature films. Tourneur detested television, whose tight schedules made it almost impossible, he said, to do creative work: a 25-minute series episode was generally scheduled for two and a half or three days, each day lasting ten to twelve hours. Tourneur noted: "So, these poor actors, after three in the afternoon, they no longer know what they're doing, they're as if in a cloud. It's very tiring for everybody and the result isn't worth much. But I think that television can't exist otherwise. It's a commercial enterprise, and nothing else."[1]

It is hard to see Tourneur's TV work today; apart from *Bonanza* and *Twilight Zone*, the series he worked on are now obscure, and prints of his TV films are rare. Of the ones I've managed to see, several, unsurprisingly, are mediocre exercises in plodding hackwork, bearing out Tourneur's contempt for the medium. He must have found it painful and humiliating to direct, for example, "A Bride for the Captain" (*Adventures in Paradise*, 1962) or his *Northwest Passage* episodes (1958-59).

Yet if the conditions under which he had to work frequently got the best of him, Tourneur remained more than equal to the challenges of the occasional well-wrought script that came his way. The near-impossibility, under current conditions of film distribution and exhibition, that anyone will see these films except in archives makes me almost hesitate to write this, but "The Martyr" (*The General Electric Theater*, 1955), "The Stopover" (*Walter Winchell File*, 1958), and "Aftermath" (a.k.a. "Mr. Preach," an unsold pilot shown as an episode of *The General Electric Theater*, 1960) are small masterpieces in which Tourneur's visual authority is not only clearly in evidence but more apparent than in some of his theatrical features of the period. The same is true of "Night Call" (*Twilight Zone*, 1963), which, fortunately, is widely available. There is something miraculous about the flourishing of Tourneur's artistry in these works.

"The Martyr" (1955)

The earliest known representative of Tourneur's TV work is "The Martyr," an episode of *The General Electric Theater* broadcast on January 23, 1955. "The Martyr" is based on a story of the same name by Frank O'Connor. Set in 1922, during the civil war that followed the signing of the Anglo-Irish Treaty, O'Connor's story is narrated by a Free State colonel, named Raftery in the film and played by Brian Aherne. After a deadly ambush against the narrator's men, they capture a rebel commander, Colonel Jack Hartnett, believed to have plotted the ambush. To save himself from execution, Hartnett betrays to the colonel the real leader of the ambush, Morgan, who is captured. Hartnett then tries to organize an escape, but the plan is found out, and Morgan is executed. At the end of the story, the colonel returns to the barrack from a conference to find that Hartnett has been shot trying to escape.

The tersely written story contains many ambiguities and contradictions, all related to the central dilemma of the loss of a basis for principled action, a dilemma that Hartnett's act of informing brings into focus and that the narrator states thus: "That's the curse of civil war. No matter what high notions you start with, it always degenerates into a series of personal quarrels, family against family, individual against individual, until at last you hardly mind what side they're on."[2]

In the film, the dilemma becomes one of personal conscience in a world where, as the offscreen narrator says at the beginning (the words sound curious coming from Ronald Reagan), there is "nobody wrong, nobody right":

> HARTNETT: In the old days it was simple. It was all of us
> against the Black and Tan.
> RAFTERY: But now each man must judge for himself.

Leo Davis's teleplay follows the story but leaves the point of view of the colonel to concentrate on the anguish of Hartnett (Reagan, wearing glasses), abandoned to a solitude in which he thinks up his paradoxical double "bargain," one with Raftery to deliver Morgan and one with himself to try to free him. Davis adds scenes in which Hartnett and Morgan plot their escape, in which Morgan, just before leaving the cell to be executed, realizes that Hartnett is the informer, and in which Hartnett goads the brutal Captain Morrissey (Lee Marvin) into killing him.

Tourneur capitalizes on the starkness of the settings to create the atmosphere of a chamber play, in which the almost exclusive restriction to enclosed spaces supports the interior nature of the drama. Most of the film takes place in the grim barrack, lit by naked electric bulbs and dominated by a heavy stone staircase and by the bars on the window and door of the converted tool shed that serves as Hartnett's cell. The opening shot is a crane shot that briefly sets forth the limited possibilities of this architecture before a truck drives into the shot, depositing the captured Hartnett.

The brief excursion to the village where Raftery and his men arrest Morgan is merely an extension of the same dark, hermetic space, suggesting that all Ireland is a prison in which men work out purely personal dilemmas. This point is reinforced by the shot in which Hartnett, in the foreground outside the house, looks in through a window at Morgan, who, deep in the background, is being disarmed and marched off. The window is a metaphor for and a frame created by consciousness, in which Morgan figures as a mental image.

In this sense, "The Martyr" is an ideal half-hour television film. Tourneur's adjustment from the large screen to the small one, from the theater to the home, takes the form of the visualization of an interior drama; the various people the protagonist meets are external projections of this drama. Morgan in particular appears as someone made up in Hartnett's head to represent an abstract political idealism for which there are no problems and no doubts. Like Morrissey, he is stupid; dedicated to a world determined by brute needs, he raises no questions except the obsessive ones about the informer's identity and about why Hartnett, with his escape plan, is willing to put himself at greater risk in order to increase Morgan's chances.

Such a script obviously places great demands on the central actor, and Reagan, in a part with more depth than those he usually played in theatrical films, strikingly conveys both Hartnett's self-hatred and the story's sense that in the not-too-distant past he has lived up to the role of patriot and leader of men. The turning point of the story is Hartnett's decision to become "the martyr," not to a cause but to his own conscience, and this is quite well rendered in Tourneur's close-up of Hartnett through the bars of the cell door, as Hartnett silently passes from the realization of the opportunity for death to the determination to accept it.

"Into the Night" (1955) and "A Hero Returns" (1956)

Two other mid-fifties TV-drama episodes by Tourneur appear to be of some interest; not having seen them, I rely on *Variety* reviews and descriptions by the critic and filmmaker Michael Henry Wilson. In "Into the Night" (*The General Electric Theater*), a vacationing couple (Eddie Albert and Ruth Roman) are hijacked by two killers (Dane Clark and Robert Armstrong), who force the couple to drive them to the Mexican border. According to Wilson, the couple undergo "a nightmarish voyage, in the course of which they discover unsuspected resources in themselves."[3] As Wilson observes, the story anticipates *Nightfall*; it also has a clear precedent in Ida Lupino's *The Hitchhiker* (1953).

"A Hero Returns" (*Jane Wyman Presents the Fireside Theater*) takes place in an Italian village just liberated by the partisans, whose leader (Dane Clark) capitalizes on the legendary, but fictive, exploits of his aviator uncle to gain prestige. Wilson sees the episode as an exercise in Tourneurian ambiguity: "Like *Berlin Express* and *Circle of Danger*, 'A Hero Returns' leads us beyond appearances, beyond Manicheanism, to force on us an uncomfortable lesson in relativism."

"Kirsti" (1956)

This episode for *The Fireside Theater* belongs to a genre that, during his post–France career, Tourneur tackled only for TV: light comedy (compare "A Bride for the Captain," a Tourneur episode for *Adventures in Paradise*). That Tourneur received such assignments either testifies to television producers' faith in his versatility or suggests that they didn't care who was given what script, as long as some member of the Directors' Guild was on the set to call "action" and "cut."

Jane Wyman (the hostess of the series) plays Kirsti Stone, the Norwegian bride of a New England assistant pastor, Rayburn (Jack Kelly). The mild drama is mostly played in encounters between the guileless, warm-hearted Kirsti and various stuffy locals, especially her husband's superior, Dr. Cutler (Charles Coburn).

Ambitious for her husband, Kirsti is impiously happy when Cutler's cold seems to offer Rayburn the chance to deliver his first Sunday sermon, but at the last minute Cutler decides he feels well enough to give the sermon himself. Kirsti substitutes the text of her husband's sermon for that of Cutler's. The sermon is well received, Cutler acknowledges his assistant's merits, and Kirsti caps things off by announcing that she is going to have a baby.

Although its theme of the outsider is reminiscent of several key Tourneur films, including "The Incredible Stranger" and *Cat People*, Tourneur can do little with the material of "Kirsti," which is basically situation comedy without humor. The restricted scope of the production — there are only three exterior shots, all brief— gives him little chance to establish a regional flavor. Moments might be taken to signify at least the presence of a director: there is a sinister angled two-shot of the town gossips in a general store; in another scene, Kirsti crosses to a window to read a written text, in the time-honored tradition of Tourneur characters. If her husband's sermon, with its reiterated river metaphor, seems to us insufficiently profound to justify the admiring reactions of everyone who reads or hears it, at least it isn't stupid, and no doubt it is preferable to the sermon that Cutler planned to give, on why the heathen Chinese must suffer eternal damnation.

As insubstantial as "Kirsti" is, Tourneur's stripped-down style can still be preferred to the empty flourishes of Sidney Lanfield (a prolific *Fireside Theater* director). Instead of camera movement, Tourneur relies mainly on varying the size and position of actors in successive shots to create visual flow. This approach gives the show a certain spareness and dry honesty that prevent it from being merely cloying. In this drab visual context, the rare unusual shot, such as the high-angle medium-long shot from behind Cutler as he preaches Rayburn's sermon, takes on special value and significance.

Tourneur presumably did not, however, direct the most worthwhile moment of the show. This comes at the end, when Wyman, in her hostess persona, announces the next week's episode, a nuns-in-Red-China story, by introducing its director as "a gentleman who has given you many hours of heartwarming entertainment. Not only is he a friend of ours, but a director we all dream about working with." The director turns out to be John Ford, slouched in a director's chair and barely acknowledging the camera from which he is half turned away. "Thank you, Jane," he says grimly. "I hope to see you all next week. Good night." (According to Tag Gallagher, Ford's *Fireside Theater* episode, "The Bamboo Cross," was "the low point of Ford's career.")[4]

Walter Winchell File (1957–1958)

Walter Winchell File was a short-lived Desilu series produced by Bert Granet and built around the imaginary/real figure of the columnist, whose knack for being in the right place at the right time involves him in 25-minute dramas of crime and punishment. The opening of each show is an atmospheric, grainy shot of Times Square at night; Winchell strides into shot from the left to light a cigarette and look around poker-faced. The camera's sharply pulling focus adds to the you-are-there excitement.

In one of the three episodes I have seen (all directed by Tourneur), "The Steep Hill," the need to integrate Winchell into a plot in which his role is merely peripheral constitutes a fatal structural flaw. The regular succession of his coincidental meetings with the hero (Michael Connors), an accountant lured astray by a femme fatale (Dolores Donlon), threatens to turn the film into absurdist farce. At the beginning of "House on Biscayne Bay," Winchell meets the protagonist, Giovanni Mancuso (William Edmunds), an elderly Italian on his way to Miami to visit his son, Steve (Grant Richards); Winchell knows, as Giovanni does not, that Steve has become a notorious gangster. Later, Winchell manages to be coincidentally present when Giovanni comes to police headquarters to denounce Steve.

Both episodes are made in a way that could be called competent but not notably Tourneurian. They have an air of cheapness, with their limited sets and routine actors. "The Steep Hill" has an evocative moment when the hero responds to the woman's matter-of-fact seductiveness by saying, "I get the feeling that this has all been staged"—a line that would not be out of character for Bailey in *Experiment Perilous*, Jeff in *Out of the Past*, or Eaton in *The Fearmakers*. The episode reaches its climax with a dark night scene on the beach, characterized by a combination of high angles, unclear human figures, and explosive violence that recalls the scene at the oil derrick in *Nightfall*.

"House on Biscayne Bay," constructed, like "The Steep Hill," out of banal material, has a few moments of power toward the end. In a tensely staged and shot scene, the evil Steve, angry that his accountant, Frank Whitman (Val Dufour), has been seeing his sister, Angela (Didi Ramati), has Frank brought into his office. Steve turns him around and backs him toward the camera; simultaneously, two hoods converge on Frank in the foreground while Steve hits him. Here, Tourneur's staging of violence, though without the rawness of Phil Karlson's, achieves a nearly equal impact with its medium-shot simplicity and elegance. Later, an interesting lateral tracking shot shows Steve going into his house; he is followed by the police, who have come with a search warrant. The camera movement ends by confronting Steve with his father, who is waiting in a relatively dark area under some trees. In this context, the movement from light into darkness for dramatic purposes suggests the theatricality of Douglas Sirk or Nicholas Ray.

The third *Walter Winchell File* episode I've seen, "The Stopover," is a quietly devastating masterpiece that ranks (along with "The Martyr," "Aftermath," and "Night Call") with Tourneur's best work for television. Unlike "The Steep Hill" and "House on Biscayne Bay," it does not repeatedly insert Winchell into the action, which is a good thing: he is merely a witness to a tragedy in which he can no more intervene than can the viewer.

The ambition of the episode is announced from the beginning: the montage of atmospheric stock shots of Mexico is abnormally protracted; the unexpected slowness initiates the viewer into a privileged experience. The montage ends with a medium shot of a single, still bell; the film holds on this shot for a noticeably long time, imprinting it on our memory (the bell will figure in the last section of the film, but not until then).

The film proceeds to introduce us to the main street of a small Mexican town and its chief of police, El Jefe (Rodolfo Hoyos, Jr.), who is on his way to pick up a law book as a present for his son's fifteenth birthday. A shot of young women congregating on the sidewalk pans up to a second-story window, where a man stands, looking balefully down at the street. He is El Gato (Rodolfo Acosta, whom Tourneur had directed in *Appointment in Honduras*), a drunken, half-crazed former boxer whom El Jefe once caught and put away for robbery and who is now out for revenge. That night, during the birthday celebration for El Jefe's son, El Gato arrives and kills the son. He is arrested and thrown in jail, but because of the heinousness of his crime, the police designate him as one of the prisoners who, in this town where capital punishment has been banned, are occasionally released so that they can be shot trying to escape. In accordance with local custom, the bell seen in the opening montage serves to announce El Gato's escape. El Jefe, for whom the law is stronger than his desire for revenge, orders his men to lower their rifles and return El Gato to the cell.

Adrian Spies's script is first-rate. Acosta's superb performance by itself would lift this entry far above the average. El Gato is believably and movingly disoriented, obsessed, driven by forces beyond his control, not merely a vicious assassin. His aggressiveness and emotionality contrast effectively with Hoyos's stolid Jefe, an equally convincing portrait.

Visually, "The Stopover" is assured and careful. The opening montage may be only stock shots, but they are artistic stock shots; the montage, as noted, surprises us with its slowness, matching the sense of impending catastrophe in Winchell's quietly mournful narration. The town exteriors, though obviously sets, are dressed and lit (by Maury Gertsman) convincingly, making good use of trees, archways, and passersby; we believe no less in the reality of this Mexican town than we do in the reality of the town in *The Leopard Man*. Throughout the film, Tourneur emphasizes height: the pan up from the sidewalk to El Gato in the window; the high angle from his point of view of El Jefe, in the street, leafing through the law book; the high shot of El Gato, drunk, leaning on a tree trunk on his way to El Jefe's house; the recurrent image of the stone steps leading from El Jefe's house to the plaza; the pan up to the bell as the lieutenant rings it; El Gato's clambering over the rooftops after his release from jail.

The scene of the birthday party at El Jefe's house is a model of mise-en-scène. As is his wont, Tourneur shows us only parts of the set, in logical sequence, each at the moment when, and not before, we need to see it. A fine composition shows El Jefe and his wife in the middleground beneath an interior arch; an ornamental clock is in the right foreground. As El Jefe turns, the camera tracks left past a table lamp and pans down to frame a two-shot of the father leaning proudly over his son, who is studying his new law book under the lamp. A cutaway shows the drunken Gato approaching the front door. The doorbell rings; both father and son say, simultaneously, "I'll get it." The son goes to the door while the father joins his wife in the next room and turns out the light in preparation for lighting the candles on the cake. The son opens the door; El Gato enters and holds his gun on the boy while both stand in silence. The parents, lighting the candles, are at first oblivious to what is going on in the front room; the camera tracks back in front of them through the archway when they emerge. "You came to *my* house," El Gato recalls compulsively. In a close shot that frames him under the arch, El Jefe says calmly and evenly, "Not the boy." This cuts to a medium group shot: El Gato, in the background, shoots El Jefe as he moves forward.

The sound of the gunshot cues cuts to exterior shots: Winchell and his party of traveling Americans; a policeman. More shots are heard. Then we cut back to a high interior shot framed by El Gato's legs at left, by his arm, at a downward slant, still holding the gun, by a low table at right, and by the boy lying, his face invisible, in the space between El Gato's body and the table. The mother rushes into the shot and kneels by her son, then the father steps into the shot at right; we pan up his body and see that he has been wounded by El Gato's first shot. After El Gato runs out, a high shot shows the open law book on a table in the foreground, the son's body and the mother dark in the background. Obviously, Tourneur isn't afraid of exploiting the oppressive pathos of the scene, but he does so in such a visually rigorous way that we feel the pathos is earned. Moreover, the restraint of the actors and the terseness of the dialogue make the situation credible and involving.

El Gato's release (harrowingly visualized, with the police lieutenant entering grimly and slowly under a single light hung from the ceiling while El Gato crouches in a pool of stark light against the wall of his cell) leads to a protracted montage of deserted spaces (the courtyard, marked by a tree, through which El Gato flees; the stone steps; the empty tables of the outdoor café), returning repeatedly to a shot of the tolling bell. Echoing the decor of the jail cell, the film shows the mourners for the dead boy through the bars of a balustrade. The final confrontation reaffirms Tourneur's humanism: the high-angle close shot of the two policemen's rifles being lowered recalls the shot in *Stars in My Crown* of the noose intended for Uncle Famous.

The vengefulness of the townspeople links "The Stopover" to both *The Leopard Man* (which also takes place in a Hispanic community) and *Canyon Passage* (which also portrays the situation of a prisoner escaping), as well as to Tourneur's later TV masterpiece "Aftermath," whereas the theme of the rule of law links it to *Stranger on Horseback* and *Wichita*.

Northwest Passage (1958-1959)

MGM-TV produced this relatively high-budget color series, based on Kenneth Roberts's epic of the French and Indian Wars, a book that had already provided material for King Vidor's 1939 feature of the same name. Tourneur, who directed several episodes of the series, noted: "Our work consisted only in matching our shots with those of the film shot way back when by King Vidor. We took shots in which thousands of Indians and a few hundred Rangers appeared and we matched them with our own shots which contained no more than six or seven actors."[5]

The series was not a success, but MGM found a way to recoup its expenses by repackaging several of the episodes into three features to fill out its European theatrical release schedule for 1959. The first of the features, *Frontier Rangers*, consists of three Tourneur-directed episodes; the other two, *Mission of Danger* and *Fury River*, contain one part each by Tourneur.

Frontier Rangers begins in a way that suggests a Tourneur film: first a lateral tracking shot of three Indians making their way through a forest, followed by a shot that cranes backward from a burning wagon as a wounded white man crawls toward us — we're not far from the dry visual grandeur, the terseness in presenting disaster, of *Canyon Passage* and *Way of a Gaucho*. We quickly realize, however, that the narrative that unfolds and the characters who people it are without depth or contour. It is not cinema but merely spectacle, and rather thoughtless spectacle at that: one image succeeds another, rarely in a way that suggests the internal logic and control that come from mise-en-scène, usually in the fatally *believable*, almost-but-not-quite random manner of a producer's film, a commodity film (of which *Frontier Rangers*, by its production history and nature, represents a peculiar type). This arbitrary succession of images, which we must merely accept and not try to interpret or interrupt, is at its most nakedly factitious in the many moments when shots from the Vidor film are cut into Tourneur's footage.

Major Robert Rogers (Keith Larsen) is a cold, repellent automaton — not only as distant a figure as can be imagined from Spencer Tracy's quietly obsessed professional adventurer in Vidor's film but less charismatic even than Victor Mature and Steve Reeves in their performances for Tourneur. Larsen's beefcake robot presence makes the racism of the script play in an extremely unpleasant way. For example, in the first episode ("The Gunsmith"),[6] Rogers and his sidekick, Sergeant Hunk Marriner (Buddy Ebsen), become suspicious of the gunsmith Rivas simply because Rivas is half–Indian (and their suspicions prove justified). Both this episode and the third one, "The Burning Village," deal with Natula (Lisa Gaye), a white woman who was captured by Indians, is seemingly involved in a sexual relationship with an Indian chief, and is eventually returned to white society. People who think that John Ford's handling of the same situation in *The Searchers* and *Two Rode Together* is politically incorrect are in for an eye-opener if they ever see *Frontier Rangers*.

Tourneurian flashes occur throughout the film, but without a meaningful context. For example, the sequences at the Indian village in "The Burning Village" contain a few shots in which the orchestration of movement and the compositional placement of a sacrificial pyre and some torches are distinctly in Tourneur's style, yet their effect is mitigated by everything that surrounds them: the nonexistent choreography of the Indians' dance; the mediocre acting by the principals. The slightly pejorative connotations of the word "pictorialism," applied to Tourneur by Andrew Sarris, are justified in the case of *Frontier Rangers*.

Only the second episode, "The Bond Women," allows an opportunity for sustained development, although even here it is only a matter of, perhaps, two or three minutes of successfully realized scenes. The relative success of this part of the film is due partly to the presence of Angie Dickinson, although Tourneur's failure to use her effectively also makes this segment more frustrating than the rest of the film; he brings out little more than a hint of the personality that would unfold less than a year later in *Rio Bravo*. In this segment also, Buddy Ebsen is allowed to do a broad drunk routine that is particularly un–Tourneurian and anticipates the over-acting in which Tourneur would indulge the cast of *The Comedy of Terrors*. Since Ebsen's character is *simulating* drunkenness in order to get the better of a pair of villains, the scene can be said to work, again, on an "innocent" level, where excess is a conventional sign of deception (similar to the theatrical aside); but still we're thrown back on the fact that Tourneur's is not, as a rule, an innocent cinema and is not intended for a primitive reading.

"The Vulture," Tourneur's episode in *Fury River*, is of little interest and is barely distinguishable in style from those of "george waGGner," Alan Crosland, Jr., and Otto Lang. The beginning of the episode contains a line that sums up the premise of the series: "All he's interested in [this is spoken of Major Rogers] is licking the French and their Indian allies, and as quickly as possible, so he can find his northwest passage to the Pacific Ocean, which doesn't leave much time for the ladies." I haven't seen *Mission of Danger*, which contains one episode by Tourneur ("The Break Out") and two by "waGGner."

"Aftermath" (1960)

It is pleasing to find that a Tourneur TV drama from 1960 is a major work, entirely and unmistakably reflecting Tourneur's themes and principles. "Aftermath" was apparently the pilot for an unsold TV series called *The Code of Jonathan West*; it aired as part of *The General Electric Theater*. The film takes place just after the Civil War, in a small southern town — war-ravaged, impoverished, and seething with hatred and resentment. The itinerant hero, Jonah (Fess Parker), nicknamed "Preacher" because of his compassionate treatment of wounded and dying members of his platoon, is clearly no other than Parson Gray, from *Stars in My Crown*, in a different guise. At the beginning of the film, he arrives on the scene of an apparent homicide just after it takes place; the victim, Frank Colter (John Cole), has left behind a wife, two children, and a vengeful, half-insane brother, Hardy (James Best, in a performance that is almost a rehearsal for his berserk southerner in *Shock Corridor*), who leads a posse to find his brother's killer. Joined by the Preacher, who comes along to try to restrain Hardy, the posse captures the killer, Redway (William Challe), who claims that the killing was an accident. The Preacher overpowers the rest of the posse to prevent them from lynching Redway.

The care and scope of the production, and Tourneur's hand, are evident throughout "Aftermath," from its opening high-angle shot of Redway walking along a stream in the woods, through the elliptical, enigmatic presentation of Redway's encounter with Frank Colter and the Preacher's discovery of Colter's body. The subsequent scenes develop a contrast between the threat of further violence and an almost unearthly tenderness: visiting the Colter house to deliver the belongings of the deceased, along with some food donated by the town storekeeper, the Preacher finds two frightened children alone in the house, where a single Tourneurian lamp burns on a small table in the middle of a dark room. Meanwhile, Hardy stirs up the townspeople, in a series of night scenes that evoke the tortured atmosphere of *Great Day in the Morning*. Back at the house, the Preacher, putting the little girl to bed, tells her the story of Noah; the camera tracks left behind him across darkness to frame, in close-up, the boy looking in through the window with curiosity.

In another atmospheric high-angle shot, the posse rides away from the camera at night through a landscape of twisted bare trees and scattered remnants of broken war equipment. Tourneur's direction is assured: the Preacher's successive victories over the members of the posse are handled as authoritatively and as neatly as in a Budd Boetticher film. Finally (in a scene that recalls the denouements of both *The Leopard Man* and *Appointment in Honduras*), he confronts Hardy as a dislocated voice coming from somewhere in a landscape filled with dead trees and other potential hiding places. After the ordeal, the dissolve to a day scene creates a powerful relief: Colter's young widow is on the porch of the house; her two children emerge through the door, the camera panning and tracking with the daughter as she runs from shadow into bright sunlight carrying the Preacher's hat, which she hands up to him (he is on horseback).

The margins of the piece expose its TV-drama limitations: a certain patness in the story development; the rather bald close-ups of the Preacher and his side-kick, Ernie (Sammy Jackson, Jr.), at the end. In general, however, John Paxton's script suits the format excellently. The tense drama takes place within a single day-night-next-morning period. The script uses to advantage the fact that the viewer knows no more about events than the Preacher does, making it a device to let the issues gradually unfold.

Ernie is one of Tourneur's insider/outsider figures. He even has two names and, apparently, a different persona for each: as the village idiot Galoot, he is a grotesque caricature of debility; as Ernie, the Preacher's wartime friend, he is thoughtful and humane and adroitly assists the Preacher in the maneuver to overcome the posse. Like Hi Linnet, the Kid, Carrefour, the medium in *Night of the Demon*, and others, Ernie is associated with communication: he first hears the news of Lincoln's assassination and informs the posse.

The end of the film links it to *Wichita* and "The Stopover" (and to Ford's *Young Mr. Lincoln*) as well as to *Stars in My Crown*. Riding away from town with Ernie, the Preacher says he thought about being a preacher before the war and then gave up the idea, unsure of his ability to live up to what he would have to preach. He has decided that "the Bible's God's law; the next best is man's law." "You aim to go to lawyering?" Ernie asks. The Preacher answers: "It's one way of preaching, I guess. It may be a way to preach away the differences between men. Anyway, it's a living." Further adventures of the character weren't forthcoming, but one feels that Tourneur said, in the pilot, all that needed to be said about him.

"Sergeant Kolchak Fades Away" (1962)

Tourneur considered this episode of the series *Follow the Sun* one of his three best films for television (with "The Martyr" and "Night Call").[7] Produced by William H. Wright, the producer of *Stars in My Crown*, "Sergeant Kolchak Fades Away" stars William Bendix (who here, Tourneur said, "demonstrated an unsuspected sensitivity") as a Marine sergeant who massacred thirty Japanese in a fit of rage during World War II. The sole survivor of the massacre comes to Hawaii (where the sergeant is stationed) for revenge but relents when he discovers that the sergeant, to expiate his act, has been secretly supporting a Japanese orphanage. The denouement perhaps recalls Clay Douglas's renunciation of vengeance in *Circle of Danger*, and the theme of postwar reconciliation may link this film to *Berlin Express*, *Stars in My Crown*, and "Aftermath."

"A Bride for the Captain" (1962)

Tourneur started his career by accompanying his father to Tahiti in 1924 for the shooting of *Never the Twain Shall Meet*. Did he look back on that trip with nostalgia while toiling in the MGM studio on this episode of *Adventures in Paradise?* This now deservedly forgotten light-comedy series features Gardner McKay (who looks a little like Mel Ferrer with a hipper haircut) as Adam Troy, free-living captain of a boat-for-hire in Tahiti. McKay slouches a lot, puts his hands on his hips, and has bad diction, slurring the ends of phrases in a rotten "cool" act.

In the Tourneur episode, Frank (Ray Walston), an old friend of Troy's, arrives in Tahiti obsessed with the project of getting Troy married. He plays matchmaker between Troy and his friend Claudine (Maggie Pierce) by arranging for her to receive a forged marriage proposal apparently written by Troy. Claudine, who has long had a crush on Troy, is so excited and happy that Troy can't bring himself to tell her the truth. Then Troy falls in love with Claudine, but Frank misreads the situation and tries to undo everything, forging a letter from Troy to Claudine's boyfriend, inviting him to step in and replace Troy.

Tourneur fails to make anything of this material and these characters. The frequent back projections increase the general air of triviality. The last half of the film has a few good shots. The scene of Troy showing Claudine around his boat is better looking than the rest of the episode, with well-composed two-shots and careful lighting and decor. The scene closes on a strange effect: after a zoom-in on one of Troy's buddies singing a shanty, there is a dissolve to a shot that tracks in slowly on Claudine sleeping on a couch, the singing still audible but now mixed with reverb (indicating that the singing cannot "really" be heard in Claudine's room). The subsequent scene in Troy's cabin is also interesting visually, with Troy's shadow projected on a wall as he takes a drink. A scene at an airport unexpectedly employs a crane; then there is a nice shot of Troy (in the foreground) watching through a doorway partially obscured by a plant as Claudine embraces her estranged fiancé.

Jack Edmund Nolan observed that "A Bride for the Captain" has thematic similarities to two of Tourneur's French films: *Pour être aimé* and *Les Filles de la concierge*.[8]

"Night Call" (1963)

This *Twilight Zone* episode, produced by Bert Granet and written by Richard Matheson, is another major Tourneur work. Like *Night of the Demon*, it recapitulates a number of the director's career-long concerns in a profoundly elegant form.

Miss Keane (Gladys Cooper), a lonely, elderly invalid, is harassed by enigmatic phone calls from an unknown man. The phone company can't trace the calls or even verify that they have taken place. Eventually, Miss Keane learns that the calls may be the result of interference on a broken phone line at a nearby cemetery. Arriving with her nurse to investigate, she discovers that the line has fallen beside the grave of her fiancé, who died years ago in a car crash. Convinced that he is trying to communicate with her, she now impatiently awaits his calls, but they cease to come: in her panic, she had earlier ordered him to stop calling. He says, signing off, "I always do what you say."

In "Night Call," both the presence and the absence of sound cause anguish. At first, there is sound — the ringing of the phone, always at an unnaturally high volume on the soundtrack — where there should be none: it is two o'clock in the morning; Miss Keane is habitually alone, has no close friends, and is only intermittently in contact with a sister. She answers the phone and instead of the expected response, we have to strain to hear a sound that is practically no sound: the intermittent crackle of white noise.

Later phone calls transmit moaning, then repetitious fragments of speech ("Hello, hello"), a parody of an attempt to establish contact (the "phatic" function of language, in Roman Jakobson's scheme: "Where are you? I want to talk to you"). Finally, we hear a complete, distinct, and meaningful utterance ("You said to leave you alone. I always do what you say") that merely declares the suspension of the dialogue. Cut off from Miss Keane's desire, the caller's voice can only answer the letter of her demand. By breaking contact after she has come to long for it, the voice perfectly exemplifies Lacan's dictum about communication: Miss Keane gets her own message back in an inverted form.

The caller's communications progress from a noise that is virtually a metaphor for the silence it mysteriously interrupts to sentences that enunciate and enact their own fallback into silence. At the end of the film, silence takes over where sound is now desired and expected. (Narrator Rod Serling's voice-over violates the silence and the film's symmetry, however: the film starts with a shot that tracks right from a rocking chair to the bed and ends with a shot that reverses this movement, but the voice-over is present only in the second shot.)

The cutoff status of the fiancé's voice is structural. It is a "voice-off" that can never be "on," an absence that can never be present. This absence is invariably linked, however, with a visually present element: the telephone receiver, always shown in the frame when the voice occurs on the soundtrack. The receiver connects the scene — the hollowed-out space of Miss Keane's house — with its "other scene" of drives and intensities.

Significantly, this connection works only when an accident (the storm) disrupts the normal functioning of the apparatus (just as, in Tourneur's unrealized scenario *Whispering in Distant Chambers*, the voices of the dead can be detected only when the recording equipment malfunctions). The point of the film, and its irony, are that an interruption is needed for a contact to take place. "It's not a connection, it's a man," Miss Keane asserts. Speech, the body, memory (Miss Keane recounting the car crash that killed her fiancé and left her paralyzed) — all surge forth as ruptures of a calm that, at the beginning of the film, the ferocious storm already disturbs. Miss Keane's dread of this rupture turns into desire and anticipation, whose violence is marked by three short, unexpected zooms that collapse close and middle distance into pure psychological space.

The search for the source of the voice leads to the fabulous image of the gravestone, the fallen cable, and the telephone pole. The umbilical implication of the image fits one of the film's subtexts: the dead fiancé's voice takes the place of the son Miss Keane never had. The voice's progressive independence from Miss

Keane's utterances, the progressively increasing quantity of information in its messages, strongly resemble a child's linguistic development, the progress from vocalization to imitation to mastery.

"Night Call" could aptly stand as the title for a number of Tourneur films. The tormented body of Miss Keane, wracked by sound, recalls other unquiet sleepers in *Cat People*, *Days of Glory*, *Easy Living*, *Anne of the Indies*, *Appointment in Honduras*, and *The Fearmakers*. Most of Tourneur's protagonists — including Teresa in *Way of a Gaucho* and Natalie in *Timbuktu* as well as Betsy in *I Walked with a Zombie* — are called on at night to acknowledge and incarnate desire, to become bodies capable of desiring and being desired. In some cases this becoming carries anguish rather than pleasure: an extreme case, Holden in *Night of the Demon* discovers that he is desired by death.

"Night Call" not only is a tour de force for actress Gladys Cooper but also is a triumph of sound design: the force of the episode resides largely in the extreme contrast between virtual silence and the high-decibel phone ringing that shatters it. The way we hear the nurse leaving for the night while the camera holds on Miss Keane (the sound of the nurse's key turning in the lock, then footsteps up the walk, then a car door opening and closing and the ignition starting) testifies to the care taken to build up the dramatic and emotional role of sound in the film.

Matheson's script is ideally suited to the small-screen format: the miniature, largely interior drama takes place entirely in two rooms of Miss Keane's house, except for two exterior shots of the house, one insert of the telephone company representative talking on the phone, and the crucial visit to the cemetery.

Tourneur demonstrates an acute judgment of when to pull back from tense close shots (inevitably, the dominant visual mode of the film) to his signature textured medium shots so that rather than dissipating the dramatic tension, the latter crystallize the anguish of the situation that gives birth to the drama. In the brief shots that provide relief by escaping from the inside of the house to the open air, the camera prowls restlessly, as if the respite from Miss Keane's interior hell could only occasion an impatience to resume it.

Afterword

Asked in 1977, a few months before he died, what place he thought his films had in the history of cinema, Jacques Tourneur replied: "None. Nothing is more evanescent than an image in celluloid.... I'm a very average director, I did my work the best I could, we're all limited. On the one hand, one shouldn't have a false modesty; on the other, one shouldn't seem to boast; I'm somewhere between the two."[1]

Tourneur's willingness to consign himself and his works to oblivion is typical of him. Throughout his career he was a soft-spoken, self-effacing artisan; later, he was happy to tell interviewers that he never turned down a script. That he was far from an "average" director, however, is apparent not only from his films (several of which, despite his own final assessment, are likely to endure as long as the cinema) but also from his interviews, which invariably betray the concerns and the point of view of a self-conscious, precise artist.

The 1977 interview was conducted in French; the word "average" is an unavoidable (in context) translation for a word, *moyen*, that has other meanings more appropriate to Tourneur's achievement. *Moyen* also means "middle" or "medium"— words closely related (like the phrase "somewhere between the two") both to the themes of thresholds, borders, and transformations that Tourneur treated consistently in his films and to his view of his own role as an artist, a role that he saw as similar to that of a medium. "You must be more modest, try to handle as well as possible what you are given and let your subconscious work.... This attitude forces you to be open, receptive to all genres, to all forms of narration. It's a way of refusing to specialize."[2]

Tourneur's insistence on the "evanescent" nature of film is also significant, since his work is so preoccupied with, and so brilliant at tracing, the invisible and the absent. His films not only embrace their own obscurity and the risk of their disappearance but seem to make these the conditions of their existence. Tourneur's cinema, though remaining the most "average" of Hollywood cinemas, also finds the most elusive way imaginable of dispersing the limits that Hollywood imposed on representation.

Notes

Introduction

1. Sarris, *The American Cinema*, p. 141; Wood, "The Shadow Worlds of Jacques Tourneur," p. 64.

2. Johnston and Willemen, *Jacques Tourneur*, p. 5.

3. Siegel, *Val Lewton*, p. 23.

4. Telotte, *Dreams of Darkness*, pp. 12–13.

5. Willemen, "Notes towards the Construction of Readings of Tourneur," p. 16.

6. Quoted in Manlay and Ricaud, "Jacques Tourneur et le métier de cinéaste," p. 48. Except where contrary indication is given, all translations from works whose titles appear in French are mine.

7. Willemen, "Notes towards the Construction of Readings of Tourneur," p. 23.

8. McNiven, "Jacques Tourneur," p. 332.

9. Lourcelles, "Note sur Jacques Tourneur," pp. 52, 54.

10. Tavernier, "Murmures dans un corridor lointain," p. 6; Wood, "Jacques Tourneur," p. 1008.

11. Gilles Deleuze and Félix Guattari, *Kafka: Pour une littérature mineure* (Paris: Les Editions de Minuit, 1975), pp. 51–52.

12. Lourcelles, "Note sur Jacques Tourneur," p. 55.

13. Wood, "Jacques Tourneur," p. 1008.

14. Henry, "*Berlin Express* de Jacques Tourneur," p. 14.

15. Farber, *Movies*, p. 49.

16. Marc Vernet, "*Film Noir* on the Edge of Doom," in *Shades of Noir: A Reader*, ed. Joan Copjec (London: Verso, 1993), p. 9.

17. Margaret Fitts, *Stars in My Crown* (script), in the Cinema-Television Library, University of Southern California, Los Angeles; and Margaret Herrick Library, Academy of Motion Picture Arts and Sciences, Beverly Hills, California.

18. See Guinle and Mizrahi, "Biofilmographie commentée," p. 73.

19. Tourneur, "Propos," p. 13. See also Guinle and Mizrahi, "Biofilmographie commentée," p. 73.

Maurice Tourneur

1. Much of the information given here on Maurice Tourneur's life comes from Geltzer, "Maurice Tourneur."

2. "Idealist and Artist," *Motion Picture Classic*, February 1920, p. 81.

3. Geltzer, "Maurice Tourneur," p. 204.

4. *Trésor de la langue française: Dictionnaire de la langue du XIXe et du XXe siècle (1789–1960)*, s.v. "tourneur."

5. Quoted in Brownlow, *The Parade's Gone By...*, p. 353.

6. Ibid., pp. 140–41.

7. Maurice Tourneur, "Stylization in Motion Picture Direction," *Motion Picture Magazine*, September 1918, pp. 101–2; unidentified news clipping dated March 25, 1917, in the Robinson Locke Collection, the Billy Rose Theatre Collection, New York Public Library for the Performing Arts, New York City.

8. *Motion Picture World*, April 13, 1918; "Are Stars Only Meteors? Tourneur Believes the Play's the Thing and Stars Must Go," *New York Times*, June 16, 1918.

9. Dorothy Nutting, "Monsieur Tourneur: Otherwise Accurately Called 'the Poet of the Screen,'" *Photoplay*, July 1918, p. 55; "Idealist and Artist," *Motion Picture Classic*, February 1920.

10. Geltzer, "Maurice Tourneur," p. 204.

11. Tourneur, "Propos," p. 10.

12. Brownlow, *The Parade's Gone By...*, p. 153; Tourneur, "Propos," p. 10.

13. "Brought into Focus," *New York Times*, December 26, 1920.

14. "Maurice Tourneur," Geltzer, p. 202; Clarence Brown remembered that Tourneur "fell off a parallel" (Brownlow, *The Parade's Gone By...*, p. 144).

15. Geltzer, "Maurice Tourneur," pp. 205–6.

16. Brownlow, *The Parade's Gone By...*, pp. 418–20.

17. Brion and Comolli, "Un Cinéma de frontière," p. 35.

18. Geltzer, "Maurice Tourneur," p. 210.

19. Brownlow, *The Parade's Gone By...*, p. 153.

20. Manlay and Ricaud, "Entretien avec Jacques Tourneur," p. 53.

21. Tourneur, "Propos," p. 10; studio publicity sheet in the *Anne of the Indies* clippings file at the Margaret Herrick Library, Academy of Motion Picture Arts and Sciences, Beverly Hills, California.

Jacques Tourneur: I

1. Tourneur, "Propos," pp. 9–10.

2. Christiane Tourneur and Jacques Miermont, unpublished interview with Philippe Roger, Bergerac, France, July 31, 1992.

3. Tourneur, "Propos," p. 9.

4. Guinle and Mizrahi, "Biofilmographie commentée," p. 56; Brion and Comolli, "Un Cinéma de frontière," p. 42; Brion, "Biofilmographie de Jacques Tourneur," p. 44.

5. "Tourneur Jr. Found Guilty in Gin Party," *Los Angeles Examiner*, May 12, 1928; "Tourneur Jr. Given 10 Days as 'Drunk,'" *Los Angeles Examiner*, May 13, 1928.

6. Manlay and Ricaud, "Entretien avec Jacques Tourneur," p. 54.

7. Ibid., p. 53.

8. Telephone interview with the author, November 9, 1996.

Jacques Tourneur: II

1. Guinle and Mizrahi, "Biofilmographie commentée," p. 61.

2. Tourneur, "Taste without Clichés," p. 10.

3. Telephone interview with the author, February 20, 1996.

4. Bert Granet, letter to the author, July 21, 1996 (all subsequent quotations from Bert Granet in this chapter are from this letter, except as noted); Charlotte Granet, interview with the author, Santa Monica, California, November 6, 1996 (all subsequent quotations from Charlotte Granet are from this interview).

5. Christiane Tourneur and Jacques Miermont, unpublished interview with Philippe Roger, Bergerac, France, July 31, 1992 (all quotations from Christiane Tourneur and Roger in this chapter are from this interview).

6. Interview with the author, Burbank, California, November 7, 1996.

7. Christiane Tourneur and Jacques Miermont, unpublished interview with Philippe Roger, Bergerac, France, July 31, 1992 (all quotations from Miermont in this chapter are from this interview).

8. Tourneur quoted in Brion and Comolli, "Un Cinéma de frontière," pp. 35–36; Bernard Eisenschitz, *Nicholas Ray: An American Journey*, trans. Tom Milne (London: Faber and Faber, 1993), p. 106; "An Oral History with Richard Goldstone," interviewed by Douglas Bell, 1995, in Margaret Herrick Library, Academy of Motion Picture Arts and Sciences, Beverly Hills, California, p. 676.

9. Brion and Comolli, "Un Cinéma de frontière," p. 39; Tourneur, "Taste without clichés," p. 10.

10. Guinle and Mizrahi, "Biofilmographie commentée," p. 73.

11. Ibid.

12. Jane Greer, interview with the author, Santa Monica, California, November 6, 1996; Rhonda Fleming, telephone interview with the author, January 24, 1996; Paul Valentine, telephone interview with the author, February 13, 1996; Dick Moore quoted in Doug McClelland, *Forties Film Talk*, p. 136.

13. Hedy Lamarr, *Ecstasy and Me: My Life as a Woman* (N.p.: Bartholomew House, 1966), p. 123; Virginia Mayo, letter to the author, December 30, 1995; Robert Stack, letter to the author, February 17, 1996; Gregory Peck quoted in letter from Victoria Haupenthal to the author, December 18, 1995; Peter Graves, telephone interview with the author, February 13, 1996; Richard Matheson, letter to the author, December 14, 1995.

14. Randolph quoted in Mank, *Hollywood Cauldron*, p. 220; Tourneur, "Propos," p. 10; Manlay and Ricaud, "Entretien avec Jacques Tourneur," p. 59.

15. Flinn, "Screenwriter Daniel Mainwaring Discusses *Out of the Past*," p. 45; Bert Granet, interview with the author, Santa Monica, California, November 6, 1996; Heyward quoted in Tom Weaver, *Science Fiction Stars and Horror Heroes: Interviews with Actors, Directors, Producers, and Writers of the 1940s through 1960s* (Jefferson, N.C.: McFarland & Company, 1991), p. 161.

16. Quoted in Brion and Comolli, "Un Cinéma de frontière," p. 40; Tourneur, "Taste without clichés," p. 9.

17. Brion and Comolli, "Un Cinéma de frontière," p. 40.

18. Tourneur, "Taste without clichés," p. 9.

19. Quoted in Guinle and Mizrahi, "Biofilmographie commentée," p. 73.

20. Tourneur quoted in Brion and Comolli, "Un Cinéma de frontière," p. 39; Bert Granet, interview with the author, Santa Monica, California, December 6, 1996; Siegel, "Tourneur Remembers," p. 24.

21. Cf. Brion and Comolli, "Un Cinéma de

frontière," p. 42; Tourneur, "Taste without Clichés," p. 10.

22. Brion and Comolli, "Un Cinéma de frontière," pp. 35-36.

23. Tourneur, "Taste without Clichés," p. 11.

24. Brion and Comolli, "Un Cinéma de frontière," p. 42; Tourneur, "Taste without Clichés," p. 11; Wicking, "Entretien avec Jacques Tourneur," p. 13; Tourneur, "Murmures dans des chambres lointains"; Guinle and Mizrahi, "Biofilmographie commentée," pp. 76-77.

25. Brion and Comolli, "Un Cinéma de frontière," p. 42.

26. Tourneur, "Propos," p. 16.

27. Tourneur, "Taste without Clichés," p. 11.

28. Wicking, "Entretien avec Jacques Tourneur," p. 13.

29. Quoted in Brion and Comolli, "Un Cinéma de frontière," pp. 39-40.

30. Manlay and Ricaud, "Entretien avec Jacques Tourneur," p. 57.

31. Jacques Manlay, letter to the author, November 21, 1995.

French Films (1931-1934)

1. Quoted in Guinle and Mizrahi, "Biofilmographie commentée," p. 60.

2. Tourneur, "Taste without Clichés," p. 9.

3. Quoted in Guinle and Mizrahi, "Biofilmographie commentée," p. 60; Tourneur, "Propos," p. 10; quoted in Brion and Comolli, "Un Cinéma de frontière," p. 42.

Second-Unit Work (1934-1938)

1. Guinle and Mizrahi, "Biofilmographie commentée," p. 61.

2. Quoted in Higham and Greenberg, The Celluloid Muse, p. 246.

3. Ibid. See also Guinle and Mizrahi, "Biofilmographie commentée," pp. 61-62.

4. Patricia King Hanson and Alan Gevinson, eds., The American Film Institute Catalog of Motion Pictures Produced in the United States, Feature Films, 1931-1940 (Berkeley: University of California Press, 1993), pp. 2122-23.

5. Quoted in Guinle and Mizrahi, "Biofilmographie commentée," p. 61.

MGM Shorts (1936-1942)

1. Quoted in Guinle and Mizrahi, "Biofilmographie commentée," p. 63.

2. Richard Goldstone, telephone interview with the author, February 20, 1996.

3. Quoted in Guinle and Mizrahi, "Biofilmographie commentée," p. 62.

4. Ibid.

5. Ibid.

6. Ibid., p. 64.

7. Ibid.

8. Lotte H. Eisner, Murnau (Berkeley: University of California Press, 1973), p. 219.

They All Come Out (1939)

1. Guinle and Mizrahi, "Biofilmographie commentée," p. 65; Tourneur, "Taste without Clichés," p. 10; Douglas W. Churchill, "Espionage in Hollywood," New York Times, February 5, 1939.

The Nick Carter Films

1. Guinle and Mizrahi, "Biofilmographie commentée," p. 66.

2. Don Miller, B Movies (New York: Ballantine Books, 1988), p. 178.

3. Patricia King Hanson and Alan Gevinson, eds., The American Film Institute Catalog of Motion Pictures Produced in the United States, Feature Films, 1931-1940 (Berkeley: University of California Press, 1993), p. 1506.

Doctors Don't Tell (1941)

1. Tourneur quoted in Guinle and Mizrahi, "Biofilmographie commentée," p. 66.

2. Don Miller, B Movies (New York: Ballantine Books, 1988), p. 181.

Cat People (1942)

1. For accounts of the production, see Bodeen, "Val Lewton," pp. 211-18; Higham and Greenberg, The Celluloid Muse, pp. 247-48; Siegel, Val Lewton, pp. 26-39; Siegel, "Tourneur Remembers," pp. 24-25; Bansak, Fearing the Dark, pp. 121-29.

2. Quoted in Siegel, "Tourneur Remembers," p. 24.

3. Bodeen, "Val Lewton," pp. 213, 215; Higham and Greenberg, The Celluloid Muse, p. 247.

4. On the budget, see RKO production files, Special Collections, University of California at Los Angeles; for Ostrow and the Hawaii Theatre, see Siegel, "Tourneur Remembers," p. 24; for the domestic gross, see Fred Stanley, "The Year in Hollywood," New York Times, December 26, 1943.

5. Telotte, Dreams of Darkness, p. 24.

6. Alice's presence has left a trace on the scene, in the form of the woman standing with

her back to the camera next to Oliver when Irena's littering causes him to notice her. The woman resembles Jane Randolph in hairstyle and physique; Alice's dialogue with Oliver was probably shot but eliminated in editing.

7. Siegel, *Val Lewton*, p. 32; Willemen, "Notes towards the Construction of Readings of Tourneur," pp. 23–24; Telotte, *Dreams of Darkness*, p. 22.

8. DeWitt Bodeen, *Cat People* (shooting script), in the Val Lewton Collection, Library of Congress, Washington, D.C.

9. Ibid.

10. Quoted in Mank, *Hollywood Cauldron*, p. 222. Bodeen goes on to say that Lewton was indignant at the inference but that he himself (Bodeen) "rather liked the insinuation," which he had anticipated.

11. Charles Higham and Joel Greenberg, *Hollywood in the Forties* (New York: Paperback Library, 1970), p. 64; Siegel, *Val Lewton*, pp. 101–2; Siegel, "Tourneur Remembers," p. 24.

12. Siegel, *Val Lewton*, p. 106.

13. Quoted in Higham and Greenberg, *The Celluloid Muse*, p. 248.

I Walked with a Zombie (1943)

1. Siegel, *Val Lewton*, p. 41.

2. Ibid.

3. Ardel Wray and Curt Siodmak, *I Walked with a Zombie* (shooting script), in the Val Lewton Collection, Library of Congress, Washington, D.C.

4. Tzvetan Todorov, *The Fantastic: A Structural Approach to a Literary Genre*, trans. Richard Howard (Ithaca, N.Y.: Cornell University Press, 1975), p. 33.

5. Tavernier, "Murmures dans un corridor lointain," pp. 4–5.

6. Tourneur, "Taste Without Clichés," p. 10; Higham and Greenberg, *The Celluloid Muse*, p. 248.

7. Wood, "The Shadow Worlds of Jacques Tourneur," p. 69.

8. Tourneur, "Propos," p. 16.

9. James Agee, *Agee on Film* (Boston: Beacon Press, 1958), pp. 84–85.

10. Wood, "The Shadow Worlds of Jacques Tourneur," p. 69; Telotte, *Dreams of Darkness*, p. 50.

11. Pierre, "The Beauty of the Sea," p. 46; Wray and Siodmak, *I Walked with a Zombie*.

12. Pierre, "The Beauty of the Sea," p. 47.

13. Cf. Bansak, *Fearing the Dark*, p. 153.

14. Pierre, "The Beauty of the Sea," p. 46.

15. The shooting script suggests a possible explanation for the jarring cut-in of a static shot of Betsy and Paul in the middle of the track-in on Ti-Misery. The script called for the scene to fade out on "the glistening sad face of the saint." Then there was to be an epilogue with Betsy on an Ottawa street corner, her voice-over explaining how, after the "sad time at Fort Holland," Mrs. Rand managed to pick up the pieces and carry on. Paul was to have emerged from an office building and apologized for having been delayed by invoices and stock lists; a light-hearted ending would have closed the film (Wray and Siodmak, *I Walked with a Zombie*). This banal scene was apparently shot: a still exists showing Tom Conway and Frances Dee on a sidewalk set in a fake snowfall. Presumably, during editing, the filmmakers decided that it would be better to end the film with the last scene at Fort Holland. But the duration of what then became the film's final shot, the track-in on the figurehead, may have been seen as overly impersonal, prompting the decision to insert the two-shot of the principals.

The Leopard Man (1943)

1. Siegel, *Val Lewton*, pp. 115–16.

2. Quoted in Higham and Greenberg, *The Celluloid Muse*, p. 249.

3. Eisenschitz, "Six Films produits par Val Lewton," p. 60.

4. Farber, *Movies*, p. 49

5. Eisenschitz, "Six Films," p. 61.

6. "The way in which dreams treat the category of contraries and contradictions is highly remarkable. It is simply disregarded. 'No' seems not to exist so far as dreams are concerned." Sigmund Freud, *The Interpretation of Dreams*, trans. and ed. James Strachey New York: Avon Books, 1965), p. 353.

7. Telotte, *Dreams of Darkness*, p. 74.

8. Ibid., p. 72.

9. Bansak, *Fearing the Dark*, p. 175.

10. Telotte, *Dreams of Darkness*, p. 75.

11. Quoted in Brion and Comolli, "Un Cinéma de frontière," p. 36.

12. Bansak, *Fearing the Dark*, p. 178.

Days of Glory (1944)

1. Quoted in Higham and Greenberg, *The Celluloid Muse*, p. 246; Siegel, "Tourneur Remembers," p. 25.

2. Quoted in Guinle and Mizrahi, "Biofilmographie commentée," p. 68.

3. Letter to the author from Victoria Haupenthal, December 18, 1995.

4. James Agee, *Agee on Film* (Boston: Beacon Press, 1958), p. 102.

5. Bernard F. Dick, *The Star-Spangled Screen: The American World War II Film* (Lexington: University Press of Kentucky, 1985), pp. 161–63.

Experiment Perilous (1944)

1. On the costumes, see Frank Daugherty, "Hollywood Letter," *Christian Science Monitor*, October 6, 1944; Fellows and Tourneur quoted in Thornton Delehanty, "'Experiment Perilous,' but Not to Lamarr," *New York Herald Tribune*, August 20, 1944; for the cut scene, see Higham and Greenberg, *The Celluloid Muse*, p. 249, and Warren Duff, *Experiment Perilous* (shooting script), in RKO Collection, Special Collections, University of California at Los Angeles.
2. Delehanty, "Experiment Perilous"; Brion and Comolli, "Un Cinéma de frontière," p. 40; Daugherty, "Hollywood Letter."
3. Cf. Manlay and Ricaud, "Entretien avec Jacques Tourneur," pp. 56, 64.
4. Vernet, "La Mise en scène de l'homme-araignée," pp. 90–91.
5. Biette, "Revoir Wichita," p. 43.

Reward Unlimited (1944)

1. Quoted in Manlay and Ricaud, "Entretien avec Jacques Tourneur," p. 63.

Canyon Passage (1946)

1. A. H. Weiler, "Random Notes about the Screen," *New York Times*, May 6, 1945.
2. All information on the preproduction and production of *Canyon Passage* comes from the Walter Wanger Archives, State Historical Society of Wisconsin, Madison, and from the Universal Collection, Cinema-Television Library, University of Southern California, Los Angeles.
3. Tourneur, "Taste without Clichés," p. 10.
4. Skorecki, "Tourneur n'existe pas," p. 7.
5. McNiven, "Jacques Tourneur," p. 336.
6. Wood, "Jacques Tourneur," p. 1008.
7. Skorecki, "Tourneur n'existe pas," p. 7.
8. McNiven, "Jacques Tourneur," p. 338.
9. "It will be unacceptable either to show or to suggest that the two Indian girls are bathing in the nude. Their persons should be adequately covered at all times. Also, the expression on Bragg's face, as he pursues the girls, should not be excessively lustful." Letter from Joseph I. Breen to Maurice Pivar, July 24, 1945. In a letter to Walter Wanger dated April 1, 1946, Breen gave the film his formal

"certificate of approval"—"based upon our understanding that the first shot of the girls in the pool, in which it is clearly established that the girl wears a brown suit, is to be used in all prints to be put into circulation."
10. The others include *My Darling Clementine, The Virginian, Duel in the Sun,* and *California.*

Out of the Past (1947)

1. Schwager, "*Out of the Past* Rewritten," p. 16; Flinn, "Screenwriter Daniel Mainwaring Discusses *Out of the Past*," p. 45; Tourneur quoted in Guinle and Mizrahi, "Biofilmographie commentée," p. 69; Biette, "Trois morts."
2. Alain Silver and Elizabeth Ward, eds., *Film Noir: An Encyclopedic Reference to the American Style* (Woodstock, N.Y.: Overlook Press, 1979), p. 218; Danny Peary, *Cult Movies: The Classics, the Sleepers, the Weird, and the Wonderful* (New York: Dell, 1981).
3. Tourneur, "Propos," p. 12.
4. On the title, see Turner, "*Out of the Past*," p. 36; Mainwaring quoted in Flinn, "Screenwriter Daniel Mainwaring Discusses *Out of the Past*," p. 45; Greer quoted in McClelland, *Forties Film Talk*, pp. 77–78.
5. Flinn, "*Out of the Past*," p. 38; Robert Ottoson, *A Reference Guide to the American Film Noir: 1940–1958* (Metuchen, N.J.: Scarecrow Press, 1981), p. 132; Grist, "*Out of the Past*, p. 212; Michael Walker, "Film Noir: Introduction," in *The Movie Book of Film Noir*, ed. Ian Cameron (London: Studio Vista, 1992), p. 20.
6. Jean Renoir, *My Life and My Films*, trans. Norman Denny (New York: Atheneum, 1974), p. 238.
7. Quoted in Higham and Greenberg, *The Celluloid Muse*, p. 250.
8. Legrand, "Une Solitude labyrinthique," p. 56.
9. Oddos, "Murmures devant un miroir," p. 123.
10. J. A. Place and L. S. Peterson, "Some Visual Motifs of *Film Noir*," in *Movies and Methods: An Anthology*, ed. Bill Nichols (Berkeley: University of California Press, 1976), pp. 325–38.
11. Ibid., p. 328.
12. Ibid., pp. 331, 336.
13. Ibid., pp. 336–37.
14. Skorecki, "Three Tourneurs," p. 15.

Berlin Express (1948)

1. Information on the production of *Berlin Express* comes from Bert Granet, letter to the author, July 21, 1996, and from Lightman, "The Story of Filming *Berlin Express*."
2. Lightman, "The Story of Filming *Berlin Express*," p. 233.
3. Henry, "*Berlin Express* de Jacques Tourneur," p. 14.
4. Quoted in Higham and Greenberg, *The Celluloid Muse*, p. 250.
5. Quoted in Wicking, "Entretien avec Jacques Tourneur," p. 14.
6. Henry, "*Berlin Express* de Jacques Tourneur," p. 14.

Easy Living (1949)

1. Bernard Eisenschitz, *Nicholas Ray: An American Journey*, trans. Tom Milne (London: Faber and Faber, 1993), p. 106.
2. Quoted in Higham and Greenberg, *The Celluloid Muse*, p. 250.
3. Quoted in Guinle and Mizrahi, "Biofilmographie commentée," p. 70.
4. See material on *Easy Living* in RKO Collection, Special Collections, University of California at Los Angeles, and in Production Code Administration files, Margaret Herrick Library, Academy of Motion Picture Arts and Sciences, Beverly Hills, California.

Stars in My Crown (1950)

1. Tourneur, "Taste without Clichés," p. 11.
2. Quoted in Guinle and Mizrahi, "Biofilmographie commentée," p. 70.
3. Ibid., p. 71.
4. Willemen, "Notes towards the Construction of Readings of Tourneur," pp. 32–33.
5. Ibid., p. 34.
6. Tourneur, "Propos," p. 14.
7. Biette, "*Stars in My Crown*," p. 34.
8. Quoted in Manlay and Ricaud, "Entretien avec Jacques Tourneur," p. 56.
9. Legrand, "Malgré les ombres, la mémoire," p. 71.

The Flame and the Arrow (1950)

1. Videotaped interview included in *Biography: Burt Lancaster* (Arts & Entertainment cable network, 1996).
2. Mikhail Bakhtin, *Rabelais and His World*, trans. Helene Iswolsky (Cambridge: MIT Press, 1968), p. 8.

Circle of Danger (1951)

1. *Circle of Danger* anticipates *Night of the Demon* in other ways: Hamish's mother, seemingly oblivious to the mystery surrounding her son, is the prototype for Mrs. Karswell; Sholto, whom Douglas calls Hamish's "mouthpiece," gives voice to what Hamish must keep silent and also to the dead (he remembers Hank as "loud") and thus resembles the medium in *Night of the Demon*, played by Reginald Beckwith, the same actor who plays Sholto's assistant, Oliver.

Anne of the Indies (1951)

1. Sarris, *The American Cinema*, p. 142.
2. Tourneur, "Propos," p. 10.
3. Information on the production of the film comes from the Philip Dunne Collection, Cinema-Television Library, University of Southern California, Los Angeles, and the 20th Century–Fox Collection, Special Collections, University of California at Los Angeles.
4. Tom Stempel, *Framework: A History of Screenwriting in the American Film* (New York: Continuum, 1988), p. 82.
5. Philip Dunne, *Take Two: A Life in Movies and Politics* (New York: McGraw-Hill, 1980), p. 71.
6. Pascal Bonitzer, "Hitchcockian Suspense," in *Everything You Always Wanted to Know about Lacan (but Were Afraid to Ask Hitchcock)*, ed. Slavoj Žižek (London: Verso, 1992), pp. 20–22. Bonitzer cites, among other examples, the bloodstain that haunts *Marnie* and Hitchcock's unfilmed idea of suggesting a murder in a tulip field with a huge close-up of a drop of blood falling on a petal. Tourneur's films are filled with such "stains": the spot left by pitchblende on a photographic plate in "Romance of Radium"; the voodoo patch dangling from the tree branch in *I Walked with a Zombie*; the blood flowing under the door in *The Leopard Man*; the bloodstain on the back of the fake clown in *Berlin Express*; the reflection of the attack on Bernhardt in the train window in the same film; and the cloud/demon in *Night of the Demon*.
7. Johnston, "Femininity and the Masquerade," p. 40.

Way of a Gaucho (1952)

1. Unless otherwise noted, information on the production of the film comes from the Philip Dunne Collection, Cinema-Television Library, University of Southern California, Los Angeles; the 20th Century–Fox Collection, Special

Collections, University of California at Los Angeles; and Diego Curubeto, *Babilonia gaucha: Hollywood en la Argentina, la Argentina en Hollywood* (Buenos Aires: Planeta, 1993), pp. 25–26.

2. Manlay and Ricaud, "Entretien avec Jacques Tourneur," p. 63; Philip Dunne, *Take Two: A Life in Movies and Politics* (New York: McGraw-Hill, 1980), p. 257.

3. Dunne, *Take Two*, pp. 258, 263–64.

4. Ibid., p. 264; Tourneur quoted in Manlay and Ricaud, "Entretien avec Jacques Tourneur," p. 63.

5. Dunne, *Take Two*, p. 47

6. Quoted in Brion and Comolli, "Un Cinéma de frontière," p. 39.

7. Ibid., p. 42.

Appointment in Honduras (1953)

1. Richard B. Jewell and Vernon Harbin, *The RKO Story* (New York: Arlington House, 1982), p. 256.

2. Peter Bogdanovitch, *Allan Dwan: The Last Pioneer* (New York: Praeger Publishers, 1971), pp. 154–55.

3. Don Siegel, *A Siegel Film: An Autobiography* (London: Faber and Faber, 1993), pp. 148–49.

4. Bogdanovitch, *Allan Dwan*, p. 167.

5. Simon Mizrahi, "Entretien avec Allan Dwan," *Présence du cinéma*, no. 22–23 (fall 1966): 21–22.

6. Tavernier, "Murmures dans un corridor lointain," p. 2.

7. Quoted in Guinle and Mizrahi, "Biofilmographie commentée," p. 72.

8. The film has no specific historical basis. In 1953, the year it was made, the main concern of the United States in Central America was the socialist government of Arbenz in Guatemala, whose rule was overthrown in the following year in a CIA-backed coup that used Honduras as a staging ground.

9. Rosenbaum, "Then and Now," p. 25.

Stranger on Horseback (1955)

1. Quoted in Guinle and Mizrahi, "Biofilmographie commentée," p. 74

Wichita (1955)

1. Willemen, "Notes towards the Construction of Readings of Tourneur," p. 21.

2. Biette, "Revoir Wichita," p. 41.

3. Daniel B. Ullman, *Wichita* (shooting script), Walter Mirisch Collection, State Historical Society of Wisconsin, Madison.

4. Quoted in Guinle and Mizrahi, "Biofilmographie commentée," pp. 74–75.

5. Skorecki, "Three Tourneurs," p. 15. The French original reads, "*et cependant cet instant est toujours cloisonné*" (Skorecki, "Trois Tourneur," p. 37). A *cloison* is a partition or membrane (Skorecki doubtless had in mind the door behind which Mrs. McCoy dies), and thus a truer, though less striking, translation might be "and yet that instant is always closed off."

Great Day in the Morning (1956)

1. Sarris, *The American Cinema*, p. 142. In his entry on Sam Peckinpah, however, Sarris acknowledges a "Tourneur-McCrea tradition," whose confluence with the "Boetticher-Scott tradition" resulted, he says, in Peckinpah's *Ride the High Country* (ibid., p. 219). Given Sarris's silence on the subject of *Stars in My Crown* and his denigration of *Stranger on Horseback* and *Wichita*, this reference is mysterious. The three films have little in common with *Ride the High Country* in any case (apart from McCrea's presence and Peckinpah's having worked as Tourneur's assistant on *Wichita*).

2. Andrew Sarris, "Notes on the Auteur Theory in 1962," in *Theories of Authorship: A Reader*, ed. John Caughie (London: Routledge & Kegan Paul, 1981), p. 64.

3. Brion, "Biofilmographie de Jacques Tourneur," p. 45.

Night of the Demon (1957)

1. Cf. Carlos Clarens, *An Illustrated History of the Horror Film* (New York: Capricorn Books, 1968), p. 115; Siegel, *Val Lewton*, p. 24; Bansak, *Fearing the Dark*, pp. 434–40.

2. Tourneur, "Propos," p. 14.

3. Pat McGilligan, *Backstory: Interviews with Screenwriters of Hollywood's Golden Age* (Berkeley: University of California Press, 1986), p. 45; Tom Weaver, *Attack of the Monster Movie Makers: Interviews with 20 Genre Giants* (Jefferson, N.C.: McFarland & Company, 1994), pp. 24–25; Higham and Greenberg, *The Celluloid Muse*, p. 251.

4. Guinle and Mizrahi, "Biofilmographie commentée," p. 76; Borst and MacQueen, "Curse of the Demon," pp. 32–33.

5. Mrs. Karswell recalls Uncle Charlie's admiring sister in *Shadow of a Doubt* and the ineffectual, adoring mother of Bruno in *Strangers on a Train*. The antagonist of the hero in Tourneur's *Circle of Danger*— produced by Joan Harrison, previously another of Hitchcock's regular story collaborators and,

incidentally, cowriter with Charles Bennett of *Foreign Correspondent*— also has a mother who, like Mrs. Karswell, seems uninformed of the dark background to the two men's relationship.

6. Higham and Greenberg, *The Celluloid Muse,* pp. 251–52; Siegel, "Tourneur Remembers," p. 25.

7. Quoted in Borst and MacQueen, *"Curse of the Demon,"* p. 33.

8. Two deleted moments noted by Ronald V. Borst and Scott MacQueen, who had access to the continuity script of the British-release version of the film, have not been restored: the conclusion of the opening narration ("Through the ages, men have feared and worshipped these creatures. The practice of witchcraft, the cults of evil, have endured and exist to this day") and the continuation of Karswell's card game with his mother after Harrington leaves (see Borst and MacQueen, *"Curse of the Demon,"* pp. 33, 35). Since both these moments occur in the first reel, it seems probable that the distributors of the new version left this reel unrestored in order to retain the American title card.

9. Tourneur, "Taste without Clichés," p. 10.

10. Quoted in Wicking, "Entretien avec Jacques Tourneur," p. 14.

11. Quoted in Siegel, "Tourneur Remembers," p. 25.

12. V.F. Perkins, *Film as Film* (Harmondsworth, England: Penguin Books, 1972), p. 174; Fieschi, "Le Médium," pp. 64, 66.

13. Tourneur, "Taste without Clichés," 10.

14. Quoted in Guinle and Mizrahi, "Biofilmographie commentée," p. 76.

15. Slavoj Žižek, "'In His Bold Gaze My Ruin Is Writ Large,'" in *Everything You Always Wanted To Know About Lacan (but Were Afraid To Ask Hitchcock),* ed. Slavoj Žižek (London: Verso, 1992), pp. 236–37.

16. Bellour, "Believing in the Cinema," p. 99.

17. Ibid., p. 100.

18. Tourneur, "Propos," pp. 9–10.

19. Bellour, "Believing in the Cinema," p. 98.

The Fearmakers (1958)

1. Guinle and Mizrahi, "Biofilmographie commentée," p. 77; Jacques Tourneur, "Propos," p. 12.

2. Quoted in Guinle and Mizrahi, "Biofilmographie commentée," p. 77.

Timbuktu (1959)

1. Ian Cameron, *Adventure in the Movies* (New York: Crescent Books, 1973), p. 39.

2. Tourneur, "Propos," p. 11.

La Battaglia di Maratona (1959)

1. Brion and Comolli, "Un Cinéma de frontière," p. 39; Wicking, "Entretien avec Jacques Tourneur," pp. 14–15; Guinle and Mizrahi, "Biofilmographie commentée," pp. 77–78; Siegel, "Tourneur Remembers," p. 25.

2. Siegel, "Tourneur Remembers," p. 25.

The AIP Films

1. Tourneur, "Taste without Clichés," p. 9.

2. Quoted in Guinle and Mizrahi, "Biofilmographie commentée," p. 79; quoted in Higham and Greenberg, *The Celluloid Muse,* p. 252.

3. Richard Matheson, letter to the author, December 14, 1995.

4. Tourneur, "Taste without Clichés," p. 9; quoted in Wicking, "Entretien avec Jacques Tourneur," p. 16.

5. Tom Weaver, *Science Fiction Stars and Horror Heroes: Interviews with Actors, Directors, Producers, and Writers of the 1940s through 1960s* (Jefferson, N.C.: McFarland & Company, 1991), pp. 160–61.

6. Hart quoted in Tom Weaver, *Attack of the Monster Movie Makers: Interviews with 20 Genre Giants* (Jefferson, N.C.: McFarland & Company, 1994), p. 136; Heyward quoted in Weaver, *Science Fiction Stars and Horror Heroes,* p. 161; Tourneur, "Propos," p. 11.

7. Higham and Greenberg, *The Celluloid Muse,* p. 252.

8. Quoted in Weaver, *Attack of the Monster Movie Makers,* p. 25.

Television Films

1. Quoted in Guinle and Mizrahi, "Biofilmographie commentée," p. 82.

2. Frank O'Connor, "The Martyr," *Collected Stories* (New York: Vintage Books, 1982), p. 624.

3. Michael Henry Wilson, unpublished program notes (original in French).

4. Tag Gallagher, *John Ford: The Man and His Films* (Berkeley: University of California Press, 1986), p. 537.

5. Quoted in Brion, "Biofilmographie de Jacques Tourneur," p. 45.

6. The episodes are not distinguished in

the film, but their titles can be found in Guinle and Mizrahi, "Biofilmographie commentée," pp. 82–83.

7. Guinle and Mizrahi, "Biofilmographie commentée," p. 81.

8. Nolan, "Tourneur on TV," p. 27.

Afterword

1. Quoted in Jacques Manlay and Jean Ricaud, "Entretien avec Jacques Tourneur," p. 64.

2. Tourneur, "Propos," p. 10.

Filmography of Jacques Tourneur

Note: Establishing the correct running time of a film is often difficult. For this filmography, I have relied on (in descending order of authority) the following: timings from studio cutting continuities; my own timings of prints believed complete; and secondary sources such as trade reviews, *The American Film Institute Catalog of Motion Pictures Produced in the United States*, Patrick Brion's "Biofilmographie de Jacques Tourneur," Pierre Guinle and Simon Mizrahi's "Biofilmographie commentée de Jacques Tourneur," and the filmography in the San Sebastian International Film Festival catalog, *Jacques Tourneur*. When contradictory timings suggest an error in one or more sources or the existence of alternate versions of a film, I give the shorter running time in parentheses.

FEATURE FILMS AS DIRECTOR

Tout ça ne vaut pas l'amour (1931)
Pathé-Natan
Working title: *Un Vieux Garçon*
Director: Jacques Tourneur. Screenplay: René Pujol. Decorations: Lucien Aguettand. Music: Hugo Kirsch.
Cast: Marcel Levesque (Jules Renaudin), Josseline Gaël (Claire), Jean Gabin (Jean Cordier), Mady Berry (Mme. Cordier), Jeanne Lourie (Léonie), Delphine Abdala (Mme. Triron), Gilberte Savary, Robert Tourneur, Valiès.
Production: July 1931.
87 minutes.

Pour être aimé (1933) Pathé-Natan/Via Films
Director: Jacques Tourneur. Director of Production: Jacques Natanson. Screenplay: Jacques Célérier. Dialogue: d'Erlanger. Photography: Georges Raulet, Cauteret. Music: Georges Célérier. Songs: Leo Lelièvre, Jr. Assistant Director: Maurice Vaccarino.
Cast: Pierre-Richard Willm (Gérard d'Ormoise), Suzy Vernon (Edith), Marguerite Moreno (Marie-Josèphe des Espinettes), Colette Darfeuil (Maud), Paulette Dubost (Maryse), Pasquali (Emilien), Jean Hubert (Victor), Marthe Sarbel (Mme. Costebrave), William Aguet (Anthénor de la Chaulme-Percée), Heritza (singer), Pierre Juvenet (Costebrave), Georges Treville (Weston), Gaby Basset, Paul Azaïs, André Roanne, Pitouto, Jean Fay, Pierre Hot, Henry Trévoux, Hubert Daix, Michel Goyot, Michel André.
75 minutes.

Toto (1933) Pathé-Natan
Director: Jacques Tourneur. Screenplay: Herman Kosterlitz. Adaptation: René Pujol. Photography: Raymond Agnel, René Colas. Decorations: Jacques Colombier. Music: Jane Bos. Sound Engineer: Sivel. Assistant Director: Charles Barrois.
Cast: Albert Préjean (Toto), Renée Saint-Cyr (Ginette), Robert Goupil (Carotte), Jim Gérald (Bruno), Félix Oudart (policeman), Ginette Leclerc, Prince-Rigadin, Gabrielle Fontan, Mercédès Brave.
80 (68) minutes.

301

Les Filles de la concierge (1934) Kaysersmann/Azed Films

Director: Jacques Tourneur. Director of Production: Oscar Danciger. Screenplay: Jean Georges Auriol, based on a story by Georges de la Fouchardière. Dialogue: Georges de la Fouchardière. Photography: Michel Kelber, Marcel Soulié. Decorations: Robert Gys, Georges Wakhévitch. Music: Georges Van Parys. Assistant Director: Maurice Vaccarino.

Cast: Jeanne Cheirel (Mme. Leclercq), Josette Day (Suzanne Leclercq), Germaine Aussey (Ginette Leclercq), Ghislaine Bru (Lucie Leclercq), Paul Azaïs (Albert), Marcel André (Gaston Rival), Pierre Nay (Jacques), Prince Youca Troubetzkoy, Maximilienne, Emile Saint Ober.

85 minutes.

They All Come Out (1939) MGM

Director: Jacques Tourneur. Producer: Jack Chertok. Original story and screenplay: John C. Higgins. Directors of Photography: Clyde De Vinna, Paul C. Vogel. Art Director: Elmer Sheeley. Music: David Snell, Edward Ward. Editor: Ralph E. Goldstein. Wardrobe: Dolly Tree. Recording Director: Douglas Shearer. Assistant Directors: E. J. Babille, Herbert Glazer.

Cast: Tom Neal (Joe Z. Cameron), Rita Johnson (Kitty Carson), Bernard Nedell (Clyde "Reno" Madigan), Edward Gargan (George "Bugs" Jacklin), John Gallaudet (Albert "Groper" Crane), Addison Richards (warden, Atlanta), Frank M. Thomas (superintendent, Chillicothe), Ann Shoemaker (Dr. Hollis), Paul Fix (Vonnie), George Tobias (Sloppy Joe), Charles Lane (psychiatrist), Adrian Morris (judge in kangaroo court), Fay Helm (Mamie Jacklin), Joseph Crehan (judge), Homer S. Cummings (himself), James V. Bennett (himself), Edward Keane (social service inspector), Harry Worth (Atlanta psychiatrist), Roy Barcroft (federal marshal), Joe Yule (bailiff), Dick Wessel (Moxie), Harry Hayden (educational director), Sherry Overton (Charity), Dora Clements (beauty operator), Fuzzy Bradley (Bugs's son), James Flavin (guard).

Location filming: Bank of America, Beverly Hills branch; U.S. Hospital for Defective Delinquents, Springfield, Ohio; Women's Reformatory, Alderton, West Virginia; Federal Prison, Atlanta; Chillicothe, Ohio, Reformatory; Alcatraz Prison.

Production: January 9–June 10, 1939. Premiere: July 14, 1939.

70 minutes.

Nick Carter, Master Detective (1939) MGM

Director: Jacques Tourneur. Producer: Lucien Hubbard. Screenplay: Bertram Millhauser, based on a story by Bertram Millhauser and Harold Buckley. Director of Photography: Charles Lawton. Assistant cameraman: Luther Bradley. Art Director: Cedric Gibbons. Associate Art Director: Howard Campbell. Set Decorator: Edwin B. Willis. Music: Edward Ward. Editor: Elmo Vernon. Recording Director: Douglas Shearer. Unit Manager: Jerry Brecher.

Cast: Walter Pidgeon (Nick Carter), Rita Johnson (Lou Farnsby), Donald Meek (Bartholomew), Stanley Ridges (Dr. Frankton), Henry Hull (John A. Keller), Addison Richards (Hiram Streeter), Henry Victor (J. Lester Hammil), Milburn Stone (Dave Krebs), Martin Kosleck (Otto King), Frank Faylen (Pete), Sterling Holloway (bee catcher), Wally Maher (Cliff Parsons), Edgar Dearing (Denny), Frank Ball (Peake), George Meeker (Hartley), Richard Terry (Cain), William Newell (taxi driver), Andrew Tombes (Robinson), Richard Lane (Vaughn).

Location filming: Lockheed Airplane Works, Burbank, California.

Production: began September 1939. Premiere: December 15, 1939.

60 minutes.

Phantom Raiders (1940) MGM

Director: Jacques Tourneur. Producer: Frederick Stephani. Screenplay: William R. Lipman, based on a story by Jonathan Latimer. Director of Photography: Clyde De Vinna. Art Director: Cedric Gibbons. Associate Art Director: Malcolm Brown. Set Decorator: Edwin B. Willis. Musical Score: David Snell. Editor: Conrad A. Nervig. Recording Director: Douglas Shearer.

Cast: Walter Pidgeon (Nick Carter), Donald Meek (Bartholomew), Joseph Schildkraut (Al Taurez), Florence Rice (Cora Barnes), Nat Pendleton (Gunboat Jacklin), John Carroll (John Ramsell, Jr.), Steffi Duna (Dolores), Cecil Kellaway (Franklin Morris), Matthew Boulton (John Ramsell, Sr.), Alec Craig (Andy MacMillan), Thomas Ross (Dr. Grisson), Dwight Frye (Eddie Anders), John Burton (Steve Donnigan), Holmes Herbert (Sir Edward), Harry Tyler (waiter), Hugh Beaumont (seaman), Nestor Paiva (inspector).

Premiere: June 7, 1940.

70–71 minutes.

Doctors Don't Tell (1941) Republic

Director: Jacques Tourneur. Associate Producer: Albert J. Cohen. Screenplay: Theodore Reeves, Isabel Dawn, based on an original story by Theodore Reeves. Photography: Ernest Miller. Art Director: John Victor

Mackey. Musical Director: Cy Feuer. Editor: Edward Mann. Supervising Editor: Murray Seldeen. Wardrobe: Adele Palmer. Production Manager: Al Wilson.

Cast: John Beal (Dr. Ralph Sawyer), Edward Norris (Dr. Frank Blake), Florence Rice (Diana Wayne), Douglas Fowley (Joe Grant), Ward Bond (Barney Millan), Grady Sutton (Dr. Peter Piper), Bill Shirley (Tom Wayne), Joseph Crehan (judge), Paul Porcasi (Montes), Russell Hicks (Superintendent Duff), Howard Hickman (Dr. Watkins).

65 (53) minutes.

Cat People (1942) RKO

Director: Jacques Tourneur. Producer: Val Lewton. Screenplay: DeWitt Bodeen. Director of Photography: Nicholas Musuraca. Art Directors: Albert S. D'Agostino, Walter E. Keller. Set Decorators: Darrell Silvera, Al Fields. Music: Roy Webb. Musical Direction: Constantin Bakaleinikoff. Editor: Mark Robson. Costumes: Renie. Sound Recordist: John L. Cass. Assistant Director: Doran Cox.

Cast: Simone Simon (Irena Dubrovna), Kent Smith (Oliver Reed), Jane Randolph (Alice Moore), Tom Conway (Dr. Louis Judd), Alan Napier ("Doc" Carver), Jack Holt (Commodore), Elizabeth Russell ("cat woman" in restaurant), Teresa Harris (Minnie), Elizabeth Dunne (Miss Plunkett, pet-shop owner), Mary Halsey (Blondie), Alec Craig (zookeeper), Dot Farley (Mrs. Agnew, cleaning woman), Charles Jordan (bus driver), Don Kerr (taxi driver), Betty Roadman (Mrs. Hansen).

Production: July 28–August 21, 1942. Premiere: December 1942.

71 minutes, 27 seconds.

I Walked with a Zombie (1943) RKO

Director: Jacques Tourneur. Producer: Val Lewton. Screenplay: Curt Siodmak and Ardel Wray, based on scientific information from articles by Inez Wallace. Director of Photography: J. Roy Hunt. Art Directors: Albert S. D'Agostino, Walter E. Keller. Set Decorators: Darrell Silvera, Al Fields. Music: Roy Webb. Musical Director: C. Bakaleinikoff. Editor: Mark Robson. Sound Recordist: John C. Grubb. Assistant Director: William Dorfman.

Cast: Frances Dee (Betsy Connell), Tom Conway (Paul Holland), James Ellison (Wesley Rand), Edith Barrett (Mrs. Rand), Christine Gordon (Jessica Holland), James Bell (Dr. Maxwell), Teresa Harris (Alma), Sir Lancelot (calypso singer), Darby Jones (Carrefour), Jieno Moxzer (Sabreur), Richard Abrams (Clement), Martin Wilkins (Houngan), Jeni LeGon (dancer), Arthur Walker (Ti-Joseph), Kathleen Hartfield (dancer), Clinton Rosemond

(coachman), Alan Edmiston (Mr. Wilkens), Norman Mayes (Bayard), Melvin Williams (Baby), Vivian Dandridge (Melisse).

Production: October 26–November 19, 1942. Premiere: April 1943.

68 minutes, 33 seconds.

The Leopard Man (1943) RKO

Director: Jacques Tourneur. Producer: Val Lewton. Screenplay: Ardel Wray, based on the novel *Black Alibi* by Cornell Woolrich. Additional Dialogue: Edward Dein. Director of Photography: Robert De Grasse. Art Directors: Albert S. D'Agostino, Walter E. Keller. Set Decorators: Darrell Silvera, Al Fields. Music: Roy Webb. Musical Director: C. Bakaleinikoff. Editor: Mark Robson. Sound Recordist: John C. Grubb. Assistant Director: William Dorfman.

Cast: Dennis O'Keefe (Jerry Manning), Margo (Clo-Clo), Jean Brooks (Kiki Walker), James Bell (Dr. Galbraith), Abner Biberman (Charlie How-Come), Ben Bard (Chief Robles), Margaret Landry (Teresa Delgado), Tula Parma (Consuelo Contreras), Ariel Heath (Eloise), Richard Martin (Raoul Belmonte), William Halligan (Brunton, rich man), Jacqueline De Witt (Helene), Robert Anderson (Dwight), Kate Lawson (Señora Delgado), Fely Franquelli (Rosita), Tola Nesmith (Señora Contreras), Brandon Hurst (gatekeeper), Jacques Lory (Philipe), Bobby Spindola (Pedro), Russell Wade (man in car), Margaret Sylva (Marta), Charles Lung (Manuel, kindly shopkeeper), John Dilson (coroner), Mary MacLaren (nun), Tom Orosco (window cleaner), Eliso Gamboa (Señor Delgado), Joe Dominguez (cop), Betty Roadman (Clo-Clo's mother), Rosa Rita Varella (Clo-Clo's sister), John Piffle (flower vendor), Rene Pedrini (frightened waiter), Rose Higgins (Indian weaver), George Sherwood (police lieutenant), John Tettemer (minister), Belle Mitchell (Señora Calderon).

Production: February 9–March 8, 1943. Premiere: May 1943.

65 minutes, 59 seconds. (At some point subsequent to its initial release, the film was cut to 59 minutes. The full version is now generally available in the United States.)

Days of Glory (1944) RKO

Director: Jacques Tourneur. Producer: Casey Robinson. Screenplay: Casey Robinson, based on an original story by Melchior Lengyel. Director of Photography: Tony Gaudio. Production Designer: Mordecai Gorelik. Art Directors: Albert S. D'Agostino, Carroll Clark. Set Decorators: Darrell Silvera, Harley Miller. Music: Daniele Amfitheatrof. Musical Director:

Constantin Bakaleinikoff. Orchestrations: Leonid Raab. Editor: Joseph Noriega. Gowns: Renié. Makeup Artist: Mel Berns. Sound recorded by Richard Van Hessen, rerecorded by James G. Stewart. Assistant Director: William Dorfman. Special Effects: Vernon L. Walker. Special Sound Effects: Roy Granville. Technical Adviser: George Johansen. Additional Direction: Casey Robinson (uncredited). Additional Photography: Frank Redmond (uncredited).

Cast: Gregory Peck (Vladimir), Tamara Toumanova (Nina), Lowell Gilmore (Semyon), Maria Palmer (Yelena), Alan Reed (Sasha), Hugo Haas (Fedor), Igor Dolgoruki (Dmitri), Glenn Vernon (Mitya), Dena Penn (Olga), Edward L. Durst (Petrov), Lou Crosby (Staub), William Challee (Duchenko), Joseph Vitale (Seminov), Erford Gage (Colonel Prilenko), Ivan Triesault (German lieutenant), Maria Bibikov (Vera), Edgar Licho (Anton), Gretl Dupont (Mariya), Peter Helmers (Von Rundholz), Gene Reading (German sentry), Rudolph Lindau (German sergeant), Charles Faber (German corporal), Sonny Boy Williams (boy), Peter Seal (Captain Mitkin).

Location filming: Cedar City, Utah.
Production: July 7–December 9, 1943.
86 minutes.

Experiment Perilous (1944) RKO

Director: Jacques Tourneur. Producer: Warren Duff. Executive Producer: Robert Fellows. Screenplay: Warren Duff, based on the novel by Margaret Carpenter. Director of Photography: Tony Gaudio. Art Directors: Albert S. D'Agostino, Jack Okey. Set Decorators: Darrell Silvera, Claude Carpenter. Music: Roy Webb. Musical Director: C. Bakaleinikoff. Editor: Ralph Dawson. Gowns for Hedy Lamarr: Leah Rhodes. Other Gowns: Edward Stevenson. Sound recorded by John E. Tribby. Rerecording: James G. Stewart. Assistant Director: Dewey Starkey. Special Effects: Vernon L. Walker. Second Unit Director: Warren Duff (uncredited). Second Unit Cameraman: Harry Wild (uncredited).

Cast: Hedy Lamarr (Allida Bederaux), George Brent (Dr. Huntington Bailey), Paul Lukas (Nicholas Bederaux), Albert Dekker ("Clag" Claghorne), Olive Blakeney (Cissie Bederaux), George N. Neise (Alec Gregory), Carl Esmond (John Maitland), Margaret Wycherly (Maggie), Stephanie Bachelor (Elaine), Julia Dean (Deria), Mary Servoss (Miss Wilson), William Post, Jr. (District Attorney MacDonald), Billy Ward (Alec Bederaux), Broderick O'Farrell (Frank), Alan Ward (Shoes), Nolan Leary (bellhop), Mark Cramer (guest at Clag's), Larry Wheat (caterer), Sam

McDaniel (porter), Edward Clark (train steward), Joel Friedkin (brakeman), Jack Deery (doorman), Almeda Fowler (clerk), John Elliott (telephone operator), Charles McMurphy (cop), Michael Orr (Nick, age 3), Peggy Miller (Cissie, age 8), Evelyn Falke (Cissie, age 5), Janet Clark (Deria as a girl), Georges Renavent (voice instructor), Adrienne d'Ambricourt (voice instructor), John Mylong (Nick, Sr.), Perc Launders (ambulance man), Michael Visaroff (ballet master).

Production: July 11–October 7, 1944.
91 minutes.

Canyon Passage (1946) Universal

Director: Jacques Tourneur. Producer: Walter Wanger. Associate Producer: Alexander Golitzen. Screenplay: Ernest Pascal, based on the novel by Ernest Haycox. Director of Photography: Edward Cronjager (Technicolor). Art Directors: John B. Goodman, Richard H. Riedel. Set Decorators: Russell A. Gausman, Leigh Smith. Music Director: Frank Skinner. Songs, "Rogue River Valley," "I'm Gettin' Married in the Mornin'," "Silver Saddle": music and lyrics by Hoagy Carmichael; "Ole Buttermilk Sky" by Hoagy Carmichael and Jack Brooks. Editor: Milton Carruth. Costumes: Travis Banton. Hair Stylist: Carmen Dirigo. Makeup Director: Jack P. Pierce. Sound Director: Bernard B. Brown. Sound Technician: William Hedgcock. Dialogue Director: Anthony Jowitt. Assistant Director: Fred Frank. Special Photography: D. S. Horsley. Technicolor Color Director: Natalie Kalmus. Associate: William Fritzsche. Second Unit Director: Charles Barton. Production Manager: Perk Ikerd.

Cast: Dana Andrews (Logan Stuart), Susan Hayward (Lucy Overmire), Brian Donlevy (George Camrose), Patricia Roc (Caroline Marsh), Hoagy Carmichael (Hi Linnet), Ward Bond (Honey Bragg), Andy Devine (Ben Dance), Lloyd Bridges (Johnny Steele), Stanley Ridges (Jonas Overmire), Victor Cutler (Vane Blazier), Onslow Stevens (Jack Lestrade), Rose Hobart (Marta Lestrade), Dorothy Peterson (Mrs. Dance), Fay Holden (Mrs. Overmire), Halliwell Hobbes (Clenchfield), Ray Teal (Neil Howison), James Cardwell (Gray Bartlett), Virginia Patton (Liza Stone), Tad Devine (Asa Dance), Denny Devine (Bushrod Dance), Francis McDonald (Cobb), Erville Alderson (judge), Ralph Peters (Harry Stutchell), Wallace Scott (McIver), Chief Yowlachie (Indian spokesman), Peter Whitney (Cornelius Van Houten), Harry Shannon (McLane), Frank Ferguson (minister), Chester Clute (proprietor), Jack Rockwell (teamster), Gene Stutenroth (miner).

Location filming: Oregon.
Production: August 20–December 20, 1945. Premiere: July 1946.
92 minutes.

Out of the Past (1947) RKO

Director: Jacques Tourneur. Producer: Warren Duff. Executive Producer: Robert Sparks. Screenplay: Daniel Mainwaring (and Frank Fenton and James M. Cain, uncredited), based on the novel *Build My Gallows High* by Geoffrey Homes (pseudonym for Mainwaring). Director of Photography: Nicholas Musuraca. Art Directors: Albert S. D'Agostino, Jack Okey. Set Decorator: Darrell Silvera. Music: Roy Webb. Conductor: Constantin Bakaleinikoff. Editor: Samuel E. Beetley. Costumes: Edward Stevenson. Makeup: Gordon Bau. Sound: Francis M. Sarver, Clem Portman. Assistant Director: Harry Mancke. Special Effects: Russell A. Cully. Second Unit Director: Lynn Shores (uncredited). Second Unit Cameraman: Harold Stine (uncredited).

Cast: Robert Mitchum (Jeff Bailey/Markham), Jane Greer (Kathie Moffat), Kirk Douglas (Whit Sterling), Virginia Huston (Ann Miller), Rhonda Fleming (Meta Carson), Paul Valentine (Joe Stefanos), Richard Webb (Jim), Steve Brodie (Jack Fisher), Dickie Moore (the Kid), Ken Niles (Leonard Eels), John Kellogg (Lou Baylord), Wallace Scott (Petey), Mary Field (Marny), Teresa Harris (Eunice), Oliver Blake (Mr. Tillotson), Tony Roux (José Rodriguez), Harry Hayden (Mr. Miller), Adda Gleason (Mrs. Miller), Caleb Peterson (man with Eunice), Lee Elson (policeman), Frank Wilcox (Sheriff Douglas), Wesley Bly (headwaiter), William Van Vleck (cigar-store clerk), Phillip Morris (porter), José Portugal (waiter), Jess Escobar and James Bush (doormen), Charles Regan (mystery man).

Location filming: Lake Tahoe, Bridgeport, California; second unit: San Francisco, Mexico City, Acapulco.

Production: October 21, 1946–January 9, 1947. Premiere: November 25, 1947.
96 minutes, 37 seconds.

Berlin Express (1948) RKO

Director: Jacques Tourneur. Producer: Bert Granet. Screenplay: Harold Medford, based on a story by Curt Siodmak. Director of Photography: Lucien Ballard. Camera Operator: Richard Davol. Art Directors: Albert S. D'Agostino, Alfred Herman. Set Decorators: Darrell Silvera, William Stevens. Music: Frederick Hollander. Musical Director: Constantin Bakaleinikoff. Choreography: Charles O'Curran. Editor: Sherman Todd. Merle Oberon's Gowns: Orry Kelly. Makeup: Gordon Bau.

Sound: Jack Grubb, Clem Portman. Assistant Director: Nate Levinson. Special Effects: Harry Perry, Russell A. Cully, Harold Stine. Assistant to the Producer: William Dorfman.

Cast: Robert Ryan (Robert Lindley), Merle Oberon (Lucienne Mirbeau), Charles Korvin (Henri Perrot/Holtzmann), Paul Lukas (Dr. Heinrich Bernhardt/Otto Franzen), Robert Coote (James Sterling), Roman Toporow (Lieutenant Maxim Kiroshlov), Reinhold Schunzel (Professor Johann Walther), Peter Von Zerneck (Hans Schmidt), Otto Waldis (Kessler), Charles McGraw (Colonel Johns), Fritz Kortner (the fake Bernhardt), Michael Harvey (Sergeant Barnes), Richard Powers (major), Marle Hayden (Maga), Eric Wyland (clown), Willy Wickerhauser (Frederich), Richard Flato (master of ceremonies), Hermine Steiler (Frau Borne), William Yetter and Robert Boon (German youths), William Allister (Richard), Bert Goodrich and George Redpath (acrobatic team), Robert Dalban (French police commissioner), Cécile Barrette (French woman), Leonid Snegoff (Russian colonel), Jim Nolan (train captain), Arthur Dulac (dining car steward), Ray Spiker (first husky), Bruce Cameron (second husky), Buddy Roosevelt (M.P. sergeant), David Clarke (army technician), Roger Creed, Rick Williams, and Paul MacWilliams (M.P.'s), Gene Evans (train sergeant), Robert "Buddy" Shaw (sergeant), Paul Stewart (narrator).

Location filming: Paris, Berlin, Frankfurt.
Production: July 6–November 25, 1947.
86 minutes.

Easy Living (1949) RKO

Director: Jacques Tourneur. Producer: Robert Sparks. Screenplay: Charles Schnee, based on the story "Education of the Heart" by Irwin Shaw. Director of Photography: Harry J. Wild. Art Directors: Albert S. D'Agostino, Alfred Herman. Set Decorators: Darrell Silvera, Harley Miller. Music: Roy Webb. Musical Director: Constantin Bakaleinikoff. Editor: Frederic Knudtson. Gowns: Edward Stevenson. Makeup Supervision: Gordon Bau. Sound: Earl Wolcott, Clem Portman. Assistant Director: James Lane.

Cast: Victor Mature (Pete Wilson), Lizabeth Scott (Liza Wilson), Lucille Ball (Anne), Sonny Tufts (Tim McCarr), Lloyd Nolan (Lenahan), Paul Stewart (Dave Argus), Art Baker (Howard Vollmer), Jeff Donnell (Penny McCarr), Jack Paar (Scoop Spooner), Gordon Jones (Holly Holloran), Don Beddoe (Jaegar), Dick Erdman (Buddy Morgan), Kenny Washington (Benny), William "Bill" Phillips (Ozzie), Charles Lang (Whitey), Julia Dean (Mrs. Belle Ryan), Everett Glass (Virgil Ryan),

Jim Backus (Dr. Franklin), June Bright (Billy Duane), Steven Flagg (Gilbert Vollmer), Audrey Young (singer), Robert Ellis (urchin), Alex Sharp (Don), Russ Thorson (Hunk Edwards), Edward Kotal (Curley), members of the Los Angeles Rams football team.
Production: July 7–August 20, 1948.
77 minutes.

Stars in My Crown (1950) MGM

Director: Jacques Tourneur. Producer: William H. Wright. Screenplay: Margaret Fitts, based on the novel by Joe David Brown. Director of Photography: Charles Schoenbaum. Camera Operator: John Schmitz. Art Directors: Cedric Gibbons, Eddie Imazu. Set Decorators: Edwin B. Willis, Alfred E. Spencer. Music: Adolph Deutsch. Vocal Arrangements: Robert Tucker. Editor: Gene Ruggiero. Wardrobe: Walter Plunkett. Assistant Director: Dolf Zimmer. Second Unit Director: James C. Havens. Special Effects: Warren Newcombe. Assistant to the Producer: Sergei Petschnikoff.
Cast: Joel McCrea (Josiah Doziah Gray), Ellen Drew (Harriet Gray), Dean Stockwell (John Kenyon), Alan Hale (Jed Isbell), James Mitchell (Dr. Daniel Kalbert Harris, Jr.), Lewis Stone (Dr. Daniel Kalbert Harris, Sr.), Amanda Blake (Faith Radmore Samuels), Juano Hernandez (Uncle Famous Prill), Ed Begley (Lon Backett), Charles Kemper (Professor Sam Houston Jones), Connie Gilchrist (Sarah Isbell), Jack Lambert (Perry Lokey), Arthur Hunnicutt (Chloroform Wiggins), Norman Ollestad, Jr. (Chase Isbell), James Arness (Rufe Isbell), Adeline DeWalt Reynolds (elderly parishioner), Ben Watson (Gene Caldwell), Polly Bailey (Mrs. Belsher), William Clauson (Cado Isbell), Ralph Hodges (Tom Isbell), Charles Courtney (Jed Isbell, Jr.), Jimmy Moss (Bobby Sam Carroll), Jessie Grayson (Bessie), Wilson Wood (Thad Carroll), Snub Pollard (bartender), Victor Killian (Ned), Connie Van and Buddy Roosevelt (townspeople), Marshall Thompson (narrator).
89 minutes.

The Flame and the Arrow (1950)

Warner Bros./Norma-F.R. Productions
Director : Jacques Tourneur. Producers: Frank Ross, Harold Hecht. Associate Producer: Norman Deming. Story and Screenplay: Waldo Salt. Director of Photography: Ernest Haller (Technicolor). Art Director: Edward Carrere. Set Decorator: Lyle B. Reifsnider. Music: Max Steiner. Orchestration: Murray Cutter. Editor: Alan Crosland, Jr. Wardrobe: Marjorie Best. Makeup: Perc Westmore. Sound: Francis J. Scheid. Assistant

Director: Frank Mattison. Technicolor Color Consultant: Mitchell G. Kovaleski.
Cast: Burt Lancaster (Dardo), Virginia Mayo (Anne of Hesse), Nick Cravat (Piccolo), Robert Douglas (Alessandro, Marchese of Granezia), Frank Allenby (Count Ulrich of Hesse), Gordon Gerbert (Rudi), Norman Lloyd (troubadour), Victor Kilian (apothecary), Aline MacMahon (Nonna Bartoli), Francis Pierlot (Papa Pietro), Lynne Baggett (Francesca), Robin Hughes (skinner), Philip van Zandt (counselor), Sue Casey (Anne's maid), Phil Pine (sweep), Alex Sharp (tinker), Michael Roy (baker), Russ Conklin (butcher), Gaunt and Allan Matthews (twins), John Pallette (arrowsmith), Mel Archer (bambino).
Production: October 4, 1949–January 18, 1950.
88 minutes.

Circle of Danger (1951) Eagle-Lion/Coronado Productions (G.B.)

Director: Jacques Tourneur. Producer: Joan Harrison. Executive Producer: David E. Rose. Screenplay: Philip McDonald, based on his novel *White Heather*. Director of Photography: Oswald Morris. Camera Operator: Arthur Ibbetson. Additional Photography: Gilbert Taylor. Settings: Duncan Sutherland. Music: Robert Farnon. Song "Buttonhole for Baby": music by Walter Ridley, lyrics by Hal Halifax. Choreography: Betty and Philip Buchel. Editor: Alan Osbiston. Wardrobe Supervisor: Phyllis Dalton. Makeup: Jim Hydes. Hair Stylist: Nina Broe. Sound Recording: Alan Allen, Red Law. Production Manager: Fred C. Gunn. In Charge of Production: John R. Sloan. Assistant Director: Kenneth K. Rick. Continuity: Betty Forster.
Cast: Ray Milland (Clay Douglas), Patricia Roc (Elspeth Graham), Hugh Sinclair (Hamish McArran), Marius Goring (Sholto Lewis), Naunton Wayne (Reggie Sinclair), Marjorie Fielding (Mrs. McArran), Edward Rigby (Idwal Llewellyn), John Bailey (Pape Llewellyn), Dora Bryan (Bubbles Fitzgerald), Reginald Beckwith (Oliver), Colin Gordon (Colonel Fairbairn), Michael Brennan (Bert Oakshott), Philip Dale (Jim Stoner), David Hutcheson (Tony Wrexham), Archie Duncan (Angus), Nora Gordon (Sheila), George Margo (Sim), Ben Williams (mine director).
86 minutes.

Anne of the Indies (1951) 20th Century–Fox

Director: Jacques Tourneur. Producer: George Jessel. Screenplay: Philip Dunne, Arthur Caesar, based on a story by Herbert Ravenel Sass. Director of Photography: Harry

Jackson (Technicolor). Art Directors: Lyle R. Wheeler, Albert Hogsett. Set Decorators: Claude Carpenter, Thomas Little. Music: Franz Waxman. Orchestration: Edward B. Powell. Editor: Robert Fritch. Wardrobe: Edward Stevenson, Charles LeMaire. Makeup: Ben Nye. Sound: B. Clayton Ward, Harry M. Leonard. Assistant Director: Horace Hough. Special Photographic Effects: Fred Sersen. Technicolor Color Consultant: Leonard Doss. Fencing Master: Fred Cavens. Technical Advisor for Whipping Scenes: Dave Kasher.

Cast: Jean Peters (Captain Anne Providence), Louis Jourdan (Captain Pierre François La Rochelle), Debra Paget (Molly La Rochelle), Herbert Marshall (Dr. Jameson), James Robertson Justice (Dougall), Thomas Gomez (Blackbeard), Lester Matthews (Wherry), Olaf Hytten (Captain Harris), Francis Pierlot (Herkimer), Sean McClory (Hackett), Holmes Herbert (English sea captain), Byron Nelson (bear handler), Douglas Bennett (bear wrestler), Mario Siletti (auctioneer), Bob Stephenson (tavern host), Carleton Young (pirate mate), Lynn Davies (Carib woman), William Walker (servant), Sheldon Jett (innkeeper), Gene Ramey (singer), Harry Carter, Harry Wilson, Steve Pritko, William Schallert, and Michael Ross (pirates), Stuart Holmes and Major Sam Harris (English officers), Hera Sonkur, Chabing, Lillian Molieri, and Noel Toy (slave girls), Roberta Haynes (Indian princess).

Production: February–May 1951.
81 minutes.

Way of a Gaucho (1952) 20th Century–Fox

Director: Jacques Tourneur (and Henry Levin, uncredited). Producer: Philip Dunne. Associate Producer: Joseph C. Behm. Screenplay: Philip Dunne, based on the novel by Herbert Childs. Director of Photography: Harry Jackson (Technicolor). Art Direction: Lyle R. Wheeler, Mark Lee Kirk. Set Decorators: Thomas Little, Bruce MacDonald. Music: Sol Kaplan. Musical Director: Alfred Newman. Orchestrations: Bernard Mayers. Editor: Robert Fritch. Wardrobe Direction: Charles LeMaire. Costumes designed by Mario Vanarelli. Makeup: Ben Nye. Sound: Eugene Grossman, Harry M. Leonard. Assistant Director: Jack Stubbs. Special Photographic Effects: Ray Kellogg. Technical Advisers: Eleodoro Marenco, Coronel Landa.

Cast: Rory Calhoun (Martín Penalosa), Gene Tierney (Teresa Chavez), Richard Boone (Major Salinas), Hugh Marlowe (Don Miguel Aldeondo), Everett Sloane (Falcón), Enrique Chaico (Padre Fernández), Lidia Campos (Tía

María), Roland Dumas (Julio), Claudio Torres (Florencio), Jorge Villoldo (Valverde), Chuck Roberson (Brutos), Hugo Mancini and Nestor Yóan (army lieutenants), Raúl Astor (police lieutenant), John Paris (railroad foreman), Alex Peters (driver), John Henchley (gaucho tracker), Kim Dillon (sentry), Lia Centena (hacienda guest), Anthony Ugrin (beadle), Douglas Poole (pallbearer), Mario Abdah (horse dealer), Teresa Acosta and Oscar Lucero (dancers at hacienda), Tom McDonough Anderson (gaucho), Douglas Brooks (Jiminez), David Fresco (corporal), Salvador Baguez (sergeant).

Filmed in Argentina and California.
Production: October 1951–March 1952.
91 minutes.

Appointment in Honduras (1953)
RKO

Director: Jacques Tourneur. Producer: Benedict Bogeaus. Screenplay: Karen De Wolf, based on a story by Mario Silveira and Jack Cornall. Director of Photography (Technicolor): Joseph Biroc. Art Director: Charles D. Hall. Set Decorations: Alfred E. Spencer. Music: Louis Forbes. Music Associate: Henry Jackson. Editor: James Leicester. Wardrobe: Izzy Berne. Makeup: Frank Westmore, Dave Grayson. Production Supervisor: William Stephens. Assistant Director: Ralph J. Slosser. Special Effects: Lee Zavitz. Script Supervisor: William Ord.

Cast: Glenn Ford (Jim Corbett), Ann Sheridan (Sylvia Sheppard), Zachary Scott (Harry Sheppard), Rodolfo Acosta (Reyes), Jack Elam (Castro), Ric Roman (Jiménez), Rico Alaniz (Bermúdez), Stuart Whitman (radio operator), Paul Zurumba (Luis), Stanley Andrews (Captain McTaggart), Mel Welles (General Hidalgo), Robert Brown (helmsman), John Mansfield and Ron Kennedy (lieutenants), Julian Rivero (President Prieto).

78–80 (76) minutes.

Stranger on Horseback (1955) United Artists/Leonard Goldstein Productions

Director: Jacques Tourneur. Producer: Robert Goldstein. Screenplay: Herb Meadow, Don Martin, based on a story by Louis L'Amour. Director of Photography (Ansco-Color): Ray Rennahan. Art Director: Albert Hogsett. Set Decorator: Victor Gangelin. Music: Paul Dunlap. Editor: William B. Murphy. Makeup: Jack Byron, Willon Fields. Sound: Frank McWhorter. Assistant Director: Frank Parmenter.

Cast: Joel McCrea (Judge Richard Thorne), Miroslava (Amy Lee Bannerman), Kevin McCarthy (Tom Bannerman), John McIntire (Josiah Bannerman), John Carradine (Colonel

Buck Streeter), Emile Meyer (Marshal Nat
Bell), Nancy Gates (Caroline Webb), Robert
Cornthwaite (Arnold Hammer), Jacklyn Green
(Paula Morrison), Walter Baldwin (Vince
Webb), Roy Roberts (Sam Kettering), Emmett
Lynn (drunk), George Keymas (Joe Fly), Lane
Bradford (Rusk), George De Normand (Tay-
lor).

Location filming: Sedona, Arizona.
Production: July 12–31, 1954.
66 minutes.

Wichita (1955) Allied Artists

Director: Jacques Tourneur. Producer:
Walter Mirisch. Associate Producer: Richard
Heermance. Story and Screenplay: Daniel B.
Ullman. Director of Photography: Harold
Lipstein (Technicolor, Cinemascope). Art
Director: David Milton. Set Decorator: Joseph
Kish. Music composed and conducted by Hans
Salter. Song "Wichita": music by Hans Salter,
lyrics by Ned Washington, sung by Tex Ritter.
Music Editor: Eve Newman. Film Editor:
William Austin. Makeup: Edward Polo,
Robert Dawn. Hairdresser: Mary Westmore-
land. Recorded by Ralph Butler. Sound Edi-
tor: Del Harris. Production Manager: Allen K.
Wood. Assistant Director: Austen Jewell. Dia-
logue Director (?): Sam Peckinpah (uncred-
ited). Set Continuity: Mary Chaffee.

Cast: Joel McCrea (Wyatt Earp), Vera Miles
(Laurie McCoy), Lloyd Bridges (Gyp Clem-
ents), Walter Coy (Sam McCoy), Wallace Ford
(Arthur Whiteside), Edgar Buchanan (Doc
Black), Peter Graves (Morgan Earp), Keith
Larsen (Bat Masterson), Carl Benton Reid
(Mayor Andrew Hope), John Smith (Jim
Earp), Walter Sande (Clint Wallace), Robert J.
Wilke (Ben Thompson), Rayford Barnes (Hal
Clements), Jack Elam (Al Mann), Mae Clarke
(Mary McCoy), Gene Wesson, Bob Swan, and
Rory Mallinson (bandits), George Sherwood
(marshal), I. Stanford Jolley (Stanton), William
Newell (bartender), Sam Peckinpah (teller),
Dorothy Tennant (Mrs. Stanton), Al Wyatt
(cowpuncher), Jody McCrea.

Location filming: Newhall and Thousand
Oaks, California.
81 minutes.

Great Day in the Morning (1956)
RKO

Director: Jacques Tourneur. Producer:
Edmund Grainger. Screenplay: Lesser Samuels,
based on the novel by Robert Hardy Andrews.
Director of Photography: William Snyder
(Technicolor, Superscope). Art Director: Jack
Okey. Set Decorations: Albert S. D'Agostino.
Music: Leith Stevens. Editor: Harry Marker.
Hair Stylist: Annabell Levy. Makeup: Larry

Butterworth. Costumes: Gwenn Wakeling.
Sound: Jack Grubb, Terry Kellum. Assistant
Director: Jimmy Casey. Production Super-
visor: Cliff Broughton. Unit Manager: John E.
Burch. Sound Effects: Walter Elliott.

Cast: Robert Stack (Owen Pentecost), Vir-
ginia Mayo (Ann Merry Alain), Ruth Roman
(Boston), Alex Nicol (Captain Stephen Kirby),
Raymond Burr (Jumbo Means), Leo Gordon
(Sergeant Zeff Masterson), Donald MacDonald
(Gary Lawford), Regis Toomey (Father Mur-
phy), Carleton Young (Colonel Gibson), Peter
Whitney (Phil the Cannibal), Dan White
(Rogers), Burt Mustin (doctor), William
Phipps (Robinson).

Location filming: Silverton, Colorado, and
California.
92 minutes.

Nightfall (1957) Columbia/Copa Produc-
tions

Director: Jacques Tourneur. Producer: Ted
Richmond. Screenplay: Sterling Silliphant,
based on the novel by David Goodis. Director
of Photography: Burnett Guffey. Art Director:
Ross Bellah. Set Decorators: William Kiernan,
Louis Diage. Music: George Duning. Orches-
trations: Arthur Morton. Conductor: Morris
Stoloff. Song "Nightfall": music by Peter
DeRose and Charles Harold, lyrics by Sam M.
Lewis, sung by Al Hibbler. Editor: William A.
Lyon. Wardrobe: Jean Louis. Makeup: Clay
Campbell. Hair Styles: Helen Hunt. Record-
ing Supervisor: John Livadary. Sound: Ferol
Redd. Assistant Director: Irving Moore. Fash-
ion show by J. W. Robinson Company of Cali-
fornia.

Cast: Aldo Ray (Jim Vanning/Art Ray-
burn), Anne Bancroft (Marie Gardner), Brian
Keith (John), James Gregory (Ben Fraser),
Rudy Bond (Red), Jocelyn Brando (Laura
Fraser), Frank Albertson (Dr. Edward Gurston),
George Cisar (bus driver), Eddie McLean (taxi
driver), Orlando Beltran and Maria Belmar
(Spanish couple), Walter Smith (shoeshine),
Lillian Culver and Maya Van Horn (women),
Gene Roth (bartender), Monty Ash (clerk),
Art Bucaro (cashier), Arline Anderson (host-
ess), Winifred Waring (fashion M.C.), Jane
Lyn, Betty Koch, Lillian Kassan, Joan Fotre,
Pat Jones, and Annabelle George (models).

Location filming: Bridgeport, California.
Filming completed: April 9, 1956. Premiere: January 23, 1957.
78 minutes.

Night of the Demon (1957)
Columbia/Sabre Film Productions
(G.B.)

U.S. title: *Curse of the Demon*

Director: Jacques Tourneur. Producer: Frank Bevis. Executive Producer: Hal E. Chester. Screenplay: Charles Bennett, Hal E. Chester (and Cyril Raker Endfield, uncredited), based on the story "Casting the Runes" by Montague R. James. Director of Photography: Ted Scaife. Camera Operator: Kenneth Peach. Production Designer: Ken Adam. Assistant Art Director: Peter Glazier. Music Composer: Clifton Parker. Music conducted by Muir Matheson. Editor: Michael Gordon. Hair Stylist: Betty Lee. Sound Recordist: Arthur Bradburn. Production Manager: R. L. M. Davidson. Assistant Director: Basil Keys. Special Effects: George Blackwell, Wally Veevers. Special Effects Photography: S. D. Onions. Sound Effects Editor: Charles Crafford. Casting: Robert Lennard. Continuity: Pamela Gayler.

Cast: Dana Andrews (Dr. John Holden), Peggy Cummins (Joanna Harrington), Niall MacGinnis (Dr. Julian Karswell), Athene Seyler (Mrs. Karswell), Liam Redmond (Professor Mark O'Brien), Maurice Denham (Professor Henry Harrington), Reginald Beckwith (Mr. Meek), Peter Elliott (Kumar), Ewan Roberts (Lloyd Williamson), Brian Wilde (Rand Hobart), Rosamund Greenwood (Mrs. Meek), Janet Barrow (Mrs. Hobart), John Salew (librarian), Charles Lloyd Pack (chemist), Richard Leech (Inspector Mottram), Lloyd Lamble (Detective Simmons), Peter Hobbes (superintendent), Percy Herbert (farmer), Walter Horsbrugh (Bates), Lynn Tracy (air hostess), Ballard Berkeley and Michael Peake (reporters), Shay Gorman (narrator).

Location filming: England.

U.S. premiere: February 1958.

95 minutes. (*Note:* The film was originally released in the United States at 82 minutes. Since the 1980s, prints running about 95 minutes have become generally available. The longer version has been said to be that of the British release of the film. Ronald V. Borst and Scott MacQueen report, however, that the film was originally released in Great Britain at 7,350 feet [about 82 minutes], having been cut from 8,582 feet [about 95 minutes]. The footage and timings they give were noted on "the British release script" [Borst and MacQueen, *"Curse of the Demon,"* p. 33].)

The Fearmakers (1958) United Artists/
Pacemaker Productions

Director: Jacques Tourneur. Producer: Martin H. Lancer. Associate Producer: Leon Chooluck. Screenplay: Elliot West and Chris Appley, based on the novel by Darwin Teilhet. Director of Photography: Sam Leavitt. Lighting: James Almond. Art Director: Serge Krizman.

Set Decorator: James Roach. Music: Irving Gertz. Music Editor: Herry Eisen. Editor: J. R. Whittredge. Associate Editor: Paul Laune. Wardrobe: Frank Roberts. Makeup: Dave Grayson. Sound: John Kean. Assistant Director: Eugene Anderson, Jr. Sound Effects Editor: James Nelson. Script Supervisor: Dolores Rubin.

Cast: Dana Andrews (Allen Eaton), Marilee Earle (Lorraine Dennis), Dick Foran (Jim McGinnis), Mel Torme (Barney Bond), Kelly Thordsen (Harold Loder), Veda Ann Borg (Vivian Loder), Joel Marston (Rodney Hillier), Roy Gordon (Senator Walder), Oliver Blake (Dr. Gregory Jessop), Robert Fortier (Colonel Buchans), Janet Brandt (Senator Walder's secretary), Fran Andrade, Dennis Moore.

84–85 minutes.

Timbuktu (1959) United Artists/Imperial
Pictures

Director: Jacques Tourneur. Producer: Edward Small (uncredited). Screenplay: Anthony Veiller, Paul Dudley. Director of Photography: Maury Gertsman. Art Director: William Glasgow. Set Decorator: Darrell Silvera. Music: Gerald Fried. Supervising Editor: Grant Whytock. Wardrobe Man: Frank Beetson. Wardrobe Woman: Elva Martien. Makeup: Layne Britton. Sound: John Kean. Assistant Director: Al Westen. Special Effects: Joe Zomar, Alex Weldon, Al Bird. Technical Adviser: Feridun Colgecen. Effects Editor: Al Bird. Music Editor: George Brand. Casting Director: Betty Pagel. Script Supervision: John Dutton.

Cast: Victor Mature (Mike Conway), Yvonne DeCarlo (Natalie Dufort), George Dolenz (Colonel Dufort), John Dehner (the emir), Marcia Henderson (Jeanne Marat), James Foxx (Lieutenant Marat), Paul Wexler (Suleyman), Leonard Mudie (Mohammed Adani), Robert Clarke (Captain Girard), Willard Sage (Major Leroux), Mark Dana (Captain Rimbaud), Larry Perron (Dagana), Steve Darrell (Nazir), Larry Chance (Ahmed), Allan Pinson (Sergeant Trooper).

Production: May 5–30, 1958.

91 minutes.

La Battaglia di Maratona (1959)
MGM/Titanus-Galatea (Rome)/Lux Films (Paris)

U.S. title: *The Giant of Marathon*

Director: Jacques Tourneur (and Bruno Vailati and Mario Bava, uncredited). Producers: Bruno Vailati, Massimo de Rita. Executive Producer: Ferrucio de Martini. Screenplay: Ennio de Concini, Augusto Frassinetti, Bruno Vailati, based on an idea by Alberto Barsanti and Raffaello Pacini. Photography (Dyaliscope, Eastmancolor) and Special Effects: Mario Bava. Cameraman: Massimo Terzano. Cameraman, Underwater Scenes (Totalscope): Massimo Manunza. Set Architect: Marcello Del Prato, from sketches by Massimo Tavazzi. Music: Roberto Nicolosi. Conductor: Pierluigi Urbini. Film Editor: Mario Serandrei. Wardrobe Supervisor: Marisa Crimi. Makeup: Otello Fava. Hair Styles: Mara Rocchetti. Recording Supervisor: Giulio Tagliocozzo. Production Supervisor: Renato Angiolino. Production Manager: Ferruccio De Martino. Assistant Production Manager: Massimo De Rita. Assistant Directors: Ottavio Oppo, Odoardo Fiory, Armando Govoni.

    Cast: Steve Reeves (Philippides), Mylène Demongeot (Andromeda), Sergio Fantoni (Theocritus), Daniela Rocca (Karis), Ivo Garrani (Creusus), Alberto Lupo (Miltiades), Daniele Varga (Darius), Philippe Hersent (Callimachus), Gianni Loti (Teucrus), Miranda Campa (Karis's servant), Sergio Ciani (Euros), Anita Tedesco (Andromeda's friend), Franco Fantasia, Carlo Lombardi, Gianpaolo Rosmino, Ignazio Balsamo, Walter Grant.

    Filmed in Italy and Yugoslavia.

    92 minutes.

The Comedy of Terrors (1963) American-
    International Pictures/Alta Vista Productions

    Director: Jacques Tourneur. Producers: James H. Nicholson, Samuel Z. Arkoff. Coproducer: Anthony Carras. Associate Producer and Screenplay: Richard Matheson. Director of Photography: Floyd Crosby (Pathecolor, Panavision). Camera Operator: Harry Underwood. Art Director: Daniel Haller. Set Decorations: Harry Reif. Music: Les Baxter. Editor: Anthony Carras. Costume Supervisor: Marjorie Corso. Wardrobe: Jerry Alpert. Makeup: Carlie Taylor. Hairstyles: Betty Pedretti, Scotty Rackin. Sound: Don Rush. Assistant Directors: Robert Agnew, Lew Borzage. Production Supervisor: Joe Wonder. Script Supervisor: Emile Ehrlich. Special Effects: Pat Dinga. Dialogue Director: Wayne Winton.

    Cast: Vincent Price (Waldo Trumbull), Peter Lorre (Felix Gillie), Basil Rathbone (John F. Black), Boris Karloff (Amos Hinchley), Joyce Jameson (Amaryllis Trumbull), Joe E. Brown (cemetery keeper), Beverly Hills (Mrs. Phipps), Paul Barselow (Riggs), Linda Rogers (maid), Luree Nicholson (Black's servant), Buddy Mason (Mr. Phipps), Luree Holmes, Alan DeWitt, Doug Williams.

    83 minutes.

War-Gods of the Deep (1965) American-
    International Pictures/Bruton Film Productions (U.S./G.B.)

    G.B. title: *City under the Sea*

    Director: Jacques Tourneur. Producer: Daniel Haller. Executive Producer: George Willoughby. Associate Executive Producers: James H. Nicholson, Samuel Z. Arkoff. Screenplay: Charles Bennett, Louis M. Heyward, based on the poem "City in the Sea" by Edgar Allan Poe. Additional Dialogue: David Whitaker. Director of Photography (Pathe-Color, Colorscope): Stephen Dade. Director of Underwater Photography: John Lamb. Underwater Photography: John Lane, Neil Ginger Gemmell. Art Director: Frank White. Set Decorations: Colin Southcott. Scenic Artist: Peter Wood. Music: Stanley Black. Editor: Gordon Hales. Makeup: Geoffrey Rodway, W. T. Partleton. Sound: Ken Rawkins, Colin LeMesurier. Assistant Director: David Tringham. Production Manager: Pat Green. Special Effects: Frank George, Les Bowie.

    Cast: Vincent Price (Sir Hugh Tregathion, a.k.a. "The Captain"), Tab Hunter (Ben Harris), Susan Hart (Jill Tregellis), David Tomlinson (Harold Tufnell-Jones), John LeMesurier (Reverend Jonathan Ives), Henry Oscar (Mumford), Derek Newark (Dan), Roy Patrick (Simon), Anthony Selby (George), Michael Heyland (Bill), Steven Brooke (Ted), William Hurndell (Tom), Jim Spearman (Jack), Dennis Blake (Harry), Arthur Hewlett, Walter Sparrow, and John Barrett (fishermen), Barbara Bruce, Hilda Campbell Russell, Bart Allison, and George Richarde (guests).

    85 (84) minutes.

SHORT FILMS AS DIRECTOR

The Jonker Diamond (1936) MGM
    Explanatory Remarks: Pete Smith.
    A Miniature
    10 minutes.

Master Will Shakespeare (1936) MGM
    Screenplay: Richard Goldstone. Music: Herbert Stothart. Commentation: Carey Wilson.
    A Miniature
    10 minutes, 40 seconds.

Harnessed Rhythm (1936) MGM
Explanatory remarks: Pete Smith.
A Sports Parade Subject
9 minutes, 40 seconds.

Killer-Dog (1936) MGM
Narrator: Pete Smith.
Cast: Babs Nelson.
A Pete Smith Specialty.
Approx. 10 minutes.

What Do *You* Think? (1937) MGM
Told by Carey Wilson.
A Miniature.
10 minutes, 25 seconds.

The Grand Bounce (1937) MGM
Narrator: Pete Smith.
A Pete Smith Specialty.
Approx. 10 minutes.

The Rainbow Pass (1937) MGM
Story: Richard Goldstone. Told by Carey
Wilson.
Cast: Ching-Wah Lee (Yuan), Bessie Loo
(Yuan's wife), Walter Soo Hoo (Yuan's son).
A Miniature
10 minutes, 37 seconds.

The Boss Didn't Say Good Morning
(1937) MGM
Screenplay: Douglas Foster. Narrator:
Carey Wilson.
A Miniature
Approx. 11 minutes.

Romance of Radium (1937) MGM
Screenplay: Richard Goldstone, N. Gayle
Gitterman.
Narrator: Pete Smith.
A Pete Smith Specialty.
9 minutes, 40 seconds.

The King without a Crown (1937)
MGM
Screenplay: Herman Boxer. Historical com-
pilations: Charles E. Whittaker. Photography:
Charles Lawton. Told by Carey Wilson.
An Historical Mystery.
Approx. 10 minutes.

The Man in the Barn (1937) MGM
Screenplay: Morgan Coxe. Historical com-
pilations: Charles E. Whittaker. Told by Carey
Wilson.
An Historical Mystery.
10 minutes, 15 seconds.

**What Do *You* Think? (Number
Three)** (1937) MGM

Screenplay: Carl Dudley, Jack Woodford.
Told by Carey Wilson.
Cast: Mary Howard (Mary Dosier), Arthur
Rieck (John Dosier).
A Miniature.
10 minutes, 29 seconds.

The Ship That Died (1938) MGM
Screenplay: George Sayre. Historical Com-
pilations: Charles E. Whittaker. Director of
Photography: Lester White. Told by John
Nesbitt.
Cast: Leonard Penn, Rhea Mitchell, Harry
Allen, Lee Prather, Dick Alexander, Ed Kilroy,
Frank Shannon, Claude King, Ralph Bush-
man, Charlie Sullivan, Joan and Diane Gor-
don.
An Historical Mystery.
10 minutes.

The Face behind the Mask (1938)
MGM
Screenplay: Milton Lowell Gunzburg. His-
torical Compilations: Charles E. Whittaker.
Photography: Paul Vogel. Told by John Nes-
bitt.
Cast: Lyons Wickland (the mask), Leonard
Penn (Louis XIV), Mary Howard (La Vallière),
George Sorel (Count Mattioli), Edward Keane
(Fouquet), Harry Worth (Louis XIII), Michael
Mark (peasant), Thomas Mills (governor),
George Jiminez (Spanish king), Ival Hender-
son, Fred Warren, Andre Marisaudom, Carlos
Devaldes, Jack Deery.
An Historical Mystery.
Approx. 10 minutes.

What Do *You* Think? Tupapaoo
(1938) MGM
Screenplay: Carl Dudley. Photography:
Harold Lipstein. Music: David Snell. Told by
Carey Wilson.
Cast: Moroni Olsen (Kurt Larsen).
A Miniature.
10 minutes, 46 seconds.

Strange Glory (1938) MGM
Screenplay: Morgan Cox. Historical Com-
pilation: Charles E. Whittaker. Photography:
Harold Lipstein. Music Score: David Snell.
Told by Carey Wilson.
Cast: Fay Helm (Anna Ella Carroll), Frank
McGlynn, Sr. (Abraham Lincoln), Addison
Richards and Byron Foulger (senators), Jack
Gray (General U. S. Grant), Roger Moore,
Doc Dearborn, Granville Bates, Boyd Gilbert,
Harrison Greene, Cedric Stevens, Edward
Stanley, Charles French, Gene Coogan.
An Historical Mystery
Approx. 11 minutes.

Think It Over (1938) MGM

Original Story and Screenplay: Winston Miller. Photography: Paul Vogel.

Cast: Lester Matthews (leader), Charles D. Brown (Inspector Wilson), Donald Barry (blackmailer), Dwight Frye (fire-starter), Robert Emmett Keane (Johnson), Frank Orth (clothing-store owner).

A Crime Does Not Pay Subject

19 minutes, 45 seconds.

Yankee Doodle Goes to Town (1939) MGM

Original story: Richard Goldstone, Alvan Sommerfield. Screenplay: Joseph Sherman. Music Score: David Snell. Film Editor: Harry Komer.

Cast: Albert Russell (Abraham Lincoln), Josiah Tucker.

John Nesbitt's Passing Parade

Made in cooperation with *Collier's, The National Weekly*

10 minutes, 38 seconds.

The Incredible Stranger (1942) MGM

Screenplay: Douglas Foster. Director of Photography: Jackson Rose. Art Director: Richard Duce. Editor: Harry Komer.

Cast: Paul Guilfoyle (the stranger), Dorothy Vaughan (Mrs. Brewster), Walter Baldwin (doctor), Sam Ash (storekeeper), Connie Leon (woman), Roger Gray and Joe Mack (townspeople), Henry Sylvester (stationmaster).

John Nesbitt's Passing Parade.

10 minutes, 50 seconds.

The Magic Alphabet (1942) MGM

Director: Jacques Tourneur. Original Story and Screenplay: Robert Lopez. Photography: Alvin Wyckoff. Art Director: Paul Youngblood. Editor: Harry Komer.

Cast: Horace McNally.

John Nesbitt's Passing Parade.

Produced in conjunction with the U.S. Government Office of War Information.

Approx. 10 minutes.

Reward Unlimited (1944) Vanguard Films (David O. Selznick)

Director: Jacques Tourneur. Producer: B. P. Fineman. Screenplay: Mary McCall, Jr.

Cast: Dorothy McGuire (Peggy), Aline MacMahon (Mrs. Scott), James Brown (Paul), Spring Byington (Peggy's mother), Tom Tully (Peggy's father), Jackie Jenkins.

Produced for the U.S. Public Health Service. "Distributed and exhibited under the auspices of the U.S. Government Office of War Information as a public service by the War Activities Committee — Motion Picture Industry."

10 minutes.

TELEVISION EPISODES AS DIRECTOR

The Martyr (1955) Revue Productions/ MCA TV/CBS-TV

Producer: Z. Wayne Griffin. Executive Producer: Mort Abrahams. Screenplay: Leo Davis, based on the story by Frank O'Connor. Director of Photography: John L. Russell. Art Director: Martin Obzina. Set Decorator: Armor E. Goetten. Music Supervisor: Stanley Wilson. Editor: Edward A. Biery. Editing Supervisor: Richard G. Wray. Wardrobe Supervisor: Vincent Dee. Makeup: Howard Smit. Sound: Stanley F. Cooley. Assistant Director: Jack Corrick. Program Supervisor for General Electric: Ronald Reagan.

Cast: Ronald Reagan (Colonel Jack Hartnett), Brian Aherne (Colonel Raftery), Lee Marvin (Captain Morrissey), J. M. Kerrigan (Jimmy), James McCallion, Noel Drayton, Pat O'Malley.

Episode for *The General Electric Theater.*

First broadcast: January 23, 1955.

25 minutes.

Into the Night (1955) Revue Productions/ MCA TV/CBS-TV

Producer: Leon Gordon. Screenplay: Mel Dinelli, based on a story by Charles Hoffman. Director of Photography: Ellsworth Fredricks. Art Director: Martin Obzina. Set Decorator: James S. Redd. Editor: Michael R. McAdam. Editing Supervisor: Richard G. Wray. Sound: Hugh McDowell. Program Supervisor for General Electric: Ronald Reagan.

Cast: Eddie Albert, Ruth Roman, Dane Clark, Robert Armstrong, Jeanne Bates, Wallis Clark, Bill Fawcett, Nora Marlowe, Jerry Mathers, Larry Blake, Bob Bice.

Episode for *The General Electric Theater.*

First broadcast: May 1955.

25 minutes.

A Hero Returns (1956) Lewman Productions/NBC-TV

Producer: William Asher. Screenplay: John Fante, based on a story by Indro Montinelli. Director of Photography: John MacBurnie. Editor: Edward Haire.

Cast: Dane Clark, Sebastian Cabot, Serena Sande, Penny Santon, Anna Navarro, Danny Richards, Lee Erickson, Edward Manduk, Louis Mercier, Joanne Rio, Eugenia Paul.

Episode for *Jane Wyman Presents the Fireside Theater.* First broadcast: January 1956. 25 minutes.

Kirsti (1956) Lewman Ltd./NBC-TV

Producer: William Asher. Screenplay: Jameson Brewer, based on a story by Gladys Hasty Carroll. Director of Photography: John MacBurnie. Art Director: George Patrick. Set Decorator: Ralph Sylos. Music Supervisor: Stanley Wilson. Editor: Daniel A. Nathan. Editorial Supervisor: Richard G. Wray. Wardrobe Supervisor: Vincent Dee. Makeup: Jack Barron. Sound: Perc Townsend. Assistant Director: Jack Corrick. Story Consultant: William Kozlenko.

Cast: Jane Wyman (Kirsti Stone), Jack Kelly (Rayburn Stone), Charles Coburn (Dr. Cutler), Edith Evanson (Mrs. Horton), Burt Mustin (Ruggles), Minerva Urecal (Mrs. Adams), Kate MacKenna (Mrs. Madison), Robert Peterson.

Episode for *Jane Wyman Presents the Fireside Theater.* First broadcast: February 1956. 25 minutes.

The Mirror (1956) Lewman Productions/ NBC-TV

Producer: William Asher. Screenplay: Jack Hanley, based on a story by Jack Schaefer. Director of Photography: John MacBurnie. Editor: Edward Haire.

Cast: Joanne Dru, Tom Tryon, Carleton Young, Harry Harvey, Rosa Turich, Lisa Montel, Mimi Gibson, Tim Graham.

Episode for *Jane Wyman Presents the Fireside Theater.* First broadcast: February 1956. 25 minutes.

Outlaw's Boots (1957) Revue Productions/ CBS-TV

Producer: Frank Rosenberg. Screenplay: N. B. Stone, Jr., based on a story by Tommy Thompson. Director of Photography: Lionel Lindon. Editor: Gene Palmer.

Cast: Steve Cochran, Keenan Wynn, Whitney Blake, Roland Winters.

Episode for *Schlitz Playhouse of Stars.* First broadcast: December 1957. 25 minutes.

The Steep Hill (1957) Desilu Productions/ NTA/ABC-TV

Producer: Bert Granet. Executive Producer: Desi Arnaz. Associate Producer: Edward Hillie. Screenplay: William Bruckner. Director of Photography: Maury Gertsman. Art Director:

Claudio Guzman. Set Decorator: William Stevens. Music Supervisor: E. C. Norton. Editor: Robert L. Swanson. Editorial Supervisor: Dann Cahn. Assistant Director: Don Torpin. Production Supervisor: W. Argyle Nelson. Production Manager: James Paisley.

Cast: Michael Connors (Davey Hopper), Dolores Donlon (Libby Wicks), Walter Winchell (himself), Stephen Joyce (Toby), Mush Solomen (Buster), William Hughes (Deputy).

Episode for *Walter Winchell File.* First broadcast: December 25, 1957. 25 minutes.

House on Biscayne Bay (1958) Desilu Productions/NTA/ABC-TV

Producer: Bert Granet. Executive Producer: Desi Arnaz. Associate Producer: Edward Hillie. Screenplay: Martin Berkeley, Clark E. Reynolds. Director of Photography: Maury Gertsman. Art Director: Claudio Guzman. Set Decorator: William Stevens. Music Supervisor: E. C. Norton. Editor: Robert L. Swanson. Editorial Supervisor: Dann Cahn. Assistant Director: John E. Burch. Production Supervisor: W. Argyle Nelson. Production Manager: James Paisley.

Cast: William Edmunds (Giovanni Mancuso), Grant Richards (Steve Mancuso), Didi Ramati (Angela Mancuso), Val Dufour (Frank Whitman), Walter Winchell (himself), Phil Tully (Captain Bruckman), John Close (sergeant), Len Lesser (Mike), Ken Alton (Hanigan), James Logan (butler).

Episode for *Walter Winchell File.* First broadcast: January 31, 1958. 25 minutes.

The Stopover (1958) Desilu Productions/ NTA

Producer: Bert Granet. Executive Producer: Desi Arnaz. Associate Producer: Edward Hillie. Screenplay: Adrian Spies. Director of Photography: Maury Gertsman. Art Director: Claudio Guzman. Set Decorator: William Stevens. Music Supervisor: E. C. Norton. Editor: Edward Biery. Editorial Supervisor: Dann Cahn. Assistant Director: Don Torpin. Production Supervisor: W. Argyle Nelson. Production Manager: James Paisley.

Cast: Rodolfo Hoyos, Jr. (El Jefe), Rodolfo Acosta (El Gato), Alex Montoya (Alfredo), Renata Vanni (Lupe), Edward Colmans (Judge Juan Mercado), Rita Conde (Carla), Tony Terry (Raphael), Walter Winchell (himself), Robert Carricart (chauffeur), Francis Villalobos (Doctor Bermudez).

Episode for *Walter Winchell File.* First broadcast: March 28, 1958. 25 minutes.

Cool and Lam (1958) CBS Productions/
Paisano Productions
Producer: Edmund Hartman. Executive
Producer: Gail Patrick Jackson. Screenplay:
Edmund Hartman, based on characters created
by A. A. Fair (Erle Stanley Gardner).
Cast: Billy Pearson (Donald Lam), Benay
Venuta (Bertha Cool), Maurice Manson (Dr.
Listig), Maggie Mahoney (Marion Danton),
Judith Bess Jones (Elsie Brand), Sheila Bromley
(Flo Mortonson), Don Megowan (John Har-
bet), Movita (Carmen), Allison Hayes (Evaline
Dell), John Mitchum (bartender), Tristram
Coffin (Thatcher), Alex Sharpe (plainclothes-
man).
Unsold pilot.
25 minutes.

Episodes for *Northwest Passage* (1958–59)
MGM-TV/NBC-TV
The Gunsmith (released theatrically as part
of *Frontier Rangers*)
The Burning Village (released theatri-
cally as part of *Frontier Rangers*)
The Bond Women (released theatrically as
part of *Frontier Rangers*)
The Break Out (released theatrically as
part of *Mission of Danger*)
The Vulture (released theatrically as part of
Fury River)
The Traitor
The Assassin
The Hostage
Producer: Adrian Samish.
Cast: Keith Larsen (Major Robert Rogers),
Buddy Ebsen (Sergeant Hunk Marriner), Don
Burnett (Ensign Langdon Towne), Philip
Tonge (General Amherst).
(*Note:* for more information about the epi-
sodes released theatrically, see section below,
"Feature Films Reedited from Television
Episodes.")

The Devil Makers (1960) Warner Bros./
ABC-TV
Episode for *The Alaskans*.

The Mink Coat (1960) Edelman-Barwick
Productions/NBC-TV
Producer: William Wright. Screenplay:
Blanche Hanalis. Director of Photography:
Nicholas Musuraca. Editor: Carl Peirson.
Cast: Barbara Stanwyck, Stephen McNally,
Tenen Holtz, Lewis Martin, Jack Nicholson,
Michael Whalen, Hal Smith, Anna Lee.
Episode for *The Barbara Stanwyck Show.*
First broadcast: September 1960.

Aftermath (1960) CBS-TV
Alternate Title: "Mr. Preach."
Producer: Harry Tatelman. Screenplay:
John Paxton. Director of Photography: Paul
Ivano. Art Directors: George W. Davis,
Gabriel Scognamillo. Set Decorators: Henry
Grace, Otto Siegel. Music: Fred Steiner. Music
Editor: Gene Feldman. Editor: Harry Gerstad.
Makeup: Jack Dusick. Production Manager:
Harry Templeton. Assistant Director: George
Templeton. Sound Effects Editor: Gene Eliot.
Sound Mixer: Larry Jost.
Cast: Fess Parker (Jonah), James Best
(Hardy Coulter), Sammy Jackson, Jr.
(Ernie/Galoot), Bill Phipps (Hicks), Steven
Joyce (Murray), John Hambrick (Gordon),
Maurine Dawson (Sarah), William Fawcett
(Harris), Tim Graham (storekeeper), Burt
Mustin (Wilson), John Cole (Frank Coulter),
Gina Gillespie (Bessie), Larry Gillespie
(Thomas), William Challee (Redway).
Unsold pilot for series *The Code of Jonathan
West.* Presented as an episode of *The General
Electric Theater.* First broadcast: April 17, 1960.
25 minutes.

Denver McKee (1960) NBC-TV
Producer: David Dortort. Associate Pro-
ducer: James W. Lane. Screenplay: Fred Frey-
berger, Steve McNeill.
Cast: Lorne Greene (Ben Cartwright), Per-
nell Roberts (Adam Cartwright), Dan Blocker
(Hoss Cartwright), Michael Landon (Little Joe
Cartwright), Franchot Tone (Denver McKee),
Natalie Trundy (Connie McKee), Ken Mayer
(Miles), Stephen Coutleiger (Harley).
Episode for *Bonanza.*
Approx. 50 minutes.

Sergeant Kolchak Fades Away (1962)
20th Century–Fox Television/ABC-TV
Producer: William H. Wright. Associate
Producer: Carl Pingitore. Screenplay: Gene L.
Coon. Director of Photography: Kenneth
Peach. Art Directors: Jack Martin Smith, Jack
Senter. Set Decorators: Walter M. Scott,
Edward M. Parker. Music: Arthur Norton.
Conductor: Lionel Newman. Main Theme:
Sonny Burke. Music Editor: Leonard A. Engel.
Editor: Joseph Silver. Story Editor: Orville H.
Hampton.
Cast: Brett Halsey (Paul Templin), Gigi
Perreau (Kathy Richards), William Bendix
(Sergeant Major Kolchak), Nobu McCarthy
(Tamiko), Howard Smith (General Fulton),
James Yagi (Seigo Tachikawa), Conlan Carter
(guard), George Takei (Hideo), Les Damon
(adjutant), Dick Sargent (Lieutenant Collins).
Episode for *Follow the Sun.*
52 minutes.

A Bride for the Captain (1962) 20th
Century–Fox Television/ABC-TV
Producer: Art Wallace. Screenplay: Jean
Holloway. Director of Photography: Lloyd
Ahern. Art Directors: Jack Martin Smith,
Charles Myall. Set Decorators: Walter M.
Scott, Norman Rockett. Music: Lionel New-
man. Music Editor: George Korngold. Editor:
Fred Feitshans, Jr. Assistant Director: Wilbur
McGaugh. Story Editor: Earl Booth.
   Cast: Gardner McKay (Captain Adam
Troy), Maggie Pierce (Claudine), Ray Walston
(Frank), J. Pat O'Malley (McPheeny), Arthur
Malet (O'Toole), Marcel Hillaire (Inspector
Bouchard), Guy Stockwell (Chris Parker),
James Holden (Clay Baker), David Brandon
(George), Carl Don (Louis), Lani Kai (Kelly).
   Episode for *Adventures in Paradise.*
   Approx. 50 minutes.

Night Call (1963) Cayuga Productions/
CBS-TV
   Producer: Bert Granet. Screenplay: Richard
Matheson. Director of Photography: Robert
Pittack. Art Directors: George W. Davis, Wal-
ter Holscher. Set Decorator: Henry Grace,
Robert R. Benton. Editor: Richard Heer-
mance. Sound: Franklin Milton, Philip N.

Mitchell. Production Manager: Ralph W. Nel-
son. Assistant Director: Charles Bonniwell, Jr.
   Cast: Gladys Cooper (Elva Keane), Nora
Marlowe (Margaret Philips), Martine Bartlett
(Miss Finch), Rod Serling (host and narrator).
   Episode for *Twilight Zone.*
   25 minutes.

The Ring of Anasis (1966) NBC-TV
   Screenplay: Herman Miller.
   Cast: Robert Loggia, William Daniels, Ross
Hagen, Michele Carey.
   Episode for *T.H.E. Cat.* First broadcast:
December 30, 1966.

   Tourneur also directed episodes for *The
Californians* (1958, NBC-TV), other episodes
for *The Barbara Stanwyck Show* (1960,
Edelman-Barwick Productions/NBC-TV), and
other pilots (titles unknown). Tourneur proba-
bly also directed other episodes for *Schlitz
Playhouse of Stars* (1952–59), *General Electric
Theater* (1955–60), *Jane Wyman Presents the
Fireside Theater* (1956), *Walter Winchell File*
(1957–58), and *The Alaskans* (1960). He may
have also directed other episodes for *Follow the
Sun* (1961–62) and *Bonanza* (1960–62).

FEATURE FILMS REEDITED
FROM TELEVISION EPISODES

Frontier Rangers (1959) MGM
   Director: Jacques Tourneur. Producer: Adrian
Samish. Executive Producer: Samuel Marsh.
Screenplay: Gerald Drayson Adams, based on the
novel *Northwest Passage* by Kenneth Roberts.
Directors of Photography: William W. Spencer,
Harold E. Wellman (Metrocolor). Art Directors:
William A. Horning, Merrill Pye. Set Decora-
tors: Henry Grace, Richard Pefferle, Otto Siegel.
Editors: Ira Heymann, Frank Santillo. Music:
Raoul Kraushaar. Song "Make Way for the
Rangers" by Howard Dietz, Arthur Schwartz.
   Cast: Keith Larsen (Major Robert Rogers),
Buddy Ebsen (Sergeant Hunk Marriner), Don
Burnett (Ensign Langdon Towne), Lisa Gaye
(Natula), Angie Dickinson (Rose Carver),
Larry Chance (Black Wolf), Pat Hogan
(Rivas), Philip Tonge (General Amherst), Lisa
Davis (Elizabeth Browne), Emile Meyer (Ben
Klagg), Claude Akins (Caleb Brandt), Charles
Horvath (Klagg's henchman).
   Reedited feature version of three episodes
of the TV series *Northwest Passage*: "The Gun-
smith," "The Bond Women," and "The Burn-
ing Village."
   83 minutes.

Mission of Danger (1959) MGM
   Directors: Jacques Tourneur, george waG-
Gner. Producer: Adrian Samish. Executive
Producer: Samuel Marsh. Screenplay: Gerald
Drayson Adams, based on the novel *Northwest
Passage* by Kenneth Roberts. Directors of Pho-
tography: William W. Spencer, Harold E.
Wellman (Metrocolor). Art Directors: William
A. Horning, Merrill Pye. Set Decorators:
Henry Grace, Richard Pefferle. Editors: Ira
Heymann, Frank Santillo. Music: Raoul
Kraushaar. Song "Make Way for the Rangers"
by Howard Dietz, Arthur Schwartz.
   Cast: Keith Larsen (Major Robert Rogers),
Buddy Ebsen (Sergeant Hunk Marriner), Don
Burnett (Ensign Langdon Towne), Philip
Tonge (General Amherst), Patrick Macnee
(Colonel Trent), Taina Elg (Andrea), Alan
Hale, Adam Williams, Sandy Kenyon, Mau-
rice Marsac.
   Reedited feature version of three episodes
of the TV series *Northwest Passage*: "The Red
Coat" (waGGner), "The Break Out" (Tour-
neur), and "The Secret of the Cliff" (waG-
Gner).
   79 minutes.

Fury River (1959) MGM

Directors: Jacques Tourneur, george waG-Gner, Alan Crosland, Jr., Otto Lang. Producer: Adrian Samish. Executive Producer: Samuel Marsh. Screenplay: Gerald Drayson Adams, Antony Ellis, Sloan Nibley. Directors of Photography: William W. Spencer, Harkness Smith (Metrocolor). Art Directors: William A. Horning, Merrill Pye. Set Decorators: Henry Grace, Richard Pefferle, Keogh Gleason, Jack Mills. Editors: Ira Heymann, Frank Santillo, Jack Kampschroer. Music: Raoul Kraushaar. Song "Make Way for

the Rangers" by Howard Dietz, Arthur Schwartz.

Cast: Keith Larsen (Major Robert Rogers), Buddy Ebsen (Sergeant Hunk Marriner), Don Burnett (Ensign Langdon Towne), Philip Tonge (General Amherst), Jay Novello (Link), Harry Wilson, Paul Picerni, Rayford Barnes, Paul Langton.

Reedited feature version of three episodes of the TV series *Northwest Passage*: "The Vulture" (Tourneur), "Stab in the Back," and "Fight at the River."

74 minutes.

FEATURE FILMS AS SECOND-UNIT DIRECTOR

The Winning Ticket (1935) MGM

Director: Charles F. Riesner. Producers: Jack Cummings, Charles F. Riesner. Screenplay: Ralph Spence, Richard Schayer, based on a story by Robert Pirosh and George Seaton. Director of Photography: Charles G. Clarke. Second-Unit Director: Jacques Tourneur (uncredited).

Cast: Leo Carrillo, Louise Fazenda, Ted Healy, Irene Hervey, James Ellison, Luis Alberni, Purnell Pratt, Akim Tamiroff.

Production: November 14–mid-December 1934. Released: February 8, 1935.

A Tale of Two Cities (1935) MGM

Director: Jack Conway (and Robert Z. Leonard, uncredited). Producer: David O. Selznick. Revolutionary War sequences produced by Val Lewton and directed by Jacques Tourneur. Screenplay: W. P. Lipscomb and S. N. Behrman, based on the novel by Charles

Dickens. Director of Photography: Oliver T. Marsh.

Cast: Ronald Colman, Elizabeth Allan, Edna May Oliver, Reginald Owen, Basil Rathbone, Blanche Yurka, Henry B. Walthall, Donald Woods, H. B. Warner, Lucille LaVerne.

Production: June 4–August 19, 1935. Released: December 1935.

Marie Antoinette (1938) MGM

Director: W. S. Van Dyke II. Producer: Hunt Stromberg. Screenplay: Claudine West, Donald Ogden Stewart, Ernest Vajda. Director of Photography: William Daniels. Second-Unit Director: Jacques Tourneur (uncredited).

Cast: Norma Shearer, Tyrone Power, John Barrymore, Robert Morley, Joseph Schildkraut, Anita Louise, Gladys George.

Production: December 30, 1937–May 25, 1938. Released: July 1938.

FEATURE FILMS (IN CAPACITIES OTHER THAN DIRECTOR)

AS BIT PLAYER

Scaramouche (1923) MGM
Director: Rex Ingram.

The Fair Co-ed (1927) MGM
Director: Sam Wood.

Love (1927) MGM
Director: Edmund Goulding.

The Trail of '98 (1928) MGM
Director: Clarence Brown.

AS SCRIPT CLERK

Never the Twain Shall Meet (1925)
Cosmopolitan–Metro Goldwyn
Director: Maurice Tourneur.

Sporting Life (1925) Universal
Director: Maurice Tourneur.

Clothes Make the Pirate (1925) Sam
Rork–First National
Directors: Maurice Tourneur, Alfred E. Green.

Aloma of the South Seas (1926) Paramount
Director: Maurice Tourneur.

Old Loves and New (1926) Sam Rork–
First National
Director: Maurice Tourneur.

The Mysterious Island (1929) MGM
Directors: Maurice Tourneur, Benjamin
Christensen, Lucien Hubbard.

AS ASSISTANT DIRECTOR
OR EDITOR

Das Schiff der verlorenen Menschen
(1929) Maestro-Staaken
Director: Maurice Tourneur. Screenplay:
Maurice Tourneur, based on the novel by
Franzos Keremen. Photography: Nicholas
Farkas. Assistant Director: Jacques Tourneur.
Cast: Gaston Modot, Marlene Dietrich,
Fritz Kortner, Vladimir Sokoloff.

Accusée, levez-vous (1930) Pathé-Natan
Director: Maurice Tourneur. Screenplay:
Jean José Frappa, based on a story by Mary
Murillo. Photography: Victor Armenise.
Decorations: Jacques Colombier. Editor and
Assistant Director: Jacques Tourneur.
Cast: Gaby Morlay, André Roanne, Camille
Bert, Jean Dax, Charles Vanel.

Maison de danses (1931) Pathé-Natan
Director: Maurice Tourneur. Screenplay:
Paul Reboux. Photography: Victor Armenise
and Marc Bujard. Editor: Jacques Tourneur.
(*Note:* In 1977, Jacques Tourneur denied having edited this film, saying, "or else I really
have a bad memory" [Manlay and Ricaud,
"Entretien avec Jacques Tourneur," p. 54].)
Cast: Gaby Morlay, Charles Vanel, José
Noguero.

Partir! (1931) Pathé-Natan
Director: Maurice Tourneur. Screenplay:
Maurice Tourneur, based on the novel by
Roland Dorgelès. Photography: Georges Benoit,
Barreyre. Decorations: Jacques Colombier. Editor and Assistant Director: Jacques Tourneur.
Cast: Simone Cerdan, Jean Marchat,
Lugné-Poe, Ginette d'Yd, Prince-Rigadin.

Au nom de la loi (1932) Pathé-Natan
Director: Maurice Tourneur. Screenplay:
Maurice Tourneur, based on a story by Paul
Bringuier. Photography: Georges Benoit, Marc
Bujard. Decorations: Jacques Colombier. Editor and Assistant Director: Jacques Tourneur.
Cast: Marcelle Chantal, Gabriel Gabrio,
Charles Vanel, Jean Dax.

Les Gaîtés de l'escadron (1932) Pathé-
Natan
Director: Maurice Tourneur. Screenplay:
Georges Dolley, based on the military revue by
Georges Courteline and Edouard Norès, from
the novel by Georges Courteline. Photography: Victor Armenise, René Colas, Raymond
Agnel. Decorations: Jacques Colombier. Editor: Jacques Tourneur.
Cast: Raimu, Jean Gabin, Fernandel, Henry
Roussell, Mady Berry.

Les Deux Orphelines (1933) Pathé-Natan
Director: Maurice Tourneur. Screenplay:
René Pujol, based on the novel by Adolphe
d'Ennery and Cormon. Photography: Georges
Benoit, Roger Lucas. Editor: Jacques Tourneur.
Cast: Yvette Guilbert, Emmy Lynn, Rosine
Deréan, Renée Saint-Cyr.

Lidoire (1933) Pathé-Natan
Director: Maurice Tourneur. Screenplay:
Maurice Tourneur, based on a one-act play by
Georges Courteline. Assistant Director:
Jacques Tourneur.
Cast: Fernandel, Rivers-Cadet.

Obsession (1933) Pathé-Natan
Director: Maurice Tourneur. Screenplay:
André de Lorde, based on a play by André de
Lorde and Charles Binet. Photography: Raymond Agnel, René Colas. Decorations: Jacques
Colombier. Editor: Jacques Tourneur (uncredited).
Cast: Charles Vanel, Louise Lagrange, Paul
Amiot, Georges Paulais.

Le Voleur (1933) Marcel Vandal and
Charles Delac
Director: Maurice Tourneur. Screenplay:
André Lang, based on the play by Henry
Bernstein. Assistant Director: Jacques Tourneur.
Cast: Madeleine Renaud, Victor Francen,
Jean Worms, Jean-Pierre Aumont.

La Fusée (1933) Via Film-Pathé-Natan
Director: Jacques Natanson. Screenplay:
Henry d'Erlanger. Editor: Jacques Tourneur.
Cast: Firmin Gémier, Pasquali, Lucien Gallas, William Aguet.

Rothschild (1933) Escalmel
Director: Marco de Gastyne. Screenplay:
Jean Guitton, based on a story by Paul Laffitte.
Photography: Marius Roger, Parguel, G. Brun.
Editor: Jacques Tourneur.
Cast: Harry Baur, Pasquali, Pauley, Philippe
Hériat.

Bibliography

António, Lauro. *Jacques Tourneur: Entre a luz e as sombras.* Fantasporto, 1985. 67-page booklet in Portuguese, with 24 pages of filmography and an essay consisting substantially of passages from Tourneur interviews from other sources.

Bansak, Edmund G. *Fearing the Dark: The Val Lewton Career.* Jefferson, N. C.: McFarland & Company, 1995.

Bellour, Raymond. "Believing in the Cinema." Translated by Dana Polan. In *Psychoanalysis & Cinema,* edited by E. Ann Kaplan, pp. 98–109. New York: Routledge, 1990. English translation of "Croire au cinéma."

_____. "Croire au cinéma." *Caméra/stylo,* no. 6 (May 1986): 35–43. On *Night of the Demon.*

Biette, Jean-Claude. "Revoir Wichita." *Cahiers du cinéma,* no. 281 (October 1977): 40–43.

_____. "Stars in My Crown." *Cahiers du cinéma,* no. 309 (March 1980): 33–34.

_____. "Trois Morts." *Cahiers du cinéma,* no. 285 (February 1978): 58–63. On Tourneur, Chaplin, and Hawks.

Bodeen, DeWitt. "Val Lewton: Proved That Even Low-Budget Films Can Have Artistic Integrity." *Films in Review* 14, no. 4 (April 1963): 210–25.

Borst, Ronald V., and Scott MacQueen. "*Curse of the Demon*: An Analysis of Jacques Tourneur's Supernatural Masterpiece." *Photon,* no. 26 (1975): 31–41.

Brion, Patrick. "Biofilmographie de Jacques Tourneur." *Cahiers du cinéma,* no. 181 (August 1966): 44–69. Detailed filmography with critical commentary on Tourneur's films.

Brion, Patrick, and Jean-Louis Comolli. "Un Cinéma de frontière." *Cahiers du cinéma,* no. 181 (August 1966): 35–43. Interview with Tourneur.

Brownlow, Kevin. *The Parade's Gone By....* Berkeley: University of California Press, 1968. Includes material on Maurice Tourneur.

Caméra/stylo, no. 6 (May 1986). Special issue on Tourneur, including many previously unpublished essays and two unproduced treatments by Tourneur.

Comolli, Jean-Louis. "Vanité de l'art." *Cahiers du cinéma,* no. 142 (April 1963): 54–57. On *The Flame and the Arrow* and *Great Day in the Morning.*

Coursodon, Jean Pierre, and Bertrand Tavernier. *50 Ans de cinéma américain.* Paris: Nathan, 1991. Includes an essay on Tourneur.

Curubeto, Diego. *Babilonia gaucha: Hollywood en la Argentina, Argentina en Hollywood.* Buenos Aires: Planeta, 1993. Includes a chapter on *Way of a Gaucho.*

Eisenschitz, Bernard. "Six Films produits par Val Lewton." In *Le Cinéma américain: Analyses de films,* edited by Raymond Bellour, vol. 2, pp. 45–85. Paris: Flammarion, 1980.

Farber, Manny. *Movies.* New York: Stonehill, 1971. Includes an article on *The Leopard Man.*

Fieschi, Jean-André. "Le Médium." *Cahiers du cinéma,* no. 190 (May 1967): 64–66. On *Night of the Demon.*

Film Ideal, no. 176 (September 1965). Special issue on Tourneur; includes Spanish translations of articles previously published in France and an essay by Javier Sagastizábal, "La curva como distancia más corta."

Flinn, Tom. "*Out of the Past.*" *Velvet Light Trap,* no. 10 (fall 1973): 38–43.

_____. "Screenwriter Daniel Mainwaring Discusses *Out of the Past.*" *Velvet Light Trap,* no. 10 (fall 1973): 44–45.

Geltzer, George. "Maurice Tourneur: Believed Beauty Should Be a Component of Even a Programmer." *Films in Review* 12, no. 4 (April 1961): 193–214.

Grist, Leighton. "*Out of the Past,* a.k.a. *Build My Gallows High.*" In *The Movie Book of Film Noir,* edited by Ian Cameron, pp. 203–12. London: Studio Vista, 1992.

Guinle, Pierre, and Simon Mizrahi. "Biofilmographie commentée de Jacques Tourneur." *Présence du cinéma*, nos. 22-23 (fall 1966): 56–83. Detailed filmography and extensive interview with comments by the director on most of his films.

Henry, Michael. "*Berlin Express* de Jacques Tourneur." *Dossiers du cinéma: Films III*, pp. 13–16. Paris: Casterman, 1975.

_____. "The Garden of Forking Paths." In *Jacques Tourneur*, edited by Claire Johnston and Paul Willemen, pp. 7–12. Edinburgh: Edinburgh Film Festival, 1975. Largely on *Berlin Express*.

_____. "Jacques Tourneur." *Dossiers du cinéma: Cinéastes III*, pp. 193–96. Paris: Casterman, 1974.

_____. "*Rendez-vous avec la peur* (*Night of the Demon*) de Jacques Tourneur." *Dossiers du cinéma: Films II*, pp. 153–56. Paris: Casterman, 1972.

Higham, Charles, and Joel Greenberg. *The Celluloid Muse: Hollywood Directors Speak*. New York: New American Library, 1972. Includes an interview with Tourneur.

Horak, Jan-Christopher. "Good Morning, Babylon: Maurice Tourneur's Battle Against the Studio System." *Image (Journal of Photography and Motion Pictures of the International Museum of Photography at George Eastman House)* 31, no. 2 (September 1988): 1–12.

Jacques Tourneur. San Sebastian: Festival Internacional de Cine de San Sebastián; Madrid: Filmoteca Española, 1988. Catalog published in conjunction with the Tourneur retrospective at the 1988 San Sebastian International Film Festival; includes Spanish translations of numerous previously published texts, a filmography, and a previously unpublished essay by Bernard Eisenschitz.

Johnston, Claire. "Femininity and the Masquerade: *Anne of the Indies*." In *Jacques Tourneur*, edited by Claire Johnston and Paul Willemen, pp. 36–44. Edinburgh: Edinburgh Film Festival, 1975. Republished in *Psychoanalysis & Cinema*, ed. E. Ann Kaplan (New York: Routledge, 1990), pp. 64–72.

Johnston, Claire, and Paul Willemen, eds. *Jacques Tourneur*. Edinburgh: Edinburgh Film Festival, 1975. Includes an English translation of Tourneur's "Propos" and several critical texts.

Joly, Jacques. "Esther et les autres." *Cahiers du cinéma*, no. 122 (August 1961), pp. 17–25. Discusses *La Battaglia di Maratona*.

Koszarski, Richard. "Maurice Tourneur: The First of the Visual Stylists." *Film Comment* (March/April 1973), pp. 24–31.

Král, Petr. "Tourneur ou le suspens hagard." *Caméra/stylo*, no. 6 (May 1986): 8–17.

Legrand, Gérard. *Cinémanie*. Paris: Stock, 1979. Includes an article on Tourneur.

_____. "Malgré les ombres, la mémoire (*Stars in My Crown*)." *Positif*, nos. 341-42 (July-August 1989): 70–71.

_____. "Une Solitude labyrinthique." *Positif*, no. 85 (June 1967): 54–57. On *Out of the Past*.

Leguèbe, Eric. *Le Cinéma américain par ses auteurs*. Paris: Guy Authier, 1977. Includes an interview with Tourneur.

Lenne, Gérard. *Le Cinéma "fantastique" et ses mythologies: 1895–1970*. Paris: Henri Veyrier, 1985. Discusses Tourneur's supernatural films.

Lightman, Herb A. "The Story of Filming *Berlin Express*." *American Cinematographer* 29, no. 7 (July 1948): 232–33.

Lourcelles, Jacques. "Note sur Jacques Tourneur." *Présence du cinéma*, nos. 22-23 (fall 1966): 52–55.

Mangravite, Andrew. "A Light on *Nightfall*." *Big Reel* (March 1991): B10–B11.

Mank, Gregory William. *Hollywood Cauldron: Thirteen Horror Films from the Genre's Golden Age*. Jefferson, N. C.: McFarland & Company, 1994. Includes an essay on *Cat People*.

Manlay, Jacques, and Jean Ricaud. "Entretien avec Jacques Tourneur." *Caméra/stylo*, no. 6 (May 1986): 51–66.

_____. "Jacques Tourneur et le métier de cinéaste." *Cinéma*, no. 230 (February 1978): 42–52. Different version of the interview also published as "Entretien avec Jacques Tourneur."

Massuyeau, Michel. "Jacques Tourneur, français d'Hollywood." *Cinematographe*, no. 35 (February 1978): 19–22.

McCarty, John. "The Parallel Worlds of Jacques Tourneur." *Cinefantastique* 2, no. 4 (summer 1973): 20–29.

McClelland, Doug. *Forties Film Talk: Oral Histories of Hollywood, with 120 Lobby Posters*. Jefferson, N. C.: McFarland & Company, 1992. Includes interviews with Jane Greer and Dick Moore, who comment on Tourneur and *Out of the Past*.

McNiven, Roger. "Jacques Tourneur." In *American Directors*, edited by Jean-Pierre Coursodon and Pierre Sauvage, vol. 1, pp. 330–39. New York: McGraw-Hill, 1983.

Nolan, Jack Edmund. "Tourneur on TV." *Film Fan Monthly*, no. 139 (January 1973): 26–28. Brief survey of Tourneur's work for television.

Oddos, Christian. "Murmures devant un miroir." *Caméra/stylo*, no. 6 (May 1986): 115–30. On *Out of the Past.*

Peary, Dannis. "Mark Robson Remembers RKO, Welles, & Val Lewton." *Velvet Light Trap*, no. 10 (fall 1973): 32–37.

Pierre, Sylvie. "The Beauty of the Sea." In *Jacques Tourneur*, edited by Claire Johnston and Paul Willemen, pp. 45–47. Edinburgh: Edinburgh Film Festival, 1975. On *I Walked with a Zombie.*

Pym, John. *"Easy Living." Monthly Film Bulletin* 46, no. 549 (October 1979): 215–16.

Roger, Philippe. *"Appointment in Honduras* de Jacques Tourneur." *Jeune cinéma*, no. 223 (July-August 1993): 45–46.

———. "Du suspense au suspens." *CinémAction*, no. 71 (1994): 142–48. Largely on Tourneur's conception of sound.

———. "Entretien avec Serge Daney." N.d. Unpublished interview containing reminiscences of Tourneur and comments on his work.

Rosenbaum, Jonathan. "Then and Now: The San Sebastian International Film Festival." *Independent* 12, no. 3 (April 1989): 24–25. On the Tourneur retrospective at the 1988 San Sebastian International Film Festival.

Sabatier, Jean-Marie. *Les Classiques du cinéma fantastique.* Paris: Balland, 1973. Includes an article on Tourneur.

Sarris, Andrew. *The American Cinema: Directors and Directions, 1929–1968.* New York: E.P. Dutton & Co., 1968. Includes a short article on Tourneur.

S[chroeder], B[arbet]. "Tourneur." *Cahiers du cinéma*, no. 142 (April 1963): 34–35. On *Timbuktu.*

Schwager, Jeff. *"Out of the Past* Rewritten." *Film Comment*, January/February 1991, pp. 12–17.

Siegel, Joel E. "Tourneur Remembers." *Cinefantastique* 2, no. 4 (summer 1973): 24–25. Interview.

———. *Val Lewton: The Reality of Terror.* New York: Viking Press, 1973.

Skorecki, Louis [Noames, Jean-Louis]. "Three Tourneurs." In *Jacques Tourneur*, edited by Claire Johnston and Paul Willemen, pp. 13–15. Edinburgh: Edinburgh Film Festival, 1975. English translation of "Trois Tourneur."

———. "Tourneur n'existe pas." *Caméra/stylo*, no. 6 (May 1986): 5–7. Short essay on Tourneur's conception of sound and on *Canyon Passage.*

———. "Trois Tourneur." *Cahiers du cinéma*, no. 155 (May 1964): 35–37. On *Anne of the Indies, Appointment in Honduras*, and *Wichita.*

Tavernier, Bertrand. *Amis américains: Entretiens avec les grands auteurs d'Hollywood.* Lyon: Institut Lumière; Arles: Actes Sud, 1993. Includes Tavernier's "Murmures dans un corridor lointain" and Tourneur's "Propos," along with a short preface.

———. "Murmures dans un corridor lointain (sur Jacques Tourneur)." *Positif*, no. 132 (November 1971): 1–8.

Telotte, J. P. *Dreams of Darkness: Fantasy and the Films of Val Lewton.* Urbana: University of Illinois Press, 1985.

Tourneur, Jacques. "Murmures dans des chambres lointaines." Translated by Agnès Folgoas. In *Caméra/stylo*, no. 6 (May 1986): 131–36. Treatment for the unproduced *Whispering in Distant Chambers.*

———. "Propos." *Positif*, no. 132 (November 1971): 9–16. Interview.

———. "Taste without Clichés." *Films and Filming* 12, no. 2 (November 1965): 9–11. Interview.

Turner, George. *"Out of the Past." American Cinematographer* 65, no. 3 (March 1984): 32–36.

Vernet, Marc. "La Mise en scène de l'homme-araignée." *Caméra/stylo*, no. 6 (May 1986): 85–91. On *Experiment Perilous.*

Walsh, Michael. *"Out of the Past*: The History of the Subject." *Enclitic* (Double Film Issue) 5, no. 2/6, no. 1 (fall 1981/spring 1982): 6–16.

Wicking, Chris. "Entretien avec Jacques Tourneur." *Midi-minuit fantastique*, no. 12 (May 1965): 11–16.

Willemen, Paul. "Notes towards the Construction of Readings of Tourneur." In *Jacques Tourneur*, edited by Claire Johnston and Paul Willemen, pp. 16–35. Edinburgh: Edinburgh Film Festival, 1975.

Wood, Robin. "Jacques Tourneur." In *Cinema: A Critical Dictionary: The Major Film-makers*, edited by Richard Roud, vol. 2, pp. 1006–9. New York: Viking Press, 1980.

———. "The Shadow Worlds of Jacques Tourneur." *Film Comment* 8, no. 2 (summer 1972): 64–70. On *Cat People* and *I Walked with a Zombie.*

Zlatoff, Dominique. *"La Féline." Caméra/stylo*, no. 6 (May 1986): 94–107. Excerpts from a shot-by-shot analysis of *Cat People.*

Index